Let this book speak for millions of unnamed addicts to gambling, for their own pain, as well as for the grief and misery they've inflicted on so many others, *for the 'little guy' who in an innocent although blind search for a night's fun, an evening's entertainment, puts his own and his family's resources at risk, or even throws it away, i.e. gambles it down the cesspool of electronic gaming machines. In pursuing their own addiction, gambling addicts lead to impoverishment instead of wealth, to pain instead of joy, to trouble and misery instead of fun.*

This book speaks for the Millions who've fallen prey to pie-in-the-sky dreams of riches, to false promises and dashed hopes, incited by corporations only interested in profit, in the dollar.

This book is a cry for ***Americans to wake up and see where the addiction of gambling is leading.*** *It's for citizens, for legislators, to take a good look at what the Trojan Horse of gambling really brings, and to look at what travels with gambling, the demons of divorce, bankruptcy and neglect. It's an ode to children and families raped by the colossus of gambling, the multi-headed corporate giant, enabled and created by the gods of greed and the money-hungry, insatiable forces that gambling ignites and fans into fire.*

Let's look with a clear eye and see ***what gambling brings, not prosperity but economic and moral decline.*** *Once we look and see, then we can vanquish the devil from one more of his hiding places within our midst, ourselves.*

Many, many thanks to* Dianne Berlin*, vice-chairperson of the National Coalition Against Gambling, *for her invaluable e-mail service, for her efforts to bring the truth about gambling to the public eye and for her compassion to gamblers and their families.*

I would also like to thank the many others involved in this struggle to bring light to the tragedies that are occurring and to stop future heartbreak and catastrophe for others.

May God preserve the country that invites in the forces of darkness and bids them welcome, that considers money more important than lives and profit more valuable than hearts.

TABLE OF CONTENTS

INTRODUCTION

Gambling is a 'financial vampire,...
A time bomb in a pretty package. 1
Rex Rogers, President, Grand Rapids Corn. Univ.

This isn't economic development and it isn't an acceptable funding source for anything. ***(Gambling) is a life-shattering addiction*** *for millions,* ***fueled by a state*** *that seems* ***addicted*** *to the promise of easy revenues. 2*
State Senator Frank Padavan (R-NY)

The ***odds*** *of winning Power ball is* ***1 in 80 Million*** *tickets. 3*

*"****Gambling*** *is just as bad an* ***addiction*** *as* ***alcohol*** *for* ***cops*** *on this force," 4*
a source familiar with the 2004 Toronto police investigation.

"It's so ***sad****," Erie Country Judge Timothy J. Drury, sentencing people who embezzled because of gambling addictions. "****These aren't people doing car-jackings or dealing drugs. They're otherwise worthwhile people*** *who just somehow bought into these advertisements. They feel a rush...The state encourages it." 5*

****

Gambling has become a new self-induced, scourge upon our society. Whether we call it Entertainment or whether we call it raising money for Education, Gambling is raping the American public out of Billions of dollars of hard-earned money and ravishing our society of needed funds, resources, and energy.

In the last 25 years, gambling has expanded on a scale never before seen in our country or around the world. Since the advent of the Atlantic City, New Jersey, casinos in 1978, gambling has expanded exponentially. Previously Las Vegas was the only gambling locale in America having opened its doors in 1931. Since 1978 and especially since the 1990s, casinos have opened in 28 states, Lotteries are run in 38 states plus D.C., and riverboat casinos first floated in Iowa in 1991. Although various cultures have had gambling of one kind or another throughout history, this is gambling on a scale and breadth never conceived of before.

In 2001, gambling revenue, money paid to the casinos by the public, had grown to more than ***$40 Billion dollars****, up from $9 Billion in 1991. (This is revenue to the casino after player winnings). 38 state lotteries generated nearly $38 Billion in 2001; pari-mutuel horse and greyhound racing more* *than 3.25 Billion and $550 million respectively. Americans spend more money in casinos than on golf, movies, CDs, sound equipment and cable TV all together. (American Gaming Assoc. www.Americangaming.org). 6*

Correspondingly, the ills committed in the name of gambling, the so-called **Social Costs**, *have become widespread, yet are often silent and escape our notice and awareness. This book is an effort to bring them to our attention. Once we are aware of the COSTS of the legalization of gambling in our society, then we can decide if this is really what we want to do. We can see with a clear eye where we are walking and whether this is where we want to go.*

Can we even conceive of people in the U.S. losing or spending $40 Billion dollars? Now that number has escalated again to an estimated $80 Billion worth of losses annually by Americans, according to Dr. Joel Rose of CACGEC. The numbers are mind-boggling. The enormity of these losses by citizens usually escapes our notice. The media doesn't publish stories about individual tragedies and people are not forth-coming about telling others when their homes are about to be foreclosed upon or they have to file for bankruptcy.

About 53 Million people in the US participate in some way in casino gambling alone. This equals 27% of the 21 or older population, or, slightly over one quarter of adults. ***That's one in every 4 adults gamble!*** *8* Casino Gambling in America, *Thomas A. Garrett.*

This is what a lot of people are doing with their time and their money. This is big business - really big. This new epidemic hurts children, the elderly, minorities, recent immigrants, and women, with a disproportionate influence. 9 (Lesieur, Henry, President, Institute for Problem Gambling, 12/13/98 www.gamblingproblem.org/ kidsgamblin.htm)

This **$80 Billion** *is money that people miss, income that needs to be spent on more constructive aspects of life, ranging from money for basic necessities such as rent, and food, to meals at restaurants, and other material aspects of life. All this becomes unavailable when money is lost through gambling. Nobody has an infinite amount of money. Money spent on gambling can't then be spent on other things, such as the rent, tuition, food, and children's endless needs.*

Money spent on casino meals won't be spent on neighborhood restaurants and other small businesses. When casinos move in, these restaurants and businesses then go out of business at an alarming rate (Gambling Causes Economic Decline, p. CACGEC Website). 10

Americans gamble more money each year than they spend on groceries and food. *(US Census Bureau, Stat. Abstract of the US: 1997, 117th Ed, Wash. DC p.769) More than $600 Billion is gambled in the US annually. Christiansen, op.cit. p. 3 Hotel Online. 11 Look for yourself at the area surrounding Atlantic City for proof of this thesis that gambling destroys all the business around it.*

Gambling provides no product, i.e. the money spent in gambling builds nothing, provides no long lasting goods and services, and, in short, returns nothing to the community. Gambling only gives to the coffers of wealthy shareholders and to the few top executives it creates. Donald Trump gets richer and richer. Steve Wynn is one of the wealthiest men in America.

***Current estimates** of the number of gamblers range from about **53 million to 100 Million within the US in 2003**. Of these numbers, researchers estimate that between 3% and 10% are either problem or pathological gamblers. Pathological gamblers are defined as people who obsess about their gambling, who spend much of their time gambling, and who are dysfunctional as a result of gambling excesses. Pathological gamblers, people like you and me, are routinely involved in any or all of the following, bankruptcy, suicide, crimes of various sorts including embezzlement, theft, murder, child neglect, and divorce, as a consequence of their gambling.*

*Problem gamblers are defined as people who are very close to becoming involved in illegal activities to finance their gambling habits and who have spent money earmarked for other areas such as home or family. It's a matter of degree, of being further along on the continuum. Since gambling is a **progressive** disease, n.b. the American Medical Association's definition, the problem gambler sooner later becomes the pathological gambler.*

*Another **15 Million people are defined as at risk** of becoming problem or pathological gamblers soon. It's only a matter of time before they'll be pathological gamblers and generating big trouble for themselves and their families. On paper these numbers mean little. Yet for a country to have these kinds of numbers of people with serious problems translates to enormous personal suffering and pain, incredible amounts of lost revenue, and wasted resources. On paper these numbers, although astronomical, mean little, are just a statistic. In real people's lives, they mean everything.*

These statistics translate into parents not home for children, husbands not there for wives. They equate to people who had satisfactory marriages, now embroiled in divorce. What's behind these statistics are the Social Costs, the children left in hot cars during the day and neglected to sleep there during the night while parents gamble. They mean Seniors with Social Security checks who think they can play poker and win on the Internet. How wrong can they be. These statistics are a disguise for college students gambling and losing college tuition. Pathological gamblers are people who embezzle from their jobs and later find their way into bankruptcy courts. And they all could be you and me. Or our children, or husbands. Why would we ever make something like this available to our fellow, also struggling, human beings?

***Social costs** can be translated into people who have lost life savings, who have gone to prison for crimes to support their gambling habits, who have lost wives and children to divorce because of their gambling. In short, gambling foreshadows and instigates almost every type of social ill. Do we want to make our society less potentially damaging to our fellow citizens? Then let's return to a time 20 years ago when gambling was only in Las Vegas, or even Las Vegas and Atlantic City. Not when every corner was another available venue for every person who never learned that there's no free lunch and that Casinos win every time.*

People think they can win. They think they can make money from the casinos, the Internet, the Riverboats, the Lottery, the Bingo halls. The gambling industry is very pleased that you think you can win, that you have a fighting chance. That's what they want you to think. The New York Lottery psyches you up with their ad campaign, 'Hey, someone's gotta win.' But it's a sucker's bet. You will never, never win in the long run.

The only ones who win in the long run are the casinos, their financiers, their managing companies. Do we really think the opulent casinos with their solid marble walls, plush carpeting, enormous chandeliers, and solid window walls, are built by allowing people to win. Of course not. No one wins. The casinos, sooner or later, take everyone's money. The only question is how long before they do it. No one wins.

What is the nature of the beast of gambling? It's thought to be entertainment, something interesting and fun, perhaps amusing. It passes for our friend, a game, we think we're having a good time. We're led to believe that gambling will help our towns and cities revive economically and that it will give people something to do in their leisure time. Nothing could be further from the truth. You think you're doing something acceptable, but you're truly 'sleeping with the enemy', 'in bed with all the demons in hell'. When you gamble, you think you can do it responsibly. But make no mistake, sooner or later, you'll get hurt, you'll sustain a loss much greater than you ever thought possible.

You may think you're slick, knowledgeable, and smart, but you're really 'small fry' compared to the brains and the collective influence and monies behind gambling.

Would you think you could outsmart Big Business, Big Tobacco, and our very government? No way! There's no way you can win against organized casinos. This industry has the top brains in business, in technology, in marketing, people who eat, sleep, and breathe, just thinking and scheming of ways to separate you from your hard-earned money. They only want something negative for you, for you to lose.

No, they don't come right out and say that's their goal. They stealthily pose as your best friend. Your 'rep' makes sure to remember your wife's birthday with flowers and your birthday with a big cheese and cracker or fruit and chocolate assortment. They pass, disguise themselves, as your friends and associates.

At first they just try to get their 'foot in the door'. 'Just a few machines in an isolated part of the state' and in turn, they agree to 'kick back' what sounds like astronomical amounts of revenue to the state. We allow the industry to sell us this bill of goods. We encourage them to come in, to set up shop. We give them so much leeway, so much freedom to pedal their wares.

Yet the reality is that we're encouraging and licensing 'pushers', people who want you to become hooked, to become addicted. The industry does nothing for the American people. It acts as a parasite on the American economy. The industry helps only one group of people – its own entrepreneurs, its own high management, its own stockholders. It's a self-centered, money-driven industry with no high-minded goals other than its own enrichment, at any cost. Rex Rogers, president of Cornerstone University, Grand Rapids, Michigan, notes that gambling is a "financial vampire" and a "time bomb in a pretty package." 12

The state of Michigan alone has 20 casinos, 7 horse tracks and a Lottery. Gambling 'on every corner', so to speak. Who could fail to succumb to the sheer convenience of gambling, to the pervasive quality of this commodity being so available? Associated Press, 4/18/04. http://www.mlive.com/newsflash/michigan/index.ssf?/base/news-14/1082292241257990.xml

Let's propose, for argument's sake, that the gambling industry is a business, like any other. Let's say that when you spend your money you make your 'choice' of what you want to do with your money. So you've chosen to spend your money this way. Do you normally choose to spend $1,000, for example, on a night of fun? Do you usually choose to spend $50, $100, $500. or even $10,000. on recreation, on something that you'll never see again? No, I imagine not. Don't you usually think, plan, consider, and research, at least look at Consumer Magazine, before you buy something, before you travel somewhere? Yet when you're in a casino, you and your money are soon parted.

Or do you go to a casino planning to lose? Do you set aside a certain amount and say you're okay with losing this much. Why would you go to a place where you were programmed to lose? For what? What product does it give you?

The truth is you're not making an ***informed*** *choice. You think, your fantasy is, that you can win. That's exactly what the casinos want you to think. They want you to think you can win. You think that you're gambling a certain amount of money to possibly gain a life-changing amount. Yet what you don't realize is that the odds are so stacked against you that the probability that you will win is so small as to be negligible. It's a sucker's bet! There's no way you're going to win. One author calculated the odds of winning the progressive jackpot. He said "If you play every day for the rest of your life, at age 75, you have a 1% chance." 13 Do you really think those odds are going to pay off for you? And the other side of the coin is, let us remember, that for you to win, incredible numbers of people have to lose. Do you really want to make money off the losses of others.*

And what is the ***product****, the end result, a night's fun, entertainment. There's no product. No gain to society, no marketable material result. Is a night's fun worth $1000.? Is it worth your children's college tuition or your family's food budget? Your family rent? Your inheritance? Your good credit rating? Or, conversely, is your win so important as to cause or to benefit from the losses of others, from someone else's poorly spent rent money, or someone else's food budget, or someone else's life? When gambling becomes convenient, suicides escalate significantly. One in 5 compulsive gamblers attempt suicide! Do you want to have your hands in the same pie, the same pot, that might precipitate others to commit suicide?*

The myth that casinos perpetuate, is that people gamble what they can 'afford to lose'. The casinos suggest to us that we 'gamble with our head', implying rationality. The reality is far different. People spend what they can't afford and then they borrow more. They spend money that is not theirs and then they embezzle more. The stories of respected town controllers, lawyers, accountants, mayors, secretaries, wives, husbands, stealing from each other, from their jobs and businesses and even from their children are widespread, numerous, and easily documentable. The amounts of money thrown away and even stolen in order to gamble, are staggering. The numbers of people who get hooked on this latest addiction are innumerable.

The illusion that people can afford to lose what they lose is advocated by gambling interests. But, in fact, who among us can afford to lose $500. a week, $20,000 a month? Many of us live from check to check. This doesn't allow room for gambling losses. The casinos weren't built on people losing $20. or $100 or more and walking away. Casino buildings are among the most opulent and extravagant in our society, much more beautiful than government offices, more luxurious than *hotels, more striking than any schools or churches. These Atlantic City or Las Vegas casino-buildings are more ornamental than the buildings of any society* ***thus far in the history of mankind****.*

They resemble palaces with glittering ballrooms, marbled interiors, sink-into-carpeting, gigantic interiors, with telephones and TV's in the bathrooms. These buildings are the most expensive, sybaritic buildings that any society has ever built. Construction costs on these buildings are astronomical. This is where the rent money goes, to marble baths. This is where old people's Social Security checks go to, for glittering chandeliers, what people's foreclosed homes and mortgages pay for, mirrored ceilings.

The amounts of our hard-earned money and resources diverted to casino profits from gambling is staggering. Gambling, or 'Gaming' as euphemistically called, diverts Americans hard-earned money and energy into the pockets of the already rich, from constructive, positive areas into destructive and negative pathways.

Government & Gambling

By the act of licensing these casinos, these slot emporiums, these racinos, our government is ***enabling people*** *to uncover and then to succumb to their addictive tendencies. My husband would never have become hooked on gambling if it wasn't first made* ***very available*** *and* ***very attractive.***

What an 'attractive nuisance'. The government makes a known addictive activity, i.e. gambling, available to its citizens. Research has shown definitively that a certain percentage of people, anywhere from 1% to 10% of people, depending on various factors involved, will become addicted when gambling becomes available. And gambling as addiction, as all addictions, is a sentence to 'hell', a surefire formula for misery, destroyed hopes and dreams, and endless tragedy for the gambler, his wife, his children, and innumerable others he's in contact with.

We're led to believe that our government functions in the interests of its people, 'by and for the people', 'for their inalienable rights for the pursuit of happiness.' Yet when our elected officials sell licenses to provide an acknowledged addictive activity to citizens, then it's hard to understand how it is acting 'in the best interests' of its people. ***Our very government provides the gambling interests with the wherewithal to enable people to destroy themselves.***

Our elected officials knowingly legalize something, which will in the end be destructive for some, and a hardship for others. Being a democratic society, we have values about free choice. Yet I don't have access to cocaine or heroin. Do I have free choice to kill myself? Many people have killed themselves after a particularly destructive bout of gambling. Many people have lost homes, marriages, their children's love, merely because they followed a very predictable course of action, i.e. losing, while engaging in an activity sanctioned and licensed by their elected officials.

Values & Gambling

Do we really want to go in the direction of such an opulent, 'decadent' lifestyle? How can we justify dropping a couple of hundred dollars in the pursuit of mindless pleasure when we have the faces of starving children in Somalia, Biafra, or Afghanistan, staring up at us in the face with our morning paper and cup of coffee.

In what direction as a society do we want to go? Do we want to seek never-ending mindless pleasure? Will we be the next Sodom and Gomorrah? Are we as obtuse as Queen Mary of France who said of her starving masses. 'If they don't have bread, let them eat cake.' Maybe instead of throwing our money away gambling, we decided to go down in history as the first culture that, even after they achieved material affluence for their people, yet still concerned themselves with helping others acquire that same freedom.

As we continually expand the range of available gambling, i.e. with the increased proliferation in all the states, more and more people will start to gamble. We could choose instead to become more involved in other pursuits to stimulate the mind or add to the real value and comfort of our homes. Or we could spend more time with our family or do community work. Although gambling looks like a cooperative, social activity, in fact, it's really a solitary sport with the extreme highs and lows, the wins and losses, all drama on an individual basis. An elderly person hunched over a slot machine for hours is not interacting with others or doing anything for himself or for others.

This country was not founded by people interested in pleasure seeking but by hardworking individuals with strong, solid values. What will make this country great, what will advance each person, is not a narcissistic concern for fun and pleasure, but energy spent in more positive pursuits with more long lasting value.

*I **indict the churches, the synagogues**, in our society, for **complicity** in partaking themselves in bingo, 'Las Vegas nites', and in the passive acceptance of this addictive pastime. If the churches don't stand strong and denounce this evil, then how will people be sure about what actions are beneficial, what values are good and* *what are not. Many people suffer from a lack of direction and emptiness, lack of meaning in their lives. They're not sure what is right and what is wrong. How is the average citizen to know what is right, what is dharmic, if the churches themselves indulge in gambling? If gambling is not wrong, then when someone loses, as they will, when they get hurt, who's to blame? Who was wrong and what sin was incurred? We're building a materialistic culture on the backs of the poor, the elderly, the immigrants, who think that 'something for nothing' is possible in this country where the streets are 'paved with gold'.*

The government allows, licenses, and profits from gambling. It's like the government passing around a loaded gun. When someone uses it and kills themselves, we shouldn't be surprised. Instead, we just invoke that old slogan, 'free choice', and blame them for ruining themselves. Blame the victim, as in the old rape scenarios. Let the weak beware, goes the unsaid thoughts. 'If you can't control yourself, don't play,' its said. This addiction is just as malevolent, if not more so, than drinking or drugs. It's just as destructive in the long run.

****

This book is a story about my husband, $3 Million dollars and me, his wife. It's about my husband gambling and losing his entire fortune, my entire fortune, his children's money, his relatives' money and his clients' money. Money that was not his to touch. He gambled whatever money he could get his hands on - and then some. My husband, as I've learned, is a compulsive gambler. He put mortgages on our home, spent our children's inheritance, invaded our life insurance, spent our stock portfolio, and embezzled client's funds. And he did all this without my having a clue as to what was happening! My husband is not that unusual. There are Millions of stories just as devastating as ours. These are the 'social costs' of gambling, the social impact. This is part of the tip of the iceberg of the suffering that gambling creates. It does so across all economic levels and all classes of people. We are the unseen statistics, the silent costs.

****

The first inkling I had that he had lost money gambling was when my mother-in-law sued us for 1.3 Million dollars. Imagine my shock when a deliveryman had me sign a receipt for the notice of the lawsuit. I signed the receipt, opened the envelope, and found—a lawsuit against us!

I always thought I had the perfect marriage! Wonderful husband, great children, beautiful house, a good retirement plan, and a dog. Finances looked good, the house had been paid off 20 years ago, we had a big stock portfolio, and secure jobs. To my mind we were in great shape financially.

Yet as the story of my husband's compulsive gambling unfolded, I suddenly realized that I had no money, a husband who had lied to me for the last10 years, who had a serious addiction problem, and children with no inheritance! One side of the extended family no longer spoke to us, and we had a $5,000./month mortgage payment and no money to pay it with! Just as I was about to retire, to stop working, I found out I now had nothing. No stocks, no money in the bank, no savings, no insurance, and no credit. Our 2 houses, which I thought were free and clear, had multiple mortgages, we had an additional $150,000. of credit card debt on 20 cards I never even knew we had, 3 casinos were suing us for another $50,000, and we had $50,000 in our children's student loans which were supposed to have been paid already! As far as I was concerned, this was Disaster!

Yes, this story is about how at the age of 55 years old, my husband and I were again starting from scratch—having given $3 Million dollars of our money and other people's money to the Atlantic City casinos!

This is what I call a ***modern tragedy****. Yet it's one that could have and should have been avoided. It's a story that revolves around a new level of greed in our society. Yes, old-fashioned greed, ignorance, and stupidity. Greed on the part of casinos, for misrepresenting gambling as entertainment. Greed on the part of our government for licensing an incredibly addictive activity. Ignorance, on my part, for believing my husband when he told me he always won, and finally, greed, ignorance and stupidity on my husband's part for thinking he could win, that he could make money without working for it, that he could best the casinos at their own game.*

****

I hold everyone responsible. ***I hold our government and our elected officials responsible*** *for this tragedy. The preamble to the Constitution says clearly that Congress shall make laws for the "general welfare of the people". If 5% (a commonly agreed upon figure), of all people who gamble, end up seriously addicted and engage in activities that are blatantly self-destructive to themselves, others, and their society, then the licensing of casinos can hardly be called in the 'general welfare' of our society.*

I hold ***organized religion responsible****. Churches and synagogues have been co-opted by this new menace and are complicit in trying to make money this way. Churches often run 'bingo' nights or trips to Atlantic City, giving the impression that there's nothing wrong with this activity. Yes, it seems an easy way to have fun and* *make money. But make money at whose expense? Only the Islamic religion regards gambling as a sin and forbids its people to engage in it. Islamic people don't even gamble in the stock market. Methodists also tell their people not to gamble. However, as a clear statement of do's and don'ts, Christians have not formulated or promulgated a clear statement to their people that gambling is wrong.*

A few churches have recently become aware of gambling as the true wolf in sheep's clothing that it is. Recently a Catholic priest in Indiana decreed that his parish would have no more bingo. Despite the uproar, now 3 years later, his parish is in better economic shape than ever. The Salvation Army recently refused to accept a 5 Million donation from a casino saying that the money was tainted. Yes, it's tainted, impure, blood money, taken from the psychologically weak, money that should have been used to pay rent, to build homes, to feed people.

***I hold the Casinos and the gambling industry responsible**. They misrepresent people's chances of winning. They pay people to buddy up to you, to act like your best friend. They build the most expensive buildings in the world—all in the interest of getting your hard-earned money. They give you almost anything you want or need, childcare, hotel accommodations, food, shows, and loans (called credit), in an effort to get you to stay with them. Then, after they have you in their grasp, they will surely divest you of all your money. At that point, you are in their power, in their hold. You give over your power to them. They don't want your betterment, your welfare, they only want your money.*

*And, finally, **I hold my husband responsible**. My husband is a compulsive gambler. This is the man who I planned my retirement with, discussed my future life with, picked and chose responsible investments with, and discussed what charities to give our money to. He's now thrown away all of our hopes and dreams, flushed our money down the toilet, so to speak, and left us not only penniless, but in fact, still owing casinos and credit cards. I would've trusted my husband with my life. I did trust him with my children and with my money. And he blew it all.*

Yet let me hasten to add that my husband is a good man, always solicitous of the children and me, never abusive. He always tried to help others. He gave a lot in charity, was a professional in the community. He returned extra change at stores that gave us back too much. He would never think of breaking the law—except around his gambling and his need to feed his habit. He's a respected and valuable member of our community – except in this one instance! In terms of gambling, he's an addict! An addict cannot be trusted, cannot be relied upon, and gives little thought to others. Were it not for the good graces of a very special family member, my husband would've gone to prison for many years.

So how could this happen? How can a good person completely change from being a law-abiding citizen interested only in the well-being and welfare of those around him, to one who blows all his family's savings, and commits whatever crimes he needs to get money? What mad beast possessed him? What Dr. Jekyll and Mr. Hyde did he become?

****

This book is the story of our **complete financial ruin** *at the hands of the Atlantic City gambling casinos. It's a story that can happen to anyone, that is happening as we speak, to millions and millions of innocent people. Their only mistake is believing the casino's hype. We got out lucky, we still have our house and hopefully will be able to keep it. We still have our marriage and, God willing, it will last more than its current 32 years. Our children still love us and 'understand' as best they can, that their father still puts them first, has always put them first, in spite of the fact, that he spent all their money. As unfathomable as that is.*

Gambling does not fill state coffers with money, as has been said. It's a game of substitution, of mirrors, 3 card Monte, a game that looks like you can win - but few people really do.

The money that gambling brings in for education merely allows the money earmarked for education to be spent another way. Substitution. In the meantime, tax money that comes in must be spent by the State, on the 'Social Costs' of gambling. Gambling revenue to the states, what turns into our tax money, goes for the courts for the bankruptcies, for the divorces, the many crimes, for children who are placed because their parents are in jail or have no money to support them. The government's money is spent on the prisons to hold the people indicted for embezzlement, murder, for theft, for child neglect. Let's imbibe every one of these words fully, not skimming over phrases or paragraphs. Each word is real, each word has the history of many, many individuals behind it.

Estimates vary widely on the **cost to the taxpayer** *of these 'social costs' but they range from $.43 to $3.00 to $13. for every $1.00 of gambling generated revenue. So the revenue is hardly a gain for the state, i.e. the taxpayers. In fact, it's a net loss. It's a gigantic gain to the industry operators but a net loss to the taxpayers. That's the part that's not understood. Of course, the casinos don't exactly publish these statistics.*

Gambling is no cash cow for society, as often touted. It's only good for the industry owners. In this book, we'll explain the Economics of Gambling. Gambling, as we're just now beginning to realize, is 'fool's gold'. It looks good but it's really false. Gambling is inconsistent with solid values like perseverance, hard work and integrity. It's inconsistent with the values that a person of faith would hold dear. It's inconsistent with humility, with trust, with good Stewardship of what we have, of putting our thoughts in the 'highest' possible place. Only the casino owners benefit from gambling. No one else.

Gambling is a **redistribution of wealth** *on a vast scale. A perversion of the American Dream with its contrived hope of getting something for nothing. Words such as sordid, sleazy and corrupt, describe this new phenomenon. It's catering to our baser instincts such as our desire for money, more and more wealth, and our craving for sex and power. It does nothing for the general good. The jobs created are low level and not geared toward a career ladder. Gambling is designed to pander to the psychologically weak, the lonely, the people who don't have anything better. It's materialism at its most blatant and most perverted. It's materialism run amok.*

In this book, we'll look at research studies, true stories, and economic facts, and we'll see what gambling is all about and who it truly serves. Read and become aware of where your money really goes. See where all this leads and where our society is headed. History says that 'Nero fiddled while Rome burned', referring to the increasing debauchery and corruption of the great Roman empire. Similarly in the name of entertainment, and 'having a good time', we deny and ignore the excesses of Gambling. We not only allow but encourage this blight upon our society and open the doors for it to spread its evil upon all.

****

CHAPTER ONE

HOW IT ALL BEGAN

The modern slot machine is one of the best ways to remove money from ***suckers*** *known to man. 1*
Charles Munger, Vice Chairman, Berkshire Hathaway, Shareholders meeting, 5/1/04

Gambling is based on the ***victimization*** *of people losing money over and over again. 2*
State Repres. Matt Baker, Pa, 4/29/04

It all began innocently enough in 1982 when we took a family trip to Cape May, on the New Jersey shore. On the return trip, my husband, Alan, asked if we could stop in an Atlantic City casino, which had opened a few years earlier. So I watched our 2 young children play in the sand on the beach and Alan entered the casino.

If I'd known how it would end, I would never have stopped the car. This would be the first stop on the road to ruin 20 years later. But I was young and naive. Little did I know of the road we had just turned down. Little did I realize that all the demons of man's negativities, all the hounds of hell in all their frenzied craziness, were about to be let out. Yet they would remain invisible for the next decade, slowly eating the guts out of our family life, sapping my husband's soul, insidiously tapping all our financial reserves, trying to gain a toehold into the destruction of our marriage, one by one, until there was nothing left.

Alan came out of the casino 2 hours later and showed me $100 that he won. To me, this was, big money, it was great! I was happy to watch my children for $100. for 2 hours! I eagerly let him go the next time he asked, and the next, and the next...Soon he was going to Atlantic City regularly on the casino bus every Friday night. He made a few friends on the bus and would hang out with them when he went. Meanwhile after I had worked all day, I stayed home and took care of our two young children. I would have preferred to have his company but he told me he was winning. I felt duty-bound to allow him to make money for the family. This became our routine. Every Friday night, he would go to Atlantic City. We thought of it as his 'second job'.

On the bus he would pay $30 and get $20 worth of coins, a coupon for dinner and the bus trip. A small time gambler. He would come home around 4 am in the morning and put bills on my night table, signifying that he'd won. When I woke up the next morning, I would look on the night table to see if there was any money. The next morning, Saturday morning, I'd let him sleep late knowing that he'd been up late the night before. Of course, there wasn't always money on the table, but often enough there was. Overall, he told me that we were making 'good' money. Sometimes there were several thousands on the table.

After a few years of this, he decided that he would take the family with him and we would stay the weekend. He explained that this would be a family vacation for all of us. We would eat meals free at casino restaurants, 'comped', our room would be comped, free again, and we could even buy clothes or toys for the children at the casino shops which the casino also comped. This sounded great to me. I calculated that we didn't have to pay for groceries or take-in food that weekend and we even got some clothes and toys for free. Alan would take us to the 'spa', we'd go swimming for free and play in the exercise rooms where they treated us like celebrities.

After a few visits, we graduated to huge 'suites' with a living room, 2 bedrooms and 2 baths. These rooms were in the expensive section of the casino-hotel. They overlooked the Atlantic Ocean with incredible views, totally marble baths, sumptuously decorated. They were often larger than many people's residential apartments. The children had unlimited movies on wide screen TVs. We had 'salon' privileges with regular haircuts, facials, perms, and massages. As the Mother, I saw value in not having to pay for a whole family's haircuts and food. I was into it 'small time'. The casino had bought me for 'small change'.

I often didn't want to go for the weekend as I was in the middle of a busy life back on Long Island and I didn't really want to leave my own full schedule of activities and plans. So I'd be resistant for the first day. After a day, though, I surrendered to enjoying the self-indulgent luxuries and would start planning to extend our stay. It was always amazing what the casinos were happily willing to give us. Food, drinks, rooms, clothes, gifts, haircuts, pool and spa privileges. Now we know why.

And then there was our 'rep', a family man, like ourselves, who was always there to get us whatever we wanted. He introduced us to everyone, and was always interested in greeting us and eating with us at the door. He seemed genuinely concerned about our welfare. He asked about the children, and their schooling. He acted like a 'Dutch uncle'. We didn't have that much extended family so it was nice be treated as 'special,' to have someone so interested in us.

At night when we stayed there, he sent up chocolate chip cookies and milk for the children. He always remembered us lavishly at holidays. At Christmas, he would send big baskets of holiday goodies to our home. Several Christmases we received a voucher giving us 5 hours at the local Christmas Store in the nearby suburbs. This voucher was a real plum as it included limousine round-trip, $500. worth of free Christmas purchases, and a champagne and desert buffet. Not a bad way to spend an evening.

On other holidays like July 4th or New Year's Eve, there were plenty of parties and BBQ's to go to with extravagant firework displays. At our birthdays, he would send 1 or 2 dozen long stemmed roses. At Easter, he would make sure the children got Easter bunnies and baskets. We were never neglected. When we left the casino at the end of the weekend, he made sure we had sandwiches and drinks, 'we shouldn't starve', for the 3-hour ride home. We didn't count the leftovers wrapped up from the other enormous meals.

Often we would travel by limousine. Sometimes the children would go earlier with me in one limo and Alan would come home a few hours later in another. Getting limos was no problem. Once a limo picked me up at my job at a public elementary school on a Friday afternoon. The driver was supposed to be there at 3 pm but arrived early. So he went inside the school to let me know he was there. The school office let me know 'my limo' was there and I almost died of embarrassment. Other times, limos would pick me up in Manhattan after I'd gone to a play or lecture and then drove me down to meet up with Alan and the rest of the family. Of course, the limos were fully stocked with drinks, snacks and movies.

When we graduated to higher levels, we began to be part of the 'clubs'. Inside the clubs are lounges where 'serious players', actually top-rated losers, enter by swiping a card. All the food and drinks in huge buffets are free, again, with wide-screen TV's, tropical fish tanks, magazines, newspapers, and books, all there for your entertainment. Our rep often allowed us to 'sneak' the children in. The clubs were officially open only to 18 and older because they served alcohol. So we ate as a family all we wanted at these free smorgasbords. On Saturday nights, we always made sure to go for the jumbo Shrimp. We would eat our fill and then put extra in cups to take home. Later, much later, we realized that those shrimp probably cost us about $1000. each!

On Sunday mornings, we'd choose another club at another casino, for example, the one on the 20th floor of the Taj Mahal casino, and sit and eat a leisurely individually cooked breakfast overlooking the Atlantic Ocean. Everyone looked well dressed, wealthy, and very important. They all acted like they were having the time of their lives. Now I realize it was all a show, a sham, designed to paint a certain picture, calculated to impress poor stupids like me.

By this time, the casinos were also giving out free gifts as enticements to come down for the weekend. Twice my husband was fitted for and received a free tailor-made suit of clothes. Another time, he got a free entire casual outfit. Again there were free tailor-made, individually fitted leather coats for me and then another for each of the children. So the whole family got expensive leather coats. Of course all these 'giveaways' were coupled with lavish, obscenely plentiful food and drink, all you could eat. If the gifts and the lavish food weren't sufficient, little lucrative giveaways were often on the tables to take, such as expensive lighters or other gifts. Decorations would be beautiful with ice statues, flowers to excess and service in abundance.

We were introduced to Willie Mays once, who autographed, unasked for, a baseball card for my son. Frequently there were giveaways involving gold bracelets or diamond pendants, for the ladies and TV-VCR's, DVD's, computer accessories like printers and scanners, for the men. At one time we had so many TV's from casino gifts that we were selling them at garage sales at home.

Then came the ***airplanes****. The casinos would happily charter a small private plane so Alan and a few friends could fly down Friday afternoons. The planes would depart the local airport around 4 pm and return around 2 am. Alan met a lawyer and a couple of men who had their own small businesses on the planes and they soon became 'gambling buddies.' Next, he started taking the family on the planes down with him. So he'd be asking for, and getting, 5 or 6 round-trip plane tickets for us and friends. Or, since Alan had his private pilot's license, the casino would rent him* *a plane for him to fly down and let him fill it with whoever he wanted. All for free, of course. It was a weekend away for free and usually Alan won extra money—or so he said. It was hard for me to argue with this kind of apparent success.*

We also went to shows when they had a performer that we enjoyed. As a family we saw Diana Ross and individually shook her hand during the show due to our front-row seats. A girlfriend and I went to see Smokey Robinson, he's still as great as ever. There were numerous skating and Magic Show extravaganzas including internationally famous illusionist, David Copperfield. But the best night was when we went with friends to see Neil Diamond. We were so close we could see him sweating profusely under the lights. I wondered if he was so expansive and feel-good as his songs seemed to indicate, Crackling Rosie, Sweet Caroline, Coming to America, why did he look so contorted and hard when he sang?

We also went to the Bahamas several times, to Paradise Island Resorts, Crystal Palace, and to Puerto Rico, staying at the El San Juan Hotel and another beautiful (gambling) resort in the country, El Conquistador. Many of the hotels had little 'hospitality suites' on each floor where one could get drinks, and snacks, fruit, at any time of day. Free, of course. The El Conquistador resort had been built on the top of a mountain and had a European tram car that carried guests from the main hotel area on top of the mountain to the sea level beach. Then a small private boat would take you to other beaches on a separate island. The breakfast buffet was exquisite at this resort, perched on the side of this mountain with views of the Atlantic Ocean below and the dense jungle around. We would sit and sip Bloody Mary's, eat steak and eggs, and take in the view.

We also took **gambling cruises** *around the Caribbean where there was a casino on board. At night when the ship was out at sea, it would open. If you played enough - or if you lost enough - you would receive discounts on the price of the cruise tickets. The cruise lines gave us an outside cabin with an outside deck. We would sit on our private deck, have a drink, and watch the waves go by. Very luxurious. Of course, we were always addressed by our proper names, with a certain amount of deference and courtesy. It all certainly turned my head, country girl that I am. Naturally, the spa privileges, haircuts, massages, gifts, all were continued on the cruises.*

The trade-off was that Alan would spend long hours in the casinos and the family had to find their own entertainment without him. In Atlantic City, he would be in the casinos both in the afternoons and evenings. In the afternoons, we often went to the malls by limo with extra money to buy things that he gave us, that he said he won. In the evening, we would go out to a restaurant all together and then at night I would collapse with a movie or book. Then the night in the casino would really start for him.

Alan stayed long hours in the casino gambling, calling it his 'work'. I used to feel guilty about his having to 'work' all the time and I'd say to him, was it really worth it, even if he was winning. He replied that he enjoyed it, and for me not to worry about anything. And truly he did seem to be a different person when we went, more alive, more excited and awake, 'charged up' and energized. On the return plane ride home, he'd fall asleep immediately and I would be left alone again admiring the twinkling stars or watching the lights of Long Island come alongside the plane.

Alan admitted that he could gamble all night without sleep in Atlantic City or Vegas. But at home he often fell asleep in front of the TV by 10 pm. This irritated me. He would seem uninterested in talking, or too tired to do anything. But in Atlantic City, he woke up big-time. Taking Alan on that plane, was like giving Popeye a can of spinach. Instant explosion. Even the thought of going would soup him up and he became A-L-I-V-E!

So after the first 5 or 10 years, and it had become a pattern, I began to wonder. In the early years of his gambling, he used to win big. One summer we sent the children to expensive day camps near us and paid the $10,000 bill in cash. Amazingly, the camp was full at first, but when we said we wanted to pay with cash, they suddenly found openings for our children. I never knew that it could work like that.

But I remained a 'homebody', and never wanted to go away. So Alan continued to go on Friday nights, religiously (!), and the children and I found things to do by ourselves. How could I argue with the extra money, the food and gifts he brought home. He even allied the children against me saying that they wanted to go too, that they had a lot of fun there. So how could I make a big deal out of it?

Yet sometimes we had long discussions and I told him at what cost this was all happening. I figured that he gambled big money from the perks they gave him. He admitted that he gambled big money and never let us watch as he played at the tables. He liked Blackjack, Slots and especially Craps. Craps was exciting to him. As the table turned toward the players, as the players started winning, the action got loud and boisterous. I didn't like that side of my husband. But he said one had to bet big to win big. Sounded logical to me. He said that although he bet a lot, he won a lot too. So—I believed him.

Yet I would have conversations with him when I wondered whether we finally had enough money and whether what we really wanted now was to have him home with us all the time. I would explain to him that since his energy was all bound up in gambling, it didn't leave time or energy for other interests. He replied that there wasn't ***that much exciting*** *to do around our small home town, so we might as well go to Atlantic City. (We've been sold a bill of goods that life is supposed to be 'exciting'.) I countered with the thought that if we stayed home and participated in community events, other things would open up also. We'd stopped going to church and synagogue by now since the children were grown. We participated in one large meditation community but it didn't occupy all our time as it had previously.*

I told Alan that I wasn't happy always going to Atlantic City and wondered what kind of values we were teaching our children. Yet we had a harmonious household and he persuaded me that this was just another form of entertainment. He rationalized that 'surely we had to have some fun...' Sounded just like casino propaganda. I tried to limit him to going once every other week or once a month. He would sometimes become surely and resistant when I broached the topic too vigorously and I'd end up backing down.

Somehow I knew it wasn't great but I was powerless to stop it. I never dreamed that he wasn't telling the whole truth. I never entertained the idea, for even a split second, that he could be losing money. We had a standing joke about him suddenly dying and my finding a mortgage on the house and then going up to heaven to kill him. But it turned out to be no joke.

I never thought of looking at our finances. Alan was a CPA, that was his area of expertise, and he knew how to do financial planning par excellence. I secretly prided myself that he handled our money affairs so well. We used to discuss that some people had a lot of money yet didn't handle it well, and consequently never really felt like they had any money. Yet he handled our money so well, I thought, that the money went even further than most peoples' money.

Alan never viewed his gambling as getting 'something for nothing.' He figured that he had to 'work' at it, that he had to stay there for long hours (although he was loving it), and be judicious about what bets to place and when to place them. He said it was his 'skill' that enabled him to win. He had a 'system' whereby he would 'press', bet more money, when he was winning and bet less money, when losing. So that all he had to do was to wait for a winning streak and then keep betting. If he could wait out a losing streak, then bet big on a winning streak, he had it made, or he made money. Or so he said... We figured that he was 'smarter' than other people, that he had special good money karma. We knew others lost but didn't feel that was us. He was smarter than them. After all, he was a respected CPA, right? Finances were his 'forte', his strong point, or so we thought.

This idea that the gambler is 'smarter' than other people, 'special', that he has perfected a certain system, is a common fantasy among gamblers. With this rational, the gambler can then deny and ignore his losses because his mental system allows for losses. He feels the losses are part of the game but that his system is foolproof and will eventually succeed. The illusion of 'specialness' has tripped up many people along the way and not only in gambling.

The fallacy is that each bet has its own odds of winning or losing and stands on itself. There are really no such things as winning and losing streaks. The law of random numbers says that each time you bet, you have the same odds of winning or losing. Those odds are always less than even so you can never come out ahead in the long run.

I'd been brought up without much money so one of my personal desires was to have money and not to have to worry when I spent it. So, I thought, he was making my dream come true. In the final years of his gambling, he used to persuade me that I was now a wealthy woman, that I could spend what I wanted and not worry. (I still preferred to buy store brands and penny-shopped whenever I could. Ordering the cheapest thing on the menu when we went out was de rigueur for me).

I used to talk to him about how grateful I was that we were in a good financial position, that our house was paid off, our vacations were paid for, we had money in investments, and that we didn't have to live hand-to-mouth, like so many people. He would solemnly agree that we'd been wise with how we managed money and we were in a good place financially. We even planned how much money we'd have in retirement, about 5 - 10 years away and the number came up beyond my wildest projections. It seemed as if it would be a more than comfortable retirement. Inside I wondered why so many people seemed to find it so difficult to get ahead. All you had to do, I felt, was to be consistent, live within your means, and save a little regularly. That's what I though we were doing.

It certainly never entered my head to look at our books, to look at our checkbooks, our stock certificates, bank accounts, etc. I'd once tried paying the bills each month and found it boring and time-consuming. So I duly gave him my pay-check every month. We had agreed that we would save my salary every month and live on his. I figured that he knew what he was doing, this was his area of expertise, finances, right? A smart CPA, right? My husband whom I trusted implicitly, right? Well, he knew what he was doing—but it was hardly what I thought it was.

Statistics show that more men than women become compulsive gamblers. This is possibly because they have access to household finances and more freedom to move about in the world. Women are often expected to be home with the children. Also, this action-type adventure seems more a man's thing.

The Gambler's Anonymous groups are full of men and the Gam-Anon meetings, the spouses and families of the gamblers, are full of women. This is another area where women have been victimized by virtue of their traditional roles and responsibilities within the household. Many women are literally at the mercy of their husbands financially speaking. If the husband does well, they have money. If he does poorly, they and their children suffer. If he spends all the money that both have amassed over the course of a long marriage, then that's too bad. Women have no legal recourse. Another women's issue.

I also realized later that while I thought I was being virtuous, playing the role of traditional wife, deferring to what my husband wanted, letting him make family decisions, allowing him to decide where we went for vacations and what we did, it was not a role that would help us get out of the grip of this addiction he had. If I'd been more assertive, more of a modern woman, involved in family finances, determined where we spent family vacations, then this tragedy might not have been played out so easily.

Alan had a lot of freedom due to my giving it to him, to my allowing him his 'nights out' with the boys. In being a traditional woman and wife, I often acquiesced to what he wanted to do, deferred to his supposed, better judgment. If I hadn't been so solicitous of what he wanted to do, he might not have been able to squander our fortune, to take what wasn't his, to act so irresponsibly. I thought I created harmony in the family by allowing him to make decisions. I found out that in the end, my playing 'good wife' only made for going down the wrong road and getting lost. Women often sacrifice their own needs and desires in favor of husband's wishes. Yet often women have the wiser values, are more intuitive, put their children's needs first. In this instance my acquiescence resulted in him spending all our money, it allowed him freedom, in the interest of his addiction.

Many marriages operate similarly, with the unspoken agreement, that the husband's judgment is better than the wives, that he's smarter, more clever, and so is deferred to. However we know that women are more intuitive, more sensitive, more in tune with the important values and real priorities in life. This has all proved to me that my judgment was better, my values rooted in a solid foundation. This was a revelation to me, that my judgment was sounder and my ideas smarter than his. I hadn't had the courage of my convictions. Only later did I realize that I'd been right about everything.

Now that all had changed, the balance in our marriage, in our relationship, shifted. This was all not what I'd bargained for, nothing in our marriage vows had said anything about the enormity of all this.

The traditional, women's role had not served me well. It had kept me enslaved into a role that allowed this tragedy to happen. The role of a traditional wife had enslaved me. We'd both agreed that traditional marital roles had worked smoothly for us. But now it seemed that the Women's Rights groups were right all along. By staying in traditional roles, we give away our power and our strength. By giving away our power, we allow ourselves to be in bondage to another and to be vulnerable to his weaknesses and idiosyncrasies. By not seizing our power, we weaken ourselves and so don't do as much as we could for our families, who need us at our best, at our most intuitive and most capable.

The funny thing was, towards the end, before this all blew up in our faces, we'd started looking at very expensive homes on the North Shore of Long Island. I wanted a large home in the woods. By my calculations, with all his wins, with my salary saved, our investments, and what had been left us in inheritance, we now had enough money to buy an estate—for cash. So we looked at Million dollar houses and began to agonize over the question of whether we wanted to undergo the torture of moving, enough to live in one of these mansion-types. Well—we didn't need to agonize...

****

That Spring day, I was home and a deliveryman rang the doorbell. He gave me a large envelope and another for Alan. I opened them up absent-mindedly and saw that it was a lawsuit against us, by his mother-in-law—for 1.3 Million dollars, plus our Florida home! I was sure that this must be some mistake and called Alan. He had always fixed everything in the past, so I was sure he'd be able to fix this also.

He muttered that this wasn't a good time to talk and for once I yelled at him that it certainly was a good time. He said, "I hope you'll continue to love me," which in the coming months I had reason to wonder about. He admitted that he'd borrowed money from his step-mother without her knowing, to cover gambling losses. He hastened to add that he fully intended to pay her back. I began getting the picture. I asked how was he going to pay her back 1.3 Million dollars on an accountant's and a social workers salary?

This is another common fallacy, that of thinking that the money taken is a 'loan', that it will be repaid in the future. Of course a loan is only a loan if both parties know and agree to it. In this case only one party, my husband, knew about it. This rationalization works to combat the fact that the person is 'stealing'. Normally, his own set of moral principles would not justify taking the money any other way. I fully believe that my husband really intended to repay her when he got ahead. It's just that he never got ahead. He never would get ahead. The casinos knew that for sure.

This was the beginning of the end. The end of my hopes and dreams. The end of my innocence, of my believing in Peter Pan, Santa Claus, and the tooth fairy. I grew up a lot in the next few months and learned the real meaning of the word, R-e-s-p-o-n-s-i-b-i-l-i-t-y.

I also learned the meaning of the word - Pain. In the first few days I felt like my heart broke. My husband, whom I'd totally believed in, completely trusted and loved, had had all the faith in the world in, had now admitted that he'd lied to me for the last 10 years of our marriage. And then, as if that wasn't enough, I found out that we were swamped with gigantic bills, that we couldn't pay the mortgages, and that the lawsuit was threatening foreclosure on our Florida house.

In the next few weeks, the full story came out. He admitted that although he'd gambled for the past 15 years, in the past 10 years, he'd started losing badly. After he was losing, he started 'chasing' his losses (trying to recoup the lost money with even more money, seeking to jumpstart the winning momentum again). Chasing losses can be really destructive. By this time, the gambler has lost any acumen or judgment that he might once have had. He's now filled with anxiety and dread of being discovered. So he's playing with even less 'smarts' than before. Alan said he had wanted to tell me but he knew that I'd stop his gambling. He felt he had to hide it from me. He said he couldn't stop gambling at the time and felt he would start winning again at any moment.

This need for secrecy and denial of the significance and amount of the losses is common and a part of the destructive nature of this addiction. As a gambler falls deeper in debt, his need for silence about his activities and their malevolent nature must be concealed even more. Consequently he becomes even more isolated from others who could help stop him, he becomes even more panicked and alienated from others who could help him and whom he is hurting.

Meantime Alan put 2 mortgages on our prime residence, which until now had been free and clear. He went through our stock portfolio to the tune of about $300,000. He got money out of our life insurance. He put 3 mortgages on our vacation home in Florida. He spent money we had in savings for the children's college tuition and our daughter's wedding. When a distant Aunt died a few months earlier, leaving me $20,000, money which she'd saved all her life, he spent that too.

He spent money his parents had left him for his inheritance and money my father had left me.

I couldn't believe it. I was dumb-founded, totally in shock. We'd protected ourselves from almost every eventuality, fire, theft, earthquake, flood, thieves, and yet, in the end, had succumbed at Alan's own hand. He'd done it himself. How self-destructive. As research is beginning to show, the road to hell has been paved and well-greased by the casinos and their misrepresentations.

Alan's rationalizations were carefully nurtured by the casinos and his decline was astutely planned by them in the innumerable ways the casinos have developed to part people from their money. Alan was a small fry in their ocean. There was no way that he could've swum against the prevailing current and not drowned.

As I shared the news with a few relatives and friends, they were also completely dumbfounded. Alan was the one person whom everybody turned to in time of trouble. He was the one who always knew what to do about any problem and who was very willing to handle it for you too. Alan was a conservative guy, and could be trusted with matters. Or so we thought.

Quite a few clients of his had asked him to be their Estate Trustee or Executor. He just radiates calm, trustworthiness and sensitivity to others. This whole story was so unbelievable that at first I think some of our relatives thought I'd lost my mind and was making it all up. People depended on Alan for emotional support as well as financial acumen. It was really hard to believe that he had lost all our money. And impossible to believe that he had spent and lost other people's money as well. He just wasn't like that. He was a regular guy.

Alan wasn't alone in needing to get money for gambling. The number of crimes associated with the need to obtain money for gambling routinely escalates radically about **3** *years after a casino opens.*

> *As Maura J. Casey notes in an article in the Buffalo News, 11/19/03: In the last decade, public officials of 5 area towns in Connecticut, near the 2 giant Indian casinos, several of them tax collectors, all... respected women, have been charged with embezzling hundreds of thousands of dollars from the towns that they (later) spent at casinos." 3*

I never would have believed that Alan would have succumbed to gambling. Even now, a year and a half later, it's hard to believe. Yet such noted people as Paul Merson, football player, and William Bennet, author, have all yielded to the irresistible lure of the lights and action of casinos. But to me, Alan was just a regular guy. He was always there for anyone who needed him. Alan was r-e-l-i-a-b-l-e in the fullest sense of the word. Many people counted on him in many ways, felt that he listened with real compassion to them, and then helped them decide what to do. When our children were little, he was assistant Cub Master and Little League coach. He regularly sang Christmas carols to shut-ins at our church sing-along even though he was Jewish. He would take the children and go along and sing carols and I would stay home! Our church pastor probably knew him better than he knew me. This was all really uncharacteristic of him.

But true it was and gradually the whole story came out. In the beginning when he was winning, it was all fine. But then, in the last 10 years, his luck changed and he started losing. Then he didn't know what to do with this new turn of affairs. So he kept gambling, convinced that his luck would turn again. But it never did. He ended up losing around 3 Million dollars despite occasional wins that he threw back in the pot.

After this all came out, I was depressed for months. When I confided in my family doctor about this, while seeking anti-depressants, he started telling me about his own tale of getting hooked on 'the ponies' when he was younger and how he had barely escaped that addiction. The doctor added, "How are you going to do something good out of something bad?" alluding to the question of how was the State going to fund Education, something good, from the fruits of something bad, harmful to people?

I was depressed because of the loss of my husband, as I had known and believed in him. I was also depressed because of the loss of our estate, i.e. all my money which meant the loss of all my dreams and hopes and plans. All my life I'd worked at jobs that I wasn't crazy about just because they paid the bills and paid them well. I'd given everything I had back to the family, not buying what I'd wanted, feeling that the money was better saved than spent. Now I realized that I had sacrificed for nothing, that the money I'd scrimped and saved so hard for, for our future, had been thrown away anyway.

****

I'd planned to retire from my job in a few years and spend retirement managing a farm. Both of us had thought a lot about how this would be done and we had elaborate plans. This was now impossible. We'd also planned to travel which we hadn't done. We had a lot of hopes and dreams. These were all now impossible. I didn't know where to go or what to do. Our lives had been planned down to the last detail and those plans now had just gone right out the window. Literally right into the slot machines, figuratively down the cesspool. And they had given nothing in return.

Gambling respects no age barriers. It destroys lives of young people, of seniors, with no concern. This is not an isolated or a particularly unique story. In fact, there are many situations much worse involving permanent losses, murder, child neglect, rape, prostitution, all to get money for the person's addiction, in Alan's case, gambling.

Gambling addiction is as cutthroat as drug addiction. It incites people do uncharacteristic, willful, and self-serving things to get their fix. Anything is fair game in the service of the addiction. A recent drug addiction case on Long Island, New York, shows the depths to which addicts will stoop. In February, 2004, a drug addiction case in Newsday, the Long Island paper, detailed how a grandmother, watching her 15 year old granddaughter, didn't have money for her cocaine fix of the day. So she traded the drug dealer her granddaughter, for him to do with as he pleased sexually, in exchange for cocaine. 4 To most of us, this is almost inconceivable. Yet it happened.

Another tragedy. That's what addictions do to people. They respect no one's rights, possessions, or feelings. The drug, the substance, or the activity, gambling, becomes more important than anything or anyone, even than one's loved ones. In this case, a drug addiction changed a grandmother's love from seeing another, her granddaughter, as someone to be protected, to something to be used, a vehicle with which to secure drugs. This is addiction.

I couldn't believe that my husband, in whom I had trusted all my hopes and dreams, money and schemes, could have disappointed me so much. The loss of the man I thought I knew was overwhelming. There were times when I felt like crying all day. To top it off, he wasn't functioning so great either and he had no energy to try to pull us out of this mess. I'd always thought I had a great marriage. We never argued much and when we did, we resolved it fairly easily. We'd been married for 32 years which was more than most of our friends and acquaintances. I couldn't believe that I was just now seeing a new, very vulnerable side of him.

I didn't want to see this side of him. I didn't want him to stop managing our lives and resources as well as it seemed he used to do. Alan had always managed our affairs and our family well, ensuring peace within the family and ample resources for all. When I was disheartened, I'd talk to him and feel better. When there was a problem, we all told Alan and he made it right. So now, without warning, this man was having his own mini-breakdown. And I was having my own mini-breakdown. All due to the excesses that gambling had wrought.

The pain in my heart was unbelievable. It was kind of a cross between the pain you feel when someone dies and the physical pain of someone putting a hot branding iron inside your chest. I would sit there and meditate on the pain as if it were a palpable entity. I thought sometimes that my pain would explode out of my heart and break me apart. In an intellectual way, I would be nauseous thinking of the money he'd thrown away, and the good that could've been done with it. I was broken-hearted thinking of what the children, at the time 20 and 24 years old, could be thinking of their Father, their idol. I didn't tell my son for 3 months as I wanted to wait until the end of his college semester before he found out. My daughter overheard us talking the first night and knew it all from the beginning.

The pain was unlike any other pain I'd ever had. I've lost my share of people in this world but this went beyond that. It was an active kind of pain, scouring out my heart and leaving it empty and barren, the psychic equivalent of physical pain, emotional pain. I felt like I had after 9/11, the demise of the World-Trade Center, that the worst had happened, my innocence gone, destroyed forever. Moments of grimness and searing pain were my constant companion, my ever present state of mind. I felt that if Alan could do this, anyone could do anything.

Yet this pain sowed seeds of compassion, of love. When I wasn't being too overwhelmed by my hurt, I realized that if Alan and I could get messed up, us with our advanced degrees, our family support, our own 'smarts', and sizable inheritance, then anyone could. Besides wondering how it could have happened, I began, very slowly, to accept that it had happened and that now I had to cope - somehow. I wished that he had just gotten in trouble with another woman. It would have hurt less, been cheaper, more understandable, and caused less long-term damage. Yet I had to accept that it had happened, decide what to do next, try to implement a plan to make more money.

I shared the news with few people but I did tell one counselor I knew. She commented on how much Alan loved me, which I was beginning to doubt. She assured me that his gambling wasn't about me. This helped a little if anything could. I couldn't fathom that Alan had such difficulties. He'd always been the rescuer – not the one who needed rescuing.

Another friend told me that she knew of many accountants and lawyers who succumbed to temptation when handling other people's money. I'd never heard of any before myself. After this, I heard about many. Now I was learning about ***the***

underside of the belly of the beast of Gambling. *About its seaminess, its rapaciousness, its constant hunger for more. The glitz is a hoax, entertainment is a sham, it's all about money. The constant, unending search for money. Other people's money. But this understanding didn't come easy.*

In the midst of dealing with my husband and our relationship, I had to cope with ***the bills.*** *The $150,000. worth of credit card debt, the $50,000 worth of judgments the casinos were collecting against us, and the fact that I, who had worked at well-paying jobs all my life, and saved my money constantly, was now poor. I'd become one of the world's poor, like the millions who live in the Bronx, in all the world's major cities. What hopes do they have for the American Dream as seen on TV, our mass media and culture builder. I'd worked all my life, and I still didn't have a dime.*

Trust had always been a big thing with me. I always knew that I trusted Alan as I'd trusted no one else – ever. When I found out I couldn't trust him any more, I questioned myself, ourselves, and our marriage. I said, what is a marriage if you can't trust? Yet my pain was my awakening. It was the point at which I finally grew up. No more little kid wanting to please people. Now it was me talking to lawyers, mortgage brokers, attorneys. Alan wasn't functioning well any more. I realized that if I didn't do it, it wasn't going to get done. A common woman's condition.

We had to try to salvage the little we had left. I knew that if we had to sell our house that it would break up our family, our older children would leave home and then go who-knows-where. I was determined not to let that happen. I was determined to have our lives continue with as little overt disruption as possible. I think the woman always tries to manage things, to resurrect the hope, they're the homemakers, the nest builders, the stronger of the two sexes.

Financially, I'd always had a 'pay-as-you-go' philosophy and thought that we'd agreed that this was how we'd handle our monetary affairs. In retrospect, I learned that he certainly didn't have this same understanding, or at least, didn't implement it. So now I insisted on my way, we cut up all our credit cards and started paying cash for everything – or not buying it. We eliminated extravagant gift-giving at Christmas. I'd tried to do this before, but been overruled by everyone else. Previously we'd had an orgy of materialism every Christmas morning. He finally agreed to this idea since we had no money anyway. I encouraged buying older cars, they still get you where you're going, rather than new ones. I said we could have a 5' or 6' Christmas tree not an 8 or 9' tall tree.

I found that actually I didn't need most of what I saw advertised in the stores. Before I'd spent a lot of time shopping, feeling that it was my job to create a beautiful house. Now I didn't feel the stress of making a beautiful house since we were just trying to get by. I found I liked not 'shopping till I dropped'. I suggested we use up our seemingly endless stocks of food supplies. We had cans of food bought at sales that we never used and didn't have sufficient cabinet space to hold it all. So we started using up inventory and found we now had places to put food when we came home from grocery shopping.

I realized that we weren't poor but we certainly had no money! When I was young we'd had no money but we didn't feel poor. Now I literally had no money to pay bills with and I felt poor. When I went to the store for food, I'd give the clerk, bill after bill, unrolling them slowly and carefully, so as not to make any mistakes and give too much. I felt deprived and hopeless, like I'd lost my zest and my fun-loving spirit. Sometimes I'd feel numb, like I was just going through the motions. I didn't know where to go now since he'd thrown out my money and my dreams, my hopes and my plans. I'd worked my whole life, for the past 30 years, and all that savings had been blown. I'd worked my whole life and didn't have a dime. I didn't think I had the energy to get out of bed in the morning, much less start again.

I tried to sell assets we had but there wasn't much. Alan's energy hadn't been in buying things for the house and my energy had been in saving money for the future. I wanted to sell my car and thought I could get some cash out of it. But it took me 9 months to sell my Chrysler Convertible. It had been bought in a different time, when appearances were important, looking well-to-do. Now I knew that it was really about just getting along and the appearance of things really didn't matter. Alan had bought my convertible a few years earlier saying that he paid cash for it and I believed him. Now I asked and found we were still making monthly payments on it. That was another sore spot.

I'd believed in pay-as-you-go and here I found out that for the last 5 years, we'd been making payments on a car I was led to believe was bought free-and-clear. So I put the car on the market thinking I would get good money for it. I found out that American cars didn't hold their value and the car wasn't worth much. But I sold it anyway and used an old car we had around. I learned there's a surcharge on car insurance for convertibles. More knowledge of what I learned.

I asked Alan to show me our monthly budget and to review our bill structure. It turned out we had no monthly budget and that he just paid bills as they came in, willy-nilly. I insisted on a budget. It took him 6 months to get everything written down for us just to discuss. I highly suggest everyone have a written-down budget. Otherwise you don't have an informed awareness of how you're operating financially.

This is another area where wives whose husbands are financially irresponsible or die unexpectedly are really at a loss. They've never learned to manage their financial affairs. I grew up some more. I said that there could be no expenditures over $50. without my knowledge. As we learned to scrutinize purchases, we found that there were many things we didn't need, could well live without. I started shopping for clothes, toys, and household items at thrift stores. I never would've done this before but now I felt good about 'recycling' items. The shopping is much speedier and to the point.

In my desperation, I still had to function, to go to work, to take care of my older children, and even our new 2 year old adopted child whom we'd gotten in better times. I started taking over bill-paying. I thought about this whole scenario every waking moment. It burned its way through me all the time. I couldn't think about anything else. I felt I had to be working on this problem all the time in order to solve it. I couldn't get it out of my mind.

I couldn't understand how it'd happened that my husband had betrayed me and spent all our money. I knew he loved me and that he knew that money was important to me. It's important to all of us. It's about survival and meeting our very basic human needs. Yet this is what the casinos prey on. People dropping their guard, their normal caution, in the 'thrill' of the moment, and spending what they shouldn't.

We started to make many changes in our lives. We stopped going out as we had no money. We stopped seeing friends as we felt we couldn't share the awful news and we found we were all on different wave lengths. I wanted to tell them but felt they'd never understand. When we began to broach the topic, they often changed the conversation. People are not comfortable with other's challenges.

For a while I wondered if I'd ***enabled*** *him through my interest in money. I wracked my brain for instances where I'd said it was okay to do anything for money. Finally I decided, that no, this was not about me. It wasn't about my desire for money and for the good things in life. Just like all of us, sure, I'd like to have the good things in life, an assured future. But I certainly wouldn't have ever jeopardized my existing money, my savings, for unreliable future money.*

No, I wasn't an enabler, but I think I know who was. ***The casinos enabled him****. They fed him lies that he could win, that the 'big one', was just around the corner, that gambling was a respectable activity, that he could continue going to Atlantic City just as millions of other people were doing. That he wouldn't lose forever. Yet it was a forever loss. When the money is gone, it's gone. No one's going to make it up to you. The casinos don't give it back.*

As in all losses, I went through various stages in my grief reaction, as Elizabeth Kubler-Ross, Death and Dying, writes. First I went through the denial stage – 'no, this is not really happening, I'll wake up in the morning and it'll be gone.' Sometimes in my denial, I imagined that I would enter a different field, perhaps real estate, and make a high salary and pay everything off. Sometimes I imagined we would start a class action suit against the casinos and they would give us 3 Million dollars to drop it. But we couldn't find a lawyer interested in working with us. Even extended family members went through this denial phase. They often said to me that they 'couldn't believe it', and they were sure that they'd awake and find it to be a bad dream.

This denial stage, however, didn't last long since the evidence of the lawsuit was staring up at me all the time. Then I went through the depression phase. For a long time, I had no energy, and physically was just too drained to do anything. A few times I became very angry at Alan and told him so. After I vented it to him, and he admitted it all, I would feel better inside. But that still didn't get us any money. There was a point at which it appeared that we might lose the house we'd lived in for the past 30 years and in which we'd invested our sweat by the bucketful and ourselves and our love. These were not good times.

Then I went through the bargaining and fantasy phase. I thought that if I worked hard enough, I'd make enough money to cover our losses. I thought that I could make a couple of hundred thousand dollars a year and pay off all our debt. Pure fantasy. I rationalized away my loss saying maybe I wasn't supposed to have money in this lifetime. I got a part-time job in addition to my full-time job but then found I didn't have enough time for our 2 year old. It wasn't fair to him to have me working all the time just because his father was an addict. So I cut down on my part-time job. Alan got a part-time job in addition to his very full CPA practice. So he was working all the time, during the day and now at night too. Very bad, really bad - karma, I said.

Just as we were thinking about retirement, about stopping work, about living on the 'fruits' of our labor, then suddenly we find that we have no money, everything is mortgaged to the hilt and then some, and we're looking at bankruptcy! What a kick in the gut. It took the next 6 months of my life just to begin to get over the trauma. And this trauma occurred while Alan was engaging in an activity that's completely legal, that our churches and synagogues smile upon, and millions of people engage in.

My children lost their inheritance, we almost lost our house, my husband and I could've easily gotten divorced, all our savings were gone, my husband had to declare bankruptcy, and lost business clients, just to name some of the fall-out from his gambling. These are called the 'social costs' and the impact of Gambling. These facts are 'statistics with a face', as someone said. It happened to us and is happening to many others. If it can happen to my smart accountant -husband, believe me, it can happen to anyone.

But how could it happen to us? We were insured against every possible catastrophe. We thought we had it all covered. Think again - we're all going die and we all have to go through life's difficulties. We're all human and vulnerable. What was this demon of addiction that my husband had fallen prey to? My loving husband, the one who didn't drink or smoke, never took drugs, never looked at other women, and was always caring and considerate? What could make him become so crazy as to lie to his wife and children, take money that didn't belong to him, and put us into financial ruin? Only one thing could have incited him to lose his good judgment, his morals, his common sense, and his truthfulness. His ***addiction - to gambling****!*

One can say that gambling was his own free choice. His addiction was of his own making. However I submit that free choice is not really a choice, not really a clear decision, based on weighing both alternatives and then making an educated decision, unless - its ***informed,*** *unless we're* ***aware*** *of the possibilities, the larger picture. We think we know both sides of the gambling picture, but we really don't. We're not aware of the multitude of small and large misrepresentations, lies, and half truths, that the casinos and gambling interests feed us. Sooner or later, we succumb to the propaganda until we begin to adopt their values, their mind-set, their way of thinking. We begin to believe their lies until we accept them as truth, and then 'rationalize' these untruths to ourselves.*

This is the nature of addiction. Addiction that's carefully cultivated, deliberately planned and skillfully and manipulatively developed and nurtured - until people are hooked. And when people are hooked, i.e. addicted, they loose all their money. That's the casino's aim, intention and goal. Their strategy is to adopt every half-truth, every deception, every con, until you squander all your money.

It's that simple. This is what gambling is all about - money. Gambling leads to addiction. The more available gambling is, the faster it leads to addiction. The same gambling that our states are rushing to license, that our legislators are pushing on us as an economic miracle, the supposed answer to high taxation, is the same demon that ensnared my husband and millions of others. If you can get someone addicted, the rest, the part about their money, becomes child's play. Probably legislators will want to license crack-cocaine next, if it gets enough money from the masses. Addiction is the demon that we let out of Pandora's box. The more available gambling is, the more people will engage in it. The more people gamble, the faster they'll become addicted.

****

This is not my hunch, my idea or even my opinion. It's been documented in study after study, by expert after expert. Gambling breeds addiction. Addiction breeds social costs. Social costs like divorce, bankruptcy, children neglected, domestic violence, homelessness. Addiction breeds social costs like crime, embezzlement, theft, murder. Social costs cost the taxpayer big bucks. Nothing is for free. There's no free lunch – ever! It just a matter of how fast the addiction occurs and for how much the gambler gets hooked into the industry. When, where, why and who.

The costs are always there, whether they're hidden from view or not. Whether we want to look at them or not. Whether or not we want to see. ***Our government has licensed an addictive activity - for profit.*** *Cocaine is an addictive substance. Gambling is an addictive activity. Both lead to ruin. Why is one legal and the other not? It's all about the money. A lot of money.*

****

CHAPTER TWO

THE PSYCHOLOGY OF ADDICTION

THE ADDICTION OF GAMBLING

Gambling interests don't bring out the best in society.
Warren Buffett, Chairman, CEO, Berkshire Hathaway Inc. [1]

***A**ddiction* *is the superglue in the quicksand of Gambling. It's the adhesive that holds all the pieces together, the common bond that ties all the threads into their mosaic. If there was no addiction, there would be no problem. But the reality is that there is addiction, plenty of it. Addiction is what's responsible for casino's incredible profits, for gambling's Pied-Piper appeal, and its death-like grip on people. Addiction is the devil's spell, his hypnotic trance and reverie.*

In this chapter on Addiction, certainly an extensive subject, we'll examine an overview of various aspects in regard to gambling. We'll look at such issues as how addiction occurs, why to some people and not others, and what addiction feels like. We'll also explore the issue of how many people are currently addicted to gambling, what groups might be especially susceptible to addiction, and what aspect of gambling is most addictive for people. Finally we'll discuss the big question - ***the role of the casinos in addiction****.*

As we delve into the addiction of gambling, we'll show it for what it is, a many-headed hydra enticing people onto the rocks of destruction and ruin, like sirens of old who lured sailors to their deaths on the shoals, the rocks, of barren islands. Gambling is the monster from the depths, a Medusa whose face is so terrible that once you view it, you turn to stone. Once you are exposed to gambling, once you start, you're ensnared and your fate is sealed. How can what looks like so much fun, so beautiful a goddess, be the haunting mermaid singing beautiful songs, luring people to their death?

From a clinical point of view, ***perception*** *is the beginning of addiction. The mind is led to false perceptions or views leading to incorrect, i.e. wrong, expectations. These false expectations guide the person's behavior, gambling, toward a hoped for and expected, but impossible outcome, that of winning. This feeling that you're 'going to win', the* ***deception,*** *sets the stage for the whole misguided phenomena called Addiction to begin, unfold, and spring full-blown into existence.*

Who sets up the deception to begin with? This is part of the big question. Does the person set the stage himself with his own hopes and dreams and schemes? Or does the casino bring out the stage, build it, advertise it, make it attractive and enticing, and pay the mermaids to sing? Does the gambler in his own unique weakness draw the sword that he'll use to stab himself, or do the casinos present it to him, all polished and shined, and offer it to him, looking like a halo?

These are the questions we'll discuss as we ponder what an addiction is and how it unfolds. Gambling qualifies as the quintessential addiction. It straitjackets the soul and keeps it bound. It binds up the spirit, entraps it, and lets it beat itself to death on the rocks of expectation, seeking to regain its freedom. It's one more attraction on the highway towards death, keeping us bound souls, unable to see the light for the obscuring darkness. The darkness that we've constructed ourselves, trip by trip, bet by bet...We call upon the darkness and say to it, I seek the night, my restless soul yearns for meaning in Excitement and Money, the fiends of illusory sense pleasures. What kind of enlightened existence is this?

****

In casinos, people ***look*** *like they're having the time of their lives – the illusion, the first step in the brain-washing. What isn't so apparent is the heart of the addiction, the loss of irreplaceable monies. What's unseen, what we don't tell others is that we're addicted and have lost hundreds or thousands or even millions of dollars. Similarly, communities don't advertise their increased spending for social programs, for the costs of bankruptcy to businesses and to individuals. They advertise the lights and the glitter. But the effects are there, they can be seen. Misery doesn't show its face to the public, it doesn't open it to the light. It hides in* *private, masquerading as depression, neglect, homelessness and a million other demons.*

What is the addiction of gambling? Is it similar to other addictions? What are the characteristics of addiction - is it a disease or an excuse? How do we cope with it in a productive and aware manner? What theories about human behavior and addiction make sense when it comes to gambling and what involvement do casinos have in people becoming addicted? If casinos have a role in people's addiction, are they culpable, are they liable? Can they be sued in a court of law? Why do some people become addicted, spending all their savings and going to great lengths to embezzle and various crimes, and other people walk away without a parting glance?

When gambling first became widespread in this country, in the 80's and 90's, we weren't as sophisticated as now, we didn't have the body of research we do now. We didn't realize the nature and intensity of what the addiction could become. When there was just Las Vegas, a destination resort, a resort people had to journey to, gambling wasn't as widespread or as convenient. Now with the advent of casinos in almost every state, and gambling as very convenient, the impact of the disease of addiction has become full-blown, widespread, and pervasive.

WHAT IS ADDICTION?

***Addiction** is what makes gambling the monster that it is, the fly-in-the-ointment that makes gambling so destructive and hard to control for people. If it wasn't for Addiction, then gambling would be just the 'Entertainment' that the casinos promote it as and not the devastating social problem, even Public Health concern, that it's become. Yet gambling is addictive, and like any other addiction, it carries the seeds of people's destruction within it.*

***Addiction** is **gambling's micro-effect** on the individual. The subsequent chapter, **Economics,** will detail the effect on **society**, the impact on **communities**. **Community impact is its macro effect - economic decline.** Both, economic decline and individual deterioration, are silent, hidden, deteriorative effects. Both are opposite sides of the same coin. Both imperceptible to the eye, yet felt by the heart.*

*Being addicted to something, **the state of being addicted**, in this case, gambling, is a state of mind. It totally affects how you look at your life events, the 'cast' or 'slant' you put on them, the mental understanding you have of the whole picture. It determines your thoughts, your perception.*

***Being addicted is also a state of being**. It describes how you **feel,** your emotional and physical sensations. How you feel inside is the sum-total of your* *thoughts, your emotional feelings, and your physical feeling. For someone addicted, they're constantly feeling, on an internal level, the effects of the addiction, whatever it is.*

An addiction, by definition, dictates that you feel agitated, 'needy', anxious, nervous, not peaceful, not content, dissatisfied in some way, bored, at loose ends,...Otherwise, you wouldn't be addicted, you wouldn't be in the grip of something that forces you to progressively invest yourself more and more into an activity not beneficial for you and yours, and to engage in this activity to the extent and to the excesses that you need to pursue it.

The more the drug addict gets addicted, the more he has to take of the drug to get his high. The more agitated he is that he won't be able to get what he needs to get high, the more desperate he becomes to obtain the necessary substance. This is part of the progressive aspect of the disease.

***Addiction is being in a state of need and of neediness.** It's a lack of inner resources to be able to cope with the world without a significant infusion of pleasure and excitement, or whatever it is that the particular addiction provides to the individual. The entity needs, or thinks he needs, what the addiction provides to him, to function in this world. The addiction allows him to achieve the degree of sense pleasures that he thinks he needs or, perhaps just wants. Characteristically, the state of mind and the state of being of individuals with addictions comes from a more negative place, than people who don't have addictions, or at least, not so obvious ones.*

*The issue of the **negativity**, on whatever level, is what gives the understanding that addictions are not helpful to the individual, don't bring contentment, peace, and happiness, but rather insecurity, fear, physical ill-health, and dis-ease. Addictions force us to turn away from our higher selves, from seeking to fulfill our potential, and turn us to increased levels of frustration and suffering. Addictions are **negative passions**. They lead us in the direction of our 'darker' selves. Once we become addicted to something, we become as a plaything in the hands of the Devil, a toy in his grasp to do with as he wishes. We lose our humanity, our self-control, our concern for others, our basic compassion, our good judgment, our awareness of where we're going and how to get there, i.e. goals and direction, as well as our basic honesty and integrity.*

****

The most commonly accepted definition of Addiction, that of the American Medical Association, first noted in 1980, that compulsive gambling is an addictive illness in which the subject is driven by an overwhelming, uncontrollable impulse to gamble. According to this definition, the impulse ***progresses*** *in intensity and urgency, consuming more and more of the individual's time, energy and emotional and material resources. Ultimately it invades, undermines, and often destroys, everything meaningful in his life.*

DSM-IV DIAGNOSIS

DSM-IV DEFINITION – AN ILLNESS

Individuals with this Impulse-Control Disorder recurrently fail to resist gambling to such an extent that it leads to disruption of major life pursuits. The diagnostic criteria, 312.31, pathological gambling is characterized by:

A. Persistent and recurrent maladaptive gambling behavior as indicated by 5 (or more) of the following:

1. is ***preoccupied*** *with gambling (e.g. preoccupied with reliving past gambling experiences, handicapped or planning the next venture, or thinking of ways to get money with which to gamble)*

2. needs to gamble with ***increasing amounts of money*** *in order to achieve the desired excitement*

3. has ***repeated unsuccessful efforts to control****, cut back, or stop gambling.*

4. is ***restless or irritable*** *when attempting to cut down or stop gambling.*

5. gambles as a way of ***escaping*** *from problems or of relieving a dysphoric mood (e.g. feelings of helplessness, guilt, anxiety, depression).*

6. after losing money gambling, often ***returns*** *another day to get even ('chasing' one's losses).*

7. ***lies*** *to family members, therapist, or others* ***to conceal*** *the extent of involvement with gambling.*

8. has committed ***illegal acts*** *such as forgery, fraud, theft, or embezzlement to finance gambling.*

9. has jeopardized or ***lost a significant relationship****, job or educational or career opportunity because of gambling.*

10. ***relies on others*** *to provide money to relieve a desperate financial situation caused by gambling.*

B. The gambling behavior is not better accounted for by a manic episode. (Diagnostic and Statistical Manual of Mental Disorders, fourth Edition. 1994 American Psychiatric Association). 2

The important thing is that gambling was defined as an 'illness'. This was the first time it was recognized as such. This sobering definition gives some feeling for the illness it defines. It's further described as a 'behavior' disorder, meaning that the illness manifests itself in the aberrant behavior of the individual. Some authorities call it a 'thought' disorder because it's really the person's ***thoughts*** *that lead him to pursue his misguided behavior.*

What is relevant for our purposes, is that at least some of the misguided, incorrect ***thoughts are instilled there by the casinos,*** *by their misrepresentative advertising and overall marketing strategies. When a slot machine continually shows 2 out of the 3 symbols needed to win the jackpot, many people are so incited by this that they continue to push for that last symbol. People are led to believe that they can get that last symbol and thus win the jackpot. However that's also a lie, machines are programmed to frequently show 2 symbols leading people to believe they 'almost won', but very infrequently to give the required 3 symbols. This is one small example of casinos inciting addiction.*

NATURE OF ADDICTIONS

The nature of addictions is that they consist of an overwhelming urge, felt as almost uncontrollable to the person addicted, and they progress in intensity, consuming the individual's time, energy and emotional and material resources. Who would want to be at the mercy of an impulse that 'often destroys everything meaningful' in his life? One gets 'hooked' on the addictive activity or substance and then, to the extent the person is addicted, all of one's thoughts are focused on the activity.

This substance monopolizes the individual's time and thoughts, to the exclusion of other, more constructive things in the person's life. Other activities can and do distract a person from the destructive impulse of the addiction, such as religious affiliation, family, work, other interests or hobbies. But they gradually begin to get neglected and forgotten as the addiction builds in its intensity. The obsessive nature of the person's thoughts act as a catch-22, isolating the gambler and increasing the obsession and tunnel-vision with the addiction's destructive thoughts and fantasies.

This is why people say that the addiction 'takes over' their life, not allowing them time to explore other avenues of gratification in their lives, not allowing them emotional energy to look into other sources of possible interests or pleasure, not allowing them money to do other things which might divert their exclusive focus on the addiction. The person essentially has 'married' their addiction. It becomes their first priority, their first love. Their thoughts become obsessed with the activity or substance and how to get it.

All addictions are like this. They monopolize the person's thoughts, so that the person can't think clearly, can't see what is happening, is unable to take stock of where they are or where they want to go in life. When something has taken over your 'thoughts', you're are in a poor position to be able to rise above it, to come to terms with what's happening, to assess the overall situation and correct or change as needed, towards a more productive or beneficial result.

Other addictions, such as the widespread one of illicit drugs in our society, alcohol abuse, smoking, all have the common characteristic of creating ***physical dependency*** *by introducing a foreign substance into the body and the blood. Often, people need to be 'detoxed' from the toxic, poisonous effects of these alien substances. Gambling, however, is different in that there is no foreign substance introduced into the body.*

The foreign substance here is introduced into a person's ***mind.*** *The toxicity here becomes not a physical substance but a more intangible one consisting of the person's own* ***thoughts*** *and ideas about money and about winning. It's more subtle, more difficult to detect and control. Some say that money here is the abused substance, such as drugs, but in fact, it's the misguided energy that takes over a person's thoughts and mind, ensuring their lack of clarity and right direction.*

When something takes over your mind, it seems to become a part of you, like your right arm. You are led to think that those thoughts are rational, normal and logical. Our thoughts appear to be a part of ourselves to such a degree that they almost seem to become us, to have a life of their own, and to be completely in accord with things as they are. With gambling, the foreign substance introduced into the mind is in the form of a person's own misguided ideas. However, in this instance, when a person listens to his thoughts, he's being led further along incorrect and destructive pathways. However he thinks and is convinced it's the right direction, the correct course of action.

When a gambler thinks that he is 'going to win', and keeps throwing money into a slot machine, feeling that it 'must be ready to pay out', he's convinced himself of that truth. He 'knows' in his gut, he'll tell you, that this machine is 'ready' to go, that the big payout is just around the corner and it's going to be his. So he perseveres, an activity which has brought him success before in his life. He's convinced himself and if you stand there and listen, he'll convince you too.

If he's been successful previously, he's accustomed to being right and to getting what he tries for. In this instance, however, when he acts according to past patterns which have brought him success, his knowledge, perseverance and hard work, only make him poor. He cannot win on the basis of anything he does. The machines are programmed according to things out of his control. He can only helplessly keep putting money in, hoping and waiting for the illusory big payout.

As he continues putting money in the machine, he hears other people apparently winning jackpots from the multitude of lights and bells he sees going off. He's led to believe that others are winning. He feels he can do it too. But the random number generators inside the machines go off very <u>infrequently</u> for the big wins. They are not affected at all by how much he wants it, feels he's due to have it, or anything else.

His thoughts are obviously misguided. They're not the product of rational thinking, they make no sense. The thinking is not clear and goal-directed. But with the addiction of gambling, one is led to believe that one is in one's right mind, that one is coping well, and fully in control of one's actions. With alcohol there are impairment and physical symptoms such as slurred speech or slowed reflexes which make the use of the substance obvious. With the addiction of gambling, one can appear to be very much in control of the situation, not realizing how misguided or sick you are, unaware of the damage you're doing, and the hurt you're causing.

'THE HIGHS'

One question, for gambling addiction as with other kinds, is whether there's a biological, and/or genetic component. In terms of gambling, recently researchers at the Massachusetts General Hospital have found that ***gambling and drug use show similar results in the person's brain.***

This has been suspected for some time, that gambling and drug use would show similar biological indices within the brain. Scientists have recently proved this biological thesis with MRI machines that show the 'highs' of both produce similar brain activation paths and channels. This implies that both addictions operate similarly in at least some part of the brain of the person addicted. This means it's biological but does not imply its genetic since one could say that the stimulus would produce a similar effect in all people. Genetic implies that one has a predisposing tendency in one's genes, or from ones parents. Biological may encompass genetic selection but not necessarily so.

As addictions specialist at the University of Florida, Scott Teitlebaum, who has worked with compulsive gamblers for more than 30 years, said, gamblers and substance abusers suffer from a disease that seems similar. "When you look at the substance-abuse (drugs) population, brain scans and chemical studies have shown parallels between them and compulsive gamblers." This associate professor of psychiatry and director of the Shands Florida Recovery Center, noted that "Some studies have shown the high of the 'action' for compulsive gamblers is very similar to a cocaine high."3

Monitoring brain activity in volunteers playing a $50 game of chance showed that gambling "produces brain activation very similar to that observed in a cocaine addicts receiving an infusion of cocaine," researcher Hans Breiter also noted. 4 www.suntimes.com/output/health/cst-nws-gamb01.html

So if the stimulating substance or activity triggers similar areas in the brain, similar activation patterns, then we might assume that the disorders have certain things in common, namely their addictive qualities, that they trigger similar responses in people. If we assume that drug involvement or alcoholism are bona fide addictions, it would seem that gambling addiction would also be in this category. This would lead us to infer that gambling is a real, a legitimate addiction, which has some influence and produces similar effects as other addictions, in terms of physical involvement within the body. Just as drugs and their impact upon individuals is clear-cut and acknowledged to be significant, so also is gambling and its effect upon the individual, in biological terms.

Drugs such as methadone for heroine addicts, or nicotine replacement therapies, including Nicoderms for smokers, are designed to inhibit the withdrawal and physical dependence, biologically-determined symptoms, of these addictions. Are we destined to develop drugs for gambling addictions also?

In an effort to block these 'highs', scientists are developing a class of pharmaceutical drugs called opium antagonists. These block the brain's opiate receptors, preventing the 'high' an addict gets. If an addict places a bet and his body responds in a half-hearted, lackadaisical manner, then gambling wouldn't have such a powerful effect on the individual. Dr. Suck Won Kim, a psychiatrist at the University of Minnesota, says that these drugs, 'treat urges'. Dr. Kim, who recently received a National Institute of Health grant to test drugs in treating patients with pathological gambling problems, had conducted prior research showing that the drug, Naltrexone, was effective in reducing the highs and the urges to gamble. Gamblers become so intensely involved in playing that they "forget to eat, forget to go to the bathroom, and don't sleep." It puts people "almost in a trance. That's how intensely gambling desire and excitement enslaves people," said Kim. 6

This research further demonstrates, as did alcohol and drug research, 30 years ago, that the urge to gamble, can be at least partially a biologically based disorder, i.e. an illness. Over the past 30 years, "There has been a shift in the conceptualization of problem gambling," according to Marc Potenza, director of Yale University's problem gambling clinic. "It's gone from being seen as a sin to a bad habit to a ***biologically based disorder****."*

On an emotional level, psychiatrist Nancy Petry, hypothesizes that ***gambling and depression*** *are linked. She feels that treatments aimed at the depression may reduce the gambling problem. These drugs, part of a group called selective serotonin reuptake inhibitors, the antidepressants, have been used to treat mood or affective disorders, as well as obsessiveness. 7 It's felt these drugs could reduce problem gamblers' fixation over their next bets. However, I would suggest that if its* ***your*** *money that's riding on the next bet, the fixation is not totally inappropriate. So the prevention, obviously, needs to be even before the bet-placing moment.*

In terms of depression, Petry speculates that the urge to gamble hides or compensates for an underlying depression. This certainly may be possible considering that it's estimated that a majority of the American populace suffers from depression or anxiety at various times in their lives. However, I'm not sure about depression as an overall cause for the etiology, the cause of the illness of gambling addiction. While it may be a precipitating factor for some people, I can note from our experience, that Alan was never depressed a day in his life. He was the quintessential 'happy-go-lucky' guy. Until after - he realized what he'd done, where gambling had led him.

Then, he became depressed, as do many others. Then he went from the highs that the act of gambling produced, to the lows of depression with its attendant bad thoughts, lack of energy, and feelings of hopelessness. This is what the casino gambling did to him. It psyched him up and then dropped him down. Then he was very depressed and found it difficult to deal with, as this feeling was new and alien to him.

Depression is the kind of associated disorders that the research of Breen and Zimmerman, in their paper, "Rapid Onset of Pathological Gambling in Machine Gamblers," discussed. However, they felt that depression was generally a lesser factor in gambling disorders, although they acknowledged that for some people it may be significant. Rather "the social, environmental, and stimulus features of mechanized gambling" were to blame for the rapid onset of compulsive gambling. Breen & Zimmerman, p. 1 8

Of course, all of this research about the addiction doesn't begin to deal with the issue that ***most pathological gamblers would never have begun gambling if the casinos weren't there****. The majority of problem gamblers would* ***never have gambled*** *had it not been pursued by the gambling industry and legalized by our government. We have unleashed this new self-destructive demon ourselves. Our legislators continue to expand the scope of this multi-headed, omnivorous Demon.*

All because of the government's and the industry's addiction to its profits, to the money. ***'Follow the money'*** *could be the mantra not only for reporters Woodward and Bernstein in the Watergate affair, but also a watchword for gambling interests seeking to spread their culture of gambling and corruption.* ***Legality = Frequency + Availability = Addiction.***

Remember ***the National Gambling Impact Study Commission (NGISC)*** *report, 5 years ago, in 1999, estimated pathological gamblers at between 1 and 2 % of the entire adult population, now a generally agreed upon very conservative figure. Their findings portrayed* ***gambling as a 'highly addictive activity.'*** *This figure counts only pathological gamblers, not 'problem' gamblers, who are also assumed to wreck havoc of some kind and to be in the process of progressing to the pathological-gambler level. 9*

Problem gamblers, without treatment of some kind, degenerate into pathological gamblers within a few years. Remember this disorder is 'progressive'. It doesn't stay still, quiescent, passive. Gambling itself has expanded markedly in our society since the time of the NGISC commission. Since that report estimated the incidence in 1999, and we're now in 2004, we may assume that the percentage, as well as the overall number, of both pathological and problem gamblers has increased. Counting both problem and pathological gamblers, together with the quantitative increase over time and overall gambling expansion, there is probably a much greater number of the general population, inflicting their substantial damage on themselves, their families, and our society.

At this point, most researchers state figures of compulsive gamblers, as being in the 5-10% range of all gamblers. Some researchers, especially when referring to special groups, such as the elderly or youth, even cite figures as high as 20%.

> *"It's about becoming an addict and losing control over something that can destroy our lives. Advanced age and gambling can be a deadly combination, added Fowler. Gambling addicts often neglect food and medication. 10*

Beyond that risk, the suicide rate is highest among the elderly. Compulsive gambling carries with it the highest suicide risk of any form of addiction. One counselor at PTA @ Care in North Palm Beach, Florida, said that often the hard part is getting elderly to seek help. "Many are of a mind that they're going to die anyway, so what does it matter." 11 What a scary thing to hear. It could well be my mother or your father. The addiction comes and we all get bitten. Htt::/www.palmbeachpost.com/news/content/auto/epaper/editions/today/nbews 04a751069040608a007e.html

You don't know when you place your first bet, that this simple act, placing a coin in a machine, an action that looks so easy and simple, can lead you to ruin. It's not just innocent fun. It's deceptively enticing, so much so, that many gamblers feel 'at their best' when playing the machines. The ***adrenaline rush*** *they experience makes them feel self-confident, in charge of the situation, empowered, and overall, very good! Gambling, like other addictions, makes people forget about life difficulties, overlook stresses, self-doubts, chronic feelings of lack. It gives the 'hit', the 'high', the euphoric, feeling of being on top of the world. This biological state of being 'high' is stimulated and calculatedly nurtured by the total ambiance of gambling, by everything in the casinos.*

People who have the least may be suffering the most from casinos and the state lottery, new research from the Connecticut Council on Problem Gambling shows. A recent article in the Hartford Courant, 8/10/04, noted that people with little money may be losing the most. "More than a third of the problem gamblers who dialed the council's telephone help line last year earned less than $25,000 a year, and 16 percent were unemployed. Over two-thirds of those problem gamblers earned less than $45,000 annually," noted a survey by the Connecticut Council. The survey questioned approximately 600 problem gamblers who called into the Connecticut Council's 2003 help line survey. Results noted that gamblers in the survey lost $21,542 during the previous year and reported average lifetime gambling losses of $114,593. Slot machines at the two Indian casinos were the most popular choice for problem gamblers, followed by lottery scratch tickets and blackjack card games.

"Too many (problem gamblers) are going [to casinos] because they are looking to make money," said Marvin Steinberg, executive director of the problem gambling council. "There is a tremendous impact on the individual families in the community. This is no small problem."

"We don't have a full picture, but we do have a consistent picture, a picture to be really concerned about," Steinberg said. 11A The council's survey consisted of gamblers who called the telephone help line. Staff members used a 151-item questionnaire in interviewing the more than 600 problem gamblers.

The state is addicted to the money, its citizens are addicted to the 'high'. This is the 'rush' that gamblers are striving for. Clinically and emotionally, psychiatrists have noted that when the adrenaline rush is making the gambler 'high', he's likely to be in a very 'dissociated' state. This is where someone does not actually feel or be aware they are in their body, but rather feel out of themselves, totally in an escapist, relaxed not-thinking place. This is their state of mind that dictates how they feel and what they do. This is their state while dealing, and playing, with their hard-earned money.

The high that gamblers feel is master-minded deliberately and carefully by casinos in order to enhance and maintain these feelings. Everything in a casino, from the lack of clocks and the absence of windows, to the loud noises and lights that the coins or tokens make dropping into the machine's metal basin, to the reps warmly greeting gamblers by name, is carefully intended to prolong and intensify this false high. The high serves to distract and disorient the gambler. It puts him in a different time and space than he usually is in, a different reality for him. In the absence of his customary supports, in the absence of being 'grounded', his traditional values, his common sense, his normal rationality, all disappear.

Gamblers often say that gambling is a relief for them, an escape from the mundane realities of everyday life. They state it gives them a feeling of excitement and ecstasy, a glow, a state of near-oblivion. They say it's mood-altering and in the long run, perception altering. If perception is how you see things, it certainly is perception altering. If your perception is that you can win, that's a erroneous and unclear orientation for someone who goes to a casino for a night's entertainment, not anticipating the loss of any undue amount of money.

Gambling transforms your state of mind from your normal life, to an incredibly exhilarating feeling, complete with a sense of power and even a (misguided) sense of purpose. A gambler's state-of-mind becomes wrapped in an illusion of being able to make a lot of money, to be able to afford all the good things in life, the large house, the boat, expensive cruises, etc. Their perception becomes 'altered' in that they actually think that they'll be able to accomplish these goals, that they'll be able to hit that jackpot, to get their picture on the casino wall, to provide amply for their families.

Yet of course, the reality is that these thoughts are illusory. The only thing they're really doing is losing all they have and making life doubly difficult for themselves and their loved ones. These illusions are fed, nurtured, even created, by the casino hype. "Someone's gotta win", "If you don't play, you can't win." Both the verbal and the non-verbal messages, "Stay with us and be one of the beautiful people", "Be one of the in-crowd", all propel the gambler down the road to hell. All the while he thinks that he's doing something which will pay off in the end. These illusions lead to whole involved scenarios such as "I'm special, I can win," or special schemes which only he knows which he believes will allow him to win when others don't.

My husband's 'special system' involved simply pressing your advantage with the size of your bets while you were winning. In other words, bet high and fast during the winning streak. He would also say that he was just very 'gifted' to be able to always win, that he had really good money karma. He told these stories so convincingly that I believed them. He got to the point where he believed them too. He would say that 'yes, he lost sometimes, but overall he was a winner, overall he was winning more than he was losing'. Given that he was a winner, I would allow him to continue gambling. Of course it was all a lie, so as to be able to do what he wanted to do, to gamble, to prolong the thrills, the adrenaline rush, to continue his addiction.

DEFENSE MECHANISMS - DENIAL

My husband was a classic case of being ***in denial****. Many people use this particular defense of denial. Denial is a defense mechanism that people use to allow their thoughts and actions to be in sync, in accord, with each other. Defense mechanisms are strategies we use to explain to ourselves what is happening in the external world and then to validate to ourselves our response.*

They let us make sense of what happens, justify our actions, and then decide further action. They can work beneficially or not, according to how we use them, to what degree, and in the service of whatever rationalization we're trying to accommodate. If we're poor and the rest of the neighborhood is rich, we can 'rationalize' and say there are just no jobs out there. This can be true or not depending on circumstances. Defense mechanisms can work for us, or in the service of our illusions and fantasies.

Many gamblers will say 'yes, they lost today but will win tomorrow', 'it's just an off day.' This denial of the reality of the loss allows them to not look at or not face the large amount of money lost. Alan said one time when he and his friends lost a particularly large amount of money, they had an especially 'fun' time, laughing uproariously over the slightest of jokes. They were all 'denying' what had happened.

When we don't want to have to face something in our lives, denial is the defense of choice, so to speak. When we feel we either can't or don't want to do something, presumably because the alternative is not something we feel we can cope with, then we 'put it out of our minds', i.e. 'deny' it.

My husband denied how much money he lost because he didn't want to face the fact that he was losing money. He never counted up how much money he spent because then he would have had to face the extent of his losses. Many gamblers never total up their losses because that requires them to look at and take account of what's happening. Many embezzlers take money one check at a time. Once they are discovered, they're also shocked at the amount they've taken. They've been denying all along, saying to themselves that they'll 'pay it back,' when they get that big win.

They 'deny' the reality of what they're doing by rationalizing that 'with their first big win, they'll pay back all the money.' They really want to pay it back. But of course it never happens, the big win never comes. Their intentions are honorable, but their actions are not. They're so caught up in their 'highs', in the thrills, in casino propaganda, in their own drama, that they don't see the writing on the wall. They don't see that they can't ever get back even. They're caught up in something bigger than themselves but they don't realize that. They're 'small-fry' thinking that they can succeed where others have failed, that they can win when everyone else loses, that they can best the casinos at their own game. They don't admit that 'the House never loses'.

Denial can be a pathological, destructive defense when used in the service of negative and destructive scenarios. For example, when wives don't feel that they can confront a husband's abuse of a child, they 'deny' that anything is happening. Years later when children ask mother why she never said or did anything, it was because she was 'in denial'. The defense mechanism didn't allow her to plan strategy, to make alliances, even to listen to her child. Her denial didn't let her 'get to first base' in terms of handling the situation. It didn't allow her to ***admit*** *that anything was going on at all because that admission would have forced her to act.*

It's a defense mechanism that doesn't allow people to function effectively, to act in their own interests because it cuts off all communication about the negative occurrence. It effectively throttles or limits communication and actions that might mitigate or correct the situation. The individual doesn't admit to himself that there's anything to be concerned about, much less something for which action is necessary. It cuts off any possibilities to remediate the situation.

This is why when gamblers are discovered finally by their wives, either when all the money is gone or when the embezzlement has been discovered, the wives invariably say, with complete honesty, that they had no idea that the gambling was so out of control. The wives had no clue because the gambler in his denial was super-

careful not to let others have any idea of what was happening, not to let anyone close to them realize what was happening.

The gambler is in total denial that his gambling had gone way overboard. When Alan shared with me the extent of his gambling and his losses, I was in shock. I had no idea that he had lost any money at all, never mind 3 Million dollars. He had no idea that his losses had gone anywhere near that high either. He never added up losses. ***Denial is such a powerful defense mechanism that it ruins lives before it lets go of its pit-bull like grasp.***

Denial and addictions go hand-in-hand. When parents are concerned about children using drugs and the children don't want to talk or even admit that they're using them, this is denial. It shuts out the person's feelings, and closes off others' offers of help. It shuts out everything, not allowing help to get past the person's walls. This is why self-help groups say that a person must first admit they have a problem, otherwise they won't take them into treatment. Because admitting you have a problem effectively strangles the defense of denial. Without admitting that there's a problem, no one can even get in the door. The first step in the 12 Step series, states that "I am powerless over my problem." This admits that there is a problem and that the person cannot fight it alone.

Self-help groups, such as Gamblers Anonymous*, are very effective in combating the power of Denial and its fundamental role in addiction. There are self-help groups for drug addiction, Narcotics Anonymous, NA, for gambling addiction, GA, and for eating addictions, Overeaters Anonymous, OA. These groups are often more effective than individual psychotherapy because in a one-to-one situation, the gambler continues to be enmeshed in his own unclear perception of half-truths and lies, in his own vision and understanding of the problem. He can't get out of his own flawed view which is what kept him stuck for so long to begin with. He can't get out of his own head and see the larger picture. His mind and thoughts continually take him 'down' and he doesn't know how to break free of them.*

Rationalization *is another defense mechanism that travels with Denial. With rationalization, the person explains away or 'rationalizes' what is happening so that he doesn't face what is really going on. He invents explanations, overall perspectives, to mitigate and smooth over his losses. He gives excuses to himself and others. These excuses are often clever manipulations of reality in an effort to see things from a different, more benevolent, albeit false, perspective. The primary rationalization that is so common is the one that says, 'I didn't steal that money from my employer, I fully intend to pay it back when I hit big...'*

Of course, the 'big hit' never comes. Even if it does, it gets plowed right back into the machines in the hope of an even 'bigger' hit. Gamblers are sincere in their intention to pay people back. They don't believe they're stealing. But this is the rationalization, the excuse they use, the mental words they say to themselves. When found out, they say these words to others. If they didn't say this to themselves, most gamblers couldn't do what they do, couldn't justify their own actions to themselves.

Most compulsive gamblers are straight, law-abiding, prudent people with no prior record of any criminal activity. They would find it difficult to justify their behavioral excesses without these defenses of denial and rationalization. Certainly the 5 tax collectors in the small towns around Connecticut's 2 big Indian casinos found guilty of embezzling, were previously law-abiding, functional individuals who had achieved a certain degree of success in their careers. For sure, William Bennett, part of the Bush administration with published books to his credit, was a productive member of society. Obviously Pete Rose had achieved some accomplishments in his life previous to gambling. My own husband could never have taken money that didn't belong to him except that he 'rationalized' his behavior by saying he intended to pay it back. It's said that humans can invent a reason and an excuse for almost anything they do and gambling is a prime example.

FACING PROBLEMS, FACING LIFE

The gambler's own way of looking at his life, his characteristic state of mind and thoughts about his gambling, have proved detrimental and clouded his reality. He hasn't wanted to look at certain things in his life, such as why he needs to gamble so much, what he derives from it, how much money he's spending. He hasn't looked at the question of whether he really wants to spend his life and his fortune this way. Once he answers these questions, he may find that he has thrown himself into gambling so totally in order to perhaps engage in exciting activities while he simultaneously doesn't look at other, perhaps more challenging or difficult issues in his life. The difficult things don't get looked at. Who wants to look at something that's not easily amenable to solution and certainly not 'fun'. We've been led to believe that we're here 'for fun'.

Gambling takes people into a zone that seems more carefree, fun, at least in the short term. The gambler is not interested in dealing with the hard things in his life, his relationships with others, his financial situation, his career, his demanding children. He wants to have a good time, a somewhat immature orientation, the Peter-Pan syndrome, the 'I-only-want-to-see-life-as-a-tourist' syndrome. Possibly not the most 'responsible' attitude?

Entertainment is okay, except that the gambler does it to excess. He's completely focused on enjoying himself, having a good time. He spends his time and his money, both limited commodities, and uses them in the service of the voracious and many-headed hydra of gambling. If he uses his time and money to gamble, he obviously doesn't have them for other things in his life, such as his family, his obligations.

Perhaps he's ***'avoiding'*** *his other responsibilities by gambling so much. Certainly he's not being in an accountable mode, not thinking about other's needs, not trying to do anything or help anyone but himself. The gambler lacks strong self-controls and self-discipline. He's immersed in the 'instant-gratification' culture where resistance to temptation is not a priority and self-discipline is viewed as a bad word.*

This total "I" orientation is what Eastern religions call being in the 'ego.' The ego is seen as our smaller self, the self that's involved with getting and spending, holding onto things, as opposed to being and becoming, discovering ourselves, our greater Self, our spirit or soul. When we're in our ego, we're consumed by the emotions of fear and doubt. It's a gambling mentality, feeling that we need 'more', a 'scarcity' model. To addicted gamblers, there's never enough.

Our addicted gambler needs to have a total ***'paradigm shift'****, a new understanding, a different perspective, on how he handles his responsibilities, his inevitable difficulties in life. A paradigm shift is a completely new way of looking at things, qualitatively and quantitatively. It's thinking outside the 'box'.*

Gambler's paradigms are full of addictive values which lead to their undoing. *Such values as putting money and excitement as priorities, thinking that steady gambling over time will yield monetary rewards, living only in the 'hit' of the gamble, can only show the way to ruin. They lead to our unhappiness, to our drama, and our tragedy. If you want to mess up your life, to throw away what you have and not get anything in return, then go ahead and gamble. Gambling will do nothing for you. It will not make you wealthy and will not make you happy. It will not make others around you happy. Gambling unleashes the hounds of hell. It bids them 'welcome, come in and make yourself at home'. You may think you can best these foes but be wary, no one has done so yet.*

The act of gambling, the act of turning to an addictive substance or activity, is done by many so that they don't have to handle difficult issues in their life. A drug addict shoots up because he wants more excitement, more of a 'high', than his life normally gives him. He's not content with life as it is. A food addict continues eating even after he has filled his stomach because he seeks more physical pleasure than he normally gets in his life. He 'craves' something that he can't quite describe or put his finger on, but which he feels is missing in his life.

We seek to get into a state of feeling fed, being nurtured, a sensation of well-being, because we intuit that our own lives are lacking, or wanting, in something. Many people have this feeling of something missing in their lives. People say, 'Is this all there is?' or they have some inner yearnings which they can't seem to fulfill. The only problem and difference with our addicted friend, is that when he has these feelings in his life, he then acts to counteract them ***to excess****. That's another reason for addiction by some and not others, the urge to seek relief in sense pleasures and physical fulfillment.*

When we gamble on something, when we take a risk, a chance, we're turning away from the traditional mechanisms for getting what we want and need in life. We're bypassing age-old traditions of getting what we need, steady and consistent work, until we can afford it. Instead, either because we're impatient, or because we know we won't be able to achieve it the slow, incremental way, the gradual approach, or because we feel that this is an improved, faster way, we throw caution to the winds and engage in 'risky' behavior.

We seek to fulfill ourselves from external phenomena, from the sensory world of pleasure and pain. We seek happiness in money, in sex, in food, in excitement. We want the excitement and thrills that the casinos are so expert in generating, feeling our own lives a little 'boring' or slow. The casinos know this and seek in their advertisements to 'show you a good time, to show you where the action is', to incite you to leave your money in their casino ***any way they can.***

The casinos are only too happy to indulge our impatience, our instant-gratification mentality. They're not bound by any truth-in-advertising laws, any moral concerns, or anything else. They're driven by their bottom line, the statement of ***profit and loss****.*

ADDICTION—AN INTERNAL CRAVING

If there's one crucial idea in the field of addiction, it's ***DESIRE.*** *The person is faced with a sudden, overwhelming and full-blown desire for something which he has no qualms about fulfilling. Yet fulfilling our* ***own*** *desires, seeking our own way, what we want, is contrary to the wisdom of the ages which states that we should not seek for our desires to be met but those of another, 'not my will but thine...'.*

Now what is desire made of? ***Desire*** *is the* ***FEELING*** *of being pulled toward an object, usually external, which is perceived as if it will be pleasurable and which the acquisition of which seems as if it will satisfy the individual's incessant craving, his internal feeling of discontent and vague dissatisfaction. This internal state of stress in the entity will be seemingly relieved by this apparent external phenomenon, the act of gambling. Then the entity will see himself as then 'feeling' much better. This overwhelming desire can be for drugs, alcohol, sex, gambling or any of the other cravings that are so often placed in front of us. This perceived state of dis-ease, discontentment, restlessness, lack of focus, within the person seems as though it will be relieved by the external item, by the addiction, in this case, gambling.*

Thoughts are the mediator *between the external item and the internal feeling. With an addicted person, those thoughts are misleading to the individual, i.e. the item will not make him feel better, at least not in the overall or long run, but his thoughts tell him that it will.*

Desire is usually tied to ***immediacy.*** *The item is perceived to be within reach. This makes the feeling even stronger in the individual since it's seen as being almost* ***within his grasp****. He feels like he's almost beginning to feel the relief that will occur upon the goal of obtaining the item, or activity, in this case gambling. The gambler then anticipates and redoubles his efforts to win. Perseverance is seen as a positive virtue.*

With the gambler, the acquiring of his goal, the act of being able to gamble, raises his state of mind and his feeling of 'beingness' to an accelerated one, his adrenaline 'rush' comes, he feels the excitement. Its so different from his daily life, with all the lights, the colors, the spaciousness of the casinos, the surreal atmosphere - all serve to almost put him in a different state than usually. This state seems full of important, exciting decisions, of people in tuxes, and being waited on continuously. It's a 'fast', state where he feels like he's speeding along, certainly forgetting the stresses at home or at work. He enters another plane of fun, of celebrities, of pizzazz. Everything that the humdrum of our lives seems to be lacking.

The desire is overwhelming and he succumbs to it. But then he finds that in the midst of all these people apparently having the time of their lives, with bells and lights going off continuously, with everyone appearing to be winning, that our individual may sometimes win, but often not. In fact, he'll probably lose at least 5% of the time. First he'll lose 5% of 100%. Then 5% of 95, then 5% of 84, etc. until he loses all his money. Then to avoid feeling the stress that he originally felt, in addition to his new stress of losing his money, he rationalizes his loss saying, that he'll 'win it back'. He denies what happened, that he lost, and that he usually loses, and says he'll win big next time. Unfortunately this is almost impossible.

So the rationalization continues. 'We're all entitled to a little fun.' The casinos have already 'pre-educated' us with these rationalizations, they've instilled these ideas in us as we're exposed to their literature and advertising. The casinos lead us to have these types of thought processes, these new desires and to buy into them. They've indoctrinated us to want to gamble and to want to win. Then we want to win, not just a little to cover the evening, but to win BIG. It's ***dynamically progressive****. The casinos have led us to believe that all is possible and in fact, probable. 'After all, aren't those winners' pictures? If they can do it, why can't I?' The addict doesn't remind himself that the odds of winning are so slim as to be almost inconceivable and certainly not probable. Yes, one person does win, but millions and millions and millions of people don't win. And when one wins, its based on the losses of all the others. Remember, in the long run—the only winner is the casino.*

So now our individual is completely tossed by his desires, to gamble, to win, to break even, and to win BIG! His thoughts are at the whim of the latest advertisement that he passes in the casino. The casinos feed him what to think, 'Hey, someone's gotta win', '"You too could be a big winner.' He's at their mercy. He's just become an easy mark. How many books have you read about people who won big from the casinos and held onto their money? Duh...

Another thing that makes gamblers believe casino propaganda is that the ***crowds*** *are always constant. I was always amazed at the* ***hordes of people****. Constant commotion. It seemed like the whole world was there. I wondered where all the people came from. Then you think to yourself, 'Well, they're all here, so I must be in the right place.' That also tends to get you in a different mind-set, a state of mind where your good judgment and normally conservative tendencies are perhaps loosened. An environment where you're quick to have a (free) drink or two, which further loosens you up. The 'chips' in your pocket give you a charge, they look like 'funny money' even more than real money. But the truth is that they represent your hard-earned money, they're not funny money, not fake.*

The casinos don't deal with you when you're your regular stable, level-headed, feet-on-the-floor state. The casinos are very deliberate in seeking to help you to 'dissociate' from your usual self, to loosen up, and not be the same, serious intelligent, person that you are back home. Proximity translates to accessibility. ***Accessibility (A) translates to Frequency (F) which leads to Addiction. A + F = Addiction.***

It's easy to be a closet gambler and not have your addiction become known until almost the end, when all the horrendous damage has already been done, full-blown disaster, assets and resources irrevocably lost. This is what happened to us. By the time I had an inkling that his gambling was out of control, he had already lost all our fortune, all our assets, had already embezzled and had been discovered! Everything was already a fait accompli. The only thing remaining was to do damage inventory. Any attempt at damage control especially in the beginning, was a feeble effort with no real ability to mitigate events that had already occurred. Monies irretrievably lost.

We all have needs that must be met to keep us in a state of relative contentment, of passable happiness, of freedom from anxiety and stress. When these are not met, for whatever reason, then we're under a state of siege, so-to-speak, we feel beleaguered, surrounded by opposing forces, and generally backed up 'against the wall'. When people feel as if their needs aren't being met, as if they have to put out a lot more than they're getting back, they experience life from a standpoint of scarcity, of lack. They believe that they have to hold onto what they have with great tenacity.

Animals become territorial when threatened. People in offices who feel their space isn't sufficient, become acquisitive and rigid, not wanting to share their (meager) resources. This attitude of holding on tightly to what we have isn't going to allow new energy to flow through. It's like the monkey who holds onto the candy in a jar so tightly that he can't take his hand out of the opening in order to eat. Yet in doing so, he can't come up with any different methods to retrieve his desired goal, the candy.

When someone is addicted to something, he feels in a state of want, that his needs aren't being met through whatever strategies he's currently using. So he obsesses, thinking that there must be some way that he can gain the desired object. In this mindset of being totally focused on whatever it is that he thinks is going to make him happy, whether gambling, drugs, alcohol, etc., he's blocked from employing other alternatives or strategies to help him succeed at combating this addiction.

In this state of closed options, perceived limited choices, whatever presents itself to the person may possibly be seized upon with great enthusiasm. The alternative won't be examined, weighed, and looked at in terms of possible negative consequences.

This is when an individual's addiction then turns the corner and becomes not only his own problem, but a cause for concern for others in terms of their own welfare and their own integrity. When an addict becomes so fixated on his obsession that he doesn't give any weight or importance to the laws of the land, then everyone is headed for ruin. When an addict turns to ***criminal activity*** *to acquire what he needs to support his habit, he's just headed down the road to personal ruin and he usually brings at least his own family with him.*

At the point that the drug addict starts to steal to support his habit, or a gambler starts to embezzle to get money, or an alcoholic does anything he can to get money for his next bottle, then the activity has literally turned from one that was only self-destructive, into one that is now widely hurtful and harmful. This is the point at which the consequences become very negative, the point at which people start ruining lives, marriages turn into divorce, people start going to jail, becoming alienated from family members for long periods of time if not permanently, and jobs and careers are lost. It's the point from which return becomes increasingly difficult. Before this time, the individual's felt sense of lack, the person's feeling of scarcity, which led him to turn to the addiction in the first place, were primarily contained within himself. He might have felt unhappy and unfulfilled, but it was largely confined to his own interior life.

Once he starts breaking laws, he's stepped over the line of acceptability by society and understanding by other family members. We can all empathize with someone's depression, with their lack of focus and direction in their life, even with their throwing away individual opportunity. But once someone's addiction takes away other's opportunities to pursue their own goals and dreams, whether because of lack of money, or because the person was imprisoned, then the addiction has just achieved a new depth of deprivation, a new level of seriousness which is much more difficult to undue in the future.

In Australia, a wife addicted to gambling, embezzled funds from the husband's business. This act was so flagrant that it led to their divorce. What she had done was so serious that her actions forever destroyed their relationship.

In my family, my brother has been so addicted to heroin throughout his life, that he continually lands in prison due to his stealing. He's stolen from others and from his own family to such an extent that people found it hard to continue to forgive him. In the end, my brother severed family relationships himself when he found his addiction more alluring, more fascinating, more worthy of his attention and energy, than those family ties. Although there were many efforts to maintain the relationship by various family members, in the end, my brother chose to pursue his addiction and not his family. It was just too difficult to sustain the familial tie. His imprisonment itself gradually led to the de facto severance of relations.

The person has destroyed himself. It wasn't my brother's act of taking drugs that led to his being left alone. It was his act of breaking the law, not once, but repeatedly, over years and years, getting himself in prison, and then not reaching out to others as most would do in that situation. Our family was supportive, both materially and emotionally, to the extent they were able, during the years of my brother's drug obsession. Yet we're also enmeshed in our own lives, struggling to survive our own challenges, and to succeed in our own quests. We can't live his life or make his decisions for him.

We can't serve 2 masters, it's said. This wisdom of the ages is as true for us in the 21st century as for sages of old. Whatever becomes our underlying passion will become what we give our best efforts to, our juice, our essence, our 'rasa'. With addicts, their passion is their addiction. It's not their wife and children, although they would say they love them. It's not their family or their job, although they might seek to pursue them as a means to an end. Their addiction is their real passion, their primary interest in life. What 'floats their boat', is their addiction and that's what they put first. This is why addicts are seen as unreliable, untrustworthy and, overall, 'in it only for themselves.'

This is why addicts can flout the laws of society with such impunity and apparent unconcern. Their passion is not in being a good citizen, or in helping the community or their family prosper. Their passion is their addiction and they're willing and even obsessed with this all of their waking moments. This act of repeatedly flouting of laws established for the general good leads to that person being marooned, being left to navigate this world, by himself, alone and adrift, without family ties, without community support. So we can see easily why the next step for many addicts is homelessness.

After a certain amount of support, help, succorance, the person is expected to make their own way. Yet some people never seem to be able to see the correct course of action, to go their way without being a colossal drain on others and society. I imagine my brother has cost the taxpayers of the state of Connecticut millions and millions of dollars throughout his life. This is people's hard-earned money. My brother has cost his family untold heart-ache and hundreds of thousands of dollars. We're all given difficult situations in our lives from which we have no choice but to accept and proceed. Yet addicts seem to be in a constant state of screaming their need and exacerbating their pain by taking from others a hundred fold.

Addiction is something pursued in isolation and secrecy. It leads to further alienation from all that people generally hold meaningful. ***The act of addiction is a totally self-defeating, self-destructive one that cuts oneself off from recognized and generally accepted means of circumnavigating this worldly existence.***

WHICH ADDICTION?

Is there an ***'addictive personality,'*** *as it's sometimes said? If so, which of us have it and in what way? How can this addictive personality be described?*

Which addiction the person seeks depends on a number of factors, multi-determined. The factors determining which addiction is congruent with the entity's particular psychic and cognitive configuration depends on personality, really ego. He chooses which addiction he'll be susceptible to. A person who's by nature, exceedingly introspective, might adopt as something that appeals to him, which he feels comfortable with, one particular addiction over another, something more internal.

A person who likes to travel and go places, who is somewhat social, might be attracted to casino gambling with its glitter and razzle-dazzle. Someone who lived in a place where drugs were available or where his friends used drugs, would be more prone to choose that avenue as his addiction. Another person to whom alcohol was culturally approved of and beer or liquor readily available, might turn to that as their addiction of choice. Other people have stated that alcohol 'did nothing for them', and then later found in marijuana or cocaine a pleasurable experience.

Conversely, someone who was very much into cars, might find this hobby so time-consuming that a gambling addiction would be difficult to also manage. A person's strong faith foundation or bond with their religious group, find that a strong support serving to protect against an addiction.

Why does a person choose gambling? Or why does Gambling choose a specific person? *Psychiatrist Robert Custer, M.D., in his book, When Luck Runs Out, reflects some salient points. He feels that individuals who become involved in gambling are 1.* ***apt to be highly charged, energized individuals, seeking stimulation and excitement.*** *As casinos exist, with their lights, actions, noise, reps, they're stimulating, exciting places. It's easy for the adrenaline to flow. 12*

A second reason that gambling is specific to certain individuals, Custer feels, is that they've been ***2. raised to view money as 'all-important'*** *Families of origin have laid great emphasis and importance upon money seeing it as an answer to many problems. For Alan, coming from an accountant's family, he had a lifetime of working with money and numbers. It was ingrained in him and he was comfortable talking and being around large amounts of money. As he would quip, 'Rich or poor, it's nice to have money,' alluding to the fact that things could be solved with money and comfort could be bought with it.* ***Finally, some people are given to 'magical thinking'****, Custer noted, with thoughts involving illusory thinking, fantasies. These* *fantasies are ones that the casinos are all too happy to stir up, to incite. 12 Gamblers are encouraged to believe that they have some mysterious power that will enable them to win. This resort to 'fantasyland' and illusion removes our gambler even further from the world of reality. It serves to weaken the ego even more allowing his impulses to take over. So he keeps one foot in his fantasy world and one foot in the reality world. This is not enough to allow his ego to function and to maintain himself as a common sense, stable individual.*

In fact, many accountants and lawyers get in trouble this way because they have been raised to believe that they're smarter or more capable than the average person. But the machines don't know one person from another, they can't see who we are to allow us to win, they don't know about 'our special good money karma'. They only know their random number generator, what's been programmed into them.

Gambling is not that different from drug abuse. Much of the ***language*** *used in gambling and drugs has similarities to each other. Both talk about the 'highs' derived from each addiction. Mention is made of people being 'in the zone', i.e. completely focused on the activity regardless of possible consequences. In gambling one talks of having 'scored', meaning made a win. In drug language, it refers to having obtained the drug. In both instances, being 'high', refers to feeling extremely good, euphoric, pleased with oneself, feeling energized and happy with the way events are occurring. In both instances, gamblers and 'druggies' see themselves as slick, playing fast and loose, as 'cool'.*

The common language and its usage also suggests similar internal sensations associated with both, of pleasure, a release of energy, a feeling of thrill or ecstasy. When winning, even in small amounts, the addiction produces instant intense gratification, and consequent release from the downer of customary problems and stresses in life. Winning money can be very pleasurable indeed. As one always interested in acquiring money, I think many people would agree that winning money while playing a game, would be extremely pleasurable. Except - there's a time when you stop winning and start losing. The addicted gambler doesn't realize this elementary truth.

As a gambling counselor commented on the sensation derived, "For people who have a gambling addiction, gambling is a real stress release in that it works immediately." Laurie Ferguson, a nationally certified gambling counselor based in Green Bay said,

> *"(Gamblers) go into this* ***altered state of consciousness*** *at the blackjack table, the slot machine or in front of the TV watching the football game they've bet money on. While caught up in that activity, they're not thinking about... 'any stresses.'" 13*

Wisconsin *calls to their hotline number increased over last year's number and almost exclusively mentioned the ambiance, the Lights and Action, of casinos as being responsible for their downfall.*

The language involved gives some feeling for the kind of phenomenon.

I can just go there any be totally mesmerized and my brain can stop.

It was never about money. It was about a hype, a thrill, a rush. It's a roller-coaster, when you get hooked on it.

Compare this with a statement by a gambler who was later convicted for embezzling. The charge that our little gambler is talking about, 'the hype, a thrill, a rush...', could be ***physiological in*** *nature.*

Certainly we, as individuals, can't bring on a 'rush' by ourselves. I can't turn on 'a thrill' by myself. It needs something to incite it, to jumpstart it. This is what the casinos provide, 'the addictive energy, 'the spark.'

This 'charge' would appear to be at least partly based on a change in human physical chemicals, an adrenalin rush. Brain synapses start firing faster than before, the entity feels keyed up.

This is a modern perversion of the 'Fight or Flight' Syndrome, of researcher, Hans Selye, where being energized means being in a state where the body can be ready at any time, instantaneously, so to speak, to either fight, defend itself, or flee, run away. What is the gambler seeking out of a game involving the turn of a few cards, a hit, a high, a change of life?

What is the apparent 'high' *that makes people return repeatedly, continuously giving away their money until the detrimental effects are severe and the financial losses have carved great inroads of damage into a person's life, until the person has effectively thrown away things that he'd worked so long and hard for? This would appear to be the same state that an alcoholic throws himself into, that a drug abuser seeks when he throws his money away on something that he shoots into his veins, and which also ends up by causing a great similar great amount of personal and societal damage.*

These are all people, like you and me. Each has their own degree of survival instinct, of what to do and how to make life better for themselves. After the initial difficulties, one would imagine that these people would have gotten the idea and not returned to the source of their difficulties. So what's the key ingredient in the addiction, what is it that has all people with addictions 'hooked'?

Perhaps we're all addicted to something. *Some of us just hide that obsession, cover it over, better than others. The so-called major addictions, alcohol, drugs, sex, smoking, food, are the tip of the iceberg. How about people addicted to TV, who watch it at the expense of their responsibilities, such as caring for their family. Or the people addicted to clothes who derive their satisfaction from the knowledge that the clothes they are wearing make them 'look good'. Or people addicted to working, the so-called type A personality, or the ones who are addicted to 'partying', socializing excessively, to the detriment of other work that might be more beneficial for them, their loved ones and their overall life? These can be detrimental to others but not in the same, hard-core way as the commonly accepted addictions.*

Addictions are a way for the entity to gain pleasure*, satisfaction, which we all crave, from an object focused on. What is disabling for some people is that what they've chosen, happens to be, at this point in time, either* ***illegal,*** *or such that it incapacitates the entity and forces an* ***imbalance*** *in the natural state of affairs.*

It's all part of the delicate balancing act that we're forced to do while we're on this earth. We have to keep so many balls balancing up in the air, home, family, work, friends, creativity, life's purpose, individual intention, all coordinated with each getting their fair and necessary share. While we're balancing all our balls in the air, we also must be aware and conscious that ***resources*** *in the physical world, including time and energy and money,* ***are limited,*** *that we can't just put our attention wherever it wants to go at any time.*

When the balls aren't balancing, whether because there're too many to keep balanced or because they're intrinsically not well-balanced themselves, then the individual experiences ***'stress.'*** *Not wanting to experience this stress, our gambler goes after an activity or substance purely for the experience of pleasure, the opposite of stress. He 'perceives' that gambling gives pleasure and takes away stress. Yet sooner or later, he finds that it's one more ball to balance, one particularly unbalanced ball to keep in the air, and that now he experiences even more stress than before.*

This subsequent blow to his expectations, to his hopes and dreams, (that gambling was going to get him money and consequently happiness), is one additional very intense stress. This is why for some people, this disappointment and despair from gambling is the final straw, they see no outlet from the situation as its become, with gigantic debt financially, with guilt and anger on an emotional level, and you've-always-been-a-screw-up thoughts in their head. This scenario now can lead to even further self-destructive actions of many kinds, i.e. suicide.

When people go after the more obvious addictions, they become ***unbalanced*** *in their approach to life and* ***dysfunctional*** *with regard to the demands of the different areas of their lives. The addiction in itself does not necessarily have to be intrinsically bad. The act of playing cards is not in itself evil. Its greatest detrimental impact lies in absenting the entity from the other obligations of his life and wasting precious resources that exist, whether on a financial, emotional, or intellectual level. The person becomes so passionately involved with the substance or activity, whether drugs, gambling, alcohol, etc. that he focuses on it unduly, to the neglect of the other aspects of his life which are equally pressing and also require his undivided attention.*

BASIC HUMAN NEEDS

We're all seeking the same thing. We just aren't sure of the best way to secure it. Some people believe that what we're seeking can be found in clothes and other material possessions. Others seek it in Nature. But we're all seeking something, which I suspect is similar. When we find it, we say similar things, like, I "I felt like I was home," or "this is really who I am."

There are ***3 basic emotional needs****, according to psychiatrist, Dr. Custer.*

- *to be wanted, to be liked, to be loved.*
- *to be recognized as a person of worth, as important, as needed, and finally,*
- *to have confidence in our ability to deal with the problems and the people of everyday life. 14*

Gamblers find these needs to be fulfilled in their gambling. Gambling, and certainly the casinos themselves, feed into these needs. The staff in the casinos all 'cater' to the gambler making them feel important and liked. Alan was ***'recognized'*** *as a person of worth, he was given innumerable things that made him feel important and worthy. There were frequent parties to which he was invited by personal invitation. Whatever he wanted, drinks, food, restaurant reservations, show tickets, preferential seating, immediate response, he got.*

Alan was a ***VIP*** *in Atlantic City. He knew it, I knew it, and the casinos knew it. That was clear to all. This is another method of 'hooking people.' How common is being a VIP in our society? Not very common except for the wealthy, movie stars, the 'in' people. Yet with all the means at their disposal, the reps in Atlantic City would do just this. They did it well too. When we arrived, they would send wine, cheese and fruit platters, and anything else they or we could think of, up to the room. Later there would be lavish chocolates on night-time pillows, cookies and milk sent up from the kitchen, and extensive room service. All for no charge.*

In a casino of tens of thousands of people, we were individually cared for. If we wanted to eat at a casino restaurant that had a line, we called our rep and he 'walked us in'. If we wanted something at the gift shop, we 'signed' for it and it was ours. Yes, this treatment did turn Alan's head. It was carefully calculated to do so. It's hard to stay humble when the world caters to you.

Gambling made him feel liked, important, powerful. As it made him feel this way, it became even more of a pleasurable act, it fulfilled his basic needs even more. A vicious circle, a catch-22. Gambling led to feelings of being liked, being powerful, which led to more gambling because he liked the feeling. It was a vicious cycle. Many gamblers can't escape from this cycle till the money is all gone. Its so addicting, it's so fulfilling, that until some outside force, like no more money, leads to an abrupt ending, the gambler himself is powerless in the face of all these forces. Casinos are well aware of our basic human needs and cater to them.

Yet even in the face of our basic needs being fulfilled, all this that makes us feel nurtured, cared for, this state of well-being that we all crave, the gambler must remember that he's responsible for his actions. We can never be 'out-of-control', no matter how good it makes us feel. Western jurisprudence, i.e. the legal system and the courts, have said that people are responsible for their actions except in the case of 'insanity', whether permanent or temporary.

Gambler's Anonymous says that we must be responsible for our actions and has a policy of restitution or payback for all gambling losses and debts. They also regard gambling as a 'progressive disease', one that builds steadily in its craving and intensity. Restitution, paying back, alone is not sufficient. Many gamblers will never be able to pay back their gambling debts and certainly never able to pay back the pain and anguish they've caused their loved ones.

PHASES IN THE GAMBLER'S LIFE

*There are certain recognized **phases** in the life of a compulsive gambler. They're easy to recognize - afterwards. During his gambling, the gambler tries to keep everything secret. He thinks that the world is out to stop him from what he's doing so he tries to keep it all under wraps. This is one more reason why gambling is so destructive. It's not known until it's too late.*

*Initially there is the '**winning phase.**' People make a few small wins and are led to believe, erroneously, that they're 'special', that they can 'win.' During this phase, they **catch the fever**, the rocket booster phase that sends them 'high', into orbit. They're susceptible, vulnerable, at this point and it all looks like a bowl of candy. This is the 'honeymoon' phase and many people fall for it. They 'deny' that the rules of winning and losing apply to them.*

Then as it all happens, sooner or later, people stop winning and start losing. In this, ***secondary or losing phase****, they realize they lost money yet feel they can still get it back. Meanwhile the casino hype starts kicking in big time. The reps start coming around more often and being more and more friendly. People rationalize, if they won once, they can do again. They feel they just have 'to try harder'. So they try harder, throwing caution to the wind, and then lose even more.*

*Meanwhile they're continuing to '****deny'*** *the severity of their losses. Sometimes they deny their losses completely thinking that that day was just a 'fluke', or they'll do better tomorrow.* ***Stress*** *sets in heavy duty. Tomorrow comes and they still don't win. Or they don't win as much as they lost. By now, their families are beginning to be suspicious. So they resort increasingly to lies, secrecy, and other fabrications to conceal the extent of their addiction. This makes the web even more tangled, even more complicated.*

Desperation *starts to set in, the process accelerates, they become exhausted, 'chasing' their losses, the* ***third and final phase****. 14 If their thinking was not clear before, it's really confused now. They don't know where to turn or what to do. By now there's really no productive place to go except to stop and to tally up the losses. This is an even more painful process, so they don't do it. They refuse to acknowledge to themselves or others that they've lost a lot of money and that they don't have a clue as to what to do. By now, they're obsessing constantly about their money and about winning. They become really out of control, alone, desperate, and depressed. So they do what they did before. They gamble even more based on the faint hope of winning. Winning big is their only hope, the only thing that could bail them out, which could recoup their losses. Yet casinos are not designed to have people win. And they don't.*

THEORIES ABOUT GAMBLING ADDICTION

There have been various ***theories for the origin of addiction*** *in people, for how and why certain people become addicted. The theory that the casinos would have you believe is that a particular individual becomes 'hooked' because of something unique and internal to that person. They imply it's a 'personal weakness' of some kind and that the individual is to blame. Since the majority of people can gamble sensibly, gaming interests suggest, the small percentage of individuals who become addicted, do so for reasons of individual weakness. We would suggest that anyone putting their money into machines that are calculated to take their money is an act of foolishness, ignorance or lack of concern for the importance of money.*

The casinos propose that gamblers can be divided into two types, the majority who are sane, normal individuals, and the misguided, sick minority, "...one is sensibly engaged in a leisure activity whereas the other is out of control; that one is adjusted, whereas the other is maladjusted; and that one is healthy, whereas the other is Sick." 17 This suggests a dichotomy between 'social' and 'pathological' gamblers, between normal people and sick people, with the unsaid insinuation being that compulsive gamblers are not healthy, sane people.

Gambling interests propose that compulsive gambling stems from certain personality deficits or character malformations. This demarcation between healthy and not healthy is seen as supported by **psychoanalytic theories**. *The presumption is that people had early life histories which were especially difficult or traumatic in some way. This led to them having certain ego or character deficits. Then, the theory continues, they gamble because they are compensating for what they didn't get at the right time.*

These theories postulate that the individual had some degree of relationship difficulties in early life, especially with meaningful father figures. Its suggested that the damage to the person caused by the lack of adequate nurturing, appropriate role-models and/or insufficient attention to emotional needs, led to personality defects, thus leaving our gambler susceptible or vulnerable to negative, outside influences.

Women gamblers are also felt to have suffered trauma, possibly sexual, in early life and thus become vulnerable to this vague and amorphous character weakness which makes gamblers susceptible to external pressures causing them to succumb to temptation more easily than others. 18 This temptation, gambling, subsequently becomes addiction for them while others are able to resist.

Theories suggest that gamblers are consumed by anxiety, or depression, neurotic individuals moved by unconscious feelings of aggression and rebellion, and ruled by the 'pleasure principle'. Rather than deal with the causes of their anxiety and depression, compulsive gamblers avoid confronting these issues and instead distract themselves with the addiction. Thus they can blame their problems on gambling instead of themselves. Consequently they don't have to deal with them, do something about them. Of course we all do this in one way or another. We don't give our attention to things in our lives that are not easy to change, or which we see as too big to tackle.

We all do this in many ways and in our own unique way. We deal with what we can. We don't deal with what we feel we can't deal with. Actually this sounds pretty intelligent to me, its survival based. Why would we want to attempt a battle that we couldn't win. Where the excessive gambler errs is that he acts on his impulses, in secret, in measures designed to hide from others what is happening. He can't justify his actions.

The lack of openness forces him into a web of lies and untruths or half-truths, into a life lived always with an eye out for the one true love of his existence, i.e. gambling. That is his priority and on that false assumption, so rests his life. Gamblers truly build their houses on sand, not on rock. And of course it will come tumbling down sooner or later. We need to try to guide our actions by the highest principles. Gambling undercuts any ideas or aspirations toward that.

Gambling sets up the opposite framework supported by materialism and greed, with acquisition, getting and spending, and conspicuous consumption, being the watchwords instead of conserving and growing, being and becoming, living and breathing.

Excessive gambling has been seen within the whole framework of addictive behaviors such as drugs, eating, smoking, etc. In 1986 Jacobs established an ***Addictive Personality Syndrome*** *(APS) containing 2 sets of predisposing factors characteristic of persons with a high potential for developing an addiction. Jacobs based his addictive personality syndrome on addiction being defined as 'a dependent state acquired over time to relieve stress'. 18*

His ***2 predisposing factors*** *for becoming addicted were 1.* ***feeling chronically depressed****, or* ***excited,*** *(a false arousal) with the individual needing relief from stress (thus the addiction) and 2.* ***childhood experiences*** *producing deep feelings of inadequacy, inferiority and a sense of rejection by significant care-givers. The second reason could produce the first, or, the first, a sense of affective agitation, a mood disorder, could result in a false perception of the reality of earlier childhood trauma. Either can produce the other. Jacobs sees gambling as a 'family disease'. However this theory has been hypothesized but not proven. Later theorists did not find differences in the arousal state, the amount of tension or anxiety experienced on a regular basis, between heavy gamblers and the normal population distribution.*

Efforts have been made to explain excessive gambling on the basis of certain personality characteristics associated with heavy gambling. However although a few researchers have proposed certain similar personality traits, there has been ***no general agreement about personality based predispositions.***

*Also prominent is a '****medical 'disease' model*** *fostered by the medical profession. This theoretical orientation suggests that addiction, like alcoholism, or drug addiction or even food addiction, is biologically and neurologically based. It postulates that addiction is involved with the physical body just like other physical illnesses. They compare addiction to physical illnesses such as cancer or kidney disease. This paradigm became current and accepted in 1980 when the AMA declared gambling as a category on the DSM IV diagnostic criteria. Just as alcoholism is suggested by some to have a genetic basis and to run in families, this theoretical orientation would suggest that gambling or a predisposing weakness will also occur in families as a genetic component.*

A Korean psychiatrist recently reaffirmed gambling's classification as an illness. He noted the necessity for treatment, and its involvement with a host of other *difficulties in the individual's life. Psychiatrist Shin Young-chull, of the Kangbuk Samsung Hospital in Korea, said he felt that gambling addiction was a disease. "**Gambling is…a complex disorder**," Shin said, "We have to deal with so many things for the pathological gambler. There are **gambling, emotional, financial, medical and family problems."** 19*

Shin studied at the University of Minnesota under Kim Won-suck, a leading figure in gambling addiction research. In South Korea only one casino exists yet it's estimated that about 4.1 % of the adult population of Korea is addicted to gambling. Shin and Lee Hyung-si, another psychiatrist from the Korea Institute of Social Psychiatry, have studied this disease and agree that it's a major societal problem. Lee said, "The Korean dream is to be a millionaire in one day."

*These two psychiatrists feel that there are 2 kinds of gamblers. **"Action gamblers"** are impulsive, "and have an urge to gamble that they cannot resist," said Shin. They enjoy an "energy rush" that even if exposed to only once, can turn them into addicts. The other kind of gambler is the **"escape gambler"**, Shin said. "They have many emotional problems like depression or anxiety." **"Gambling should be considered as an illness treated through medication and regular psychiatric visits."** 20*

*Surveys since have showed that up to **20 % of South Korean adults** are problem or pathological gamblers, said Hyuin Hwang, program manager with Asian Counseling Services in Tacoma, Washington. In China, Hong Kong and the nearby island of Macau, with 8 casinos, gambling is popular. The horse racing industry in Hong Kong annually takes in almost $12 Billion dollars. 21*

Many Asian immigrants to the U.S. are becoming addicted to gambling. Gambling is a traditional social and an accepted cultural activity in China and other parts of Asia.

Casinos are well aware of this new market for themselves and often attempt to encourage Asian Americans with various ways including hiring Asian reps for Asian customers, Asian-themed holiday celebrations, like Chinese New Year, Asian popular musical acts, and many Asian restaurants, including sushi and Vietnamese noodle bars.

So there are many definitions and theories about the addiction known as gambling. With the endless variety of people, it could be foreseen that one theory wouldn't be applicable to all people. What everyone does seem to agree about is that gambling is an addiction and that it needs treatment. However if people agree about these two things, addiction and treatment, then why would we continue to license an activity that involves addicting people who weren't addicted before, and that has the potential to cause so much harm and damage?

Addictions are potentially devastating phenomenon in the lives of individuals both for themselves and for others. This translates to vast destructiveness of a societal level. This is what we're asking for when we continue to expand gambling, to make it more widespread, to make it more accessible to people who are already having a hard time functioning in our society.

BEHAVIORIST PSYCHOLOGY

A more recent orientation has come about as a result of the work of psychological behaviorist, BF Skinner. Skinner in the 1950's and on whom behaviorist psychology is based, states that lab animals become habituated to certain stimuli when repeated instances of those stimuli are coupled with tension reducing or pleasurable experience such as food (reinforcement). So Skinner would state that entities can become habituated to certain stimuli and their association with other stimuli.

That is, any entity can become conditioned to associate certain stimuli with reinforcement and then become intensively desirous of the stimuli itself, as well as the reinforcement. So after becoming accustomed to gratification at gambling, whether it be by lights, colors, action, deferential people, food, etc., then the activity, gambling, becomes associated with reinforcement, and reduction of stress and tension. ***An addiction is born, created and sustains itself even in the absence of the initial reinforcer****, perhaps the first win.*

The upshot of all this is that ***anyone, given enough time in a casino****, subject to its atmosphere, environment,* ***can become addicted.*** *The addicted are people who by particular personality orientation happened to get pleasure in a casino environment. But all people are subject to falling prey to an addiction if engaged in it over a period of time.*

This is the other main opposing view as to why people become addicted*. As we said, gambling interests want us to believe that it's an individual aberration, a personality weakness in a few individuals. But the theoretical framework proposed by someone looking at gambling's system of reinforcement and rewards, would suggest that* ***addiction is a natural course of events. Addiction can be seen as***

understandable behavior for the individual, given the structure of gambling with its system of play and monetary pay-offs.

If people put themselves in this kind of a situation, if we allow ourselves, or even seek, to be bombarded with stimuli and with temptation, then the very human response will be to become addicted, to become totally enmeshed in this life-style, of excitement and 'F-U-N'. If we allow others to take over our thoughts, then they can direct our actions. If we put ourselves in this milieu for a certain period of time, we'll end up adopting their values and rationalizations. That's what happens when we spend some time in a casino. We say, 'Come on, let's see what casinos are like, let's try to hit the jackpot.' But, unfortunately, the casinos do what they do, what they do best, what their prime directive is, helping to enable us to become addicted!. They take our money - all of it!

What determines what people are exposed to over time is a function of ***accessibility.*** *Is the casino near enough to go to often* ***(frequency)****? With frequency and accessibility,* ***habit*** *is built up. With habit and the many reinforcers structured into the casino environment, addiction is a short hike away. A short walk down the road to hell. Just a matter of time before the monster, let out of Pandora's box, engulfs and overwhelms our poor player. He may play VLT's or slots, the 'crack-cocaine' of gambling, and become addicted within a year or two. Other people who play table games might require a bit longer. People who play lotteries where the reinforcer occurs quite a bit of time after the initial play, days or weeks, might be able to play for much longer, years and years, with it being a habit but not an addiction.*

The ***difference between habit and addiction is a matter of frequency, intensity of craving, the amount of control the individual has over it, and degree of damage inflicted****. It's different along different places along the continuum. When William Bennet admitted that he'd "lost 8 million dollars but still had plenty of money," it wasn't called an addiction but an unfortunate occurrence. When a homeless man spends his last quarter in a casino, it's called an addiction. When an American soldier spends his salary at the post gambling hall, it's called 'stupid'. But when a Korean legislator goes on the American military post and spends his money gambling, his position becomes called into question, and it's called an addiction which the Americans catered to by allowing gambling on military bases.*

When my husband had a good night and won at gambling, it was called entertainment. When he lost our fortune, it was called addiction. Since almost everyone loses sooner or later, the amount they gamble and the damage done, the frequency they do it, and the intensity to which they become involved, all get called into question.

AUSTRALIAN THESIS

A recent researcher in Australia, Sandra Dekker, ***Commercial Gaming, The Unfair Deal****, suggested that gambling be seen, not as an individual weakness or character defect, or impulse disorder, but as a* ***general condition to which anyone could fall prey to given the right conditions.*** *22 Gambling interests would like to see pathological gambling labeled as an individual aberration, however it goes beyond that. It is a malady that anyone could be prone to under the right conditions, as we can see according to Skinnerian clinical theory.*

Stating the problem in this manner, that anyone could fall prey given the right conditions, puts the onus on the people setting up those 'right conditions' and not on the individual himself who was seen as 'weak', corrupt, etc. Correspondingly, the impetus for correcting those conditions would be seen to rest with the institutions structuring those addictive conditions instead of particular individuals who might have succumbed as an individual weakness.

This hypothesis suggests that instead of there being 2 types of gamblers, one healthy, one sick, one good, the other bad, two polarities, two extremes at the opposite ends of the continuum, there is really more of a ***process of involvement with people being at various stages on the continuum.*** *This social majority would be at a different stage on the continuum of involvement, not having reached the level of a problem or compulsive gambler.*

Everyone starts out uninvolved in terms of their time and money. People come with different motivations for playing. Some play for money while others play because of boredom or loneliness. Some gravitate more towards gambling while others lose interest because of their own intrinsic factors. But regardless of motivation, machine playing guarantees financial losses with eventual economic demise inevitable.

The only difference between habit and addiction, between regular and compulsive gamblers, said Dickerson, is that the former still have resources upon which to draw and haven't sought help, while the latter's resources are exhausted*. 23*

If there were unlimited resources, never ending supplies of money, then no one would have a problem. But of course, in our world of physical limitations, when someone runs out of money, then they either stop gambling, or turn to other ways of obtaining money. This stage of financial ruin is the cause of the gambler's despair and hopelessness. Gamblers open themselves up to more trouble when they turn to other means of getting money to continue their habit. They turn to credit card debt, to embezzling, to taking from family members, with or without their knowledge and consent. A person is entitled to spend their own money however they choose. But they're not free to spend other's money to support their habit.

Thus the statistical differentiation, whether its 1% or 5% or 10 % of the population is not an accurate way of looking at how many people are compulsive or problem gamblers, since we've seen that gambling addiction is on a continuum. The person not addicted today, may be so in six months. Then we have to count in the 10-15 significant others affected by our gambler's excessive gambling. 24

So the issue turns out to be much greater than the numbers actually represent. The ripples in the pond affected by the gambler continue to flow outward overcoming all in their path. Dickerson says there are only regular gamblers, normal people engaging in a seemingly rational activity, most of whom sooner or later, will encounter financial crisis. Only when the money runs out, and they go to counseling or financial agencies, do they become labeled as 'compulsive gamblers' with pathological problems. 25

The casinos treat as 'pathological', as sick, the people who experience difficulties with machine playing. They see them as marginal individuals, 'deviants', called 'aberrations' and 'treated' under a medical or counseling model. The gambling industry clearly says that they're not to blame for the 'addicted' gambler. In actuality, this is scape-goating the individual, blaming the victim. The gambling industry does this to maintain a low profile, to not call attention to their own involvement in this process. Yes, the gambler makes a series of poor choices and incorrect decisions. But he does this after first being offered the candy that he can't refuse.

The ***advertising, marketing and structural framework is the responsibility of the gambling industry.*** *These are designed to seduce every potential gambler, everyone who goes to the casino. Casinos cloud your good judgment by emotional and psychological manipulation and calculated misinformation. Without being aware of the truth, being informed of the real odds of gambling, we don't make informed choices.*

The casinos continue this orientation of branding the compulsive gambler as 'sick' and needing' a treatment program by giving large sums of money to 'fund' treatment programs. Actually the funds are minimal in light of their massive profits. When they give money, they try to maintain the illusion of showing themselves to be 'caring' and to be dealing responsibly with this problem. Yet this is certainly closing the barn door after the horse has left. The funding for treatment, miniscule though it is, further acts to pathologise people, as the aim is 'to cure the sick'. It's holding the individual gambler ***individually responsible for the social issue*** *of problem* *gambling. Thus the gambling industry exonerates themselves of responsibility and remain blameless for the problem gambling that they created and caused.*

The 'social majority' and the 'pathological few' - social constructs casinos use to categorize people. Implicit in these classifications are insinuations about individuals and the cause of the problem. If we accept these 2 initial constructs, social majority and pathological few, then the casino's thesis follows logically that it's an individual problem and they are not accountable for creating it.

The thesis by Sandra Dekker argues that: 1. Slots are one of the most seductive and addictive forms of gambling, much more psychologically addictive than other forms of gambling, 2. Machines are programmed for players to lose but presented as financially profitable activity, and 3. The casinos purposefully use techniques to keep people at slot machines which they are well aware will incur financial loss. 26

They do this by incentives and promotions, by training staff to keep people at machines, by deceitful advertising, and by appeals to the 'rational' motives of individuals. It's felt that casinos abuse the knowledge of human psychology, tapping into 'universal human potentialities' to encourage poker playing and incite persistent and continuous gambling.

Problems experienced in playing machines are a ***'natural outcome'*** *of playing rather than being due to gamblers' Personal deficits, Dekker adds. They are a* ***"result of the psycho-structural characteristics of the machines, the duplicitous vision of gaming; purposeful inciting of continuous participation employed by the industry; and the erosion of players' informed choices by the industry's calculated misinformation, and psychological and emotive manipulation." 26***

Much of the gambling research is ***'victim research'*** *according to Dekker. It focuses on individuals, their behavior, and the interaction with society.* ***This focus on 'victim' research diverts attention away from structural causes of social ills and scape-goats those labeled as 'victims' or 'problems.'*** *Blaming the individual diverts our gaze from broad-based social causes and thus prevents the changing of those structures. It also diverts attention from those in power who have the resources and who are benefiting from the existing structure which is causing problems for great numbers of individuals.*

The gambling industry in Australia reports that 1.16 % of the population have a gambling problem. This creates the impression that the number is very small, minimal. Actually, there are about ***100,000 problem gamblers in South Australia****. Additionally, if one adds the 'ripple effect' that each gambler affects at least 10-15 significant others adversely, then the numbers are substantially increased and the magnitude of the problem begins to take shape. Then we can see that the issue is* *much greater than the statistical evidence suggests. If fact, the numbers are probably much greater than 1.1% and many groups in Australia have much greater estimates. 27*

Reasons and causative factors are sought within the individual according to the casinos and not in the casino's actions and policies. The government is not accused of licensing an addictive activity because the massive numbers of individuals affected is never really dealt with. Yet if 100,000 people have severe problems, then something is wrong. If the individual is to blame, then vested interests and power differentials are maintained and protected and nothing changes.

By the time the gambler has lost all his money and has done whatever else he's done to try to obtain more money, he's at the end of his rope. By this time, he is depressed, overwhelmed, feeling guilty, and generally in a bad state of mind. Then he goes to GA or to clinical settings and gets private or group therapy. He's questioned and examined about his childhood, his relationships with others, his losses both financial and emotional, all of the things that clinical people do.

So these clinicians become Monday-morning-quarterbacks, they see the result – gambling and the debt – and assume the reason for the result, lies in the person's 'deep pathology'.

Then they proceed to start examining his childhood, wondering about character and personality disorders. Yet our gambler has become addicted to a social problem which if it were not available, he wouldn't have ever succumbed to. If the government had not licensed this form of addiction, if the casinos had not presented gambling in such an attractive, favorable light, then he might not have gone to excess. ***If 100,000 people in South Australia alone are addicted, then it's certainly not a unique personal weakness. Our gambler is in good company.***

For people susceptible to this constant propaganda, this unremitting hard sell, this unrelenting attack on the senses and the judgment, who are not sufficiently grounded, who perhaps are naïve and believe that they can actually win, then the casinos begin to make their real money. This is addiction carefully and deliberately incited within individuals. Some would call it business, just 'shrewd marketing strategy'. Some might say that the host of subliminal barrage in search of only one goal, i.e. your giving your money to the casino, the half-truths and misrepresentations, a way of making a living, some would say its deliberately seeking the worse in people, cold-heatedly seeking a goal that will incite very human tragedies, crimes, and family misfortunes.

By the casinos doing business, we allow them to cold-bloodedly incite people to commit crimes and other bad actions. They are inciting to addiction. Their business is inciting people to lose, which then leads them to commit bad acts. Now some people might say, no, that's not that the casinos are about, that's the person's individual choice. Yet, we know from many peer-reviewed academic studies that addiction will occur, that people are ignorant of the odds, they'll throw their money away, they'll embezzle, steal, these fraudulent, terrible acts will happen. Just as bees will come to honey, people will be attracted to gambling and will do whatever they have to do to be able to gamble. The outcome is inevitable. Gambling definitely incites some to commit bad or illegal actions, to forego family and business responsibilities. That's a given. We know in advance this will occur.

Yet because this number appears to be a small percentage, we allow it to occur, just trying to make sure that that percentage doesn't include us or our family. Yet that small percentage will hurt you as they get hurt. They will not suffer in silence, alone. They will need services, that will cost you as the taxpayer, your own hard-earned money. They will bring your society down. Their loss is also your loss, although perhaps not directly. You will feel it in your taxes if you don't have direct contact as a result of a family member or an employee.

So perhaps we better reconsider when we say that economic development of a region will be stimulated, and the entertainment value of casinos is important. We all want to have better lives; we all want our children to be successful. To do that, we must create a general scenario where all are successful, not just the brightest, the smartest or the most energetic. If only the smartest get ahead, then your child and mine, may not make it.

When my husband succumbed to the lure of the lights, the thrill of possibly making a fortune, it was a modern make-over, a complete transformation, from a guy basically good, to someone full of vices. What power of Satan, what demons could incite such a change over a relatively short amount of time in this person's life – 10 out of 55 years? He had been gambling for 20 years but only the last 10 were out of control. These were his last 10 years, the ones that should've been his best, that could have been the apex of his career. But no, they were his undoing, a good person turned to bad things, almost a family ruined.

What force could effect such a personality change? What incites each of us at times to lose our good judgment, to give in to impulsive desires? When someone is angry and commits a spur-of-the-moment murder, we can almost understand that. For anger is about not controlling our strong emotion. Or when a person commits a robbery, we can empathize thinking that he might have needed money. Our emotions often rule us one way or another.

Yet when people gamble, it's not easy to understand. We wonder whether and why it all could have happened. It's hard to understand an addiction that could go on for many years without a person 'coming to his senses' and asking for help. This book is an effort to enumerate and show the many ways that the casinos incite a person to succumb to their many blandishments, to show how even a 'good' person can become misguided and succumb to the campaign of misrepresentation, half-truths, and propaganda that the casinos are so adept at orchestrating.

Even a good person can go down the wrong road with sufficient temptation and propaganda. When kidnappers capture a person, subjecting them to their unrelenting propaganda and various 'head trips', its not uncommon for the victims to end up siding with their kidnappers, the so-called Stockholm syndrome. In the 1970's, Patty Hearst, was kidnapped by the People's Liberation Army. She ended up quasi-joining their group, carrying a rifle, dressing like her captors, mouthing their rhetoric. Propaganda, in the form of advertising and the total package, can change anyone's thoughts and orientation, i.e. their perception, given sufficient time and overall total atmosphere.

My husband was just 1 person of the 5-10% of people that could have been predicted, were bound to become addicted. 10% means that there are many, many others, many other souls who have severely messed up their lives, and the lives of others. This self-destruction occurred while engaging in an activity duly licensed and given the seal of approval of by our government, by its legislators and its citizens. ***When gambling was legalized by our legislators, we just made a vice, an addiction, both socially acceptable and physically available to much of our society.***

My husband is in good company. There are a lot of other 'bumblefucks', poor idiots like ourselves, who actually thought that they could be smarter than the corporate geniuses who built Las Vegas and Atlantic City, and the many other casinos dotting this country.

The path of chaos entranced and brought down from 5-10% of the entire population. This percentage destroyed themselves financially and brought an incredible amount of pain that didn't have to happen to their families, and to others. We could've 'made book' on the fact that this result was going to happen to a certain percentage of the population. Yet my husband's tragedy, his stupidity, was also his own. His pain unfortunately is not only his own now.

TEMPORARY INSANITY

I submit that the casinos addicted my husband in a series of moments of temporary insanity following the principles of Pavlovian psychology, propaganda, media assault and manipulation. It was 'temporary' since obviously he's not insane today. It was insanity because he was 'not himself' at the time. He was a completely different person, one created by the casinos. His actions were totally uncharacteristic of him throughout his whole life, and in all areas of his life.

This action of being careless with his finances, losing his money in reckless ways, being 'wild', was alien and foreign to the person that I've always known. The casinos stimulated, incited, and even created a Frankenstein out of an average Joe. They did that deliberately and carefully in a campaign master-minded with an overall pattern of psychological control.

The weak in our society need to be protected from the institutional thieves, the corporate pickpockets, from business corporate economic rationalist policies that take their aim at their fellow citizens that may not be as intellectually, or business minded or as capable as these owners and modern Robber Barons of our society are. The weak and less gifted in our society are no match for the Donald Trump's and the Steve Wynn's. The sheep are no match for the wolves in human form.

If we let the economic forces of our society have free rein, what will become of the vast numbers of people in our society who are not clever enough to be able to see beyond the advertisements, the hype, and everything else that's made the casinos among the wealthiest corporations in our society in a mere 20 years. What chance does the high school drop-out, the immigrant, rural people perhaps not sophisticated in the ways of the world, have in holding their own? The casinos have the lawyers, the MBA's from the top schools in the country, the people gifted with smooth and slippery tongues, the top ad agencies, what chance does the little guy have of keeping his money in the face of the best corporate business talent of Western civilization?

Casinos today are the worst example of 20th century materialism and lack of concern for the deeper, more fulfilling virtues of this world. Casinos, in their drive for money, and for worldly goods not worked for or gained in an honorable way, represent everything that's short-sighted and delusionary in this world. This false desire for acquisition of the things of this world will end up destroying people who seek for them too passionately. The things of this world, money, will destroy us if we let them.

It wasn't a fair contest when the casinos succeeded in getting my husband addicted. The casinos had the weight of their vast sums of money, their troops of lawyers, accountants, advertising executives, psychologists, all to ensnare people just like my husband and yours. In this day and age when everything has advanced to such a specialized extent, to such exact sciences, I submit that the 'regular guy', the 'average Joe', is not fair game for these mammoth, heartless corporations. The financial demise of the little guy is their goal and they have vast resources behind them. Their resources totally overwhelm any possible brain power or good judgment on an individual's part.

With the advent of high tech machines, with psychological 'entrapment', techniques, with enticingly slick and manipulative advertising, with promises thrown around like jellybeans, people need to be protected from their own ignorance and their own desires. If, as a society, we're going to put cocaine out for them to sample, then at least tell them it's cocaine, a lethal drug, and not just a good meal with a few minor inconveniences, (like bankruptcy and embezzlement). These multi-conglomerate, corporate predators need to be reined in and not allowed their excesses to drive our hard-working sincere, naive citizenry to such destructive ends as bankruptcy, embezzlement, and suicide. As Maura Casey said to the NCAL on 9/28/02,

> *"We have an industry pushing a product that is* ***guaranteed*** *– guaranteed – to make a minority of the population addicted.*
>
> *Government gets significant tax revenue (money) from the product. Yet we allow that industry nearly complete control of the research (and regulations), regarding how their marketing practices might increase or decrease that addiction. Our nation allows the gambling industry...such complete control over the bulk of research (and regulations)* ***at our peril.*** *28*

Or as economist Glenn R. Pascall noted recently in the Puget Sound Business Journal on 6/9/03, "The lottery and the slots return a fixed percentage – typically, 89 cents to 93 cents per dollar of wager. ***What would you think of a friend who purchased stocks that guarantee a negative rate of return?"*** *29 They* ***guarantee*** *a negative rate of return. We'd have to be crazy to invest in something that guaranteed you were going to lose a certain percentage of your money just because there was a possibility, an extremely slim possibility, that you just might make big money.*

But looked at realistically, that possibility is so slim as to be virtually both impossible and highly improbable. It is so improbable as to make even thinking about it, winning, a complete fantasy. People are of the opinion that 'yes, it's a fantasy but it's a realistic one'. In fact, it's not realistic in any way. The odds are so improbable as to make being struck by lightning more possible. Yet we don't think or plan on being struck by lightning. This fantasy leaves people clutching at virtually impossible straws in a haystack, thinking that possibilities exist when they really don't, not by any conceivable stretch of the imagination.

This is ***Addiction.*** *It's making people believe that something that is a virtual impossibility, (i.e. winning big money), is possible, when it really isn't, and enticing* *them to wager and lose their hard-earned money over an instigated false hope and dream. It's a response to a carefully orchestrated campaign to make the individual eschew his normal good judgment and discrimination, and give in to a succession of ill-thought and poorly planned actions designed to separate him from his money.*

Addiction makes people do what they normally wouldn't. Addiction is our own demons of fear and greed unleashed to prey upon our own better judgment and wisdom, enticing us to lose our reasoning powers, our perspicacity, our shrewdness, our own powers of self-preservation and even our instinct for survival.

'INCITED,' CREATED DESIRE

This ***stimulated demand*** *is what the casinos* ***created*** *when they produced a market for gambling when there was none before. Gambling is so pleasurable to the individual that he engages in it at his peril. When gamblers are observed at machines, they all have this dull, hypnotized look, blank states, not happy, smiling, jolly selves, laughing whole-heartedly. But this is unusual and uncharacteristic behavior of individuals. We don't normally indulge in our fantasies of becoming a millionaire and obsessing about winning jackets. We don't normally embezzle and bankrupt ourselves while obsessing about winning jackpots, and becoming rich, until we get to a gambling place, a casino of some kind.*

Then we suddenly start to think and imagine, 'What if...' and 'Maybe we'll win BIG?' In fact we know that so few people win big in comparison to the astronomical numbers of people there, that it's pretty improbable that it would ever happen. Yet we suddenly start thinking and dreaming and scheming and betting our money that it might happen. Sometimes people even engage in imaginary plans as to what they would do with the money, IF, they won. We say we indulge in these little mind-games as an exercise in fun, but yet those little mind-games of ours are where our minds are at, they're the ideas and thoughts that we've filled our head with. We end up betting our money on this vague mirage, this very distant possibility. Ultimately, we end up losing all our money in a vain attempt at obtaining something that was never really there to begin with.

*The jackpot that looked so possible, never really was a possibility at all. Yet casinos incite these fantasies and illusions by their advertising. A Borgata Hotel Casino & Spa in Atlantic City ad recently in Long Island's Newsday said, "****Win $1000. EVERY 15 MINUTES. WIN SLOT DOLLARS EVERY DAY THRU FEBRUARY.****" What a come-on. That's a promise of winning $1,000. if there ever was one. Also in the advertisement was the phrase,*

"YOU DEMANDED. WE DELIVERED. NOW EXTENDED ANOTHER MONTH." 30

Two advertisements in major newspapers indicating that people will ***win money.*** *These aren't ads for gambling, they're ads for '****winning'!*** *Perhaps some truth-in-advertising laws would be just a little appropriate here?*

Alan imagined he was going to win big. He waited for the big jackpot. He liked the excitement, the razzle-dazzle, the solicitous attention, the food and drink, the opulent feel of it all. He liked the gambling scene. He was content with our lifestyle. We made good salaries, had what we wanted, clothes, food, big house, boat, stuff, stuff, stuff! We didn't need more.

Yet when he went to Atlantic City, he would start dreaming about the jackpots, the life-changing occurrences which he was 'led to believe' were within the realm of possibility. He would become obsessed with playing. He would prefer gambling to being with his family. He wanted to be in Atlantic City over being in his own home. He believed he could win big.

Now he knows, just as rationally we all know, that winning a significant jackpot is really not within the realm of possibility. Except perhaps the kind of possibility that also includes a meteor striking earth, or the sun stopping in its path, or being hit by lighting. He knows with his own University of Pennsylvania Wharton-School-of-Economics-trained-mind, as well his own considerable financial acumen, that an incredibly small percent of the population has ever won or come out ahead, over time in casinos. Yet he thought that he could do it where so many others had failed! Where did these misguided, unclear, illusionary thoughts come from? Normally he's a feet-on-the-ground, meat-and-potatoes, excellent, hard-headed accountant not prone to idle flights of fancy and head-in-the-sky ideas.

The Gambling industry, in their advertising and marketing strategies, have a direct relationship with the development of problem gambling*. These strategies are designed to* ***seduce every potential gambler.*** *Rather than being a leisure activity of* *choice, entertainment, participation in the activity of gambling is corrupted by emotional and psychological manipulation, by calculated misinformation lacking in truth.*

Once Alan got to Atlantic City, he had this obsession, this craving to win, this addiction. He thought he could win and he knew he was going to be successful, a highly misguided desire and belief. This false idea is what's called, created desire. Desire, incited by the casino hype, the endless barrage of advertisements noting that 'Someone's gotta win,' the pictures of winners on the walls.

We don't allow liquor stores to entice their customers with free samples, or free rooms which the casinos do, we don't allow cigarette companies to advertise smoking on billboards and TV any more or to give away free cigarettes. In fact we don't allow illicit drug companies to advertise their wares at all.

How would that look? A magazine ad, enticing people-

COKE – TRY A FREE SNORT! BE ONE OF THE 'IN' CROWD!
(Become Addicted).

We run vast government programs to help people financially, to show them how to buy homes and secure mortgages, how to manage money and credit cards, and then we allow casinos to advertise for something that is sure to bring some people to bankruptcy and financial ruin. **Gambling is a poor economic choice for most people given their limited resources.** *People, especially those on fixed incomes, or with others dependent on them, as in the case of all families, shouldn't play something that would put them in trouble if they lost. Something that might have any probability of financial ruin would be a foolhardy risk for people to take. If not financial ruin, then it's certainly not a viable plan to increase savings and insure for the future.*

As Assemblywoman Crystal D. Peoples, (D-Buffalo, NY) noted on 1/26/04 the day after Gov. Pataki proposed his plan for more VLT machines and more venues in New York State:

> *I am worried about people like Preston Cloud, 42, an East Side resident who works as a contract laborer and is on disabilities. He sometimes borrows money from friends to pay for lottery tickets. Cloud has been buying 2 lottery tickets a day for the past 20 years.*
>
> *'I have that dream,' he said. 'We don't have any money and we're spending money we don't have. They say it's a dollar a dream, and I put my last dollar on that dream.' 30*
>
> ********

I suggest that our government is irresponsible and morally bankrupt to propose that gambling be licensed in the face of people who have very limited resources. Preston Cloud can barely make ends meet as it is. Yet our government decides to license this incredibly addictive phenomena right in his face, right in front of him. We're 'inciting' him to spend his limited resources to buy a 'dream' in order to balance the state's budget, at the expense of his personal finances.

A lottery takes more proportionally from his wallet than that of a person of greater income. He's trying for a dream that will probably never become actualized, yet a dream that a government agency told him was possible. The chances for him to win are so incredibly remote that I, for one, cannot even conceive of the number in my mind. He will probably never win. If he does win, he'll probably just turn around and gamble the money away as so many lottery winners have done. We're encouraging him to spend his money irresponsibly, to have unrealistic dreams and hopes, and to use his time not wisely but in planning for a fantasy with an almost nonexistent chance of occurring.

When people win big jackpots in Atlantic City, the first thing the casino does if to congratulate them boisterously and offer them a few days vacation in Atlantic City, 'On the house, of course'. As long as the casinos can get you to be there, they have a good chance of getting their money back.

*I call all this '**pushing'.** When Police departments tempt people to do something, to buy drugs, by offering them drugs first, such as when a police officer goes to a bar and offers to sell you cocaine, it's called 'entrapment'. The police officer gives you the idea, the fantasy that you will be able to buy it and get 'high'. The courts have outlawed such strategies, saying the police 'entrapped' the defendant.*

But it seems this code of conduct is okay in the larger marketplace. It seems okay for gambling corporations to offer something, to entice with a prize, to give you the idea that you will be able to win, to tell you un-truths, in order to engage you in the activity of gambling, just as the police approach the drug addict in order to engage the defendant in the act of buying the drug. Once the person makes the 'buy', he's arrested for doing the action that the police enticed him into. Once the gambler actually gambles, he is enticed into an action that he was led to believe would result in a certain outcome, winning. He's allowed himself to be involved in the activity of gambling which means that he'll end up losing.

The casinos entrap people with unrealistic fantasies and addict people with dreams of something that is really a hopeless impossibility. Our government licenses people to do this, to sell a dream of riches as being possible, when the dream is just that, a dream, an illusion, imaginary, and not real.

As C. Foreel said in l997

> ***This is licensed banditry in the guise of entertainment, given the imprimatur of legitimacy' because the victims are presumed to be willing and able (to pay) and because the community shares in the profits through taxation**.31*

How true. Licensed banditry. Modern Robber Barons. The wealthy getting even wealthier off the backs of the working man. Institutionalized robbery under the guise of entertainment.

Yet no one is immune from culpability. Despite these explanations, I want to be clear, that the one who puts the money in the machine, is the one who had the last chance - and just blew it. No one is being excused, including my husband. This book is about explaining, documenting, and highlighting the phenomenon. If we incur pain, for ourself or for others, because of our own actions, by virtue of our own blindness, the pain is still real and exists and was made manifest by what we did, by our lack of sight.

Words like immoral, seedy, and corrupt comes to mind. It's pushing unrealistic, hopelessly improbable dreams in place of constructive action and values. Whatever happened to working for your money so that little by little, you got where you want to be?

Actuaries tell us that if we save $1,000 a year, about $3 a day, at the end of 8 years, counting interest at 8%, we'll have almost $16,000. That's a sizable amount of money which could provide a nice down payment on a house or anything else a person chooses to save for. Preston Cloud has been buying 2 tickets a day for the past 20 years. That's $6 a day. If he had saved his money he would have had $102,000, at 8 %. Now he has nothing...

> ***Its shameless state governments feeding on human frailty through lawful lotteries**...Tim Sullivan, columnist noted. 32*

> *Or as Assemblywoman Peoples added:*
> ***The poor and people with low incomes are the ones who are looking the hardest for the dream of being that big lottery winner. We need to take a second look at this and find other ways to fund education, as opposed to encouraging people who can't afford to gamble.** 33*

WHY PEOPLE CONTINUE TO GAMBLE AFTER LOSING

This, of course, is the big question. Rational people would think, 'Okay, so the casinos manipulate and misrepresent the odds in their advertising, etc., but after you lose enough, wouldn't a person stop? Why do people continue even after they've lost so much? Wouldn't you think they would get the message?' The answer to this is rooted in the human response to the external world. Yes, my husband is hardly stupid, one would think that he would've gotten the idea. Yet he didn't.

One of the many answers is rooted in some of the very values that we've been taught since birth. Hard work, keep at it, persistence, a person's optimistic belief that they've done okay in the past so the future will probably turn out okay also, based on past patterns. All these ideas which Americans strongly believe in, come to play in a gambler continuing to gamble even after one would think that he had learned. Persistent and excessive gambling is a result, not only of addiction and compulsion, but of irrational thinking maintained by false beliefs. The three core beliefs that lie behind and motivate the gambler include that through knowledge and skill it is possible to win, while many fail, the gambler believes that he/she has the luck, skill and strategies to win, persistence in applying oneself to the task will ultimately be rewarded, as we've shown so far.

In fact the gambler has invested so much time already, he's lost so much of his money already, that the only way he sees to recover is to win a big jackpot. That's the only thing that will make everything all right. Remember, the casinos have been hyping him up saying that its possible to win a big jackpot, they've led him to believe that its both possible and probable. Our gambler has seen, or at least, heard in anecdotal stories from other gamblers, that someone would play a machine for a long time, then leave and another person would immediately hit a jackpot. As the saying goes, 'so much time has passed, so little time remains, keep working hard (toward the goal).'

By leaving the machine, or by stopping his play, the gambler worries that he's risking losing all his past efforts when someone else hits on the machine. Gamblers feel that if they play long enough, the machine will give back something, that after a certain amount of time, the machine is 'ready' to pay off. So if our gambler leaves after a time of putting his money in the machine, then he feels that he just set up the machine for someone else to come along and win. By his reasoning, he can't walk away. Also if he walks away, he's left with all his losses, he's stuck without any of the money he's pumped into the machine. If he continues playing, he has the hope, the possibility, incited by the casinos to begin with, of winning big and recouping all his losses. So he's almost trapped into staying if he wants a good outcome at all. Because he knows that at that moment he's lost, so it's already a bad outcome. The only way to change it, he thinks, to make it better, is to keep playing. What he doesn't account for, is that a bad outcome can worsen, much worse than he has any idea of.

Meanwhile he's continuing to lose even more money. The only sane alternative, he figures, is to continue playing. This is a rational belief, in a way, because we've been accustomed to getting what we work for, sooner or later. (Everything comes to him who waits). Yet with slot machines, this is erroneous. Past life experience has shown him to be successful in what he attempts, to be 'lucky' over the long haul, so why should this be different. We all plan the future based on the past. But, as we've learned, a slot machine pays off only when the random number generator falls on the right combination. This could happen now or far in the future. Odds are generalities over time. Each time our gambler plays, has the same possibility of winning as the last time, no more, no less. The machine has no memory of what it's done, no conception of time.

In a recent court case, a gambler alleged that a certain machine was not correctly programmed to pay off. He said that he'd been playing the machine for a certain amount of time, and it hadn't 'hit' despite the fact that it should have, according to him. By this time, his losses were larger than the jackpot would have been, several hundred thousand dollars. He'd been playing it for a few months. In court, the judge had the machine pulled and inspected. It was found to be functioning correctly. A few months later someone else 'hit' the jackpot. So there is not enough money to 'wait out' machines and you never have any idea when the random number generator which operates only by 'chance', will hit a jackpot.

These misguided ideas are part of what makes gambling so dangerous. You think that your ideas are rational because they're based on long-standing beliefs and values. Yes, hard work pays off over time but your standing at a machine pumping money in is not 'hard work'. The gambler maintains his 'illusion of control', the idea that his skill is responsible for the machine paying off, that his own strategy of play influences the outcome. He believes the locus of control is within himself.

The reality is that he has absolutely no control over when the machine hits. He forgets that the important thing, the odds of winning, do not favor him and in fact, are so outrageously low, that he'll probably never hit. But he gets caught up in the excitement of the moment, the razzle-dazzle and he doesn't take into account the whole picture. He can't see the proverbial forest for the trees. He can't see the demons of addiction for the brightly colored lights and flashing machines.

ADDICTION INHERENT IN THE ACTIVITY

As we've seen from research in innumerable studies and from our own innate common sense, we now know conclusively that gambling is a stimulus for the process called addiction to occur.

Senior Fellow Charles E. Greenawait, of the Susquehanna Valley Center for Public Policy noted,

Gambling triggers Addiction.
The more legalized gambling…available,
the more addictive behavior…produced. *34*

This common sense insight is shared by many clinical people. Recently in **Great Britain***, there have been open sessions of Parliament, their legislative body, with their legislators hearing testimony from psychiatrists and other experts in the field. As the Royal College of Psychiatrists testified:*

> ***The activity of gambling exploits the principles of intermittent reinforcement and is prone to habit formation.***
> ***Vulnerability to pathological gambling is inherent in the very activity of gambling.***
> *Pathological gambling is excessive gambling which leads to social and psychological and financial difficulty.*
> *The most important thing about whether someone becomes addicted is based on the availability of the activity.*
> ***The availability of facilities and the social pressures encouraging gambling are…crucial to the disorder." 35***

When the psychiatrists were asked the chief determinants of this disease, i.e. what made people especially vulnerable to this disease, they replied that as with all things, gambling could be seen as multi-determined with both genetic, individual, and social determinants. They allowed that this was a 'syndrome' with some people having a genetic susceptibility, internal, while others are susceptible to environmental causes, such as the lights and the action external phenomena. For most, however, they felt that the addiction would be ***inherent in the nature of the activity itself****.*

The clearest evidence, they testified, is that the potential for addictiveness of gambling is "inherent in the activity itself." 36 They noted that there are many theories about personal vulnerability ranging from character defects, to environmental triggers, but that there was generally little evidence for many of these theories.

What these British psychiatrists are saying is that **gambling produces addiction.** *We know that taking drugs leads to addiction. Not everyone who takes drugs winds up addicted but sufficient numbers do. So we feel its more beneficial not to legalize drugs, not to allow people the free choice that will kill them if they take it. Perhaps we ought not to allow people the free choice to gamble that will bankrupt them and their families, that will ruin them, if they do it.*

The doctors further listed some obvious **causes or correlates** *for this disease of gambling. One correlation often cited is that many gamblers are* **male**. *Women however are starting to be seen in increased numbers as the social acceptability of the activity increases. Another correlation is that of* **income,** *that people with lower income gamble a higher proportion of their earnings. This has been noted widely. It's assumed that people of lower income gamble more as it's seen by them as one of the few ways to escape the poverty in their lives. A win would be seen as truly 'life-changing', as opposed to people who already more financially affluent. They felt that there was little evidence for other theories about compulsive gambling such as impulsive personalities, low self-esteem, etc.*

Ultimately, they felt that the ***'activity of gambling inherently is habit forming.'*** *This correlates to our assumption linking gambling with drug abuse. If one takes an addictive drug, one will become addicted. If one gambles, one will become addicted. We have licensed in this country an activity which if pursued, will result in addiction. This may happen over time, it may happen sooner rather than later for some people. Inevitably, however, at least for a certain significant percentage of the population, if they gamble, people will become addicted.*

This thesis is similar to that of the Royal College of Psychiatrists in their submission to the Joint Committee on the Draft Gambling Bill. The Royal College submitted this report to the House of Parliament in 12/03, regarding gambling and the proposed deregulation of gambling in that country. In their report, they stated the same thing—that gambling itself leads to addiction.

> *In this behavioral disorder, the availability of gambling facilities and commercial pressures encouraging participation play very important roles...Vulnerability of pathological gambling is inherent in the very activity of gambling." The activity of gambling exploits the principles of intermittent reinforcement and therefore, by its nature, is very prone to lead to habit formation. 37*

In other words, anyone, given enough time gambling, will become addicted, according to their report. The nitty-gritty question of why some people gamble enough to cause great damage to themselves and/or their loved ones, why they gamble enough to later have to declare bankruptcy and/or embezzle to feed their 'habit', is the all-important question.

PREVALENCE

If gambling is apt to addict so many people, what is its actual ***incidence*** *in the population? Different studies have different estimates which vary by geographic locale, length of gambling in the area, age of population, and density and number of gambling facilities in the area. However generally studies cite an incidence of between 1 and 10 % of the adult population. Occasionally studies will show a higher incidence for some specific groups in the population such as seniors or adolescents. These figures reflect* ***a lot of people****. Many, many people have succumbed to this addiction and have ended up destroying themselves and/or their families. Let's look at some states and see how many citizens are involved in problem gambling.*

In Buffalo, ***New York****, it's estimated that a new casino would generate an additional 10,000 to 20,000 new problem gamblers and perhaps 20,000 to 60,000 new pathological gamblers in that area alone. This is based on national baseline prevalence for pathological gamblers of from 1.5% to 3% of the adult population. 3 % is now generally seen as a conservative estimate. 38*

In the state of ***Kentucky****, a recent report by the Kentucky Legislative Research Commission, released in 12/03, found that there were an estimated* ***15,000 addicted gamblers*** *with up to 12% of Kentuckians "at risk of developing serious gambling problems." 39*

In the state of ***California****, the number of people who are problem or pathological gamblers may be close to* ***3 Million****, according to Tom Tucker, director of the California Council on Problem Gambling, a nonprofit organization that addresses gambling addiction. 40*

The California Council on Problem Gambling, has stated that it believes there are about 1 Million Adults and about 100,000 young people addicted to gambling in the state. 41

In ***Wisconsin,*** *Rose Gruber, the executive director of the Wisconsin Council on Problem Gambling, estimated that "about* ***5% of the state's population or 265,000 people*** *are gambling addicts." 42*

In the state of ***Missouri,*** *the Missouri Dept. of Mental Health estimates that up to* ***5% of individuals*** *who participate in gambling activities experience personal, financial and social difficulties because of an obsession with these games." 43 Of this number, 2 out of 3 compulsive gamblers engaged "in illegal activities to pay gambling-related debts or to continue gambling." 43 These statistics are astonishing from the perspective that this activity can lead so many people seriously astray.*

These figures detail a phenomenon that is very similar to drug addiction. Drug addiction leads to crime, gambling leads to addiction, and gambling addiction leads to white-collar crime, such as embezzlement and other types of fraud.

No one knows where compulsive gambling will lead. In Missouri, a small-town mayor initially eagerly embraced gambling as a seeming panacea for her town's financial woes. But then it turned personal:

In ***Riverside, Missouri,*** *the town mayor there, Betty Burch, initially objected to gambling on moral grounds. In 1993, Riverside, a small economically depressed town of about 3,000 people, was approached by the Argosy Gaming Co. regarding whether they wanted casino gambling. However after hearing of the amount of money that gambling revenue could bring, she soon changed her mind. She then became an ardent advocate for gambling, convincing town people easily to pass a referendum in favor of gambling. Over the last 10 years, Riverside has received almost $50 million dollars in gambling revenue. This revenue has built a new city hall, new recreation and public-works buildings and a new sewer system.*

Yet in the process, the mayor's widowed sister began gambling herself and eventually lost the three-bedroom house that she'd owned for 25 years to foreclosure! The mayor admits 2 other family members may have gambling problems as well as a retired friend of hers. So yes, gambling brought in money, but the mayor's sister became an addict and lost a substantial amount of her money. She now lives in an apartment and lives 'payday to payday', as the mayor said in speaking about her sister. 44

The mayor's sister is a prime example of the fact that, experts note, almost ***90 % of casino revenue is received from less than 10 % of customers.*** *In other words, the profits come from the losses of the same people all the time. So it's a small group of gamblers in Riverside and the surrounding area who are actually paying for the Riverside improvements. It's the group of people who lose their houses, become bankrupt, spend their children's inheritances, and their own paychecks, i.e. the addicts.*

Would the mayor have made the same decision today knowing that members of her own family would lose their houses and probably other savings? The Mayor said recently that she feels she must separate her personal and professional life. Yet family members have said that she let money override her values. I don't think material improvements justify people crucifying themselves on the cross of gambling. It seems that there are good reasons why some people believe that gambling is wrong, that it promotes wrong values, that it puts our priorities in the wrong places. What an ironic commentary.

In the state of ***Louisiana,*** *Michael Duffy, assistant secretary of the Dept of Health and hospitals, said 11/19/03 that a recent study estimated the number of gambling addicted there as* ***74,400,*** *an increase of 20,000 from an estimate of 53,000 in 1995. 45 Will there be another 20,000 in the next 5 years? Duffy noted that for every $1 spent on treatment for gambling addiction, the state spends an estimated $5.19 in medical and criminal costs. "And that's not counting costs associated with education and social services and lost productivity, he told the state Gaming Control Board. 46*

In the state of ***Connecticut,*** *Marc Potenza, director of Yale University's problem gambling clinic, estimates that about* ***2% of all Americans are affected by problem gambling****. When the terms of 'problem or pathological gambling', are used, that indicates that an addiction has already occurred, and that there has been substantial damage of whatever kind involved, whether it be financial, social in terms of divorce or homes being lost, children neglected, or any of the myriad difficulties that gambling creates. 47*

In the state of ***Washington****, it was estimated that there were* ***95,000*** *active adult problem and pathological gamblers in 1999. Net receipts at Indian casinos totaled $1.6 Billion dollars from 2001 - 2003, according to the Washington State Gambling Commission. Private card rooms there netted $722 million. Recently funding for Washington's first treatment program to help gambling addicts get subsidized treatment, was discontinued. That program operated from 11/2002 to 6/2003 and cost $500,000. Now that funding has been discontinued, Washington is one of many* *states that license and profit from legalized gambling but do nothing to treat problem gamblers. 48*

*The **treatment program** had been funded by the Washington State Lottery's Mega Millions game. The state lottery there netted $93 million dollars in 2003. In comparison, the state spends about $90 million annually to help alcoholics and drug addicts. Ken Stark, director of the Division of Alcohol and Substance Abuse within the Dept of Social and Health Services, said recently that he is concerned over the lack of state dollars for problem gambling treatment.*

> *There's nobody in state government with the... responsibility to deal with this. Its pretty problematic for gamblers who need help.*
>
> ***(Gambling) can take over your life, much in the same way as alcoholism and drug addiction**. 49*

Indian tribes in the state of Washington as part of negotiated settlements with the state government, pay an annual 2 % 'community contribution' tax. That amounted to about $14 million in 2003. Private non-Indian licensees, paid about $44 million to local municipalities in 2003. The numbers reflect the injustices inherent in the system. If you're an alcoholic, you have access to a host of free or subsidized treatment by counselors especially trained in alcoholism. If you're a gambler, you have no subsidized state resources to turn to.

*In **Florida**, there have been an estimated **500,000 people** who at some time in their lives have suffered **serious difficulties** related to gambling, according to a 2001 study by the University of Florida for the Orlando Florida Council on Compulsive Gambling. It's felt that at this point, there are now 250,000 people who have severe gambling difficulties there. Even **the lottery** can be damaging and addictive for people.*

A 42 year old recovering addict and member of the Gainesville Chapter of Gamblers Anonymous, said that "scratch-off cards, that's where the problem is today. He said he played and lost hundred of dollars a days on them.

> *"**Scratch-offs** are so easily accessible. You can't get gas without being bombarded by the lottery. You play for gas and get $10 worth of tickets. Then you get more and more." He said often lottery addicts go to the store several times daily buying $20 or more each time, and added that he often borrowed money to buy tickets.*
> *"At a bar, if you're drinking too much, they'll cut you off. But you can buy all the lottery tickets you want." 51*

This former gambler is talking about ***accessibility.*** *The temptation is there every time he gets gas, every time he goes to the neighborhood store. This what the British psychiatrists were talking about - accessibility. When people had to travel to a 'destination' resort like Las Vegas or even Atlantic City, it was very different than gambling by going to the corner store.*

*"****What the lottery and Internet did was open up gambling to the masses,"*** *said Pat Fowler, executive director of the Florida Council on Compulsive Gambling. Fowler said her organization was formed in 1988, a year after the beginning of the lottery, as a response to the widespread problems that gambling had begun to cause people who couldn't control their lottery ticket buying.*

In 1989, ***Gambler's Anonymous*** *had 500 meetings in the U.S., according to a spokesperson for the International Service Office of Gamblers Anonymous in Los Angeles. Now* ***GA has 2,500 chapters*** *or 'meetings' in the U.S. and Canada. The rise in accessibility in the last 20 years has meant the increase of GA meetings. It has meant the increase in addicted gamblers and it translates into the increase in bankruptcy filings as well as the rise in suicides.*

Accessibility + Frequency = Addiction.

In ***Australia****, it was reported on 7/6/04 that there were* ***"250,000 problem gamblers.*** *About 90% of them are addicted to" slot machines. Adelaide MP (Member of Parliament), Nick Xenophon, feels that its not an issue of individual responsibility. He notes that "Of course the gambling industry is going to roll out the 'free choice' argument. But that just doesn't wash when you look at the devastation pokie (slot) machines have caused hundreds of thousands of Australians." Sounds familiar? Gambling is causing untold of hardships across the planet. It's not just in the U.S. 52*

In ***Maine,*** *chief of Psychiatry at Spring Harbor, a South Portland psychiatric hospital, states that gambling addiction "is a public health issue that affects nearly* ***3% of American adults*** *in any given year, with a lifetime prevalence of* ***3.5% to 5% in the general population.****" Psychiatrist Girard Robinson added that "Gamblers are at a markedly increased risk for* ***suicide,****"...that up to 70% of pathological gamblers contemplate suicide and up to 20% attempt it. Spouses of problem gamblers have a suicide attempt rate 3 times higher than the general population. 53*

In ***Canada,*** *the Canadian Foundation on Compulsive Gambling surveyed 1,300 adults in Ontario. They found that 7.7% were problem gamblers and 9% were probable pathological gamblers. After the Niagara casino was built, there was an increase in the number of people gambling and reporting problems. According to a* *study done in Windsor, Canada in 1994, the level of problem gambling was estimated at between 4.8 and 10.8% of the adolescent sample for the study. 54*

*In **Korea,** 2 Seoul psychiatrists estimated that 4.1% of the adult population is addicted to gambling. 55*

*Gambling counselor, Arnie Wexler, in **California** that "There are 5 Million compulsive gamblers and (another) 15 Million at risk in the U.S." 56*

*As **Wyoming House Speaker,** Pro Tem Rodney Anderson, R-Pine Bluffs, said recently on 2/27/04, in response to a gambling related bill passing the Wyoming Legislature,*

> ***We know we can't legislate morality, but we sure don't need to legislate immorality.*** *57*

With gambling comes a host of other immoral issues such as money issues leading to crime, and impact on family life, in the form of divorces, child neglect. As we legislate and allow the age-old vice of gambling, we'll learn all-too-well why gambling has always been called a vice and why societies historically have sought to stamp it out, not welcome it in.

We can assume that the overall number of people gambling has increased since 1999. Both the percentage and the overall numbers increase. That is to say, that 10 % in 2004 is a greater number than 10% in 1999. Tallying both problem and pathological gamblers, together with the time increase and overall gambling expansion, there is probably a much greater number of the general population inflicting their substantial damage on themselves, their families, and our society.

*Estimates vary widely regarding the number of people addicted, whether the figure is 1.5%, 3%, 5% or 10% or 20%. Given that we're talking about totals in the American population, the difference in a percentage point mean quite a significant number of people. **Experts say that when a new casino opens, the rate of pathological** gambling **doubles** within a 50-mile radius.*

If each pathological gambler is associated with one of the following for himself and/or his family, bankruptcy, alcoholism, depression, loss of homes, divorce, suicide, then even a conservative estimate of 10,000 new gamblers would mean incredible numbers of people suffering from very real social tragedies and misfortunes.

The social costs are impossible to fathom, but they're considerable. My husband comes home after Gamblers Anonymous meetings and shares with me, without names, some of the terrible stories that he's heard there. Real tragedies visited upon families, husband after husband speaking of not giving his children the attention a parent should, the love that a child needs, of families broken apart, of people losing their careers, homes and families. This is what addiction is about.

In our own case, we used to see that side of the family that Alan 'borrowed money' from, fairly regularly. Now because lawyers and Courts are involved, contact has been terminated. How much do hearts cost when they break. What do insurance companies pay to mend reputations? How long does it take to re-establish trust? Is that even possible? What price is worth the un-doing of family relationships? What incredible power gambling must have, to lead to the undoing of so many things.

Gambling sells "dreams and fantasies." But at what cost?

"It preys on the weakest, offering false hope of easy money. It is horribly addicting to some people and ruins lives and families – a small percentage of gamblers, perhaps, but enough to cause real and lasting damage to society. Making gambling ever more available, making the damage ever more prevalent, seems to be according to the columnist. 58

It's a disguised ***death wish****, for society, for communities, and for families. If an individual gambler is so self-destructive as to cause so much damage to himself and his family, what do we call it when a society looks at these figures and yet decides to go ahead and license gambling*

Addiction is a funny thing, it's hard to understand, even harder to cope with, and sometimes seemingly impossible to beat. John Cipolla found this out the hard way, from his own experience.

John had been gambling for a long time, from when he was a teenager. But until the casinos came to Rhode Island, it wasn't out of control. Once the casinos came to town, that was when his addiction and his Life became unmanageable.

"I am the ***dark side*** *of gambling.* ***Gambling took over my life*** *to the point that I was obviously out of control. What you won't hear here today are the* ***cries of my family****...the day I was led away from a courtroom in shackles."*

"I am begging someone to step to the forefront and start discussing how we mandate prevention and treatment programs."

John said this in public testimony before the Rhode Island House of Representatives on May 12, 2004. He told the House Finance Committee that a gambling addiction was the cause of him stealing more than $240,000 from a Providence, Rhode Island, city agency, the Mayor's Council on Drug and Alcohol Abuse, while he was deputy director. Cipolla spent 3 years in prison for crime related to his gambling. 59 www.projo.com/ap/ne/1084380348.htm,

John does not want casinos in Rhode Island. He's had experience with the beast of gambling, with the demon of addiction, and he doesn't want to go there again. His family's had experience with his gambling addiction. And they didn't even gamble. In our journey towards an enlightened society, perhaps we should consider whether gambling, with its associated malevolent harem of demons and things that come out in the night, is something we want to offer to people. Do we want to make something that could make life exceedingly difficult for children, wives, and gamblers, themselves, available? If gambling can do this to John Cipolla's family, to my family, it can happen to anyone.

These kinds of tragedies, divorce, suicide, loss of homes, translate into difficulties not only in the present for people and their families, but also down the road. Statistics on crime and broken homes show that most criminals suffered from dysfunctional families and single parent homes. The economic maelstrom that gambling generates for a significant percentage of the population may be expected to continue for the next 20 to 30 years in the lives of people it affects presently. Once we open Pandora's Box, it doesn't go away by itself. We'll reap the whirlwind for years to come.

Annual gambling losses of Americans totaled $1.2 Billion in 1974 when only Atlantic City and Las Vegas were operating. They increased to $40 Billion by 1995. See the National Coalition Against Legalized Gambling website for a wealth of information, www.ncalg.org, or www.casinowatch.org. 60 Joel S. Rose, in a speech on 11/21/03 to the League of Woman Voters of Buffalo, estimated that the losses are now probably about ***$80 billion dollars****. It's larger than the annual GNP of many countries.* ***Do we as Americans have $80 Billion dollars to throw away on gambling?***

Are we so wealthy as a nation and as individuals that we can afford to spend this much money in the pursuit of mindless pleasure and/or a dream? Is there nothing in our communities that couldn't be helped by a vast infusion of cash of even half of this magnitude? Have we forgotten that we still have Hunger and Homelessness in America? Could we put our money and our efforts toward those problems instead of indulging ourselves in endless entertainment, mindless stimulation?

The created world of casinos, the illusionary facade that's produced and ambitiously marketed, the glamour and the opulence, are all the social features of casinos. The hype, the lights, the noise, the action, the convenience, the appeal to sense pleasures, the accessibility, and the stimulus features of the machines themselves, are to blame for people becoming pathologically addicted. The world created by the architects of gambling, the designers of this new plastic charade called Entertainment is the culprit in people becoming hooked. This is exactly what the British psychiatrists said, what the Australian thesis noted, and what our common sense would tell us.

This artificial world of gambling has sprung up, so to speak, from the head of our materialistic society when it was having a bad decade. Now the goddess of gambling, powerful and willful that she is, exercises more influence and more of a pull to herself, than the traditional gods of home and hearth. Just as the moth is attracted to the fire, so people are attracted to the goddess of Gambling. She's seems more powerful than her creator and capable of unleashing the fire of economic destruction at her command.

In Lansing, ***Michigan*** *recently, at a press conference, there were strong comments about the proposed expansion of gambling. Legislation passed by the state House and awaiting Senate action would seek to create up to 9 new, unregulated casinos. The measure would allow up to 15,000 slot machines at race tracks, creating so-called 'racinos'. It would also allow new Internet and telephone gambling on horse racing. A U.S. Congressman, a U.S. Senator, and the former Lt. Governor, all spoke against expanded gambling and noted the negative impact it would have on Michigan.*

U.S. Representative Mike Rogers, R-Michigan, a former FBI agent and co-author of tough oversight laws governing the three non-Indian casinos in Detroit, said "This gambling legislation set up 9 new casinos without oversight, creating the potential for abuse, addiction and costly problems for the state to contend with." "This is about more prostitution, suicides, thefts, personal bankruptcies, and swelling Michigan's addicted-to-gambling population above the already staggering 350,000." 62. This ***350,000 refers to problem gamblers in Michigan already addicted****. We can only imagine how much human disruption and chaos in families is generated by 350,000 addicts.*

"It may fool some people at first, but in the long run it will hurt, not help,. Michigan's economy," added U.S. Senator Samuel Buzz Thomas, (D-Detroit). 63 Former Lt. Gov. Dick Posthumus, R-Alto., noted that the racino package is about expanding gambling and not about helping agriculture, which the bill had been advertised as doing. "This package is not about farming, and it will not build a strong foundation for agriculture in Michigan," Posthumus said 63.

*In **California** recently on 1/27/04, the California Police Chief Assoc. announced its opposition to allowing slot machines at tracks and non-Indian 'card clubs', as they're euphemistically called there. Proponents of increased slots in California wish to put 30,000 machines in 16 urban locations in counties. The Police Chiefs have opposed previous initiatives approving Indian gambling because of the "serious link between large-scale casino gambling and crime." "Californians can protect public safety by refusing to sign the casino petitions," the police chiefs urged. If we consider the police chiefs associations to be a relatively neutral group, then we have to wonder why they would take such a public stance against gambling – unless there really was something to the allegation that gambling has a history of corruption and a tradition of increasing crime. 64*

*This reminds me of the earlier assertion of quite a few district attorneys in **Rhode Island** that they've seen an alarming jump in embezzlement and other kinds of crime along with the increase in gambling there. If anything, we might expect Police Departments to welcome gambling because there would be more opportunities for career advancement as Police Departments grow larger. But in fact, they've been opposed and continue to be opposed to the expansion of gambling.*

*The **New Hampshire Chief's of Police**, the New Hampshire Sheriffs Assoc. and New Hampshire attorneys generals also oppose legalized video slots and casinos. On 1/21/04, New Hampshire Attorney General Peter Heed testified before its state Legislature that he is "unalterably opposed to any expansion of gambling." 65*

*The **Florida Sheriffs Association** also recently unanimously passed a resolution stating its opposition to expanding gambling when the racetracks there asked for VLT's. Do we think that the Florida sheriffs pass resolutions because they don't have anything else to do? Possibly they passed the resolution because they've seen first-hand the damage that the machines lead to and the crime they create. 66*

Since most of us are strongly in favor of a law-abiding society with less crime and less need for increased tax dollars to balance Police budgets, we would do well to heed the warnings of Police Chiefs and district attorneys around the country. Another example of expert testimony telling us about the fruits of gambling. More testimony from those who have seen and experienced the 'underbelly of the beast'. More people who go on record to testify to what gambling really brings, what we can really expect as the consequences of licensing gambling establishments, what will really happen as the aftermath of legalizing and inciting yet another kind of addiction.

ADDICTION & FAMILIES

As we have shown, Addiction is a powerful and widespread issue in our society. Our society gives people the means to readily avail themselves of addictive substances, such as alcohol, drugs, and now gambling. We have more availability and increased opportunity to an extent previously unheard. As people imbibe these substances, indulge in these activities, they become addicted. No surprise.

We now have extra money in our affluent society and additional time. Jobs require 35 hours a week instead of 60 hours. With this extra time and money, we have more opportunity to indulge in activities that can get us in trouble. With additional free time, we need to use extra judiciousness and discrimination in deciding how we're going to spend our time. How we spend our time today decides how our future will look. Our fathers didn't have our choices.

On a personal note, not only is my husband a compulsive gambler, but several other family members have also been addicts. In my nuclear family, i.e. my family of origin, mother, father, sister, brothers, and husband, out of 7 people, there have been 3 alcoholics, one drug addict, and one gambler, 5 out of 7.

What does this demonstrate? That we're all flawed human beings, people with weaknesses and strengths, whose weaknesses sometime threaten to overwhelm the strengths. This is what addiction is made of. It's essence. The saving grace is that we're all in this together, even though it doesn't look like that. Anyway, this is a high incidence of addictions in one family. Is it genetic? Alcoholism has been shown to have a genetic component and that certainly did carry through from one parent to one child.

However it's also said that dysfunctional families raise dysfunctional children. This is commonly called environmental influences, the Nature vs. Nurture debate, whether a person's genetic endowment is dominant or whether environmental influences are more influential.

Of these addicts, at the time they were actively addicted, they were dysfunctional people who caused damage by neglecting the performance of their roles in their families and in society. They neglected their roles as family members, they didn't support themselves, and they weren't supportive of others dependent on them. They neglected financial and emotional duties.

I'm addicted to smoking. This is penny-ante compared to some of the others which involve more immediately destructive effects. However, as is known, smoking can have long-term life-changing implications as well as present financial effects.

When we feel under stress, which seems to occur often in our fast-paced world, we turn to various addictions for emotional and psychic relief. We want to feel good, to have a good time. Drinking, gambling, smoking, drugs are billed as ways to have 'a good time,' to relax, to enjoy ourselves. We're all vulnerable.

Aside from their legality or not, addictions certainly bring more problems in the long run. Research is replete with the problems that Alcoholism brings both short and long term. Smoking has a short term, immediate gratification effect. Drugs have an immediate, pleasurable effect. However, they incapacitate a person to handle their responsibilities and, in the long run, their life. This is what addictions do. They give some escapist pleasures in the short run. Ultimately, they're so damaging that no one in his right mind would espouse them. They come at a high price. Yet we find our state governments rushing to legalize and even further expand yet another addiction—gambling.

So many of us embrace these addictions that we have to wonder why? If they're known addictive substances, why do so many people indulge in them. Obviously, for one reason or another, people's needs aren't being met. Part of the reason that need isn't being met lies in the structure of our society. How our society is structured to meet people's needs determines whether it is sensitive to those needs and tries to accommodate them.

In traditional societies, where people have less individual decision-making power, less money and less time, it would appear that the society is pre-programmed to meet overall needs on a structural level, i.e. it's built into the practices and overall culture of the society. In rural countries, such as India or some Muslim countries, religion is all-important and much of a person's life is structured around the local religious houses of worship and/or religious practices. Rural villages follow customs hundreds of years old, certainly time to refine customs that benefit people.

In villages in rural India, people lives are often organized around the local temple, its activities and programs. There they find their social outlets, their recreational and spiritual needs. People gather at temples on Saturday nights to eat, to engage in religious practices, and interact with others. This is a low cost, easy way of exchanging news, meeting and getting together with others. Marriages are still 'arranged', and while this might seem strange to us, they have a much higher success rate, lower divorce rate, than Western marriages.

Divorce, as well as compulsive gambling, are products of our modern society with its liberalized rules and touted, personal 'freedoms.' Have our many individual freedoms brought us happy marriages and harmonious families? A great spiritual leader, Ammachi, said on 7/13/04, "There is only one difference between people in wealthy countries and poor countries: while people in wealthy countries are crying in air-conditioned rooms and palatial mansions, the people of poor countries are crying on the dirt floors of their huts." These social costs are a product of our society not meeting people's needs. We're all looking for something. As we indulge in our personal freedom to gamble, we find we have the 'freedom' to destroy ourselves financially, through gambling, as well as through illicit drugs, or drinking.

Now of course primitive societies didn't always meet individual needs either. No one society was or is perfect. But when you consider the amount of very self-destructive addictions, habits, and ways of interacting that people have in our society, we have to wonder what is making this pattern of addiction so prevalent and pervasive. We have to wonder whether our 'modern' society, so full of labor-saving conveniences, material affluence, and individual liberties, is really so concerned and begins to address the issue of meeting people's deep-seated needs.

We're more interested in material affairs than with emotional, spiritual or feeling-type needs. As these needs get neglected, as we have more stress, people make poor choices looking for fulfillment and meaning. They seek in places that have no answers. Las Vegas or Atlantic City can say nothing to the search for meaning, the craving for fulfillment, felt by so many in our society.

What supports could we design to enable people to function more easily and effectively, to feel supported, and at-ease and fulfilled in their lives? What could help them avoid temptations like gambling, which the hundreds of thousands of people listed in 'Prevalence' have been unable to do? What direction can we seek to go in to meet the needs that people are seeking to fulfill when they turn to addictive substances and to addictive and/or destructive activities?

These questions are beyond the scope of this book, but are relevant for future public exploration and discussion. What is key is to note is that in allowing our governments to license this addictive activity, we're opening yet another Pandora's box of ***Social Costs****. We open and pave the way to our self-destruction. Gambling itself is not new. But the degree of technological advancement in slot machines and VLT's, the knowledge of the application of psychological principles of intermittent reinforcement, along with the savvy marketing principles, the 'Come and Win' publicity strategies, modern advancement of lights, sounds and music, all open the way to a new levels of addiction and rampant possibilities of financial and personal ruin.*

****

CHAPTER THREE

THE ECONOMICS of GAMBLING

***Casinos are a big economic and social loser**...*
More casinos will not solve the problem,
They will only make the losses greater ones. 1
William Thompson, prof. public admin.
Univ. of Nevada, Las Vegas

For every slot machine you add,
***You lose one job per year from the consumer economy**. 2*
John Kindt, business & legal policy professor,
Univ. of Illinois, Urbana-Champaign.

*Gambling has become big business as we've discussed. In 2002, Americans **spent $68.7 Billion on gambling.** That was a rise of 6.85% from 2001 and didn't even include Internet gambling. The biggest revenue came from casinos, $28 billion gross in 2002, noted Christiansen Capital Advisors. That's about 1% of the nation's entire personal annual income! The money "is absolutely enormous, and will continue to grow," 3 Eugene Christiansen, the chairman, said recently. Gambling has certainly become a major part of our economy. Its players, the private corporations, the native American corporations, have become major forces to be reckoned with in our society. The biggest growth in a particular segment of gambling in 2002 was the 11% rise in lotteries,3 said Christiansen.*

What is also enormous is the numbers of Americans spending their time and money in casinos. A Harrah's Entertainment survey in 2002 found that in

Sacramento, California, Phoenix, and Los Angeles, about ***40 % of adults*** *visited a casino at least once a year. 4 This is what Americans are doing with their leisure time and disposable income. Hardly a constructive activity. Almost half of all adults are going to casinos for their entertainment and for something to do with their time. Whatever happened to reading books, 'life-long learners,' to community, church and family activities.*

Annual gambling ***losses*** *of Americans totaled $1.2 Billion in 1974 when only Atlantic City and Las Vegas were operating. They increased to* ***$40 Billion by 1995****. National Coalition Against Legalized Gambling. 5Joel S. Rose, in a speech on 11/21/03 to the League of Woman Voters of Buffalo, estimated that the losses are now probably about* ***$80 billion dollars****. This is an astronomical amount of money. It's larger than the annual Gross National Product of many countries.*

All of those billions for an activity that provides no creature comforts, no long-term investment, nothing constructive. All of those resources for something that does not provide any product. Gambling, or trying to make lifestyle changes based on money acquired in a casino, is a natural outcome of the values of our materialistic society.

In this chapter, we'll learn about the nuts and bolts of the alleged economic development that the casino promoters offer. We'll see if their idea of economic development can really be referred to as something beneficial or whether it's all just a big public relations campaign, and the only one who wins is the casino. We'll look at the experience of many American communities across our land, from Maine to California, from Florida to Michigan and see if casinos have done what they promised, if the people who have lived with casinos in their neighborhoods feel that their lives are better off with gambling or not. After you read this economic review, supported by countless studies, you'll have a good understanding of the various economic issues and the implications of gambling in your community.

Legal betting in the United States

The increase in total dollars gambled per year in the United States from 1993 to 2002 was 99.7 percent. In billions of dollars:

	1993	1996	2002
Non-Indian casinos	$12.2	$19.2	$28.1
Lotteries	12.8	15.3	18.6
Indian casinos	2.6	5.4	14.2
Pari-mutuels (horse racing, dog racing)	3.6	3.7	4
Charitable bingo and other games	2.3	2.5	2.6
Card rooms	0.7	0.7	1
Other	0.2	0.9	0.2
Total	**$34.4**	**$47.7**	**$68.7***

*Total does not include gambling over the Internet, estimated at $4 billion worldwide in 2002.

Sources: Christiansen Capital Advisers, LLC; American Indian Culture and Research Journal Sacramento Bee/Sheldon Carpenter 6

As children, we learn from an early age that we need money to buy what we want, to acquire the desirable things in life. As teenagers, we see that money can buy prestige, a car, the attention of peers, status, all the desirable things in life. As adults, we think that money will buy us what we need in life, a home, career, clothes, and food.

Money in our society is about basic survival - the necessities of life for us and our families. Yes, we learn that money is all-important in our culture. So when we see the staggering amounts of money in a casino, we're impressed. No where else in our society are people around this much money. And it's very exciting – an adrenaline rush. So many Americans now view what was formerly perceived as sinful, gambling, as harmless entertainment, not as a vice or a sin. Yet if the figures below are correct, and they have all been researched in innumerable University studies, then we'll see conclusively that gambling not only is not 'harmless fun', but in fact a new and devastating, and worst of all, a self-inflicted, scourge on society and its innocent citizens

****

At any given craps table in a casino, or even a small blackjack table, there can easily be $300,000 out in plain sight—at each table! Each slot machine loudly advertises with lights and bells, its big jackpot, from $20,000 up to 2 or 3 Million dollars. Most people would agree this is big money. As my husband and I used to say, this is life-changing money. This is more money than most people normally see or have in a lifetime.

When we're around places with a lot of money conspicuously displayed, it can be mind-boggling. We can temporarily lose our common sense, our values. We forget, or don't remember, that these hundreds of thousands of dollars represent incredible hours of individual work, sacrifice, and labor. It's not just paper. It represents human sweat equity in lives. Casinos are places in our society where people and money meet. Gambling venues are unique in our culture in terms of flashing money and being places where large sums of money can change hands 'on the turn of a card', so-to-speak. This can be physically and mentally stimulating.

In addition to being exciting, we're led to believe that we can win. A recent newspaper bus advertisement for the Indian casino in Connecticut, Mohegan Sun, stated:

We drive. You Win. *7*

Now rationally people know that this isn't true, that they probably won't win, but it gives them the thought of going, and the rationalization that they might win. It leads people to involve themselves in the web of rationalizations and lies that allow and even encourage them to continue gambling—even when they know they shouldn't. After all, they feel there's always the chance that they might win big! No matter how slim.

So what are the economics of gambling? Does Gambling make sense for anyone? Is Gambling really able to drive economic development, to stimulate and rejuvenate communities with the roll of a dice, as it seems? Can neighborhoods and communities join the American Dream by invoking the benevolent gods of gambling? Will these gods bless our communities and rain money down upon the people? Does Gambling make sense for poor people who have no other prospects, no other realistic possibility of making it into an affluent life-style?

Or does Gambling make sense for our nation's wealthier citizens, who have some educated ideas about betting and feel that they're pretty sophisticated about how they use their money? On a macro scale, communities, and on a micro scale, individuals, does it make sense for anyone?

Let's examine some of the research done in the last 10 years as we've grown more knowledgeable about Gambling, what it is and what it isn't, what it can do and what it can't, what it does do to communities, to individuals, to families and to businesses. Let's look at this phenomenon in the hard light of numbers and see if it makes sense for anyone.

****

After all, Gambling is Big Business, VERY BIG business. The gaming industry makes nearly $51 Billion in net revenue each year. 8 In the last 20 years, since the Atlantic City casinos opened in 1979, businesses have grown into large, multi-national corporations. These corporations such as Harrah's, Bally's, International Gaming Technology, are now private businesses worth Mega Billions of dollars. They are larger than some of the Fortune 500 companies that have been around for a hundred years. They have more influence than most stocks on the Big Board.

They've been created from nothing in a short time and they now exercise their money and influence as they wish. The Indian casinos, sovereign states, have grown from small groups of people with 1/64 or 1/128 % Indian blood, to mighty corporations able to affect the fortunes of large communities and the multitude of people in them. The Indian casinos are among the largest in the world and are not hesitant to exercise their considerable influence both economically and politically!

ECONOMIC JUSTIFICATION

Economically, gambling proponents, as well as casinos, state that gambling benefits society in several ways. Let's look at these ways that they state are so beneficial and see if the research justifies their hype. When they promise jobs, community or regional economic development, state or local tax revenue, and/or tourism to an area, does any of that comes true?

Economically, gaming interests state that casinos are beneficial in 4 major areas.

1. *The overall **economic development of a community** or region, i.e. that it brings in money on all levels of society, for all groups and individuals.*
2. ***Revenue** in the form of taxes to the state, supposedly similar to 'windfall profits', the state only has to collect them, 'like rain from the sky'.*
3. ***Tourism**, assumed to bring in money to an area.*
4. *Perhaps the biggest attraction of all, is that gambling supposedly provides, as New York Governor George Pataki said in 2002 after signing the Gambling Compact, **Jobs.***

It all sounds great. Gambling employs people who are out of work, builds Convention centers, provides money for Education, has Entertainment value, nice restaurants, top shows. Who could argue with any of this? But is it all true? Is any of it true? Is none of it true?

Let's look at these ***four alleged economic benefits, 1. Overall Economic Development, 2. Revenue, Taxes 3. Tourism 4. Jobs.***

Economic development *is actually the overall rubric which drives the last 3 categories, revenue and taxes, tourism, and jobs. All of the latter are involved in and important factors in determining the economic development of an area. Each category should reinforce the others and provide for the overall growth of the region. If a community has good economic development, then its citizens should be able to provide revenue to the government in the form of taxes, for the government to be able to function for the good of its citizens.*

Tourism *is one means of economic development for some communities. Tourism looks attractive to some communities as it doesn't require a great deal of start-up capitol or a huge investment in the form of expensive factories and inventory. It's also a 'clean' industry, in that it usually doesn't pollute or require existing acreage to be converted to other uses.*

Jobs *are the means, the building blocks, of providing for economic development in an area. Jobs can be provided in various areas, whether fishing, tourism, farming, or industry. If an area has industry attuned to current markets and in demand, then it will also have jobs and subsequent government revenue. So enumerating Economic Development includes the following 3 categories, revenue, tourism, and jobs, in the overall description of the community's financial well-being.*

In 1978, when the Atlantic City casinos opened, it was widely felt that Atlantic City would be economical rejuvenated. It was felt that regional economic development would be favorable, that Atlantic City would become a tourist attraction once again, and that the casinos would solve the problems of lack of industry, scarce jobs, and poor housing. Has it done that? Could anything have done that?

Let's discuss Atlantic City and try to determine the level of its economic development based on several economic indices, crime, established businesses, the amount of homelessness, jobs, tourism and the overall 'quality of life' for the residents. Isn't that what we're all seeking, to improve our quality of life, to have the good things in life, not to have to work all the time, to make a good life for our children.

Atlantic City casino buildings are beautiful, indeed gaudy to the point of ostentatiousness. But what happens when you walk a few blocks away. We were always cautioned by our reps not to walk in the neighborhoods, only to take limos or taxis. They often said that the area wasn't safe. Whether they said that to keep us inside the casino or because it was true is uncertain. But certainly the only businesses significantly in view in the surrounding area were the ***pawnshops.*** *Their business has increased many-fold. Pawnshop owners are rolling in dough. But what does this mean and was this the goal? The neighborhood itself remains poor, dilapidated and seedy.*

The ***homeless*** *camp out in great numbers under the boardwalk in* ***Atlantic City*** *seeking shelter. Nearly 1 in 5 homeless people admit that gambling contributed to their poverty. 9 At night, the Boardwalk isn't safe to walk alone on. Yes, Atlantic City has a new physical plant for its High School, a new Convention Center, but are the lives of the residents any different than before gambling? Is their day-to-day existence significantly improved? What is their quality of life?*

Recently it was reported in the New York Times, 7/21/04, that ***Atlantic City*** *has* ***an AIDS epidemic*** *more severe than other American cities. "Drugs and prostitution - always birds of a feather - have turned Atlantic City, the gambling capital of the East Coast, into the scene of an AIDS epidemic and the backdrop for a public health emergency," according to Brent Staples, staff reporter. www.iht.com/articles/530255. htm Almost 1 in 40 residents are infected with the HIV virus, the majority of them prostitutes and drug users, and then they pass the disease on to their lovers and unborn babies.10a*

Las Vegas also has a burgeoning ***homeless*** *population. An article in Fox News, 8/3/04, "Sin City Has Become Homeless City", noted that homelessness was up 18% there. 10 What happened to casino claims of Jobs and Employment? So we see that what happened in Atlantic City occurs in other places as well. Gambling will not enrich communities but in fact will lead to their economic decline. We've been sold a 'bill of goods'. It's time we picked our heads out of the sand to see what the reality really is.*

Are we still talking about an improvement in the quality of life, in the finances of all citizens??? Let's see what acknowledged experts say about the predictable economic pattern following gambling's introduction into communities.

> *This same disappointing pattern, that there has not been corresponding* ***economic development for the communities*** *in which casinos are located, has been observed virtually wherever in America casino gambling has been adopted as an economic development tool." Joel Rose, speech to the League of Women Voters, 11/21/04 11*

The ***quality of life as measured by unemployment figures*** *has diminished.* ***Unemployment*** *in Atlantic City now is a striking* ***11.4%****, one of the highest in the nation and twice as much as the state average of 5.4%. 12 In the first 10 years of Atlantic City, 40% of the local restaurants closed. 13 In the first 20 years of gambling,* ***90% of local businesses closed****. What kind of economic development is this? This is typical and symptomatic of what occurs when casinos come into a community. In a Special to the Buffalo News, 10/19/03, Maura J. Casey wrote that the loss of area businesses can be anywhere from 10 to 30% depending on how much entertainment the casino brings in from the outside. 14*

The issue of ***jobs*** *is another economic indice and an area in which casinos were supposed to excel. To look at jobs, we have to look at the change by casinos in what they offer in terms of types of gambling. They used to concentrate on table games, such as blackjack and craps, which are labor intensive, giving many jobs. Recently casinos have turned to* ***slot machines*** *for a majority of their income. They require minimal maintenance and supervision. However, they don't offer as many jobs to community people as when table games were the big draw. Blackjack requires rotating dealers, the boss over him, and a whole staff hierarchy. Craps requires 4 dealers and pit boss. Slot machines won't give the plethora of jobs as was anticipated, especially to the minimally trained person.*

Slot machines*, which Atlantic City voters were initially promised in l977 would not come, have been found to be exceedingly lucrative to casinos. They now comprise* ***70%*** *of the casinos business. And while the rich and the powerful gamble in Atlantic City, much of the casino's money, in fact its 'bread-and-butter- is senior citizens. Buses bring in hordes of people but they stay in the all-inclusive womb of the casinos, they don't venture out to the street. They arrive by bus from community centers with their box lunches and rolls of coins for these same slot machines that were promised in l977 wouldn't come. How pathetic is this.*

Do we really want our ***senior citizens,*** *my mother, your father, to spend their last years, throwing coins in a slot machine in a vain hope of 'making it rich?' Is this the best 'culture' that America has to offer? Is this the best quality of life we have for our citizens that they should flock here in such numbers? Is this the most constructive use we have for our seniors? Or are they and their money 'throwaways' also?*

Included in this overall evaluation of economic regional and/or community development must be considerations about ***CRIME,*** *as an economic indice. Where numbers of people and their money gather, there will also be crime. A lot of it. In fact, crime rates skyrocket wherever casinos open. Atlantic City's crime rate rose an* *incredible 258 % within 10 years of the legalization of casinos. 15 FBI statistics show the crime rate per 1,000 residents tripled from 134.3 in 1978 to 450.3 in 1988.*

Where there are large amounts of money involved, people are exposed to temptation. People are not always at their highest when there's money involved. Establishing an area with gambling leads inevitably to other concomitant issues. We know that the establishment of casinos leads to **crime, corruption, prostitution.** *Casinos bring in all the unsavory elements that can exist in our society. Knowing this now, why would we ever think about expanding gambling. We should work toward decreasing or eliminating the spread of this new disease just as we would do what we could to combat rising crime rates in our neighborhoods.*

Atlantic City itself has had its share of corruption since it opened as a gambling locale. Of its six mayors since casinos opened in 1978, four were later indicted for corruption and three are presently in prison. "During 1989 the New Jersey Casino Control Commission reported huge increases in the number of assaults, rapes, prostitution activity and drug deals." That's exactly what we're trying to decrease in our society and Atlantic City attracted it like bees to honey. 16

The Las Vegas telephone book has ***20 pages of advertisements for prostitution.*** *That's incredible, isn't it? Why would any society allow that? Don't we make laws for the good of all? These are areas of corruption and negativities. We don't really want to be around this and certainly don't want to promote its expansion.*

> *In Atlantic City, homelessness increased after... casinos. Stores and restaurants declined.... The growth of crime in the Atlantic City region reduced property values by $24,000,000 for each easily accessible community. 17 Dr. Robert Goodman, "Legalized gambling as a Strategy for Economic Development"*

Property values*, another important economic indice, also* ***declined*** *substantially in surrounding neighborhoods. For many people, their property, essentially their house, is their main economic investment throughout their life-time. It helps to determine their quality of life in their old-age and can provide an inheritance for their children. So if people's 'property values' declined, then that's a significant social cost that these people suffered.*

Atlantic City itself declined 22 % in terms of ***population****. That's not good. People leaving, like rats off a sinking ship. If people leave, then they are thinking the area isn't good for them either economically or in which to raise a family. This is* *not economic development. So in the case of Atlantic City, we certainly see that a close look at all the economic indices shows clearly that economic development has not come to Atlantic City itself. In fact, Atlantic City was not the only community that experienced a jump in crime when casinos came to town.*

GAMBLING IN THE U.S.

How it compares to other things we spent money on in 2002.

Billions

- *Gambling: $68.7*
- *Furniture: $66.7*
- *Prisons: $54.3 **
- *Shoes: $48.8*
- *Car insurance: $35*
- *Coca-Cola and Pepsi-Cola: $30.9*
- *Books: $26.9*
- *50 top-grossing movies: $6.17*
- *CDs, DVDs, LPs, cassettes: $0.9*

** Local and state government share 18*

Sources: Christiansen Capital Advisers, LLC; U.S. Department of Commerce; Fortune magazine; Variety magazine; Recording Industry Association of America; Association of American Publishers.

- *In Mississippi, the Gulf Coast similarly experienced a 43% increase in crime in the 4 years after casinos arrived. 19*
- *In Ledyard, Connecticut, police department calls jumped from 4,000 calls annually to 16,700 within 5 years after the opening of the nearby Foxwoods Casino. 20*
- *In Black Hawk, Colorado, the number of police calls increased from 25 a year before casinos to between 15,000 and 20,000 annually. 21*
- *Increased crime comes with casinos. It's a natural and inevitable development. Where there's lots of money, there will be crime. Not only is crime a negative event for those who experience it directly, it's expensive in the cost of the increased staff necessary to handle the increased number of calls.*

CRIME

The costs of gambling can be measured not only in dollars and cents but also in its power to addict and bring to ruin people from all walks of life. In Canada recently, a scandal involving the Toronto Police Department showed that even they are not above the possibility of corruption. It seemed that several Toronto police officers ran up huge gambling debts. Then not knowing how to begin paying them off, the officers turned to graft and corruption to get the needed funds. The president of the Toronto Police Association, head of the 7,000 member police union, is being investigated as well as the son of the former police chief, a police officer himself. It's alleged that 'money extractions' from clubs and restaurants were done by the police officers to pay off gambling debts at Casino Rama and possibly other gambling sites. 22

"Gambling is just as bad an addiction as alcohol for cops on this force," said one source familiar with the allegations. No arrests have been made but both criminal and Police Act charges may be involved. This police department investigation was an offshoot of another investigation by the Royal Canadian Mounted Police into gambling and organized crime, where top mob bosses control the gambling trade and other rackets in Ontario as well as other places. This is the first major corruption probe for the Toronto Police Department's in its 47-year history.

So gambling places many people at risk. If gambling hadn't been available, perhaps the officers would've gotten into trouble another way but that's not really relevant. The fact is, that the police officers 'fell from Grace' by means and because of the availability and accessibility of gambling. Another example of good people, previously with no involvement in illegal activities, being brought down by gambling and its associated by-products. Gambling brings problems, the more accessible gambling is, the more frequently people indulge in gambling, the more problems it brings. It opens the door to crime, to misfortune, to dis-ease, and bids these demons welcome.

In Jacksonville, Illinois, a Roman Catholic **priest** *issued an apology for stealing $226,000 from his church to support his gambling addiction, the St. Louis Post-Dispatch said Monday, August 30,2004. Gerald Bunse, 52, resigned in January as pastor from St. Mary Catholic Church in Edwardsville, Ill., after confessing to the theft of the almost a quarter of a million dollars. So if police and priests can all fall prey to the gambling demon, it's certainly easy for lay people, the average 'Joe', to do so.*

So crime and corruption are close companions of gambling, they travel together. This completes the picture of Atlantic City's economic development, increased crime, higher unemployment, and homelessness. It's not unusual. It's not an aberration. This is the customary pattern. This is what happens. The casinos, the glitziest, most lavish buildings in our society look great. The buildings are odes to what money can buy. But the lives of the people in the community don't look so great. This is the downside of gambling, this is the 'underbelly of the beast'.

Casino profits don't stay in the community. They travel far from the glass-strewn lots, abandoned buildings and their inhabitants. They go far away to the coffers of the rich, the Donald Trumps, the multi-national corporations.

Donald Trump, owner of the Taj Mahal Casino in Atlantic City, even admitted once that area businesses die when confronted with enormous casinos. In a 1994 article, Trump stated that:

> *People will spend a tremendous amount of money in casinos, money that they would normally spend on buying a refrigerator or a new car.*
>
> *Local businesses will suffer because they'll lose customer dollars to the casinos." Donald Trump 23*

So economic development has not come to Atlantic City. Has it come to other casino areas? How about **Niagara Falls, NY***, which houses the Seneca Niagara Casino? Has it improved the overall economic development for the citizens in that area? The casino itself is a financial success, drawing larger than anticipated crowds. Has the infusion of this money reached the area's neighborhoods and its people?*

Again in Niagara Falls, New York, a few blocks from the casino, little has changed. Neighborhoods are still seedy and run-down, private sector development hasn't come and bankruptcies are up 15% to a one-year record in 2003. 24

People seeking counseling *for gambling problems also set a record at the Gambling Recovery Program run by Jewish Family Service in Buffalo. "Since the new casino opened, we've had 268 new applications for service,...53% above the previous record," said Renee Wert, dir. of the program.*

"Most of the people who come to us for counseling on gambling have filed for bankruptcy." 25

This is after just one year of operation! In terms of jobs, November unemployment figures indicated that 2,000 jobs had disappeared from the Buffalo Niagara region over a one-year period and the jobless rate rose to 6.5%. How can this be if the casinos provided so many new jobs?

- ***Economic development in Eugene, Oregon** also told a similar story. No different. A report by Dr. Jeffrey Marta, Ph.D. presented to the Lane County Commissioners 8/12/03, indicated that the annual social costs of problem gambling to the state of Oregon was approximately $3.44 Million dollars annually! 26*

*This means that the taxpayers of the state of Oregon had to pay out almost **$3 and a half Million dollars** every year to cover the costs of the newly created problem and pathological gamblers. Why should the taxpayers have to pay out for programs to help people who gambled away all their money? What a cost to taxpayers and to the society. These are taxpayer costs, you and me. Hardly economic development.*

*Let's look at this monster called gambling a bit closer. The private corporations that run gambling do so under the guise of **Economic Rationalism**. This is a theory which provides an ideological justification for laissez-faire capitalism. It states that when people act in their own best interest, then the economy will function to provide goods and services for the largest number. "Economic rationalism is a device for **redistribution from poor to rich**. Humanitarian, social and ethical considerations are subjugated to narrow economic imperatives. It serves to increase the disparities between rich and poor." 27*

*The new gambling industry is an example par excellence of corporatist economic rationalist policies. People are justified in exploiting one another in the guise of 'profits'. When someone gets hurt as do pathological gamblers, their families, their friends and businesses they're involved with, then the excuse of 'individual weakness' is cited. Those people are said to have an 'illness.' No one looks at the **gambling industry's culpability.***

The structural causes of gambling as a social problem is denied and vested interest remain the same. Blaming individuals diverts attention from structural causes. Thus gaming interests can't be blamed for what they have provided, gambling, and what it has led to. Blaming individuals prevents the corporations from being charged as 'accessories before or after the fact', from being implicated in any way in the tragedies that their gambling has led to, has made possible.

So gambling as an example of economic rationalism, simply means that casinos are in the business of making money for their shareholders and owners. Let's be clear about this. Casinos are not in the business of community economic development, jobs or increasing taxes for the state. These are byproducts which the casinos tout in order to get their foot in the door. A ***Casino's main intention, the gambling industry's chief goal in life, is unabashedly - to make money - as much and as fast as they can.*** *Profit is their most important product. Regardless of consequences.*

Now there's nothing wrong with a business seeking to make profits. Entrepreneurship is what this country was founded on. However when obtaining profits involves misrepresentation, lack of truth-in-advertising compliance, misleading ads, psychological manipulation, and increased crime, homelessness, embezzlement and bankruptcies, then perhaps we should open our eyes to the need for some regulation, truth telling, and clear thinking.

ODDS OF WINNING

The advertising is deceptive because it implies and leads people to believe that it's very possible to win a large jackpot. Yet the odds of winning are so few that the probability of winning is almost non-existent. Most casino patrons don't realize just how impossible it is to win, how heavily the odds are against them. In Keno, for example, where you pick 10 numbers, the odds of hitting that winning jackpot are Nine million to one, states John Alcamo, author of Casino Gambling Behind the Tables. 28 And even despite those outrageous odds, a $2 bet usually pays off at only $50,000.

People are led to believe that these enormous jackpots are 1. possible, 2. possible for them, and 3. are coming to their neighborhoods. They feel that surely this kind of incredible money will revitalize their communities and make life easier and more fun at the same time.

Slot machines, addictive breeding ground that they are, are often played because they offer a chance at a big jackpot. For example, a $3 bet gives you a chance at a megabucks jackpot. This usually totals many millions of dollars. However, the catch here is that the odds of winning are nearly 17 million to one. Alcamo notes that you have a better chance of being killed by an asteroid striking Earth. "Slot machines are the biggest moneymakers in the casino. That should tell the players something." 29 Yet it looks so easy, so tempting and so possible. And that's exactly what the casinos want you to think.

Life will not be made easier with gambling. As with any addiction, life only becomes more complicated when we indulge ourselves. Some basic truths are that the House always wins and we cannot gamble ourselves rich. As Tom Grey, Executive Director of the National Coalition Against Legalized Gambling, NCALG, said recently in a press release, ***"States, like individuals, cannot gamble themselves rich. But they can, and have gambled themselves poor, as demonstrated by Nevada's $870 million budget deficit in 2003."*** *30 If Las Vegas cannot balance their state deficit with the proceeds from gambling, then what makes other states think that they can do it either? Hardly terrific economic development for the state of Nevada if they have a budget deficit of $870 million dollars despite their years of experience with gambling revenues and the large amount of revenues in their state.*

We've examined several areas, slots, unemployment, local businesses, increases in counseling applications, increase in social costs, the astronomical odds, and we haven't found any positive economic development yet.

Do State Lotteries help balance the budget and provide economic development*? In terms of the odds on the lottery, the chances of* ***winning, of any possible economic development, are so slight as to be truly ridiculous. A total of 33*** *states have state lotteries. Some states have hooked up with other states to have a Mega Millions Jackpot. This is where state lotteries are connected to each other and the collective jackpots are even higher. However, of course, the downside is that the odds of winning are proportionally less, i.e. you can really never win in these.*

For example, in the state of Texas, advertisements have led people to believe that they might be the next person to win the Mega Million lottery there. However, the odds on this lottery are not favorable, to say the least.

> *"Mega Millions players have about a* ***one in 135 Million chance*** *of hitting a jackpot, compared with about one in 48 million for Lotto Texas. 31 One in 135 Million! Those odds are so staggering, so inconceivable, as to discourage us from even trying to comprehend them. One in 135 million! And people are led to believe that they actually have 'a chance'.*
>
> *As the legislative director of Texans Against Gambling, Weston Ware, said,*
>
> ***"Mega Millions is a bad idea made bigger. Every Texan ought to be ashamed and embarrassed that the state of Texas has a lottery commission whose goal is to create a frenzy of losers."*** *35*

The state of Texas decided to enter the game of Mega Millions in 2003 when the Legislature was faced with declining lotto sales and a growing budget shortfall. Texas joined 10 other states participating in Mega Millions.

In 1996 the book, True Odds, showed that "lottery players who buy 100 tickets a week starting at age 18 would have about a 1% chance of winning over the course of a life that ends at age 75." 32 Imagine, you buy 100 tickets a week for your whole life, from age 18 to age 75, and even then you have only a 1% chance of winning! If players truly understood the enormity of these odds, I don't think people would be so eager to play, to throw away their money. These incredibly lavish casinos were not built on the winnings of millions of customers. They were built on their losses, many losses, millions and millions of dollars of losses.

Slot machines, which are rapidly becoming the main focus in casinos, are a big part of the problem of gambling. People lose money incredibly rapidly on these little playthings. This is often where fortunes are lost. No, not fortunes made, just lost.

Not only are the machines addictive and people always lose, casino advertising and marketing strategy is far from truthful. 'You'll be one of the beautiful people,' 'You'll win...' It's seductive advertising, it's manipulation, and certainly not truthful. Slots look so easy. It's designed to give you that impression. But the odds of 1 to 1.2 million or 1 to over 8 million don't lie. Not too many people winning at those odds.

So slot machines, or VLTs, as the newer version are called, are not going to provide any economic development to neighborhoods or communities. In fact, these slot machines are going to be part of the external form of the ***'black hole' that sucks communities' money.*** *They* ***'cannibalize' local businesses and local individuals****, guzzling their quarters and dollars in rapid succession. Someone starts 'feeding' their machines, getting charged off the lights, music and overall action of the casino scene and then finds it's hard to stop. And the machines are voracious, eating more and more, never being satisfied, never being fulfilled. Just like the addict who's feeding them. The feeding frenzy of sharks is nothing compared to these machines' appetite for people's money.*

Another ***economic negative*** *concerning the increased expansion of slot machines and VLTs at racetracks is that in effect, by allowing their expansion at the track, the* ***state is subsidizing and supporting the horse racing industry.*** *Horse racing is not a popular activity among mainstream America any more. To allow slots to proliferate there gives a big boost to the racing industry. People will come to play slots and while they're there, they'll fill the coffers of the horse racing industry as well.*

Should this be part of our goal, to subsidize an ailing industry that most people are not in favor of anyway? The government has more important priorities than saving the horse racing industry. Suddenly, race track owners will become wealthy beyond their wildest dreams and, again, it will be at the cost of individuals who can't afford to lose.

Then there is the fundamental question leading to the catch-22 response—where does the money come from? Neither casinos nor individuals nor race tracks are printing the money themselves. It's not new-to-the-economy-money. It's ***existing money*** *that was in the hands of citizens and is now in the hands of casinos, the gambling industry and lottery officials.*

It's money that people needed to provide for their families, that people needed to pay their bills. It was in the people's hands, now it's in the hands of the gambling industry and called profit. It's gone from the people's hands, from their bank accounts, checkbooks, and will never come back. The millions and millions of dollars that the state hopes to realize from their lotteries didn't come from thin air either. It also came from the paychecks of hard-working individuals who could have put it to a much better use.

ECONOMIC DECLINE

What exactly are the economic characteristics of gambling and how does it impact upon a region in terms of overall economic development, jobs and revenue/taxes to the municipality and to state governments*?*

Research on the effect of gambling on local and regional economies clearly and repeatedly show that gambling brings ***economic decline.***

In ***South Dakota****, one year after legalizing video gambling, there were "significant declines" for selected businesses such as clothing's stores, car dealers, recreation services, etc. 33 This is exactly what we noted happened in Atlantic City, restaurants and businesses closed and pawn shops expanded tremendously. Many studies have shown conclusively that gambling triggers and instigates addiction. Addiction brings social problems. Social problems cost regional economies "billions of dollars per year because of costly social programs and damage to existing business." 34*

- *A study in 1994 on the 4 riverboat Illinois communities showed that riverboats did not create the jobs that were promised and, in fact, had little effect on reducing unemployment. 35*
- *A Univ. of Illinois professor, Dr. John Kindt, showed in his research that "nationwide you stand to lose 1.5 jobs for every job the casinos create. 36*

- *In **Chicago** the research indicated that 2 to 2.75 jobs would be lost if a land-based casino were built." 37*

- *Another researcher, Earl Grinols, a Univ. of Illinois economics professor, stated that the downside of gambling far outweighed the benefits. "**The economy as a whole would be much better off had we not allowed (casino gaming) to expand**. For every tax dollar raised from gambling, it costs society between $2.50 and $300 to pay for social programs, crime and other associated problems." 38*

*Jobs are lost because business, movies, restaurants, theaters, drug stores, pizza parlors, all close. The casino becomes the major employer in town, a monopoly. Accounting and tallying up a broad range of factors, crime, lost productivity, bankruptcy, social services and regulatory costs, Grinols writes that **each pathological and problem gambler costs the public $13,600/ year, or $180. per citizen. "That more than negates the industry's economic benefit which Grinois estimates at $50 to $70 per citizen**." 39*

- *In **Illinois**, an 1996 study by Univ. of Nevada professors William Thompson and Recardo Gazel, compiled for Chicago's Better Government Commission, also showed that gambling caused an overall economic deterioration.*

  The "state economy as a whole lost.
  There's been no identifiable economic development," 40

*The study showed that **the vast numbers of gamblers came from within 50 miles of the casino**. This means that **area citizens** support the casino with their own disposable income. Area businesses saw only $3 in spillover sales for every $100 spent and lost on board the riverboats. So the community didn't profit. It also showed that while the 10 casinos did produce $1.9 billion in annual state economic inputs, these were more than balanced out by negative multipliers resulting in a $6.7 million net loss statewide. 41*

Areas nearer the riverboats in Illinois lost the most money. Every $100 million a year in casino winnings drained $18.3 Million locally. So it was no windfall, no money falling from the sky, nothing that any informed citizenry would want or seek for their area.

*One major reason that **jobs** are lost includes this demise of existing businesses. We would expect that large casinos would have many jobs for many people. However, scratch the surface, and we find that many casino jobs are relatively low-*

paying including maids, waiters, and even card dealers. As slot machines gain in popularity, available jobs decrease...Higher echelon well-paying managerial, administrative, career jobs are often filled with imported, not neighborhood people or people with specialized skills such as computer technicians who were probably already employed.

Casinos can seem to bring jobs to an area. But the stimulative effect of those jobs is more than offset by the net flow of money out of the host community. The casino owners came into the community from the outside and will take these profits back out with them. The overall impact of a new gambling casino will be to depress economic activity. But surely, we wonder, even if there isn't all these new jobs, at least the tax revenue will significantly help state governments, and it will 'trickle down' to its citizens. However, as Dr. Thomas Garrett of the Federal Reserve Bank states in his paper, "Casino Gambling in America and its Economic Impacts,"

> *Economic development occurs when there is **increased** value to society. **Tax revenue cannot be counted as a benefit to society** because it is merely the **transfer** of revenues from casino operators to state governments. 42*

*He adds that this revenue isn't 'new money', and has no added or inherent value to society. It's just a **transfer of income** from one group to another, from people to casino operators, to state governments.*

*Below is a chart developed by a group called, **PACT, People Against a Casino Town**, in Oregon. It compares the **economic development of 4 towns** there during the time period in which casinos came to the area. The 4 towns were the cities of Florence, Lincoln City, Coos Bay, and Canyonville. The 3 latter cities, Lincoln, Coos Bay, and Canyonville, all had casinos. Florence did not have a casino.*

*The first chart describes the towns in terms of comparable economic comparison indicators, such as population, per capita income, employed/unemployed. 12 years later, the overall economic growth rate for Florence was 47 %—much higher than any of the other towns. Florence thrived without casinos. The other towns barely held their own with average growth rates of 3%, 11%, and even 26%. Remember this is over 12 years so even 26% computes to only about 2 % a year. The town of Florence's growth rate was almost **double** the highest of the others. This is pretty impressive evidence that casinos do not spur economic development, but in fact **retard** it.*

Information
Economic Comparisons

People Against a Casino Town

Census:	***Florence***	*Lincoln City*	*Coos Bay*	*Canyonville*
1990 Population	*5,162*	*5,892*	*15,076*	*1,219*
2000 Population	*7,263*	*7,437*	*15,374*	*1,293*
1990 Per Capita Income	*$10,681*	*$10,960*	*$11,240*	*$9,252*
2000 Per Capita Income	*$18,008*	*$15,597*	*$18,158*	*$14,017*
2000 Census:				
Families below poverty level (% of population)	*10%*	*12.5%*	*12.7%*	*15.8%*
Individuals below poverty level (% of population)	*14.4%*	*16.1%*	*16.5%*	*17.0%*
% of families earning less than $35,000 per year	*45.8%*	*55.4%*	*43.8%*	*55.7%*
Civilian labor force (persons 16 years and over)	*2,453*	*3,490*	*7,112*	*536*
Employed (in civilian labor force) (% of population)	*30.4%*	*41.3%*	*41.9%*	*36.0%*
Unemployed (in civilian labor force) (% of population)	*3.3%*	*5.6%*	*4.3%*	*5.5%*
Households with Social Security Income	*56.2%*	*37.9%*	*34.4%*	*40.9%*
Employment Industry - Arts, entertainment, recreation, accommodation and food service (% of total employed labor force)	*19.9%*	*38.8%*	*9.7%*	*19.8%*
Growth Rates:				
1-year growth <decline> rate (2001 to 2002)	***1.8%***	*0.2%*	*0.9%*	*<5.1%>*
2-year growth rate (2000 to 2002)	***3.5%***	*0.2%*	*1.6%*	*5.2%*
10-year growth rate (1990 to 2000)	***42.2%***	*25.9%*	*2.1%*	*6.1%*
12-year growth rate (1990 to 2002)	***47.2%***	*26.2%*	*3.6%*	*11.6%*

Data from: 2000 U.S. Census; 1990 U.S. Census; Portland State University Population Research Center. 43

One of the many reasons that the 3 towns with casinos didn't thrive is because the money gets ***diverted*** *out of the area. It literally leaves the community so it is no longer available to the people or businesses there. As we put some of our 'discretionary income' into a slot machine, we then cannot spend it somewhere else, such as at a restaurant or movie. This money winds up in the pockets of casinos'* ***out-of-town*** *share holders and owners.*

The problem increases and becomes more complicated when people spend money that isn't discretionary, i.e. available, but in fact earmarked for the rent, groceries, children's clothes or other necessary items. When that money then becomes diverted to gambling, to the industry's pockets, it's ***just not there*** *any more. It's not in the people's pockets, it's not in the businesses pockets, and it's not in the community any more. It's gone, never to be seen again.*

There was no economic development for these 3 casino towns. There was a significant amount of positive economic development for the town without casinos and for their citizens. What does this say about the casino's hype about economic development?

Why would we ever believe what the industry says about its future impact on the community? Everything the industry says will be self-serving. The industry wants to come into a community, to expand its range of business, so what do we think that they're going to say? Isn't this just human nature? If we want something, we're going to say whatever we think will help us get what we want. Truthfulness is not necessarily any casino's stock in trade. They deal in money and in addiction. A pattern of corruption has been their long-standing history and it will be their birthright and inheritance. Do we really think that they're going to deal in truth also? It's one or the other, it can't be both.

STATE REVENUE, TAX RATES

So economic development, despite being promoted by the casinos and the industry, does not come with the inclusion of casinos. How about the question of state or local government tax revenue from the gambling industry?

When this issue of tax revenue gets raised, people often are assured that the money will go for "Education", or scholarships, or social programs to benefit all of the citizenry. The New York State Lottery has advertised for years that the money it brings in goes to New York State education. Yet New York State spends among the ***least*** *of all states for education. When the casinos tout the gains for education, it's* *actually a game of mirrors or of that old New York City game of three card monte. It's Substitution.*

As money gets funneled to education, then other money, that would have gone for education, is channeled somewhere else. Bait and switch. An elaborate ruse perpetuated by the collusion of elected officials and casino interests to make gambling more palatable to the masses. After all, who would argue with spending more money on our children? However that doesn't really happen.

St. Mary's College professors, Patrick Pierce and Donald Miller, researched the question of whether lotteries provide increased funding for education budgets. They found that initially there is a boost but then those "increases quickly taper off... ***States with lotteries eventually provide less support for public education per capita than do states without them."*** *44*

Dr. James Dobson, one of 9 Federal commissioners on the National Gambling Impact Study Commission in 1997, found that state tax gambling revenue, when targeted for education was not really providing the funding that was expected. Incidentally the NGISC has been the only Federal study done so far on gambling and a relatively small amount of money, 2 Million dollars, was budgeted for it. Dr. Dobson noted that the tax revenue:

> *The promised money for schools has been a scam. Promised tax revenue doesn't always get funneled where it's supposed to go. It's all a game of bait and switch." 45*

No wonder it's said that even **legislators** *themselves can become addicted to the money or revenue that gambling can provide. Then, since we remember this is a 'progressive' disease', gamblers and even legislators, come to want more and more money, a bigger and bigger hit. People become dependent on the 'hit' from the machines and legislators become hooked on the revenues from gambling. They think that there's more and more to be had, an inexhaustible supply. This way of balancing budgets is so easy and simple that more traditional ways, such as cutting programs, don't get implemented any more. So in this same Fantasy-Island-scenario, legislators think that if gambling revenue brought in a million dollars last year, then why not 2 million dollars this year? This is addictive thinking, its unrealistic and poor budgeting practice.*

State casino revenue tax rates, the percentage that casinos have to 'kick back to the state', are interesting in their diversity*. States that have had gambling for a longer amount of time usually have older contracts with lower percentages of revenue.*

For example, New Jersey has an 8% tax on all gambling revenue with a 1.25% tax paid to Casino Reinvestment and Development Authority. Nevada's casinos, however, pay only 3% of total revenue.

Other states who came into the ballgame later than Atlantic City or Las Vegas, charge their casinos much more. Illinois has 15% on the first $25 million going up to 50% on revenue in excess of $200 million. Indiana similarly has 15% on $25 million going up to 35% on revenue in excess of $150,000 million. Iowa starts at 5% of the first $1 million rising to 32% on revenue over 3 million. Missouri is a flat 20% for state and 2% for local governments. These rates reflect somewhat the time that the state first allowed gambling in their jurisdiction with the higher rates being more recent. 45 Garrett p. 10. In Iowa, riverboats give 20 % of their revenue to the state. This will possibly rise to 21 or 22 % in the near future if the state allows the riverboats to forego 'cruising' on the rivers.

Recently in Pennsylvania, Gov. Ed Rendell and other state legislators, in their bid to allow gambling have proposed revenue percentages of up to 60% in their bid to have gambling approved by a large number of legislators. As gambling has become increasingly successful, legislators have tried to get a bigger piece of the action for the state. This has been especially obvious in the amount necessary for the initial licenses for the industry to buy in with. This lure of apparently easy money has led many legislators to see gambling as a quick, painless way to generate additional revenue and to expand services without raising taxes. This lets the legislator appear to be a hero to his constituency, thus assuring his re-election.

But in fact what is needed to balance budgets are plain, old-fashioned ***cuts.*** *Government has become so large today with so many programs, many of them 'pork-barrel', that budgets have become bloated and ridiculously large. Super-Beauocracies become institutionalized, expensive equipment and technology gets bought frequently, and programs outlive their usefulness yet stay in existence.*

Court decisions mandate large expenditures for small groups of citizens. Legislators open the door to increased immigration without considering that recent immigrants can be costly for budgets with increased need for social services.

Cutting programs is neither popular nor bound to get a legislator re-elected. Yet, as with individual and family budgets, this is what is needed. We need to balance budgets by cutting spending. Duh...When programs are allowed to proliferate and are not reviewed in terms of cost effectiveness, budgets become bloated. Then continuous infusions of large amounts of money will always be necessary. Gambling is not a bottomless revenue pit as we've seen but one fraught with many seen and unseen costs, large and small, in the short and the long term...

INTER-STATE COMPETITION

A recent development among states is that they feel a necessity to be in competition with each other, that they have to keep up with an imagined 'gambling arms race' in order not to be left behind in terms of revenue collection. They feel that 'their people' are 'crossing the river', (across state lines), to be able to gamble and that they're losing all that potential money, wrote Greg Garland in the Baltimore Sun on 2/16/04. 46

In case the states didn't realize this on their own, the casinos have been quick to point it out to them. "Pitting one state against another has proved a successful strategy as the gambling industry has expanded across the country...Lawmakers view gambling across state lines as a drain on (their) treasury." 47 This competition among states turns into a "race to the bottom," as states try to outdo each other in making their own type of gambling more attractive to people.

States do this by lifting restrictions, adding more games and more sites for gambling and new 'flashier' type of games. William R. Eadington, dir. of the Institute for the Study of Gambling and Commercial Gaming at the University of Nevada, Reno, agreed saying, "As one state relaxes its rules, others feel compelled to follow." As the article in the Baltimore Sun noted, states will do:

'Whatever it takes to keep players coming in and the money flowing.' *48*

If it sounds mercenary, cold and callous, it is. 'Whatever it takes,' conceivably could be translated by legislators as the process of expansion of gambling in general, i.e. including more variety of games, higher limits, more venues, more accessible to all, more habit-forming and more addictive to all.

EVERYONE WANTS THE ADDICTS

As legislators see immediate dollars in gambling expansion, this means more gambling sites, and hence 'increased availability.' As we've learned, more availability, translates into more gambling, increased frequency, and hence more addiction. Availability + Frequency = Addiction.

So in a way, our legislators are acting in a way that will make more people into addicts. Why? Because as they increase the prevalence, i.e. more sites, more venues, more people will get hooked. This is a time-honored pattern in addiction. Prevalence, convenience and availability, plus Frequency, of a person's trips there, which increase as it becomes more convenient, translate into Addiction. The more people addicted, the more money both the casinos and ultimately the state, will make.

We know that casinos deliberately and carefully try to make people into addicts because that's where the bulk of their business comes from. 20 % of the gamblers provide 80 % of casino income. So guess who that 20 % is. It's the addicts who blow all their life-savings, who spend their business investment, and their family's money. Some people wind up giving astronomical amounts to the casinos. My husband give them $3 Million dollars.

If studies suggest that from 5 to 10 % of everyone who subject themselves to the addictive influences of gambling, of going to Atlantic City or another casino, sooner or later become addicted, then that activity, by definition, is intrinsically addicting. We know that gambling is meant by the casinos to be addictive. How would casino's profit line look – if people weren't addicted?

If a majority of casino profits are provided by a small minority of patrons, then we can surmise that these are the addicts and they're the ones keeping the bottom lines, the profits, high. My husband was one of the 5%. The profit line of many casinos had his name on it. So without the addicts, the casinos will have a much smaller bottom line. So of course, casinos are going to want their addicts. What industry would voluntarily let go of 50 % or more of their bottom line, their profits?

Even the figure of 5% addiction rate, generally agreed upon by many in the field, may well be only the tip of the iceberg in the numbers of people addicted presently. The numbers may well climb to double what they are if the trend continues toward increased accessibility and frequency.

The numbers of people who give the casinos substantial money is high. Casinos are real happy with the person who comes and gives them $5000. every weekend. $200 doesn't fund their palatial buildings, their opulent restaurants, giant ballrooms and multitude of staff. The person who is controlled and disciplined about his time in Atlantic City, who plans ahead as to how much he will allocate and no more, this type of person does not get the Atlantic City operatives real excited. But people like Alan, who over the course of 7 years, spent more 3 Million dollars, they get very pleased and excited about him. Casinos need the addicts, they make most of their money off the addicts, they're happy to give them comps in abundance.

Alan got almost every perk or comp that they had available. One cute little perk which we used a lot, was given to him for the children. Often they would like to eat in the room, while watching a movie. But you could order from only one room service restaurant at a time, not a few items from different places. The comp was that whatever the kids wanted from wherever they wanted, they were to be able to get. This is quite a feat for a big hotel to be able to fulfill a picky customer's exact wishes. But Bally's was happy to do it for our children. I guess that tells you how much they were making off us.

The only comp we didn't get was their giant penthouse suite. There've been pictures of it in TV programs. It's about the square footage of a medium sized house, has 24 hour butler service, and is for truly 'high rollers'. At this point I'm not sure why we never got that suite with the extreme amount of money he spent. It may have been because he spread out his action among 10 different casinos.

The casinos have a good idea exactly how much you win or lose each session. There are surveillance cameras on every game. These cameras together with what you cash in and cash out, plus markers or loans you might take out, tells them your bottom figure. Their computers are programmed with state-of the-art equipment and expertise to a high level.

Yes, casinos cater to gambling addicts. And state legislators continue to act in ways that will expand more casino markets in order to 'one-up' other states. So legislators also are acting in ways that will satisfy addicts. New addicts will be created with the expansion of gambling markets. This is where the money is. The legislators won't get re-elected if the casino properties don't make money as they promised their constituents in an effort to lower property taxes or fund new education proposals. Both legislators and casino owners need to make money to survive. They're all agreed about ways that will serve to expand casino markets. Of course, market expansion will serve to separate a person from his money as fast as possible and in as great quantity as possible. Wasn't it always said, that 'politics makes strange bedfellows...'

Each has straight-forward motives, at least according to our materialistic society. Casinos are out to make money. That's clear. Legislators are out to help the state balance its budget. That's necessary. But the problem is that casinos slip into their advertising strategies, the not-so-veiled innuendo, the subtle message, that the gambler can win, make money. They're not truthful while giving the appearance that they are. It's impossible for the gambler to win because that would mean that the casino would lose. It's a win or lose game. Either the casino wins or it doesn't. Either the gambler wins or he loses. And we know that casinos always win. They have to win otherwise they'll go out of business. The House always wins. Our gambler cannot make money.

Perhaps if casinos advertisements said,

All gamblers guaranteed to lose sooner or later!

or

Gambling may lead to wealth and possibly health problems including marriage and family difficulties, possible loss of career/ home!

This would be an up up-front and a fair advisory warning. But the little bettor who buys all their hype, thinks that he actually has a chance at winning, allows himself to be blown away by the lights and the ambiance, never has a real shot at even breaking even. If he doesn't lose at first, if he wins at first, then he's doubly unlucky because he'll get hooked faster. If he loses at first, he has a possible chance of getting away while he still has his bankroll. The more he stays, the more he'll lose. Until he loses all of it, whether it takes 3 years or 20 years.

It's not surprising or even news, that the economic development of communities and regions is hardly a priority for the industry. The casino's priority is making money. To do this, casinos follow a strategy of getting their foot in the door and then expanding their sites and operations gradually. Somewhat insidious given the nature of the activity. But understandable given human nature and our society's values, that of money being important and expansion an expected way of doing business.

*The industry's goal is profit and expansion. Robert Goodman, a Hampshire College, Amherst, Mass., professor said that strategies for casino expansion are no accident. Goodman said a gambling consultant developed '**the ladder strategy**'. In this strategy, gambling companies seek to enter new markets with limited offerings that can be expanded later:*

> *You promise something very modest at the beginning...*
> *You know once you get (gambling) in that the politicians will see it as one of the few places to go to raise revenues.*
> *You could essentially call it **getting a state hooked on gambling**. 49*

*Because of the multitude of social costs related to problem gambling, Goodman notes that gambling can be very costly for a state. Opening casinos in order to stem the flow of gambling dollars across a state's borders, though an appealing argument he said, "is not based on sound economics." 50 The competition among **Maryland, Pennsylvania, Delaware, New Jersey and West Virginia**, is fierce with various* *legislators feeling that their state must build a bigger casino than their neighbors and thus not lose money to the neighbor. But this also doesn't make economic sense. Because the end result is that each state is thus acting to impoverish their own citizens in the long-run. Remember the communities hit hardest are the ones within 50 miles of a casino.*

Recently Delaware State Rep. Joseph G. DiPinto expressed his concern that Maryland and Pennsylvania were going to open slot machine casinos or racinos. He noted that "We've gotten some solid estimates that we'd lose 40 to 60 % of slots revenue if both states go (into gambling)." "If you're going to be competitive, you don't wait for your competitors to set the agenda," DiPinto said, expressing his belief that Delaware needs to strike first, so to speak. 51 Yet his reasoning is flawed and will be detrimental to Delaware's own citizens, especially in the communities nearest the gambling site.

It all becomes an increasing arms race, a self-defeating circular cycle, consisting of states trying to offer more and expanded gambling facilities, so more and more people lose, so that the government realizes more revenue, in order to fund more bloated budgets. The amount that people have to lose at casinos, in order to help the states, is little compared to how much the states actually get.

As we saw, with VLT's in the Saratoga, New York, race-track, the state gets very little out of what the gambler loses, not enough to help New York with anything substantive – unless large numbers of people lose large amounts of money. Then it mounts up. But the large amounts of money lost are a loss to people and serve to wreck havoc in various systems in the society in various ways. The large amounts of money lost by gamblers often serve to put often untenable strains on already overburdened marriages leading to divorce, family break-up, and the whole gamut of social costs leading to a further drain on an already over-taxed society. And its all paid for and built upon the many losses of each individual, the seniors, the poor, and minorities.

What a poor foundation upon which to build or fund society, what shifting sands to collapse in the form of bankruptcy, suicide and other social costs. Whatever happened to legislators creating programs for the good of the family or the individual, instead of bickering over what kinds of gambling to license, for what exorbitant licensing and annual fees, and where it will be located. Instead of enacting legislation to license casinos to provide community economic development, our legislators themselves need to think of innovative programs to enact that would more directly impact upon community and economic development. Or they could research programs successful in other states.

Instead of contracting with Casinos to enact economic development in society, as a byproduct of their primary goal, making money, why don't we just provide for economic development programs ourselves. This is a very appropriate role for states. This will eliminate the casinos's profit, the middleman, and save incredible amounts of money in the long run. Our legislators can come up with programs themselves to provide for economic development such as in the fields of low-cost, low-income housing, urban development or in the field of renewable resources and conservation.

This kind of development would then return revenue to the state in the form of jobs, consequent individual taxes, the reclamation of scarce resources, and subsequent consumer spending. This might be more challenging in the short run. It's not a 'quick fix'.

However it might provide more depth in the long run, more real economic opportunity. When states license casinos to provide economic development, what they're forgetting, what they don't account for, is ***the cost of the casino profits****, the cost of the losses to the individual and ultimately to the state in the form of dollars winging their way, even zooming out of the state. Casinos are a middle-man who end up being handsomely rewarded for his time and effort. Why should the state make these kinds of profits available to private industry?*

The huge profits that the casinos rake in, is money flying out of the state. This money will surely provide for huge deficits in someone's budget soon or later. Getting state revenue from the tax on casinos, whether its 5 % or 30 % is a very inefficient way of collecting money. It's allowing, and even encouraging, the money in-between, i.e. 70 % to 95% which consists of the bulk of the money, to go to casino profits. This huge amount of money goes to a third party, neither the state, nor its citizens. It goes to gambling industry owners. It's inserting another party, the gambling industry, to profit from people's losses.

If the state needs that 5 % so badly, then it would be wiser to tax people directly for that money. With casinos, for example, the person loses, $1,000. and $100. only goes to the state. So for the state to obtain $100, they first had to enable an extensive system of building up a whole new industry within the state, i.e. gambling, to enable its citizens to lose a great deal more of their money. The logic here is inverted and perverted and the thinking shallow and greedy. Legislators also, it looks like, don't want to work for their money but want it handed to them on a silver platter.

Dr. Garrett sums up saying that

> *Casinos, like any new business to an area,*
> *result in a* ***re-allocation*** *of consumer dollars. 52*

In a functioning economy, we would expect a consumer to know where to spend his money to get maximum benefit. In Keynesian economics, based on the economic theories of Thomas Keynes, a mainstay in Western economic theoretical models, it's felt that the laws of Supply and Demand effectively govern the most efficient use of money for consumers. Where consumers make their decisions as to what to spend their money on builds the economy in a gradual and constructive way according to people's needs and desires. But when casino patrons take their money away from local restaurants, movies, stores, and put it into games of chance, of gambling, then they're not making wise economic choices in terms of the overall good of society and their community.

The free market stops functioning in a manner to provide for the greatest economic good of the individual because the market has been interfered with. Government has provided for artificial constraints, i.e. casino licenses, and incited artificial demand for a product that doesn't produce anything, gambling. The artificial demand has come because the licensed activity is not 'goods and services,' but an addiction. When government interferes in free market enterprise and chooses to license an addiction, it's a poor choice on government's part. This is especially true when the choice, gambling, is historically a poor way for people to use their income in. Personal tragedies, consumer manipulation, and financial losses will be the result.

Consumers, i.e. citizens, are free to choose where to spend their income. This discretionary income, the amount of our income that's available for things other than necessary bill-paying, wings its way out the community as it's lost in casinos of various kinds. The gambling industry gets this money, which belonged to the community, and should have stayed there. But since there's not an inexhaustible supply of resources, of money, if poor choices are made in terms of decision-making, then that will impact upon the whole society just as wise choices will likewise impact upon the society, in terms of economic development.

Once an individual's limited supply of disposable income is gone, then there's no more money. Once an individual uses his limited income for gambling, he doesn't have it for the rent, or for clothes, or for food. He then has nothing to show for his money. He's gotten no value for it and his asset base has been reduced. He hasn't made any investments toward future income, and his own resources, including savings, and other assets, are proportionately less.

The thought that gambling was detrimental for the entire state economy was a revelation for me. I hadn't expected that there would be a large group of researchers and economists showing through field studies that gambling was bad for the entire society.

But this is exactly what a recent Supreme Court case alleges. The case states that gambling and especially machines like slots or video poker, are a 'blight' on consumers.

> *"Such gambling* ***devastates*** *the entire state economy, both short-term and long-term", said Jackson County lawyer, Larry Harless. 53*

Harless has asked the justices to consider these machines 'cannibalizing' effect on local economies. In the case, Harless quotes South Dakota researchers who estimate that in the year 2000, that video poker-style machines cost the state $63 Million from such social costs as crime, divorce, bankruptcy and loss of productivity.

These ***'social costs'*** *equaled $120 for every adult resident. They included $5.25 million caused by people who embezzled from their employers to feed their gambling habit and $8.4 million for gambling addiction treatment. The researchers suggested that these social costs, in addition to the cost of regulating and maintaining the machines, in fact yielded a* ***net annual economic loss of $89 Million dollars!*** *This is hardly economic development that anyone would want.*

These 'social costs' are most marked in the community in which the casino is located. Remember the 50 mile rule. Such communities are labeled as 'host' communities from the host- dinner guest scenario. But due to the enormity of the social costs involved, both economic and family disintegration, PACT, People Against a Casino Town, in Florence, Oregon, have recently had another interpretation of this phrase, 'host' community. They suggested on 2/22/04, that 'host' more aptly refers to the description of the 'host and parasite' biological relationship with the community being the host and the casino being the parasite. They described similarities in this way of viewing communities and casinos: They wrote that parasites must have a host from which to feed just as Casinos must have a host community to provide victims on which to prey.

They felt that parasites steal food from the host just as Casinos take their 'cut' off the top of the community's financial resources. They follow the analogy along in comparing parasites' continued growth while the host weakens.

They showed in research where casinos use profits and tax advantages to destroy competing business and weaken the community's ability to grow and prosper. Finally, they postulated that parasites create a chronic drain on the host's vital systems, reducing the host's ability to respond, while still needing protection against other parasites and bacteria.

Casinos create a chronic drain on the community's tax and social structure, reducing the community's ability to protect its citizens from other (often criminal) activities drawn to their area by the casino. The best defense felt against parasites and casinos is prevention. 54

Similarly, the language involved in Professor Kindt's research also leads to a similar conclusion, that casinos prey upon their communities, 'sucking the life-blood' out of them. Note the following excerpt from an article in the Spring/2003 Stanford Journal of Law, Business and Finance, by John W. Kindt, Prof. Univ. of Illinois. 55

> *"Gambling industry analysts delimit the 'population markets' upon which the gambling facility 'feeds' – hence the term 'feeder markets." The 35-mile radius around a casino is typically the 'primary feeder market,' or local market, commonly providing 80 % of the consumer dollars...into gambling dollars.*
> *The secondary 'feeder market' is typically a 100-mile radius around the casino...The gambling facility will be 'cannibalizing' the consumer economy within the 35-mile radius." 56*

The language and the concepts provide an interesting and dynamic analogy into what happens economically between casinos, their immediate populations and communities surrounding them.

DESTINATION VS. CONVENIENCE GAMBLING

The recent Supreme Court case filed by Attorney Harless cites a 2003 Michigan State law review article by law professor and gambling expert, John Kindt. In the article, "The Transfer of Consumer Dollars to Legalized Gambling, the study contrasts the two kinds of casinos, destination gambling such as Atlantic City, with 'convenience gambling', such as local neighborhoods, bars and clubs.

In convenience gambling, both discretionary spending and nondiscretionary 'addicted gambling' dollars were transferred from other forms of consumer expenditures. Local competing businesses lost revenue. Kindt states that local casinos cannibalize their own native businesses, and, hence their own native community people. In destination gambling, people travel to the casinos, spend vacation time and then go home. They take their problems back with them to their own home community. They may then contribute to the nation's higher bankruptcy rate. The bankruptcy rise will show itself as being more pronounced in local casino communities because that's where it's most intensified. 57

Attorney Harless cites the case of South Carolina. In 2000, South Carolina had 37,000 video poker-style machines in operation throughout the state. As the result of a case brought to the state Supreme Court, all of them were shut down in July, 2000. An economic analysis estimated that while the machines grossed $2.5 Billion a year, social costs and losses to other businesses resulted in a net annual loss of $420 million. This doesn't even begin to account for personal injury, bankruptcies, and individual loss and misery due to gambling there from the machines. So no substantive economic development occurred in South Carolina.

Other researchers concur in these findings. Professor Rose, an acknowledged expert in the field of gambling, and author of several books about gambling, states that

A casino acts like a black hole sucking money out of the local economy. *58*

Local business, i.e. local people, suffer when casino giants come in. As the money gets funneled from the many into the hands of the few, i.e. as masses of people come in and lose their money, it then goes into the pockets of the vested casino interests. It's sent 'back home', out of the communities, into the coffers of the rich. The money is not used for business, and it does not then **multiply** *as when money is spent on goods and services in the general economy. The community's money is being sucked out of the local marketplace and placed into the hands of casino entrepreneurs.*

Others have agreed that gambling is no blessing for local economies. Charles Greenawait, Senior Fellow at the Susquehanna Valley Center for Public Policy, concurs that gambling "cannibalizes local businesses."

> *One hundred dollars spent in a slot machine is $100 not spent in a local restaurant, store or theater. It's an ironclad rule:*
> *When governments legalize more gambling, taxpayers lose – whether they gamble or not.*
>
> ***For every dollar gambling produces for a regional economy, three more are lost due to the economic and social costs of gambling.*** *59*

So if casinos are supported by the surrounding communities and to some extent, by tourists, then where does the money come from? Do local residents suddenly have so much extra income to spend and to lose? Do people generally have disposable income above their needs that can be thrown away on gambling? Of course not. The Hill report, 1995 reported that when community people spend money gambling, that they're taking it from disposable income and from savings. The money spent on gambling is not going to an amusement park or a restaurant, or future savings. 60

Lower household savings in economic terms means less money invested in future assets or resources for the individual. The individual's future spending is compromised. This is economically unsustainable. "The discretionary dollar has been diverted from other leisure activities, from food venues,"...from other household expenses. 61 ***People are spending savings, i.e. selling their future, for a reckless and unstable dream.***

When money comes out of the savings of community people, the net overall economic impact is to **depress** *economic activity in the area. Money flows out of many people's hands into the pockets of a relatively few people, casino owners, developers, investors and their financiers, with some revenue going to the state. Gambling concentrates money into fewer hands and has the effect of the net flow of money out of the host community. So both the individual and the community are hurt. But the casino owners, remember, are making out like bandits, modern day pirates.*

Because of the depressing effect of the gambling on economic activity in the area, casinos typically destroy 2 or 3 jobs for every job gained, Joel S. Rose explained recently at a meeting to the League of Woman Voters of Buffalo in November, 2003. 62 The impact on the economy of the host community is significant. This activity has become a major part of our economy. Rose also noted the effect of the gambling 'revenue' to the states. This revenue is often viewed as a painless and voluntary substitute for taxation. Let's look at the path this revenue must take. First, it's income to people who live in the community surrounding the gambling venue. Then people use it to gamble with. So it becomes profit to the casinos. Then the casinos give a small percentage varying from roughly 5 % to 35 % back to the state as revenue. Let's not forget that it started as 'real money' coming from real people who needed their money and were foolish enough to throw it away. Because the poor often gamble proportionately more than other segments of the population, Rose states, gaming revenue is a regressive tax penalizing most those who can least afford it. 63

As we put our 'discretionary income' into a slot machine, then we can't spend it elsewhere. It winds up in the pockets of casinos' out-of-town owners. The problem increases and becomes even more complicated when people spend money that isn't discretionary, i.e. available, but in fact earmarked for the rent or groceries. When that money then becomes diverted, it's not entertainment any more, its addiction.

This is all the beginning of addiction. And addiction is the beginning of the end for many people. It's the beginning of the end for problem gamblers. What looked *innocent enough at first, spending $20, $50, even $100 for a Saturday night's entertainment, taking a chance to spend a little money in the hopes for a large jackpot, in the long run, translates, to spending life-time savings accounts, raiding college tuition money, selling stocks accumulated over years, and possibly even embezzling other's monies. All of this from the conviction that the jackpot is there, waiting, just around the next corner...*

STATE AND INDIVDUAL ECONOMICS

The economics of gambling don't make sense for states and for their communities although they look like they should. Gambling interests are well aware of the potential social costs to individuals but always say that the "benefits outweigh the costs.' I'm not sure that there are any benefits that could outweigh the costs of divorce, increases in homelessness, rise in bankruptcy rates, rise in embezzlements and other crimes. But putting aside the social costs for a moment, let's look at the problem from a dollars and cents view. Casinos agree to give a percentage of profits to the state. So therefore states can balance their budgets.

But the costs of the budget are driven up by the social costs of the gambling. *These are indirect, somewhat hidden costs and aren't seen as readily as the large amounts of money that the casinos give. The Florida Office of Planning and Budgeting conducted a study concluding that the costs to government of gambling addiction far outweighed all revenues that might be generated by casino gambling. 64 So then even though it was promised that property taxes would go down, in fact they may well further skyrocket as taxpayers have to pay for 'infrastructure costs,' such as costs for more roads, more police, more court time, more welfare benefits.*

- *As the Native American Press/Ojibwe News said, "Using an econometric cost-benefit analysis, economists found that, 'the costs of casinos are at least 1.9 times greater than the benefits.' In other words, a dollar worth of casino profits - and other social benefits, costs TAXPAYERS at least $1.90 in cost creating activities such as crime, suicide, and bankruptcy,' and in the expensive social problems engendered by 'problem and pathological' gamblers. 65*

- *In Portland, Oregon, it's called 'painting the pig'. This is the expression used to turn what is essentially an undesirable event, i.e. an Indian casino coming into the community, and make it look desirable. There the Indian tribe and its Las Vegas developer team highlights the positives to the community by sugar-coating their gambling projects with illusory promises. Such promises, such as expanded employment, or the supposed 'boost' that the downtown economy would get perhaps in the form of a convention hotel, are the frosting on the cake meant to allure people to vote for expanded gambling. 66*

As we've seen, the negatives far outweigh the positives once people understand what they are. A casino operating 24/7/365, in a small town or even in an urban neighborhood, quickly wears out its welcome when people discover the many negatives involved. Such downsides as increases in crime, the domination of the local economy, the overall undermining of the quality of life, and destabilization of the community's ability to manage its own growth and development all become very obvious shortly after the hyped casino opens its doors. I don't think America's small towns want to see prostitutes walking around their neighborhoods or have homeless shelters full of people.

So we see there are serious community costs associated with casinos, both in the disadvantages to local businesses and their subsequent high rate of closing. With Indian casinos there are additional problems. Tax-free Indian casinos enterprises often pay higher wages thus attracting local labor away from established businesses. Real estate comes off the tax roles, thus lowering local property tax revenue, and land use is unregulated by zoning and other use restrictions. Municipal service burdens such as police, garbage, firemen, increased social services costs, are uncompensated by 'sovereign Indian casinos' except to the extent that they choose to make contributions to the municipality.

Remember an Indian casino operates as a sovereign nation. Police and other regulatory departments of American towns, cities, and states, have nothing at all to say about what Indian casinos do or how they do it. If a crime, such as rape, occurs there, the casino 'may' call in local police but they don't have to. Environmental impact laws are not obligatory, so sewage and other wastes are discharged however the casino chooses. These sovereign casinos don't even have to provide tax revenue to the state although they usually do so in some form as a part of their initial negotiated settlements with the state.

In Manitoba, Canada, a recent University study suggested that problem gamblers costs the government about $56,000 dollars each in lost wages and health care among other costs to the public. The study felt that almost 10 % of gamblers in the Manitoba and Saskatchewan province had 'some type of addiction to games of chance.' 67

*In **Baltimore, Maryland, a study** was released 2/21/04 by the **Optimal Solutions Group**, a Baltimore economic, policy analysis firm. This study was paid for by private business groups in an effort to understand more about the issue of expanded* *gambling in Maryland. The study noted that while slots at 2 racetracks in Baltimore would bring economic benefits, there would also be* ***major social costs in the vicinity of the tracks****. "Proximity matters", said Mark D. Turner of Optimal Solutions, "People who live close by are more likely to gamble than people who live farther away." 68 This is common sense. We go where its convenient and don't go where it's not convenient.*

*The significant thing that Turner's study noted, was that putting slots at the tracks would add about "****17,000 problem and pathological gamblers in Baltimore and another 20,000 in Prince George's County****." 69 The study noted* ***other social costs related to problem gambling such as increased bankruptcies, embezzlements, divorces and lost work days.***

Groups such as African-Americans and Hispanics are especially vulnerable to be affected by these 'social costs' because these populations have a statistically higher tendency toward gambling addictions" (for many different reasons), Turner added. So before the people in Maryland vote for expanded sites for slots, they better make sure that the almost 20,000 additional compulsive gamblers in each county are not going to include their husband, or child, brother, or sister-in-law. That's a hard call to make. You may think you know someone well, but expose him to an addictive activity and then see what happens. I should know...

Another gambling tragedy showed its face In Spencer, ***Iowa*** *recently at a seminar on 11/26/03 entitled "What is the Impact of Gambling on Families." At that seminar, the speakers were Dr. Mike Hartwig from the Iowa Family Policy Center and Tom Coates, Dir. Of Consumer Credit of Des Moines. Dr. Hartwig told the story of his own life and how gambling had destroyed his family. He related that his father had been a problem gambler and abandoned the family when Dr. Harwig was 4 years old. He said after his father left, men came knocking on their door trying to collect $30,000 that the father had accumulated in debt and owed to a casino. 69*

Furthermore, he said his mother had trouble as a single parent supporting the 3 children. He and his sisters were put up for adoption! He himself was adopted by an abusive family, Dr. Hartwig related, one of his sisters became addicted to crack cocaine, and the other has been in and out of psych wards for much of her life. Dr. Hartwig said that his own life showed how gambling leads to addiction, divorce, broken families, crime, etc. What a tragic story and all because of the initial misstep, that of the gambling and addiction by the father.

The other speaker at the seminar, Tom Coates, the Director of Consumer Credit of Des Moines, Iowa, said that his message was that a casino is NOT economic development. He said a casino merely 'shuffles the deck' by preying on people within the 30 to 50 mile feeder market. He also called it ***"cannibalizing your neighbors."*** *Coates, as director of consumer credit, said that he's been trying to get credit card machines off the floors of Iowa casinos. He added that he feels that* ***6 - 7 % of the state's population are problem and pathological gamblers****. This is up from 1.7% in l989. By l995, that number was 5.4 % and now he feels it's probably almost 7 % if not more. 70*

These numbers should really jump off the page at us. Since we can assume that about 75 % of the population gamble and of that number, from 5 to 10% of people are addicted in one form or another, then that translates to ***vast numbers*** *of people. That's fathers, mothers, sisters, brothers, wives, all spending their money and their time in what is essentially a fruitless endeavor, to win and make money, spending their time and money in what is really a waste of money. This surge of people gambling doesn't come without a corresponding surge in crime. These are all stories of the incredible 'social costs' that inevitably accompany gambling. To say 'social costs' almost makes it sound okay that its just another cost of doing business. Yet to hear the stories of human tragedies, of family break-ups because of gambling, one wonders whether the term 'social costs' can ever do justice to what is involved.*

- *As a US News and World Report study found, "Nationwide, crime rates in casino areas are nearly twice the national average. "Towns with casinos have experienced an upsurge in crime at the same time it was dropping for the nation as a whole." The figures are based on FBI Uniform Crime Reports. 71*
- *Illinois State University professor, Henry Lesieur surveyed Gamblers Anonymous member in Illinois. He found 44% had stolen from work, 18% had gambling-related arrests and 17% had been sued for gambling-related debts. More than 10 years ago, Dr. Lesieur estimated that gambling-related insurance fraud costs over $1 BILLION annually in the US. 72*

So returning to the 4 basic justifications of casinos, Economic development, including Tourism, Jobs, and State Revenue, we've seen that Social Costs also need to be factored in and can be terribly expensive. They're costly economically, on a societal level, and devastating, on a human level. In fact, Social Costs turn out to be so expensive, as we've seen, that they negate the economic benefits. Even the economic benefit of additional state revenue is not nearly sufficient to make up for the social costs.

In terms of State revenue we can certainly appreciate the fact that state governments need additional revenue to balance budgets. No legislator wants to be known as the one responsible for cutting programs or reducing money to education.

In balancing budgets, when there are shortages, the arithmetic of budgets mandates that either programs get cut or additional revenue must be found. Basic economics. Cutting programs is unpopular since legislators first priority is being re-elected.

So legislators opt to seek additional revenue by other means than taxes and gambling looks easy and enticing. Yet as Les Bernal, Chief of Staff, for Massachusetts Senator Sue Tucker, said in an address on 1/10/04 at Harrah's Hotel & Casino in Las Vegas, raising revenue by getting taxes from casino gambling is bad for people and for the state's economy.

In an apt analogy, Bernal asked whether legislators would vote to increase the places where smoking is allowed, just so they could get more money from cigarette taxes. No, of course not. Should legislators vote to promote the sale of cigarettes, to make them more accessible, in order to obtain increased revenue from their sales? 73 I hope not.

The health risk from cigarettes and the subsequent cost in terms of what the long-term use of cigarettes does to people, simply do not equate with economic benefits. "We consider this a ridiculous argument at this time because now it's widely understood how harmful smoking can be. We know we wouldn't wish to do anything to widen its spread, especially among the young. We're at the beginning of understanding how destructive gambling is", he said, and we would add, how important it is to decrease its expansion, instead of continuing to help it proliferate.

TRADITIONAL CRITERIA FOR NOT RAISING REVENUE

Gambling revenue "defies the three key criteria for raising revenues for government services," Bernal added. He said that theoretically taxes that fall into this range of 3 categories are normally not implemented by government because they're not economically beneficial for the state and in the long run, cause more economic loss than they bring in. 74

These criteria include taxes that: 1. ***take away from other forms of revenue****, such as when gambling is responsible for failed businesses and people lose jobs, 2. are* ***regressive****, in that a greater proportion of low income people, including seniors, who can least afford to lose, are affected, i.e. gamble a greater percentage gamble of their incomes than wealthier people. 3. are* ***unstable*** *as a source of income, subject to the fluctuations of the economic market. This means that the revenue could increase or decrease depending on economic cycles. It doesn't make good sense to fund programs and incur the initial costs, only for programs to have insufficient funds the following year when markets decline.*

Bernal noted that gambling revenue is not only unstable but ***inefficient.*** *He says that for Massachusetts to reap $400 million in revenue from a casino, Massachusetts residents would first have to gamble and lose $2 billion. 62 This doesn't make sense as a way to raise taxes. It certainly doesn't make sense for the state to be in the business of licensing casinos so their citizens can lose, so the state can make revenue from the casino. The state is making a little, the citizens are losing a lot. As we know, none of this is 'new' money, nothing is being produced. It's just a* ***re-allocation*** *of money.*

In the state of New York, for every $20.41 gamblers play in the VLT machines at the Saratoga Gaming and Raceway casino, only $1 reverts to the school systems as revenue. 75

People in the state of **Maine** *decisively voted down, 67% to 33%, a casino referendum for their state in the 2003 elections. At that time pro-casino lobbyists said the casino would funnel 25% of its slot-machine take to the state. That was estimated at about $100 million the first year of operation. Any state seeking to balance its budget would find this tempting. But should states really balance their budgets from their own peoples' losses, on the backs of its most vulnerable citizens, so to speak? Should the budget be balanced from losses that were incurred with illegal money from embezzlements, from revenue from losses that might sometime lead to bankruptcies?*

The Christian Science Monitor, 11/5/03, noted that "State governments must look toward more stable and honest strategies to fix budget bottom lines." 76 "Public monies should not be dependent on revenue obtained from an individual's desire or addiction to bet." 76 The chairman of Maine's L.L. Bean Company put it well when he told a reporter that "casino gambling is inconsistent with ideals like perseverance, hard work, and integrity." 77

Yet casino development, with its distorted and unclear thinking, is occurring around the world. People see dollar signs and they start trying to get a piece of it. In England, there has been increased interest in liberalizing their antiquated gambling laws and allowing for casino development in different areas of the country. Two American gambling companies, Harrah's and MGM Mirage, have already begun surveying possible sites and making development deals with various companies there. These veritable gambling giants already own more than 40 casinos in America.

Great Britain *currently has gambling in various forms, such as the lottery, horseracing, small 'fruit' machines in local pubs, but no large-scale casinos. People* *from Great Britain travel to Las Vegas when they go 'on holiday'. Las Vegas estimated that they had about 100,000 English visitors last year. These large gambling operators are hoping and expecting that there will be a demand for casinos in England also. Harrah's plans to spend almost 1 Billion pounds on four 80,000 sq. ft. 'destination' casinos with hotels in 4 major cities, Glasgow, Edinburgh, Manchester, and London. They plan to build up to a dozen small casinos as well.*

MGM Mirage plans to build and open 4 large 50,000 sq. ft. resort casinos. "There is nothing in Europe that even comes close to what we are going to bring to Britain," said Alan Feldman, senior vice-president of the MGM Mirage group. MGM Grand's casino located on the Las Vegas strip, appeals to high-end gamblers. MGM also runs the $2 Billion Bellagio Casino and Hotel, Las Vegas's newest and most upbeat hotel and casino. "Paris got Disney. Britain can import the economic energy and entertainment dynamism of Las Vegas. It will make Disneyland Paris look like pretty small beer," Feldman concluded.78

The British Coalition Against Gambling Expansion has pledged to oppose new casino developments. As an American, I could certainly wish that we had expertise in other areas to export rather than something of questionable moral value and doubtful economic worth. The boldness and bravado of the gambling entrepreneurs is nothing short of amazing. With enormous casinos already in Las Vegas, with the profits going off the scale for top managers and with more and more people indulging in the new 'sport', one would think these companies would have enough to do at home to keep themselves busy. Yet expansion seems to be a by-product when it comes to gambling and no one seems satisfied with the incredibly lucrative status quo.

How much money do companies want to make? How much food can they eat or how many clothes can they wear? To contain gambling seems to be as difficult as containing the HIV virus. Gambling's scope seems to have taken over the world and everyone wants 'a piece of the action'. Gambling seems to want to expand and grow, and as it does so, it undermines people and society by its very nature. It's appetite is inexorable and all-consuming and it's drive and energy endless. Would that we could apply this to more productive and constructive activities, to projects that build up people and society instead of tearing down and wrecking all asunder.

Countries and localities are licensing this modern-day addiction, this new form of evil and self-destructiveness, as fast as they can and throwing research, experience, and history's lessons, out the window. The lure of 'easy money' looks very attractive for the individuals and very appealing for government as well. Don't we know by now, as has been oft stated, that 'if something looks too good to be true, it probably is.' Gambling is no exception to the rule.

These profits, born from the ill fortune of people like you and me, could be called 'blood money'. Who knows what crises their loss precipitated in the individual who lost the money. Perhaps that person was one of many who committed suicide. Or maybe he became divorced or lost his house, or was forced into bankruptcy as a result of losing his money. It's not clean money. Drug money is not 'clean' and neither is gambling money. It's morally bankrupt to trade in this money. It's dealing in people's misery and weakness. At the least, its promoting wrong values, that one should win money and be wealthy regardless of other's bad luck and misfortune.

BANKRUPTCIES

That gambling is a redistribution of money is possibly at its most obvious when we consider the situation involving the dramatic rise in bankruptcies that inevitably accompany gambling. Bankruptcies are an inevitable by-product of gambling. They are part of the 'social costs'. Supposedly, the benefits of government revenue outweigh the social costs both financially and emotionally. Bankruptcy for individuals is financial ruin, it's a tragedy, its life-changing, and not for the better. I'm not sure how the 'benefits' of gambling could ever outweigh the detriments of bankruptcy. Bankruptcies and their recent escalation are intimately involved with gambling.

An essential part of the economic state of the community is the solvency of its citizens. People have to feel that they are financially stable, that they can pay their bills with money honestly obtained and with income that is relatively secure. When individuals or businesses handle their money in irresponsible ways, then many people can be impacted by the losses of a few. This is what happens in personal bankruptcy. Western society has historically made provision for financial crises. Legal provisions in the law allows individuals and businesses that have had personal financial crises to have an opportunity to have their debt liquidated, so-to-speak, to start 'anew'.

There is an increasing number of Americans who are being forced to turn to bankruptcy to regain financial stability for themselves and their families. It happens to some who get in dept because of illness, lost jobs, divorce or some other unforeseen tragedy in their lives. Often people get themselves deeply in credit card debt and find the interest payments strangling them. This happens with gambling where people overdraw their credit cards, spend past savings, and mortgage houses to the hilt.

Gambling is certainly an activity which can precipitate personal financial crises. As gambling has increased dramatically in the past 20 years, so has personal bankruptcy filings in this country. Recent research states conclusively that ***the availability and accessibility of gambling in the past 25 years has been responsible for the major increase in the filing of personal bankruptcy suits.*** *The one new factor that has emerged in the past year is the opening of the new casino. To me, that sends up a red flag. 80*

Bankruptcy Court Judge Carl L. Bucki.

Other studies have corroborated the fact that with the increase in gambling has come a clear increase in the number and the percentage of people filing for bankruptcy. Bankruptcy is something that is destructive for the individual involved as well as for the overall society. In the 12 months ending ***9/30/03, a record 1.6 Million people filled for personal bankruptcy in the U.S.*** *That was 7.8 % more than in 200-02, the previous year, according to the American Bankruptcy Institute, a Virginia research organization. 81*

From 1993 through 2002, bankruptcy filings rose 93%, to 1.57 million. These are "pretty staggering" numbers said Wendelin Lipp, president of the Bankruptcy Bar Assoc. for the District of Maryland and a bankruptcy attorney. For years the filing of personal bankruptcy had been associated with personal failure and loss of status for the individual. At this time, however, the stigma appears to have abated somewhat. 82

The government, in the form of the executive branch, i.e. President Bush, is well aware of this increase and has drafted legislation that would make it more difficult and more painful financially for people to file for bankruptcy. But this legislation hasn't passed due to legislators being reluctant to raise the ire of constituencies.

On the business side of Bankruptcy, people filing for bankruptcy can be a negative scenario for businesses as well. For businesses that don't get paid, bankruptcy is associated with financial loss, possibly even disruption or forced closing. These negative factors occur to people who weren't even gamblers themselves.

Barron, Staten, and Wilshusen in their paper "The Impact of Casino Gambling on Personal Bankruptcy Filing Rates", 8/2000, state that there was a rise of nearly 50% in the number of households filing of bankruptcy protection in 1998. 81 This was about a half million more than 3 years earlier in 1995. They concluded that

"the proximity of casino gambling"...is "associated with higher bankruptcy rates." "The local impact is far more pronounced than on national rates."
"From 1992 - 1998, one out of every 20 US households filed for bankruptcy."

They note that 'destination resort casinos', such as Atlantic City or Las Vegas, are a 'net exporter' of gambling negatives. In destination gambling, the gamblers are tourists and take their financial problems back home with them. Urban casinos, such as the riverboats, the gaming clubs with video poker, etc., attract patrons from its own community. The negative effects, the bankruptcies, the embezzlements, the loss of homes or marriages, remain right there.

We found statistically significant increases at the county level in the number of personal bankruptcy filings due to the introduction of casino gambling. *83 Barron, Staten and Wilshusen*

Also significant is the fact that the large increases in bankruptcy filing rates occurred even with overall favorable economic conditions. The 1990's had relatively favorable economic conditions for Americans. Unemployment rates were low and growth was widespread. So why did so many American households have such bad financial conditions that they were forced to file for bankruptcy?

- *This research is supported by other similar studies such as done by SMR Research in 1997. They wrote that:*

Gambling was the "single fastest-growing driver of bankruptcy.*" 84*

SMR compared 298 counties in the US with at least one major gambling facility, casino, riverboat, pari-mutuel outlet, with the rate of counties without gambling. They found counties with 5 or more gambling outlets (23 counties) had filing rates of 35% above counties without gambling possibilities. Conversely, SMR noted that the "counties with the highest bankruptcy rates in New Jersey, California, and Connecticut, were those in closest proximity to major casino gambling activity."

1. *Counties with gambling outlets had a bankruptcy filling rate 18% higher than those without gambling.*
2. *Counties with more casinos had higher rates of bankruptcy filing.*
3. *Counties with 5 or more gambling outlets (23 counties in the US), had rates 35% higher than counties without gambling. 84*

- *Another study, at Creighton Univ.,* ***A County Level Analysis,*** *confirmed the link between casino gambling and bankruptcy.* ***Personal bankruptcy in counties where there are casinos are twice as high as those without casinos,"*** *said Morse and Goss, in a study of 250 counties with and without casinos. The counties were compared to analogous counties with relative similar demographics. 85*

The American Gambling Association continues to assert that "...there is no link between the rate of bankruptcy filings and the presence of casinos". I wonder how they can reason thus, seeing study after study, all continuing to say the same thing. Talk about sticking your head in the sand and keeping it there. Or are they just so wedded to profit that they can't begin to recognize reality. Possibly gamblers aren't the only ones in denial? 86

The ***Social costs of gambling****, the* ***ABCs of gambling, Addiction, Bankruptcy, Corruption and Crime****, mature in about 3 to 4 years after gambling comes and expands in an area. This only makes sense as people require some lead time. Addiction, like any illness, requires some time to germinate in the entity.*

In Melbourne, Australia, an accountant stole more than $2 Million dollars, from the company he worked for. Vince Stephen Marinkovic, 33, from Altona North, admitted that he stole more than $2.4 Million dollars from the Jotun Paint Supply Co. over a period of 6 years from 1996. to 2002. He was in charge of payroll. He used the money to feed his gambling addiction. 87

It's hard to believe that so many people allow themselves to be so badly misguided when gambling is concerned. That's one reason why I've decided that it's truly an addiction. Because nothing else could have impelled so many otherwise intelligent, lawful people, to both break and even flout society's civil and criminal laws so profoundly.

Bankruptcies, noted previously, increased 100 % in the 1990s, after gambling had invaded the heartland of America. That is, the number of people filing almost exactly doubled. Yet America's population did not double, as we know, which would justify the increase. This increase in the bankruptcy filing rate, equates to approximately half a million more people, 500,000 people per year, filing for bankruptcy every year, following the advent of gambling.

***In 1989, there were 610,000 filing** in the U.S.A. **In 1998, there were 1,400,000 filings by people**. So in ten years, the increase was 100 % with an absolute number increase of about **800,000** individuals. Assuming the number should've remained constant or even increased 4% per annum, a 40 % total, the expected number of people filing in 1999 would have been 854,000 people (610,000 + 40% or 244,000 more). But the total number of people who filed for bankruptcy wasn't 854,000 people. It was **1,400,000 Million people**, more than double in 10 years, exactly correlating with gambling's expansion across the U.S. See **Chart** below. 88*

*So the **increase of 546,000 people, can be seen as directly attributable to gambling**. Additionally, as the research of Barron, Staten, and Wilshusen, notes, this was in an affluent economic climate with no major recessionary interludes. If anything, the economic climate would have favored less people declaring bankruptcy. So an additional almost 600,000 people in the U.S. in 1998 alone filed for bankruptcy, since the introduction of gambling on a more convenient, accessible basis. Gambling has been the financial demise of more than a half million people per year in the U.S. due to their addiction. This is all because of the licensing of Gambling by our government, as well as easy credit, deliberately extended by casinos and credit card companies.*

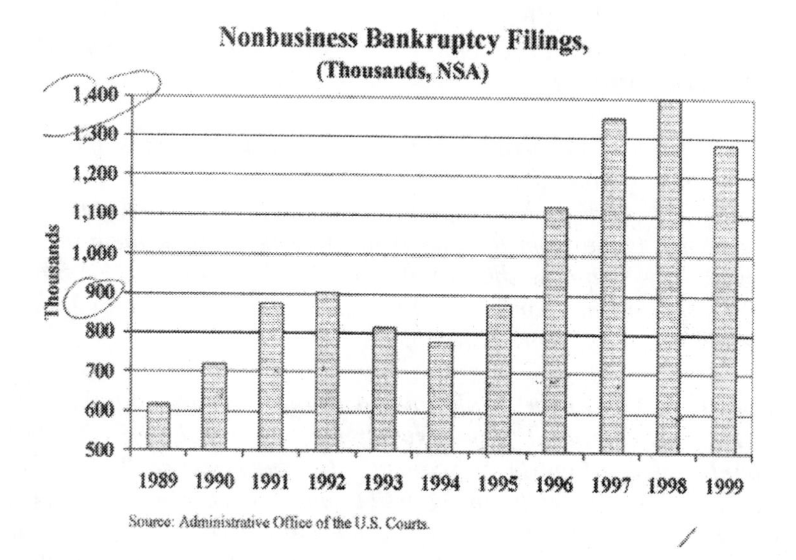

*Simply put, **where there is gambling, there is bankruptcy for a significant number** of people. I find these bankruptcy figures appalling. If we know this, and the casinos are well aware of this research, then if we put a casino somewhere, we're just waiting for people to become insolvent, with all that entails. We're enticing people into debt, into personal financial ruin, into acting irresponsibly and throwing away life savings.*

If we give a hundred people a loaded gun, I imagine that a few will use it, will pull the trigger, and will inflict great damage on themselves or others. If we allow people easy accessibility to gambling, to another addiction, I'm sure that a certain percentage will become addicts. Where does the blame lay? Whose fault is this? The person who came up with the loaded gun, the one who licensed this potential addiction, or the one who shot himself with the gun, the one who became an addict and did what addicts predictably do, lost all his money and that of others? Maybe both act irresponsibly in this world where every action has a reaction, where we all touch and impact upon each other.

Other research supports the above studies. The National Opinion Research Center (NORC), University of Chicago, was commissioned by the NGISC to compare counties in which casinos had and had not opened.

- *This study concluded that the availability of a casino within 50 miles is associated with about* ***double*** *the prevalence of problem and pathological gambling. 90*

- *These studies were further corroborated by that of Nichols, Stitt, and Giacopassi (1999). They also found that* ***the introduction of casino gambling impacted local bankruptcy filing rates in 7 out of the 8 counties they studied****.*

The largest increase occurred in the town that had casinos the longest. 91 This is a no-brainer, if gambling leads to bankruptcies, then gambling for a longer amount of time, leads to more bankruptcies. The 8th town studied was a destination resort where people came from far and then presumably took their problems back home with them. If we suppose that we are 'our brother's keeper,' then the fact that people took their problems home with them is actually not meaningful, that is, it doesn't make the losses any more palatable.

For example, in ***Wisconsin****, bankruptcy petitions increased another 12 % in the year 2003. This has continued to be a* ***steady increase for the past 3 straight years of record bankruptcy filings in Wisconsin.*** *Consumers filed* ***28,225 bankruptcy petitions in 2003****. This is really an incredible number when we consider it closely. This means that in the state of Wisconsin alone, in the year 2003, there were over 28,000 people who couldn't pay their debts and were willing to undergo the stigma of bankruptcy in order to survive financially. What does this say about people's ability to handle their money and society's ability to educate and support their citizens in handling and dealing with their money in responsible ways? 92*

A bankruptcy lawyer in Madison, Wisconsin, states that "over the years, my practice has changed, ...absolutely no doubt...I see it more and more where people *have **significant losses due to gambling, and those losses are financed by credit cards,**" said lawyer Timothy Peyton. Peyton feels the easy availability of credit cards is partly to blame for people getting in over their head. 93*

*This was our experience. After my husband went through our stock accounts and savings, he maxed out our credit cards leaving us with $150,000 worth of debt. Peyton added that he also sees gambling taking more people than ever on the road to financial ruin. **"You know…a casino's job is to take your money. That's what they do. It's great if you can afford it, but a lot of people can't."** A lot of people, Peyton notes, I would say the majority of people, 95% of them. Actually I don't know many people who have extra income.*

- *David Asbach, trustee for the Eastern District of Wisconsin U.S. Bankruptcy Court, also agreed that gambling debt is appearing more often in bankruptcy cases. "What people do, is that they go to the casino and…take advances on their credit cards." 94*

- *The Wisconsin Council on Problem Gambling feels strongly that casinos are the reasons for the increase in bankruptcy filings. Rose Gruber, executive director of the Green Bay council, said "We certainly have seen an increase in people saying bankruptcy is something they're doing as an end result of their gambling addiction." The Wisconsin Council on Problem Gambling estimates that 5 % to 7 % of people have a problem with gambling. 95*

Diana, a member of Gamblers Anonymous in southeastern Wisconsin for the last 3 years, said that once she won $5,000. dollars on a slot machine, she was hooked. After draining retirement funds set aside for her and her husband, she finally sought help when her husband threatened divorce. "My husband could have retired in another year and a half," she said. "Now he's going to have to work probably until he dies because I got into everything, bank accounts, you name it." Now all the money Diana and her husband saved for their retirement is going largely to casino owners with a small percentage to the state treasury. 96

*In **Maryland,** personal bankruptcies have also increased from 14,215 in 1993 to 34,700 in 2002, 1 of every 63 households. This is hardly surprising news given Maryland's close proximity to Atlantic City. Remember the formula, **Proximity + Frequency = ADDICTION.***

Experts feel that easy credit, poor job growth, and public policy that encourages borrowing and spending, have all fueled this surge. But the biggest contributor to people needing to file for bankruptcy would appear to be ***GAMBLING.*** *"It really is an astronomical problem," said Joseph Rubin, senior director of congressional affairs at the U.S. Chamber of Commerce in Washington. The failure of people to pay what they owe, "severely impacts small businesses…all the way up to banks and credit card companies," he said. 97*

Rep. Jerrold Nadler, a New York Democrat, responded that ***credit card companies and banks*** *'are lending money, inviting bankruptcies." 98 To me, his comment makes a lot of sense. I've seen credit companies offer my children, still in college, lines of credit up to $5,000. If they had cashed in on this credit, they would never have been able to pay the credit card back. The credit card companies themselves are to blame for offering credit to people who clearly are either unable to pay it back or poor risks of some kind. My husband had 20 credit cards from major companies all offering him, a compulsive gambler, significant credit. How in the world did they ever expect to get paid?*

Personal savings are down in our present economy and household debt rose to 18.09 % of disposable personal income, according to the Federal Reserve Board. Of the 94 Federal judicial districts nationwide, Maryland's had the 9th largest number of bankruptcy filings with 34,700 in 2002. California's central district, around Los Angeles, topped the country with 81,702. California has almost 50 gambling sites. Maryland has Atlantic City just around the corner. Gambling has certainly helped the business of bankruptcy filings.

Of course, as we discussed, when people gamble, the money goes out of the local communities, far away, to the home offices of the casino interests, the promoters. If money goes out of the community, then some people will suffer since there isn't an unlimited amount of money. This means that some people won't have any money since it's been effectively redistributed. Hence we have bankruptcies close to major casino centers such as Atlantic City and Las Vegas.

Diana threw away years and years of savings because of her misguided actions, because she became 'addicted.' Her addiction was fueled, created, greased and made possible by the casinos and by the willingness of state government to license casinos. She was an easy mark for the casinos. Her retirement money was small change for them. But for her and her husband, it was their future. Diana was addicted by the total ambiance of casinos, by their exploitative and dishonest marketing and advertising strategies, by their promulgation of false social values, by the its-just-entertainment-excuse', by her own hopes and dreams of making big money, winning a fortune. Because of her own gullibility, she and her husband are now firmly entrenched on the road to financial ruin. This is another one of millions of personal tragedies that could and should have been avoided, that we brought upon ourselves.

Connie Kilmark, a financial counselor in Madison, Wisconsin, said that from the standpoint of economics, gambling addictions go through finances much more rapidly than alcohol or drugs. ***"With gambling, the speed with which you can burn through money is absolutely without limit."*** *98 Does she mean, the speed with which one can destroy oneself is without limit, or the speed with which one can throw away years of savings, of planning? Or both?*

EMBEZZLEMENT

So bankruptcies increase directly with the accessibility of gambling. How about other financial indices, such as embezzlements? Embezzlement is when an employee of a business takes business money surreptitiously, using it for his own personal interests. To me, it's another name for stealing. Its common knowledge, that for people who are desperate to get money for drugs, stealing is a way of life. For people desperate to get money for gambling, embezzling is a common approach to getting money. This avenue seems to be used increasingly wherever gambling is found.

*Many attorney generals have remarked on this new phenomenon. Patrick Youngs, assistant Rhode Island Attorney General, says he's noticed a significant increase in gambling-related embezzlements since Rhode Island allowed slots in the 1990's. "****At least 50% of the embezzlement cases are related to gambling."*** *99*

In Wilmington, **Delaware**, *gambling addiction counselor, Melwin Slawick, in the public defender's office says gambling-related embezzlement, 'increases every year.' 100 An addiction counselor in Iowa says many of her patients have embezzled. "Even the smartest of people, when they get into the peak of this gambling high, can rationalize something that would seem crazy when they're in their right mind." She also counsels drug addicts and admits they also steal from employers. But even the worst cases of drug addicts don't approach the monetary losses a compulsive gambler can run up. "****There's no addiction…more expensive than gambling,"*** *she said. 101*

Numerous cases from around the country include embezzlements from business and from nonprofit groups, labor unions, local governments, charities, even churches and Little Leagues. "We've got mothers of Girl Scouts stealing cookie money, said Dennis Labelle, attorney in Grand Traverse County, Michigan, site of an Indian casino. Thompson, Nevada professor, says that roughly 5% of gamblers become compulsive and that of that 5%, which numbers in the millions, end up ***stealing from their employers****. So half of all people who become compulsive gamblers steal from their employers. 102*

An assistant commonwealth attorney in Jefferson County, ***Missouri,*** *says gambling is behind 1 in 3 of the cases his office has handled in which people stole $50,000 or more from employers. A lot of these people that embezzle money, "are people with otherwise clean lives." 103 The companies that are embezzled from often are then put into difficult financial positions and may end up going out of business or having to lay off non-gambling employees because of the gambling-related embezzlement. (Remember the figure that each compulsive gambler affects negatively at least 10-15 other people).*

- *A Christian County, St. Louis, Missouri Treasurer stole $650,000 from the county's building fund. St. Louis Post-Dispatch 12/29/96.*

- *The president of a sports league for youth stole $26,000 to gamble on riverboats. North County Suburban Journal 8/7/94*

- *In* ***Minnesota,*** *the Minneapolis-St. Paul Star Tribune recently reported a rising frequency of various kinds of financial crimes. Loss Prevention Specialists, In. of Minneapolis, a firm that helps employers cope with internal theft, told the paper that prior to casinos it had 'zero cases of gambling-related embezzlements,' but since it has had cases running 'well over $500,000.'"*

- *In Newark, Delaware, a trusted bookkeeper played the ponies with more than $500,000 she stole from her employer.*

- *In Wisconsin, in 1999, a 64 year old grandmother used her position as bookkeeper at a credit union to steal $289,000 to play the slots. That credit union subsequently went out of business.*

- *A printing company in Kentucky laid of seven employees after a bookkeeper there stole $180,000 to play slots. 105*

Gov. Robert L. Ehrlich Jr., pushing for the legalization of slots in Maryland, insists that the 'benefits outweigh the risks.' 106 I wonder if the people who end up embezzling or declaring bankruptcy, or both, would agree.

For these individuals, people without previous history of criminal involvement and with respected professions, I can only surmise that gambling has precipitated true tragedies in their lives. Where does a town tax collector in a small Connecticut town go after they've been convicted of embezzling? What kind of demon led these people to destroy everything they had built up in their lives for the sake of getting money for their gambling addiction? What could they say to their spouses, to their children, to their friends and their grandchildren, to their fellow churchgoers?

According to Joseph Centofanti, an accountant and president of the Connecticut Fraud Examiners, ***businesses there lost an estimated $600 Billion dollars in 2002 because of fraud with gambling problems as the primary reason****. Employee theft from companies is beginning to be a major cause for alarm with small and large businesses.*

Small businesses lost an average of $127,000 and larger companies an average of $97,000. Smaller businesses have fewer systems of checks and balances. "These people aren't looking to embezzle money. They start off with their own money and start chasing the big wins." But of course the big win never comes. "No matter how much it looks as though you're (winning), you're not," said Marlene F. McGann, exec. dir. of the Meriden and Wallingford Substance Abuse Council. "Mohegan Sun and Foxwoods ***are not in it for recreation,"*** *she added. 108*

We normally think of gambling as occurring in the big, well-publicized centers such as Atlantic City, Las Vegas, or the New Orleans riverboats. But even in American's heartlands such as Wisconsin, gambling has taken over and caused increased embezzlements.

A recent news article, 1/18/04, from Shawano County, Wisconsin, showed that gambling addiction has led to at least 10 cases of large-scale embezzlements over the past three years, according to District Attorney, Gary Bruno. "We're talking thousands of dollars—anywhere from $20,000 to $50,000 that these people are stealing from their employers. Most of it is going into gambling." 109

Recently an office manager for the Legend Lake Property Owner's Assoc. embezzled almost $71,000 from that organization. Executive director of the Wisconsin Council on Problem Gambling, Rose Gruber, added that it used to be very rare to hear of embezzlement cases. But this year alone, she has heard about more than a dozen around the state. "I'm sure there are many more out there. These are just the ones we're hearing about." 110

Recently ***Milwaukee District Attorney****, Michael McCann, and Dane County District Attorney, Brian Blanchard, got together at a press conference in Madison,*

Wisconsin on 2/10/04. District Attorney McCann was clear about the increase in crime since the Milwaukee casino first opened. Much of the crime increase has included embezzlement he said. ***"One of our parishioners has been arrested for taking $500,000 of the church's money,"*** *he said. "The money went to the Potowatomi (casino)." 111 DA Blanchard said that compulsive gambling results in more embezzlement cases. Citizens end up being affected through insurance claims and social problems.*

The 2 District Attorneys and the research Professor, John Kindt, Univ. of Illinois, had gotten together with members of the No Dane Casino, a grassroots group to stop the latest casino referendum from passing in Madison, Wisconsin. The referendum subsequently didn't pass on 2/17/04. What is interesting and significant to note is that these are really heavy hitters, 2 DA's and a university professor. So both academics and law enforcement are clearly opposed to casinos. This should certainly tell us something.

Diane Kepros, a gambling addiction counselor in Cedar Rapids, Iowa, calls compulsive gambling, ***'a disease of irrational thinking.'*** *She says many of her patients have embezzled. "Even the smartest of people, when they get into the peak of this gambling high, can rationalize." 112 So while this statement may explain the excesses to some extent, it certainly doesn't take away the prison sentences, the lost relationships, the ruined businesses that come from this devastation.*

"Most compulsive gamblers who turn to theft, do not have a criminal record", says William N. Thompson, a Univ. Of Nevada, Las Vegas professor who has studied the gambling industry. However, he reiterated, 40 to 60% of compulsive gamblers end up stealing from their employers. 113

Gambling in these instances truly destroyed lives, lives that had been productive for the community. Gambling took law-abiding, productive citizens with no history of illegal involvement and turned them into criminals, into lawbreakers, because of their addiction. I don't know of anything else that could have made these people commit illegal acts. I don't know of anything else that could have made my super-straight husband take money that didn't belong to him.

What could have possessed these fine, upstanding citizens, never previously in trouble, to turn away from the values they had traditionally espoused, to look away from the trust that was given to them, to betray the confidences that people had in them. Only an incredibly powerful addiction, only Gambling. What kind of monster has the power to make people do things that are totally uncharacteristic of themselves? Only Gambling.

Only an addiction has that kind of power. A drug addiction, an alcohol addiction, a smoking addiction, a gambling addiction. Gambling is a hidden addiction, and money is a substance people abuse.

All addictions can and have destroyed many lives, lives that have been slowly and carefully built, over the years. Only an addiction could have been more powerful than my husband's love for his wife, for his children, for his career, than his love for dharma and for doing the right thing in his life. An addiction is a powerful thing. It's like the allegory about Machiavelli and Dr. Faustus. In exchange for the riches and wealth of the world, Faustus sold his soul to the devil. With addiction, in exchange for the wealth of the physical high, the adrenaline rush, the sense pleasure of the moment, you sell your soul, your being, your identity of who you are, to the devil of drugs, or of gambling, or of alcohol. You let it take over your mind, your thoughts, your finances and your life. You become its lover and only think about your love, your passion, your obsession. Your family and job become second in importance.

And in the process of selling your own soul, you put the well-being and the lives of those around you at risk. At the least, you cause great pain and suffering to those you love, to those you have contact with. You're gambling with their well-being and their lives.

Casinos bring addiction. They do not bring economic development. Not all people become addicted, but such a significant number do that it hurts everyone in the long run. And even if no one became 'addicted', per se, the general trend of losing money which then gets sent out of communities, of businesses closing, which then forces people to lose jobs, of increased crime, which further hurts people economically and emotionally, is not a beneficial one for any community. It certainly does not contribute toward increased economic growth rates, whether in terms of jobs, or any other kind of positive development. All are incredibly negative both for individuals and for societies.

NEW YORK STATE

Let's look at the example of the State of New York. Let's see how the numbers and the figures compute. Politicians are all so eager to introduce expanded gambling in their states, let's see if it's good for New York. Recently, Governor George Pataki publicized a proposed new plan to raise funds for the state budget by increasing the number of VLTs and by selling licenses for video lottery terminal sites throughout the state. This proposal on 1/21/04 anticipated doubling the number of VLT sites to 16 with the profits going into an education fund. The governor suggested the machines would raise as much as $6 Billion over 5 years.

The video lottery terminals look like slots but narrowly sidestep the state's constitutional ban on gambling by being hooked electronically into the state lottery system and its odds. The governor estimates the terminals could generate $6 billion over the next 5 years.

Again the specter of social costs raises its ugly head. Some gambling opponents, such as Senator Frank Padavan (R-Jamaica Estates) note that in the long run, this will create more problems than it solves. The move would increase the number of the state's 1.1 million problem gamblers. It also would put more of New York's poor at risk and oversaturate the state with gambling venues, said Sen. Padavan. "The state has become addicted to gambling." 114 On 1/28/04, the Saratoga harness racetrack opened with ***1,300 new machines*** *which are being watched closely*

However legislative leaders are finally beginning to truly understand the economics of gambling and to realize that 'there is no such thing as a free lunch.' One Assemblyman, Steven Sanders-Manhattan, said that the revenue would fluctuate from year to year, making it unreliable. "To bankroll the educational system based on the gambling habits of individuals in New York is simply not the way to fund the future needs of education." 115

Other politicians also are coming to understanding the overwhelming social costs of gambling. On Long Island, Suffolk County Southampton Town Supervisor Patrick Heaney, understands well what Indian casinos would bring. According to Newsday, at a town board meeting late last month, 7/04, Heaney said about gambling: "It's a parasitic industry. You see bankruptcies increase, drug addiction increase...A lot of bad, nasty things come into a community as ***decency*** *gets sucked out." 115A*

Yet the state of New York is one of the biggest gambling operators around. It runs Off-Track Betting, owns horse tracks and relentlessly urges people to play the state lottery. This is what people mean when they say state governments are 'addicted to gambling, or to gambling revenue' at least 21 other states already use lottery proceeds to support education. But William Duncombe, a Syracuse Univ. professor who co-authored a study on NYS state education financing in 2003 called the idea 'scary.' "The education of our high-needs districts is going to depend on the whims of gamblers. What a crazy way to fund schools," Duncombe said.

> *Not only is it 'crazy', but I would suggest that it's immoral. To fund schools on the weaknesses of people who gamble, to take money which will almost certainly drive a definite percentage of people into bankruptcy and into crime, I consider to be unwise and foolish if not corrupt in terms of personal values. 116*

Senator Frank Padavan (R-Jamaica Estates), agreed. He said:

Proposals to fund education on the backs of hopelessly addicted gamblers and people of lower socio-economic status is absurd and cruel. Everyone knows gambling is a regressive form of taxation.

***"It's so sad**, said Erie Country Judge Timothy J. Drury, who had to sentence people who embezzled because of their gambling addictions.*

***"These aren't people doing car-jackings or dealing drugs**. They're otherwise worthwhile people who just somehow bought into these advertisements. They feel a rush...The state encourages it." 117*

*Gail Klepalk embezzled, or stole, **$308,000** from Buffalo Medical Group over the course of 5 years to help her with gambling debt. She pleaded guilty to grand larceny and received probation. Her sentence was lenient comparatively.*

Margaret Wollen, of Getzville, a small town outside of Buffalo, New York,, was sentenced to 2 to 7 years in prison. She had been a bookkeeper at Jet Action, a small printing company and stole more than $200,000 to fund her gambling at Casino Niagara, the casino at Niagara Falls which has just been opened for the past year. Jet Action didn't have employee theft insurance and the company had to lay off workers and nearly went bankrupt.

Casino Niagara also was the undoing of a company's trust bookkeeper. She pleaded in March, 2004, to embezzling more than $700,000. Tina had been a trusted bookkeeper there and forged checks to pay for her betting. She has not yet been sentenced. Her husband in a bid at restitution, agreed to take a $200,000 mortgage on their property and give up a $45,000 retirement account to repay part of the theft. 118

More tragedies, more family disruption, more adversity and calamities, all precipitated by the advent of gambling. Casino Niagara only opened in January, 2003, and already the tragedies are coming out of the woodwork. Isn't life hard enough without adding to its difficulties? These people were previously law-abiding, hard-working citizens. Now they could well be prison inmates, supported by the state to the tune of $25,000 dollars/year of taxpayer money, leaving husbands and families behind. These people are not two-headed monsters, they're people just like you and me. It could happen to us.

DELAWARE

In the State of Delaware, the Delaware Health and Social Service Substance Abuse and Mental Health Division issued a study in 2002 on the costs and consequence of gambling there. Delaware has had legalized slot machines since 1995. Delaware Park and Dover Downs, horse racing tracks have 2,000 machines each. Delaware gets 35% of the slot machine revenue. This has contributed about $600 million to the state general fund since 1995. "Besides...economic benefits, legalized gambling has resulted in ***substantial costs and consequences, including those associated with excessive debt and bankruptcy, divorce, embezzlement and child neglect,"*** *119 the study reported.*

The study further calculated ***annual state economic costs*** *to deal with problem and pathological gamblers at $3.1 million and lifetime costs at $20.1 million. If the economic costs aren't high enough, Delegate DeRoy Myers, asked further about the social costs.*

> *"What is a life worth? What is the value of a family worth? It isn't worth sacrificing the families," he said in a news article on 11/04/03 for the Times-News. 120*

"We need quality industry *here" (in Delaware), commented Commissioner Barbara Roque. "I don't see anything quality about the gambling industry." 121*

*The study concluded that "**problem gambling detracts significantly from the quality of life of approximately 38,000 Delaware residents** over the age of 18 years." (This is counting the numbers of actual estimated problem gamblers. It doesn't factor in the large numbers of people affected by each problem gambler). This figure of 38,000 of a state population of 720,000 estimates an incidence of about 5% of the people being problem gamblers, a generally accepted prevalence rate. "That's a very negative effect on 38,000 in a state of 720,000" said Bill Valentine, a community activist against the legalization of gambling in Pennsylvania. 122*

Similarly, a Letter to the Editor in the Jefferson County Journal, Jefferson, Missouri, on 10/11/03, notes that about 100,000 Missourians and 2.5 million Americans are probably problem gamblers. This is perhaps a low estimate consisting of a 2 – 5% of the adult population. The writer notes that in gambling there is no product and no new revenue.

> *In the case of Missouri, almost all of gambling dollars generate from the pockets of Missouri residents who pass through the casinos." This*

effectively returns "80% of all money to out-of-state gambling interests, 10% to the state and local governments, and 10% to the few 'lucky' winners, who often throw much of it back in the machines. These figures should not please Missouri residents. Does Missouri really want to be an area where out of state interests make money and take it back home with them? 122

The letter writer adds the:

"the gullibility of (people) who don't understand the dynamics of these facts leads me to say, 'Please send me your money. I will take from each of you 70% of it for myself, give the state 20% and return 10% to you. In addition, I will titillate you by saying that you may win enough money for a lifetime of comfort. Your chances are about 300 million to one." 123 Ben Bradshaw, Imperial.

****

Numerous studies have noted the economic disadvantages of gambling. Gambling is tied not to economic development but economic decline, as we've seen. The last tenet of economic development which is believed to be a lucrative by-product of gambling is ***Tourism****. We haven't devoted a lot of time to it because it's a simple area and can be discussed quickly. Chambers of Commerce might feel that their area has great natural beauty or interesting activities. Whatever the attraction, its second fiddle for gamblers. People do not go to gambling areas to spend time in the great outdoors or to sample the entertainment and historic sights of an area. Tourists may come to your area, but if you attracted them because of the casinos and the gambling, then that's the draw and that's what they're going to do.*

Gamblers will stay inside the casinos. They do not venture out of the warm womb of the casino. They eat, sleep, and gamble there. The casinos provide for every conceivable need of the tourists and do their utmost to keep the tourists inside the casino. There might be a few gas stations and pawn shops that get patronized but not very much. The casinos are not owned by community citizens so they get no profit unless the tourists patronize local businesses. Which they don't. Gamblers want to be near 'the action'. People drive to casinos, park in their lots, stay there, play there, eat and drink there, and then drive home. They do not patronize local businesses. This is the whole story about tourism. People think that it will boost the regional economic development but it really won't. It will be a boost for the casino owners and no one else.

In terms of state revenue, some may go to the state but let's remember that its just money taken from local citizens. So it's a regressive tax which means it hits poor people disproportionally, harder than people with more money. To top it all off, just a small percentage of the money the citizens lose goes to the state. Most of it goes to the industry operatives, and gets sent far away. The citizens lose much more than they would have paid had the government just raised taxes in order to get an equivalent amount of incoming revenue.

Gambling certainly provides nice profits for the industry owners, they build handsome estates and bank accounts far away. But it does not provide for community economic development. The profit for the industry comes from local people who never see their money again. The industry may provide a few jobs initially but then the net number of jobs decrease when locals businesses close and local people become bankrupt. Local businesses and local people are also hurt when their employees, other local people, embezzle funds needed for them to stay in business.

Gambling looks up-front like there is a lot of potential for communities to prosper, buildings to be constructed, jobs created, community people needed to staff the casinos. Yet, the profits from the new industry will go to out-of-town-owners and corporations. Locals who become dependent on the casino will be impoverished.

So in terms of economic development, jobs, tourism, and state revenue, I think we've gotten a much better idea of what gambling does and what it doesn't do for individuals and communities. It does provide jobs but then it takes away when those people who just got employed, become addicts and have to file for bankruptcy. It doesn't provide for Tourism. It provides some state revenue but much, much more to casino owners. It doesn't provide for community economic development but in fact serves to depress it even further. It effectively takes the community's few remaining resources and ships them out of state. Our legislative leaders need to become more sophisticated in economic terms, to call a spade a spade, and not a dollar sign.

Gambling is not an economic life-saver for poor communities. It brings in a lot of up-front promising financial activity, but the end result, simply, is the fact that everyone will lose their money. It looks like a short term at least, quick fix, but that's all it is. It creates more problems than it fixes. It creates more crime, more social problems, net unemployment, embezzlement, bankruptcy. More human heart- ache and misery.

It creates the potential for addiction for all and the actuality of addiction for at least 5% to 10 %. That minority then wrecks havoc all around, as addicts always do. If we know it brings addiction, and we do know that definitely, then why would we ever invite gambling into our household, our family, our community, and our lives? We invite addiction in and it takes over the whole scene.

Gambling is a ravenous fire, consuming everything in its path. Upfront it looks like it will help balance the budget and that seems all-important. But it balances the budget on the backs of the working people and vulnerable citizens. No positive economic development for communities, no positive economic development for individuals. Incredible profits for the gambling industry. Is this what we want?

****

CHAPTER FOUR

SOCIAL COSTS - SOCIAL VALUES

What are the values that gambling promotes? Do we want a society with these types of values? Do we want our children and our children's children to be gamblers? Would you want your grandchildren to be gamblers?

Let's take a good look at the ***values*** *that gambling promotes. Most people make a significant effort in their lives to live by certain codes of moral values. These values give our lives meaning and our actions have relevance to those values. The Ten Commandments, for example, are the basis for the Judeo-Christian traditions. Other religions have their own scriptures. All religious scriptures essentially say the same thing, in their broad outlines, to treat others with love and respect as you would want to be treated, embodying similar values of love, forgiveness, compassion, respect for others and praise and love for one's God. Our daily actions are an offshoot of this hierarchy of moral and worldly values. We work to support our* *families, to give them what they need, out of a sense of love and responsibility as well as a desire to follow the 'right' path, the honorable or dharmic thing to do.*

Does gambling promote these age-old values of love and respect for others? Or is gambling more concerned with self-gratification? Does it have a 'Me' orientation, a-what's-in-it-for-me-attitude? Serious gambling, the kind of gambling that leads to compulsive or pathological behavior, involves a series of short-term decisions revolving around immediate gratification and sense pleasures. Gambling extols such temporal, worldly values as materialism and undue thinking about money as a goal in life.

Gambling has such values as seeking to obtain money without earning it, 'easy money', playing odds to get rich quickly, rather than through steady work over time. It relies principally upon 'chance' rather than hard work, thought and planning to get ahead in life. Gambling exhorts its patrons to live for the thrill and excitement generated by casinos, for the 'hit' of winning, rather than for long-term achievement, or any other altruistic motives.

Often people innocently go to a casino to have fun, a night out on the town, certainly not meaning to engage in behavior that would cause damage to themselves or their loved ones. However in the excitement and thrill of casinos, we can all get 'carried away'. One thing leads to another and before we know it, we're headed down the road to serious Damage, amply greased by the evils of Temptation and Greed. Gambling appeals to our basest instincts, our desire for more and more material possessions, more and more affluence, more food, more drink. More! More! More! The casinos are only too happy to do their utmost to promote their addictive delivery systems, to get gamblers turned into addicts, to become 'hooked'.

The addictive elements in gambling promote poor choices, ill-informed life strategies, and lack of appropriate discernment in making personal decisions. In the process of these poor choices, in the pursuit of our fantasies, we waste our limited resources of time, money and energy. Casinos know this well, they cater to it, they aim their advertising at it and they build their net profits around these principles - or lack of them.

Gambling can be especially seductive and destructive to various segments of society. Many people have noted that youth, seniors, and lower income people are markedly vulnerable to gambling's excesses, and their losses can be extremely debilitating. It's harder for them to recover from gambling's damage than perhaps for other segments of society that might have more of a 'safety net' to fall back upon.

YOUTH AT RISK

Youth tend to be very impressionable and to see gambling in exactly the way it's presented by the casinos, as attractive, sophisticated, exciting, and lucrative – everything that the gambling interests want to present it as and everything that young people aspire towards. In Canada, there have been several studies seeking to determine the net impact of gambling on the young. In Canada, casinos are operated by the State. Studies there have found that youth are becoming addicted incredibly rapidly.

More teens engage in gambling than in other potentially addictive behaviors, such as alcohol or drugs, according to the International Centre for Youth Gambling at McGill University, Canada. More than half of Canadian youth, 12-17 already fall in the category of 'recreational gamblers'. Another 10 to 15 % are at risk for developing a severe problem and about 5% are already considered 'pathological' gamblers. The McGill study adds that ***young adults, 18-24, are 2 to 4 times more likely to develop a gambling problem than the general adult population.***

Youth specialist at the Problem Gambling Service at the Centre for Addiction and Mental Health in Toronto, John McDonald, says that "We're beginning to think that gambling is becoming something of ***a rite-of-passage activity for youth****." 1 Jeff Deverensky, co-director of McGill University's International Centre for Youth Gambling, says that "This is the first generation that will grow up their entire lives when gambling is not only legal, but endorsed, supported and even owned by the state." 2 What more legitimacy could it be given! What more endorsement could any product want in order to be seen and accepted as valid and satisfactory?*

Young people, who never went through the Depression and who have experienced the most affluent life-style thus far in the history of civilization, are not likely to frame this issue in either moral or survival terms. They see gambling as another acceptable form of entertainment. Yet most accepted forms of entertainment in our society don't serve to addict almost 10 % of the population leading to serious and long-term damages for many. Young people have been led to see it as Fun and not as dangerous. This fact, that they aren't aware of its potential destructive impact, is a cause for alarm and concern.

COGNITIVE KNOWLEDGE & GAMBLING

Interestingly, a study reported in the Ottawa Citizen 10/14/03 by Sarah Schmidt, noted that researchers attempted to test whether knowledge, cognitive rational information, of the very poor odds, the gambling probabilities, would result in a decrease in gambling behavior. Robert Williams, health sciences professor at the University of Lethbridge and research co-coordinator with the Alberta Gambling Research Institute, hypothesized that "if students really knew what the odds were, it would change their behaviors." So he involved students in a statistics class that extensively probed gambling probabilities, exploring what the actual odds were and whether it was realistic to expect to win. He found, surprisingly, that ***even rational knowledge of the incredibly impossible odds doesn't necessarily bring behavior change*** *for young people.*

Williams noted that "knowing the actual incident and statistical probabilities didn't change (student) behavior at all." 3 Even though "students learned that the odds are stacked against them in every game that exists, and they can't win in the long run," this knowledge didn't change their behavior! This result was unexpected for Williams, leading him, and us, to conclude that the atmosphere and the 'hype' of casinos must be extremely influential and powerful to get people to continue in behavior that they know cognitively is not only very likely but also almost certain, to be unsuccessful.

This is what we suggested in the Addiction chapter. We noted that gambling addiction appeared to cause 'temporary insanity', as it caused otherwise intelligent and cautious people to completely lose their normal powers of discernment, discrimination and judgment. Once my husband, normally a conservative, staid accountant, very circumspect and careful with money, entered a casino, as I learned later, he became as a child, vulnerable to whatever the casino advertising and his reps said. He lost his customary sharp acumen and perceptive skills. He would stand at craps tables for hours, believing that sooner or later he would come out ahead. Over time, of course, he always lost but he never lost the hope and the belief that he would and could win. He never learned until the money literally ran out, that this was a non-productive activity for him, a losing proposition.

So the addictive potential has more influence on individual behavior than one's own rational thoughts and even knowledge of gambling statistics*. The students knew intellectually and cognitively that they couldn't win, they knew that the odds were impossibly against them, that they couldn't win in the long run, yet they* ***continued*** *to indulge in gambling. They continued to play in the face of certain knowledge that winning was impossible. What can make us 'take leave of our senses', throw customary caution to the wind, and not listen to the wise words of people we know?*

Whatever can incite us to act completely differently than usual has got to be powerful. This powerful and obsessive thing, this addiction, certainly made my husband act the opposite of his usual demeanor and attitude, do things he normally never would've have done and act in ways that he would never have ordinarily engaged in. This was ***Addiction*** *and it captured him completely.*

Knowing well how powerful addiction is, the entire gambling industry attempts to entice people from an early age. In Australia, in September, 2003, a Dairy Farmers' advertising promotion involved the printing of 25 million Lotto tickets on milk cartons to encourage people allegedly to drink more milk. The Lottery super prize was an $18 million dollar drawing. The NSW Council on Problem Gambling said that this 'milk carton initiative' encouraged and promoted a culture of gambling, that it said to youth that it's okay to go and gamble - indoctrination of the young from an early age.

The Dairy Farmers promotion said that they were just targeting adults to buy more milk and that the milk was to be consumed by children. However I remember as a child sitting eating cereal with milk and being glued to the cereal and milk cartoon. So who would be reading and imbibing the indoctrination of these Lotto tickets? Children! Around ***94% of Australian adults*** *take part in Lotto, said Silver, head of the Dairy Farmers Assoc.*

The involvement of children on whatever level appears to be a particularly disturbing aspect of gambling. There have been many instances of children being neglected, being left in cars, ignored, or even an instance of a 7 year old girl raped and strangled in the bathroom of a Las Vegas casino while her father gambled. In Georgia, a mother left her 10 day old baby in a parked car. The baby died of heat dehydration in the car while the mother played video poker for 2 hours in a South Carolina casino. In Virginia, a 31 year old woman was arrested on neglect charges for leaving 6 young children in a car while she gambled with her mother at the slot machines at Caesar's riverboat Indiana casino. In Australia a 3-month-old baby girl was left in a car while her father gambled inside Adelaide's hotel-casino. 4

On 10/7/04, a Las Vegas mother wanted to gamble so badly that she left her 3 year old daughter in a grocer store's toy aisle while she gambled nearby. When store employees confronted the mother, the woman, Brenda Smith, then took her daughter to her car and left her there, for more than an hour in midday heat while she continued to play slots. The day's temperature was almost 90 degrees, noted Las Vegas Sun reporter, Jen Lawson.

Also in Las Vegas, another disturbing incident occurred. A mother and her boyfriend left their 11 and a 3 year children alone at night in their mobile home while they went out gambling. While they were out, teenagers broke into their home, and stabbed both children, killing one and paralyzing the other. Mother and boyfriend were charged with neglect and abuse, AP, 10/9/04.

The addiction of gambling leads people to disregard their own morals and values, in their mindless compulsion to gamble. What would incite people to engage in activities they normally wouldn't do, to neglect and abandon their own children? In the animal kingdom, mothers will protect their offspring even at the cost of their own lives. Humans, however, declare an activity that leads parents to neglect and abandon their children as within acceptable norms. All in a reckless pursuit after illusionary riches and sense pleasures. Where are we going and what have we descended to in the name of entertainment and fun?

These kinds of stories of children being neglected, of gambling being put before children, are never-ending and constant. They're not included here because they're sensational or dramatic. They're run-of-the-mill, often encountered stories about casinos and children which I receive on my e-mail frequently. www.abc.net.au/news/newsitems/s1070325.htm

At Foxwoods Connecticut Casino, there were at least 5 reported incidents of abandonment of children in cars in 2003. Meg Baxter, president of the United Way of Greater Portland, says she can't get out of her mind, the image of children left in cars in the parking lot at the Fox woods Casino. Local police confirm that leaving children in cars is a problem there. "This (the act of neglecting children in cars) shows that gambling is something that clearly does not build healthy communities," Baxter said in an editorial in the Sunday, Maine Today newspaper on 11/2/2003. Blethen Maine Newspapers Inc. 7 http://news.mainetoday.com/indepth.casinos/ 031102casino.shtml

CHILDREN & CASINOS - CHILDCARE FACILITIES

Some casinos encourage parents to bring children by having child-care facilities convenient and low-cost. The Mohegan Sun Casino in Connecticut has contracted with Kids Quest child care centers, Inc. to assume child care responsibility while parents gamble. The facts there indicate that many parents are not responsible about leaving and picking up their children. Parents attempt to drop off young children of 4 weeks of age even though the facility insists that children be at least 6 weeks old. To leave a six week old baby so the parent can gamble, seems neglectful and callous, although typical of a gambler. Many people don't even take a 6 week old out of the house.

As one child care worker said in an article on 2/22/03 in the Daily News by Heidi Evans, "More times than I care to remember, I've driven home from work watching the sun come up," implying that parents had simply not picked up children from the childcare facility until dawn. 8

"The saddest thing you see are the kids who get stuck here for 8 hours. We have our regulars," one employee said. "Some parents even pretend they don't know the closing time," indicating that they're often late. Even on weeknights, the Daily News found about 25 school-aged children on a recent night between the hours of 7 pm and 11 pm. At 11:10 pm, a young mother and her 10 year old son, the article continued, were the last ones out. "The boy walked behind the mother, fiddling with a toy, while his mother, slouched and defeated, with a cigarette in hand, didn't look back. The two shuffled past a bar, then walked toward a darkened parking lot and a desolate winter's night." 8

What kind of nurturing is this mother giving her son? What kind of real interest is she showing in him? We're putting Temptation in parents' hands, and giving them the message that this kind of behavior is acceptable. What kind of message are we giving children that this kind of parental behavior is acceptable? What kind of quality of life are we offering our next generation?

Kids Quest child care centers are located in 20 casinos nationwide and are intended to attract high-rolling parents, increase casino profits, and create the next generation of gamblers according to a Daily News article. These children "will return when they are adults with their children in tow. It becomes an intergenerational marketing ploy of tremendous success," said Dr. Durand Jacobs, a psychiatry professor at California's Loma Linda University Medical School. 8

*What kind of thinking plots '**intergenerational marketing ploys**' that take their aim at addicting the next generation, making addicts of children. What values and thinking could involve themselves in such negative and amoral attempts to undermine people? We talk about the lowest in society as being the drug pushers, selling cocaine to children, but these kind of corporate marketing techniques would seem to rival the sleaziness of drug pushers.*

These are gambling pushers. People who deliberately hope that installing childcare will lead to those children becoming future gamblers. They hope that installing kiddie casinos in casinos will familiarize and attract the current generation of children in order for them to become future gamblers. This kind of thinking leads me to believe that the only value that corporate gambling interests hold dear is MONEY.

Kids Quest child care President, Susan Dunkley, responded saying that "We are a sophisticated child-care company that understands the casino business, and realizes that we can drive up revenues and have people come to the casino who are a higher-quality gamer." So that's a pretty blatant statement about Kids Quest being in business to 'drive up revenues' and entice 'higher-quality gamers.' What about the children? Again it's all about MONEY. 8 http://www.nydailynews.com/news/story/61733p-57671c.html

Kids Quest notes that having a 'kiddie casino' will "drive more than $2 Million in additional gaming revenue to its host property every year. 80 % of our customers indicated they would not be able to visit the casinos without a Kids Quest facility." Then maybe they shouldn't be there. Kids Quest officials say the company's 20 locations had about 700,000 visits of children in 2002. Money, money, money is driving the expansion of child care facilities at casinos. Is this American culture, leaving children in child-care so parents can gamble?

- *The numbers of people under 18 years of age gambling has also increased. "In the past year, about 14 million American adolescents gambled, and about 2 million of those have serious gambling-related problems, "said Durand Jacobs, one of the country's leading experts of youth gambling. 9*

- *In New York, a recent Buffalo News article, 7/02, cited a study showing that 86% of the state's teens have gambled at least once in their lives and 75% have done so within the past year. "Teen problem gamblers are more likely to use alcohol, tobacco and marijuana and to have gotten into trouble as a result." 10 Renee C. Wert, director of the Gambling Recovery Program at Jewish Family Service said that "Kids have been exposed to gambling like no generation in the past. It has been more socially acceptable and...there are more opportunities available." 11*

Underage gambling by school children and the state's possible role in fostering it, continues to be another concern in the community bordering Connecticut's 2 major casinos. Research that came out recently at Monroe's Masuk High School revealed that 16 % of high school students surveyed said they'd gambled at least once during the preceding month. The research also found that 6 % of middle and high-school students in Monroe said they gambled daily, twice the rate found 2 years ago. 12

When students see adults in large numbers gambling and appearing as though they are having a great time, then of course they are going to want to indulge also. The activity now has legitimacy and attraction. Whatever adults do, children see and want to emulate, especially if it at all looks like it might be fun. This is called modeling. That's why experts stress that adults set high behavioral standards since those standards will be copied by impressionable young people. Do we really want our young people to think that gambling is an activity that should be copied and indulged in? Is this the highest and the best we can demonstrate for our young people—an activity of questionable moral value and certainly guaranteed to ensure negative financial results.

The article, 12/14/03 noted that Monroe, Connecticut, where this data came from, is a town where a gambling awareness group, Gambling Awareness of Monroe Through Education Our Students, has operated for several years. 4 % of students gamblers in Monroe had 'some awareness' of the problem themselves, ***4 %*** *said they had a 'serious problem', and* ***6 % said gambling was an issue*** *for them. As the article concluded, "Lottery administrators and other state officials ought to exercise more care in helping to ensure that their desires for gaming revenue are not undermining the public good." 12 http://pokermag.com/managearticle.asp?C=150 &A=6400.*

This increase in young people in Connecticut indulging in an activity with many negative connotations results from only 2 casinos! What happens in the situation of California with more Indian casinos than any other state, and with 104 federally recognized Indian tribes. San Diego County already has 9 casinos which are being built into deluxe resorts. Five more tribes are attempting to get casinos also. Thunder Valley near Sacramento is owned by the Auburn tribe and is about to build 5 mega-resorts. It's campaign promotion, 'Why Vegas?', implying that they will be bigger and better than Las Vegas, bodes ill for area people.

Rev. Tom Grey*, spokesman for the* ***National Coalition Against Legalized Gambling****, is also concerned about addiction levels among our nation's young people. He said students are "twice as likely to be addicted to gambling as adults – anywhere from 8 to 14 % of our youth are showing pathological and problem gambling symptoms". 13 Grey added that he finds the fact that gambling is being billed as entertainment, like shopping and the movies, with no warnings or awareness of the very addictive nature of the activity to be a deceptive aspect of the whole gambling culture*

Harvard Medical School researchers reviewed 9 studies of 7,700 young people, ages 15-20 years old in the U.S. and Canada. They found ***9.9 - 14.2 % already displayed gambling problems*** *and* ***4.4 - 7.4 % met the diagnostic criteria for 'pathological gambling'.*** *These figures are even greater than those reported among adults. We need to take this research seriously reaching out to teens and adults to show them that work, discipline and service are the 'ways to a meaningful and rewarding life, not dumb luck," as noted Andrew Weaver, and Christopher G. Ellison for the Sightings Bulletin of the University of Chicago Divinity School. sightings-admin@listhost.uchicago. edu.14*

One student noted that 'Just about everyone (on campus) plays poker.' 15 A senior finance major at the University of Georgia told Family News in Focus, "Different organizations on campus have been organizing big poker tournaments for charities," noted Stuart Shepard, correspondent for Family Focus. What kind of public morals are we promoting in this country? Where are we going with this whole gambling craze? And where will it stop? Certainly not in California, where casinos are fast proliferating.

South Australia is also increasingly concerned about the numbers of young people who gamble on a frequent basis as well as the number of ***senior citizens who ruin themselves financially*** *because of gambling. Recent research there has revealed that "9,000 high-school students are gambling at least once a week...and one in six of the state's students are playing games such as Keno and buying 'scratchie' tickets." Adelaide University psychologist, Dr. Paul Delfabbro, told the Sunday Mail on 3/21/04 that "****There are more problem gamblers among adolescents than adults,"*** *based on a survey of more than 500 upper-school students. "Some young people have blown their savings on gambling," MP Nick Xenophon has said. 16*

The Education Department in South Australia is spending $800,000 on a 4-year gambling education and awareness program called 'Dicey Dealings'. "Most surveys of problem gamblers indicate that their gambling problems started when they were 15 or 16," Dr. Delfabbro said. "There is strong evidence to suggest that those who gamble intensively as adolescents are more likely to go on and become problem gamblers." 17

Education Department gambling policy and program officer, Loris Glass, said that "thousands of students" were at risk of developing gambling problems. The country's taxpayers are paying for this $800,000 dollar gambling awareness program, yet the casinos are the ones raking in the substantial profits. Another example of taxpayer dollars for social programs. Hardly a bargain for the State, for the individual, or for families.

SENIORS AT RISK

In terms of older adults, 5 to 10 % of older adults who gamble are problem pathological gamblers, said Cynthia Abrams, director of the Drugs and Other Addictions Program of the United Methodist Church. 18 Older adults are especially at risk. When they go through their money, when they blow their fortunes, then they have no where to turn. Other family members are often deceased, so their support network is not as widespread as in the case of the younger person who might still have living relatives. Older citizens are unable to return to jobs, which makes building up their fortunes again impossible.

Gambling away money that's been saved over many years further complicates the depression that many seniors feel. Often seniors are perhaps not as sophisticated as younger people not having been exposed to computers, slot machines, and other video game technology, such as Nintendo, for their whole lives. I thought society was about helping seniors, easing their burdens, improving their quality of life. Allowing them to gamble away their hard-earned money hardly constitutes help.

Just as money is driving the expansion of facilities with children in mind, so is money driving the expansion of facilities with Senior citizens in mind. Seniors often view gambling as an entertaining way to spend some of their extra time, to socialize a little, and generally enjoy themselves.

However what can start out innocently enough, can soon turn into a nightmare. It certainly did so for Floridian senior citizen, Mary Cano.

At first the 71 year old widow used to just stop by the Indian casino on the way home. She didn't have a lot to do and it seemed like fun. The trouble was she kept gambling long after she knew she should stop. Then she lost 'thousands and thousands of dollars. She lost her house. She had to move in with a friend, until she finally went to Gamblers Anonymous and was finally able to get her addiction under control.

At 71 years old, she hardly has a chance to recoup her fortune, to buy another house, to regain her lost money. Now she lives from hand to mouth, worrying about whether there will be enough left at the end of the month. She thought this would be a time in her life when financial worries would be over. It would've been, except for gambling...19

Officials of the Florida Council on Compulsive Gambling, soon began hearing about the down side of gambling for seniors soon after it was started in 1988. "We were increasingly hearing about seniors maxing out their credit cards. We started to see how deep this problem was running for older adults," said council Executive Director Pat Fowler, in an article in the Sun-Sentinel by Diane C. Lade, on 3/20/04. 20

***A 2003 study commissioned by the Florida Council surveyed 1,260 Floridians, 55 or older. It found that 1 out of every 20 seniors has a serious problem with gambling**. This computes to 5% of the population, i.e. seniors. The study, by Gemini Research of Massachusetts, estimated that as many as 52,000 Florida seniors had gambling problems and as many as 205,000 were at risk. "At their age, they have little hope of recovering from their financial loses," said Fowler. Some seniors, destitute and humiliated, have committed suicide. The survey also found that men who had served in the military were especially vulnerable. 42 % of seniors who were* *veterans said they were weekly gamblers, as compared with 25 % of seniors overall. Gambling is legal on military posts and many soldiers are first initiated into gambling there. 21*

The casinos are well aware of the senior citizen influx and in fact rely on this group for mid-week business. In an effort to increase it, casinos cater to the elderly in various ways. Recently the casinos allowed flu vaccination clinics to be held there. In ***Wisconsin****, MetaStar, the company overseeing the state's health care programs, initiated the "Shot and a Slot' program. Other than churches, "Casinos are one of the most popular places for seniors to congregate," Solber, a health specialist at MetaStar said in an article by Matthew J. Malone, on 10/30/03. 22*

However allowing flu shots in casinos also makes seniors especially susceptible to becoming addicted, which is also hazardous to their health. A recent Roper ASW marketing survey of 2,000 Americans found that 57 % of gamblers are older than 50 years old. Detroit casinos are well-stocked with wheelchairs and scooters for those seniors with difficulty getting around. MGM Grand has 5 times more handicapped spots than required by law.

> *Seniors have 2 attributes that casinos find attractive: disposable income and time. 23.–Michael Pollock, publisher, Gaming Industry Observer newsletter.*

Senior citizens are an especially desirable group of people that the gambling industry, especially casinos, are interested in. A spokesman for ***Foxwoods Casino noted that 80 % of the 1.3 Million people visiting the casino annually by bus are seniors.*** *If the average senior spent $50 dollars in each visit, an expected outlay, that would amount to $52 Million per year at Foxwoods alone. Not a bad take on one group of people alone. These figures don't include seniors visiting by car.*

Gambling is a problem for some senior citizens according to the director of state-run Problem Gambling Services, Middletown, Connecticut. "Casinos typically are busier on the day of the month after people's check come in. I'm concerned that people on fixed incomes may be spending more than they can afford," said Chris Armentero. At ***(Mohegan Sun and Foxwoods), 15% of patrons meet the criteria for gambling addicts****. It's safe to say that between 10 and 15% of seniors are problem gamblers." 23*

These are serious allegations regarding the way senior citizens, people on fixed incomes with not a lot of flexibility, spend their money, their disposable income. Armentero also noted that the perceived innocuous bus trips that seniors take to gambling sites, probably include some problem gamblers but that no one knows about them. "On a bus trip of 50 people, there may be 4 or 5 with significant problems. Probably the folks who organize these trips don't have a clue that there are people in trouble," he added. 23 Armentero's figures further validate the 10 % estimated figures.

"These pensioners sell everything but the television and the bed," Charles Munger said, indicating the seriousness of the addiction and the way the gambling addiction leads senior citizens to act in foolish ways. 24 The Bristol Press, 4/26/04, Adam Wittenberg, The Herald Press

Another study by Wayne State University, also corroborated that almost 10% of seniors could be at risk of developing a gambling problem, as reported by Ankur Dholakia, in The Detroit News on 10/15/03. 25 http://www.detnews.com/2003/business/0310/15/b01-298338.htm These are serious concerns, that a group of citizens, already at risk for many serious illnesses and social difficulties, and the recipient of numerous and costly government social programs, should be faced with yet another challenge. This new activity, licensed by the government, has the potential to cause them to do significant damage to themselves and others. The difficulties or potential dangers in the activity is clouded over by statements of acceptability by government and community leaders and a shared understanding by all that the activity is F-U-N and Entertainment.

So we see that Youth and Seniors are both adversely affected by gambling and show tendencies toward indulging in this activity to excess, to the point that it's detrimental to themselves and others. Gambling can be extremely seductive, appearing to be fun and games when in fact it can be extremely damaging. Gambling sells many things, none of them beneficial or in the public interest.

See the attached cartoon and overview of The Elderly as Victims of Gambling supplied by the ***Missouri CasinoWatch!*** *This article, with every statement backed up by data on their website, conveys the heart-breaking truth of gambling and the elderly. Yes, some elderly will gamble away life-savings, some will lose their houses, some will commit suicide. They are reluctant to seek help, and they cannot get a job or start over. Casinos cater to elderly and they make money off the very people who can least afford it. As the article concludes,*

To create gambling addicts in order to raise state funds is really unethical." Valerie C. Lorenz, Compulsive Gambling Center, Inc., Maryland. 26

SEXUALITY SELLS

*Promoters of Atlantic City as a destination resort, used to refer to it as '**American's Favorite Playground'.** They have a new slogan these days, "**Atlantic City - Always Turned On**." This new slogan first unveiled on October 10, 2003, is not quite as innocuous as the former, having obvious connotations of drugs and/or sex. The executive director of the Atlantic City Convention and Visitors Authority, Jeffrey Vassar, said that tourism wanted to emphasize a 24-hour resort that is 'high voltage', 'a place to escape to'. This saucy image is the result of a 9 month long marketing research campaign. Can you imagine high-priced public relations people wracking their brains for 9 months to come up with this? The tourism agency in Atlantic City is spending a $500,000 public-relations effort to attract even more people who will lose money.*

*Las Vegas has a slogan with even more immoral connotations, **'What Happens Here, Stays Here'.** What blatant sexual intimations, what an attitude of letting all morality and sense of discrimination fly out the window...Concurrent with its new slogan is the latest hit show in Las Vegas, entitled "Zumanity". This show opened Fall, 2003, for an unlimited run, according to an article 'Cirque Du Soleil Bares All in New Vegas Erotic Show, by Reuters, on 9/29/03. http:://www.nytimes.com/reuters/arts/entertainment-stage-cirquedusoleil.html.*

In Zumanity, the master of ceremonies is a 'drag queen cabaret singer', hardly a relevant role model for anyone, who croons in the beginning of the show, 'Sex is beautiful'. The male dancers in the show indulge in long, lingering kisses, while a nearly nude female trapeze artist supposedly groans with sexual pleasure. Nubile women caress each other as they swim in a huge, see-through fish bowl. How offensive! Hardly something I would be interested in nor even have my grown children see.

Sex and business, business and sex, have always swum together, synchronized so-to-speak, in Las Vegas, 'Sin City', with each reinforcing the other. In this show, billed as another side of Cirque du Soleil, most of the performers wear little but G-strings. Topless swimming pools at Mandalay Bay and Caesars Palace are available for adults-only. Another new erotic show at MGM Grand is named 'the art of the nude' called 'La Femme'. So debauchery and decadence are getting top billing in Las Vegas and are certainly not hard to find.

These are not new issues. The trend in Atlantic City also seems to be to push the envelope in terms of sexual exposure, to offer more and more 'skin' exposed. In October, 2003, the new Borgata Hotel Casino & Spa announced they would throw an X-rated 'Pimp'n'Ho Halloween Party' for the public promising 'flesh and fantasy'. 'The Double X-rated party you've been waiting for', noted the hype, "Dress as a pimp, ho, or anything else in between". State gaming regulations specifically prohibit casino entertainment that includes actual or simulated sex acts and the exposure of private anatomical areas. The Borgata Casino would seem to be skirting the issue closely in their marketing enticements, noted Joe Weinert in the Atlantic City Business News magazine. 27

As if that wasn't enough, two months later in December, 2003, the Borgata published a calendar called "Babes of Borgata" with 8 of the casino's employees portrayed almost nude in an 11 by 14 inch glossy full-color 2004 calendar. The $15 dollar calendar includes both male and female workers. It's a way to market the Borgata, according to casino spokesman, Michael Facenda, in an article by the Associated Press. The Borgata also is one of the first hotels to have built-for-two shower stalls.

So gambling promotes the commercialization and opportunistic use of sexuality in our society. It encourages people to obsess about get-rich quick schemes, to live for the thrill of physical sensations. It's associated with crime and with personal tragedies. It suggests to people that their own lives are not exciting enough and that in order to have fun, people need to indulge in questionable activities such as going to sexually suggestive shows. This is what gambling promotes and the fall-out from it unfolds in individual tragedies. Thousands and thousands of individual tragedies. These are the values associated with gambling and which it promotes. Would that be our intention and our goal for our families, for ourselves, for our society?

The activities often associated with gambling, including the act of leaving children in cars while adults gamble, the sexual innuendoes in advertisements inviting all to forget all their morals, the specter of senior citizens losing homes to foreclosure because they're lost all their money at casinos, all are offensive, highly questionable, and not worthy of 'America the Brave.' There are countless stories on a daily basis of people forgetting or ignoring their higher ideals, their responsibilities, even their basic humanity, in an effort to 'hit it BIG', and to win.

What is our government thinking when they promote gambling as an acceptable activity? Do our legislators and governors want to see the budget balanced at the cost of innocent children, of gullible senior citizens, and of ignorant workers looking for a thrill? Do we really want to sell America as the home of gambling and the sex addict or as the home of responsible, sincere, hard-working citizens concerned with the plight of the world's poor. As the Buddhists say, no one can be happy until everyone is happy. I believe that we can't turn our back on people in the name of profits, we can't ignore their suffering in the name of money and getting rich.

We have to be very conscious of what we're promoting because the fruits of it will certainly come back and hit us in the head in the next 20 years. If we've built up, if we've been good stewards of what we have, then the future will look good. However these values of gambling, money, sex, profits, materialism are hardly what I would want for my children or for society. If we've sold our souls in the service of the dollar, then I'm not sure what the future will look like. Just because some casinos marketing strategy glamorizes Atlantic City or Las Vegas, or just because gambling is accepted as an acceptable activity, doesn't make it so. These cities are modern-day Sodom and Gomorrah's and serve to bring everyone down with them. If we approve of these activities and the values they hold implicit, we had better not go there or else we, too, may be 'turned to stone,' and lose all we hold dear.

****

SOCIAL COSTS—DOLLARS & CENTS!

*The social costs are equally horrific in terms of dollars and cents. A recent book by Earl L. Grinols, an Illinois economist, entitled Gambling in America: Costs and Benefits, Cambridge University Press, noted that the **costs of pathological and problem gambling has begun to equal nearly half the annual costs of drug abuse in the U.S.** 27 This is in only 25 years since gambling has begun to proliferate in America. Grinols writes that the social costs such as increased crime, lost work time, bankruptcies and financial hardships faced by the families of gambling addicts has reached epidemic proportions, costing the economy almost **$54 Billion dollars annually**. This compares with an estimated $110 Billion dollars cost of drug abuse, according to the U.S. Government Accounting Office. 28*

*Casino gambling causes almost **$289** dollars in social costs for every **$46** of economic benefit, according to Grinols.*

> *In 2003, society's cost of each additional pathological gambler was $10,330, based on studies in the mid-1990s. The cost of an additional problem gambler is $2,945.*
>
> *The costs of problem and pathological gambling are comparable to the value of the lost output of an **additional recession in the economy every 4 years**. 29*

Grinols, former senior economic advisor to President Reagan, felt there is "a great unfulfilled need for an economist to study the costs and benefits of casinos in society and to identify which side of the ledger is predominant." 30

Experts estimate that there are between 5 and 10 Million problem gamblers in the U.S. according to Sightings, 12/18/03, Marty Center at the University Of Chic. Divinity School, 31 Gambling is the fastest growing addiction in the U.S. In 1988 only 2 states had large-scale casino gambling. Now 27 states have casinos, 37 states operate a lottery, and some type of gambling occurs in 48 states. Advertisements for online gambling sites appear daily and in great abundance on the Internet.

Lottery sales, a dead end for the adults who play it, have increased in recent years. Looking at the figures of one state, for example, West Virginia, in 2003, total Lottery sales reached more than $1 Billion dollars, up 28 % from 2002. The state netted $411 Million dollars. Lottery players spent the equivalent of $600 for every man, woman, and child in W. Virginia, ranking the state the 4th highest in per capita lottery sales. Video lottery sales in bars which were legalized 2 years ago as well as more machines at the state's 4 racetracks, accounted for the entire increase of more than $233 million from last year.

Now most people are aware that West Virginia has a lower economic population. From what we've learned, that the poor are more likely to play lotteries, and then are more likely to be significantly impacted by the money lost, we can understand why West Virginians play the lottery, the-dollar-and-the-dream-mentality. Yet does this help the state's economy overall? No! Remember as economist, Paul Samuelson said, this is not new, it's just recycled money. No new product, no new money. Just another way for the state to get revenue at the expense of its citizens. Whether it's lottery tickets or slot machines, both behaviors are addictive and ultimately self-defeating. 32

According to evidence cited by Grinols, gambling causes addictive and destructive behavior similar to the damage of alcohol or drugs. About 10 % of the population gambles regularly and accounts for up to 80 % of the wagers in casino enterprises. Industry's profits are based on a relatively small number of addicted gamblers, who still number in the hundreds of thousands, who run up huge costs for themselves, families and society.

Recently a New Mexico casino reached the depths of corporate degenerate behavior in a TV advertisement until public criticism caused the casino to withdraw the ads. The TV advertisements, 30 second commercials by Isleta Casino located on the south edge of Albuquerque, New Mexico, suggested that people with holiday debts head to the casino in an effort to make money! The ad read: "so the holidays have passed and those credit card bills just keep piling up, and there seems to be no relief in sight? How will you pay those bills? Well, Isleta Casino Resort comes to your rescue!" The ad concludes by showing a woman smiling and laughing as someone fans a stack of cash into her outstretched palm.

This is fraud and deceit. It's suggesting that people, who already have problems paying their bills, indulge in further irresponsible behavior, that the casino knows full well is liable to put them even more in debt, behavior liable to addict them, which will then bring ruin upon themselves and their families. It's like encouraging someone who's standing on the top of a building, wondering whether to jump, to go ahead and do it, to finish the job!

Guy Clark, executive director of the New Mexico Coalition Against Gambling, called the ad 'outrageous'. He said that it leaves the distinct impression that people can make money by gambling. "You may owe (bills) for Christmas, but if you stay there (in the casino) long enough, you may lose your house," he said. Even the acting marketing manager of another local casino, the Sandia Casino, criticized the ad saying "It crosses the line between promoting responsible gaming and reckless gaming." 33

About 3 weeks later, the casino publicly apologized following criticism, saying that they did not mean to entice compulsive gamblers and that the ads were in error. But that advertisement, with its mentality of trying to tempt people already overburdened, came out of that casino's management. It didn't spring out of thin air. That's the way they think. It's the bottom line they're concerned with. The ad shouldn't have appeared at all. Between the time that the ads ran on radio and they were pulled and later publicly repudiated, what if some people did go along with that logic of winning money to pay bills at home. What if some people did act on the suggestion in the advertisement and go to the casino and lose, of course, thus getting further in debt. Not everyone in society is equally intelligent in all areas and some could be hoodwinked by this deceitful idea. 34 www.gazettetimes.com/articles/ 2004/03/27/news/the_ west/satwst04.txt

The ad encouraged people to get further into debt which would lead them to bankruptcy and/or crime in an effort to make ends meet. I could see people saying to themselves, 'Yes, I feel lucky today, I'm going there to make some of the money I need to pay bills.' Then as we've learned, the odds are such that the person will lose all their remaining money and get really in trouble. Further evidence of casinos encouraging people to engage in foolhardy and reckless behavior just so the casinos can make profits. Again - a question of MONEY!

Social costs are all about infrastructure costs that wouldn't be there without gambling. The extra costs of police and fire departments are a prime example. In Detroit, Michigan, they found this out recently. In Detroit, money collected from the casinos is ***insufficient to pay for the additional costs of Police and Fire and emergency medical gaming-related services.*** *The city's 3 casinos, Motor City, Greektown, and MGM Grand casinos pay $14 Million for municipal services as part of the contract with the city of Detroit. This year, 2004, there has been a gap between what the departments spend and what the casinos give. The gap, $1.26 Million, is due to rising costs, such as pay raises and fringe benefits. Next year's budget, 2004-5, will have an even greater gap of $2.8 Million, according to Detroit's budget director, Roger Short. 35*

This is a prime example of the definition of Social Costs. Even though casinos contribute a lot of money to defray the costs of the city's additional expenses, it's still insufficient to actually cover those expenses. And this is not even beginning to tally up other infrastructure costs such as Courts, Public Assistance, lost business income, etc. The Detroit News, May 2, Natalie Moore2004. 36

In Canada, a police department investigation was an offshoot of another investigation by the Royal Canadian Mounted Police into gambling and organized crime, where top mob bosses control the gambling trade and other rackets in Ontario as well as other places. This is the first major corruption probe for the Toronto Police Department's in its 47-year history and was precipitated by gambling. Gambling was the catalyst. Without gambling, would it have happened? 37

Gambling places many people at risk. If gambling hadn't been available, perhaps the officers would've gotten into trouble another way, but that's not relevant. The fact is, that the police officers 'fell from Grace' by means and because of the availability and accessibility of gambling. Another example of good people, with no previous involvement in illegal activities brought down by gambling and its associated by-products. Gambling brings problems. The more accessible gambling is, the more frequently people indulge in gambling, the more problems it brings. It opens the door to crime, to misfortune, to disease, and bids these demons welcome.

Gambling also contributes to physical health problems of all kinds. Gambling is stressful when people lose, and people lose all the time. Debt leads to stress, lots of stress. Actually if someone has to have a heart attack, a casino floor is a good place to have it as the casinos are equipped with state-of-the-art-equipment and skilled technicians. It's bad publicity to have people die on the casino floor. Debt, whether from gambling or any other source, can be a very negative force in people's lives. New research on the effects of debt just published in Great Britain on 5/32004, show that debt leads to both physical and emotional stress. That stress then leads to physical illness and emotional disorders. "Almost half a million people...have developed drinking problems and around 250,000 people have turned to gambling as a solution to their ongoing financial troubles," said research commissioned by Debt Free Direct. 38

Debt can lead to depression, panic attacks, the deterioration of relationships with partners and close friends and family. People who deny the reality of their own situation, who ignore the fact of large debt, see that the problem will surface in other ways such as mental or physical illness. "Those who bury their heads in the sand...find their problems manifested into physical and mental trauma," said the chief executive of Debt Free Direct, an independent company providing advice to people with debt problems.

The fact that my husband, Alan, had a heart attack while the family was in the throes of huge debt involving over a million dollars, I feel was directly attributable to his incredible stress and worry. Mind and body are interconnecting entitles, each affecting and being affected by the other. If we want to be in good physical health, capable of exploring our highest potential and exercising our strength and power, we can't be saddled with mental concerns and anxiety over how we're going to pay the mortgage, or other survival issues.

It's all part of an inter-related system with gambling being the catalyst and subsequently leading to a host of ongoing issues and problems in the life of the individual. There's no free lunch. As we burn the candle at both ends, as we throw our money away in the mindless pursuit of pleasure and more, free money, we'll experience the results of such misguided actions on many fronts in a variety of disabling occurrences. 39 www.belfasttelegraph.co.uk/news/story.jsp?story= 517113

Activities creating more social harm than good, according to Professor Grinois, "need to be regulated, monitored, and (sometimes) banned to achieve great social well-being. *The need for public intervention occurs precisely when the costs are borne by one agent or group and the benefits by another." This certainly appears to be the case with gambling with the industry reaping gigantic profits, the government reaping some revenue, and the people paying for all this out of their own pockets. 31*

As the amounts of money become increasingly large, and people take 'risks', and lose, they begin to see 'that all that glitters is not gold.' As they catch up with the truth, it can be a bit overwhelming. Anyone can become despondent as the truth sets in and they comprehend their time and money losses and how gambling has taken them, chewed them up and then spit them out, so-to-speak. The biggest social cost is suicide and its been occurring increasingly according to many reports because of gambling's excesses.

SUICIDES

When people, gamblers, have paid for casino profits out of their own pockets for several years, and the debt and stress begin to catch up, when people begin to see the holes in their denial and rationalization schemes, then sometimes the overwhelming aspects of the situation begin to take their toll. Gamblers tend to burn the candle at both ends, to play fast, stay up all night, have plenty of drama in their lives, plenty of places for false hopes and dreams to take root and multiply like weeds. Once the honeymoon is over, the summer ends, the cold winter sets in and our gamblers begin to realize the awful truth of where they're at. They have no money left, few real friends, incredible debt, and a history of double dealing.

At this point, the final phase, gamblers get desperate. They're beginning to see the writing on the wall and they're at some risk. They're not thinking about anything but winning. Their thoughts are obsessed with gambling, with the bills they can't pay, with the people they can't face or share their problems with, and with the damage they're beginning to finally realize that they've done.

As the sky begins to open, accidents of various kinds, including car accidents, become common. Casinos are well aware of this. Bally's Park Place Casino in Atlantic City used to have a few deluxe rooms with outdoor balconies. Around 1999 they locked the sliding glass doors on the balconies and never unlocked them. Even VIP's couldn't get their reps to unlock the doors. It's not good for business to have people commit suicide in their hotels. In this final desperation phase:

***One out of every 5 compulsive gamblers attempts suicide**. 40*

as Robert Custer notes in his book, When Luck Runs Out. This is a very high cost.

So much for 'just a little Entertainment.' Gambling is not the entertainment business. It's more like Russian roulette. Gambling is to entertainment as Russian roulette is to games. Gambling is certainly not entertainment and Russian roulette is no game.

Suicide is considered by many to be one of the most terrible 'social ills' that there is. Not only does it kill the person, leaving family, friends, and businesses, to pick up the pieces, but it also leaves the people left behind feeling guilty, debilitated, overwhelmed and in shock for years. The Biblical phrase about 'the sins of the fathers being visited upon the sons'...is certainly true in this instance. Doubly true for suicide.

Suicide is not only a death, a loss, but it's a loss with a kicker. It says that life was too overwhelming to continue and that the pain the person felt was more significant than their role as someone's father, husband, sister, brother. It says that their pain was greater than the person's love for the survivor. What does this say to the survivors? The victims become even more victimized.

A study by sociology professor at the Univ. of California, San Diego, David Phillips, compared suicide statistics nationwide. He traced significantly higher numbers of suicides in cities with casinos than in those without casinos. In a study, "Suicide and Life-threatening Behavior," in the 12/03 American Assoc. of Suicidology Journal, he wrote,

> *It's not a coincidence that Las Vegas, the... gambling center in the U.S., displays the highest levels of suicide in the nation. 41*

He noted that what convinced him was evidence that suicides increased significantly in Atlantic City in the first few years after gambling was legalized. Before casinos opened in 1978, the number of Atlantic City suicides was no higher than other New Jersey counties. After gambling was legalized, the numbers significantly increased.

A Las Vegas psychologist who works with problem gamblers, Robert Hunter, said that the study's results didn't surprise him:

> *There is a percentage of people who can't handle gambling. Those are the people who end up killing themselves. It's no secret...people with serious gambling problems attempt suicide.*
>
> *Our findings raise the possibility that the recent expansion of legalized gambling and the consequent increase in gambling settings may be accompanied by an increase in U.S. suicides... 42*

What a scary idea, that we have legalized in our society, an activity that causes people to engage in it to excess and end up killing themselves. An activity that is so hazardous for some that they drive themselves to desperation and to the thought, and indeed, the action, of killing themselves. Government has licensed such a destructive activity? 5% of the adult population addicted to something is not such a small number that we can cavalierly ignore the needs of such a group.

If African-Americans constituted a minority of 5% of society, instead of 25%, could we then ignore them as a group too? Why do we do research and treat such apparently minor illnesses as schizophrenia, if only a small percentage of the population suffer from it? Why not allow people to imbibe cocaine, as long as only a few do it. These ideas are blatantly ridiculous and hideously uncaring yet they're comparable to statements that we can ignore the needs of the 'small percentage' of people who become addicted. This small percentage is not small at all, especially if you or a loved one is part of that minority.

Suicide is one of the 'social problems' that come with gambling. This 'social problem' is what many politicians who favor gambling to fill state coffers, are quick to dismiss as insignificant, or not big enough to concern themselves with. But the families of the people who commit suicide don't dismiss it as 'insignificant.'

Recently the director of the ***Wisconsin State Lottery*** *was found in a motel room, having committed suicide, during an investigation into the practices of the state lottery. What a tragic end for a person and for his family. He had worked all his life in responsible position in state government. Perhaps if gambling wasn't available, this wouldn't have happened.*

> *The wife of a former compulsive gambler, Clarence Burdett, knows about the Social Costs. She should, she's lived them. Mrs. Drake, widow of Clarence Burdett, told about her husband in an article in the Capitol Gazette on 3/30/04. She said she remembered that her husband, Clarence Burdett, a retired Army sergeant major, was awarded 2 Purple Hearts during service in the Korean and Vietnamese wars.*
>
> *That was before he returned from military service in l995 and became involved in gambling. The state legalized gambling in l995. At the end of his life, after a career oj successful military service, he ended up spending his entire life's saving on gambling. He also had nearly $300,000 in gambling debts. "He went into depression as the addiction took over," said his wife.*
> *Then he got out of bed one morning at 5:30 am, made coffee, started up the cars in the garage, sat in his wife's car and waited for the carbon monoxide fumes to flood his lungs.*
>
> *"I worry about fathers, husbands, women...about little children," she said. She should know. Because oj gambling, she's been to Hell and back and ended up a widow. Is this worth balancing the state's budgets? 43*
> *http://www.capitalonline.com/cgi-bin/read/2004/0330-42/Gov*

Is her husband's life worth the revenue the state gets from the casinos for balancing the budget? If gambling had not been made available, accessible, convenient, this tragedy might well not have happened. Burdett didn't have problems that he couldn't handle in his life, he'd handled his life honorably, including career, marriage, military honors – until gambling came along. The state opened the door to his addiction by licensing gambling establishments, licensing the way for people to ruin themselves. It might have happened anyway, this person's depression might have overwhelmed him because of other issues as well, but then, at least, it wouldn't have happened from anything the State did. Tragedies happen all the time but we don't have to help them along.

Dr. Renee C. Wert, Gambling Recovery Program, a counseling agency in ***Buffalo, New York****, said "We have people with marks still on their necks from rope burns from where they tried to hang themselves." Among the clients at Jewish Family Service in Buffalo, another local counseling agency, 60 % have considered suicide and 20 % have actually tried it, according to News 4 investigative reporter, Luke Moretti on 2/5/04. 44*

In ***Ontario, Canada,*** *coroners are now for the first time tracking suicides linked to gambling. Niagara Regional coroner, Dr. Christopher Rathwell, said, "Certainly there's been enough of an evolution of this problem and concern that...stimulated us to gather proper statistics." 45*

On a personal level, the tragedies are full of heartache, human misery and suffering. One family in Canada knows this well. This mother mourns her son's gambling involvement. I'm sure she wonders why she gave birth and raised him, only to have him die at the hands of gambling.

> *Phyllis Vineberg, mother of Trevor Vineberg, talked about her son, Trevor, who gambled away hundreds of thousands of dollars and then committed suicide. She blames the government for feeding his gambling addiction. "He killed himself in the garage of our home."*
> *As Trevor Vineberg's mother said, "You're asking for tragedy, (with gambling) and believe me, there's no doubt that there'll be tragedy." 46*

Trevor's mother didn't need studies to show her the truth. She knows from her own experience. These are the social costs involved with gambling. I can't think of any amount of money worth people's lives.

- *In* ***Great Britain*** *recently, a man attempted to have controls placed on credit cards due to his father's death. His father, a gambler, had accumulated extensive credit card debt. This occurs frequently due to the credit card companies giving large lines of credit to a people who essentially have no money. After he gambled away all of the credit card loans, he had no money to repay and ended up killing himself. Jonathan*

Opalka, the gambler's son, as reported in The Guardian, a British newspaper, said it was a disgrace that his father was given up to 19 different credit cards with limits of up to 6,000. pounds each. The father hung himself in January, 2004. The family is also at risk of losing their home. Imagine the hell that this family has gone through...

- *Another incident in Great Britain recently led to more tragedy associated with gambling. On 9/21//03, a 19 year old compulsive gambler hung himself and was found by his younger brother, Christopher. He was in debt and his gambling had started to threaten his relationship with his girlfriend. His financial problems had become so serious that his Mother had tried to help him with his debts. I wonder why a 19 year old would even be allowed to gamble.*

- *In 1998, a Milwaukee man, Bob Hafemann, fatally shot himself after falling deeply into gambling related debt. His sister, Rhonda Hatefi, said her brother enjoyed life as a $45,000 a year steelworker before he became addicted to the Oregon lottery's video poker games, VLTs, electronic gambling. He lost his life's savings and then he took his life. Friends and family of his gathered on the steps of the Oregon Capitol to protest his death and to ask Oregon voters to stop the licensing of video poker lottery in their state. His death was just one individual who became addicted, became a compulsive gambler and caused great pain to himself and to many around him. Yet the casinos that addicted him, the casinos without which he wouldn't have ever gambled in the first place, are still raking in their profits off millions of people, just like Bob.*

- *In **Wisconsin**, where Bob lived, there are **17 Indian casinos**, all government sanctioned, around the state. Additional ones are being proposed. Does our society really want and need so many gambling sites? 47*

*The Rev. **Tom Gray, exec. Director of the National Coalition Against Gambling**, says that there are **70,000 Oregon citizens** who are also **compulsive gamblers**. "Obviously we have a feeding frenzy in this state." Hafemann's father said, he only knew that video poker gambling, VLTs, ruined his son's life. These are the people the state government is cashing in on, these are where the profits for the casinos and the governments come from. Corporate profits...state revenue...slot machines...VLT's... 'blood money'... Compulsive gamblers express their addiction in various ways, hopefully not all quite so destructive. But all will wreck great havoc of some kind on themselves and their families. 48*

Another Oregon resident was also unsuccessful in her fight against this addiction. But perhaps we should let her daughter tell her dead mother's story as she wrote in a letter to the Editor:

> *Does anyone realize how bad a problem the state of* ***Oregon*** *has with gambling? I felt the need to write this letter on behalf of my* ***Mother*** *and her loved ones. My mother was always a strong and sensible woman - until the casino defeated her. After losing her life savings, and then some, she finally felt cornered and* ***took her life****. It seems like there should be some regulations on Gambling. After all, if I go into a bar and have one too many, the bar is responsible if I drive. Doesn't it seem like the casinos should have some sort of an Accountability standard?*
> *Karin Doris Stubblefield, Salem. 49*
> *http://news.statesmanjournal.com/article.cfm?i=77307, 3/19/04*

In 1998, Jaszczynski, A. & Farrell, E. completed a study of 44 gambling-related suicides in the Journal of Gambling Studies, 14(2), 93-109. They noted that they found:

> ***sufficient indicators to provide strong support for the argument that gambling acted as a catalyst or played a relevant role in suicide****. 50*

They cite the case of a 34-year-old man found hanging in his garage. His loss of $13,000 to gambling had understandably created marital tensions. They noted there were additional other factors, such as not being promoted at work. But they wondered if that stress at work contributed to the gambling as an escape or whether the interest in gambling contributed to a lack of performance on the job which contributed to not being promoted. So the endless cycle continues with our having introduced another stress, another risk factor, in people's lives.

In ***Canada****, one of Montreal's leading experts on gambling addictions and related suicides, said that since 1994, the city of Quebec alone has had 156 gambling related suicides. Sol Boxenbaum commented that*

> *We know that it's the (slot and VLT)* ***machines*** *in most cases that are causing their suicide, yet they continue to put these machines out there." 51*

***Quebec's** 14,000 government-controlled VLT's make about **3 million dollars** a day for the government. The Canadian government relies on gambling as a source of substantial revenue. "The more people are exposed, the more accessibility, the more problems there are", added Boxenbaum who works in Viva Consulting, a Montreal treatment service. "The machines are accessible on every street corner and in every neighborhood." as reported in The National Post, 2/20/04, by Tom Blackwell. Another addictions counselor who treats problems gamblers at Toronto's Bellwood Health Services, Dr. Ray Steinbaum, said, "It's a very devastating process. (Gamblers) are helpless and hopeless and they see no other exit."*

The father of Eric Bishop, who committed suicide at 32 years of age, Don Bishop of Darlings Island, New Brunswick, Canada, said that gambling and its related consequences were a devastating social problem. His son, Eric, killed himself as a result of video machine addiction after losing more than $200,000 at the machines.

> ***Suicide** is the most devastating outcome of problem gambling, and it is much more common than the public is aware of.*
> ***(Gambling) is a bigger** problem than drugs, much more widespread, and every bit as devastating," Bishop added. 52*

*In **Alberta, Canada**, in 2/23/03, two provinces discovered startling statistics linking gambling to suicides. The Canadian Press learned that in the province of Alberta, gambling was noted in 10 % of suicide victims in 2001. In the province of Nova Scotia, gambling was noted in 6.3 % of suicides in the last 2 years*

*Alberta, Canada's, Medical Examiner, Dennis Caufield, said that gambling-related suicides increased after addictive VLTs - remember, the 'crack-cocaine' of gambling, were installed in 1992. **"Absolutely, without a doubt…It's almost like it was the beginning – the genesis of suicide because of gambling coincided with VLTs."** he said. The numbers collected by medical examiners are much higher than previously recorded rates. This has now raised "new questions there about the social costs of legalized betting in Canada." Canadian Press, Bailey and Elliott, 2/23/03 53*

An article in The Gazette, 12/31/03, related that a new Quebec, Canada, study about suicide suggests that it's harder to predict suicide in pathological gamblers than in almost anyone else. This is especially alarming, said Gazette writer, Aaron

Derfel, because it means that families sometimes don't even have a chance to help the gambler who has become addicted. They often don't even know that the gambler is spending his money in such a devastating manner or that he might want to commit suicide. 54

A study in the December, 2003, bulletin of the Canadian Psychiatric Association said that addicts go to great lengths to conceal their financial problems. The study also warns of the alarming increase in the number of gambling-related suicides. The researchers analyzed 75 suicides linked to gambling in Quebec, Canada from 1994-2000. Most family members were unaware of the true extent of the deceased's gambling activities. "There appear to be some possible differences between gamblers in our study who completed suicide and suicides in general," said author Dominique Bourget, a Quebec coroner and a psychiatry professor at the University of Ottawa. "These finding suggest it may be ***more difficult to predict suicide in pathological gamblers."*** *More than 60% of the victims in the study had never attempted suicide previously. 55*

*"**Gambling is a hidden addiction**", Jeff Derevensky, a McGill University psychiatry professor said, "You can't smell it on their breath or see it in their eyes. Many spouses will tell you, 'I never knew that it was out of control.'"* ***Many experts feel that many gambling-related suicides are under-reported.*** *Pathological gamblers feel "they're worth more dead than alive because of insurance policies...We need to look at this in a larger public-health framework", he concluded. 56*

Despite these high statistics, it's felt that the actual number of suicides related to gambling may be even higher. In the past, investigators didn't ask families whether the victim gambled, especially when the suicide occurs as an accident of some kind. So gambling-related suicides were perhaps under-reported due to a lack of sufficient information. However now more coroners departments and Medical Examiners, especially in Canada, are beginning to ask questions about gambling and suicides.

A Newfoundland hospital failed to report the suicide of Susan Piercey who swallowed pills and suffered from a powerful VLT habit. Only later did the coroner find out about the gambling addiction when the woman's parents spoke out about the issue in the local press.

> *Susan wagered away her student loan money, her paychecks and sold her possessions. She turned to illegal activities and had criminal charges against her. Then she stole $1,000. from an aunt. "In the last 2 years, she was totally out of control," her mother said.*
>
> *"The government is making a lot of money from these VLTs, but they're making the money on the backs oj people who can't afford it." 57 National Post, Tom Blackwell, 2/20/04*

What a tragic and senseless end for Susan and for her parents and family. Can't we do better than this in supporting people in their weaknesses and helping them follow more constructive paths in society?

The ***New Zealand*** *Herald reported on May 12, 2004, that:*

"More than 1 in 6 people seen in hospitals for trying to kill or hurt themselves have gambling problems." *58*

A recent thesis by a graduate student explored the question of gambling involvement for people who have made a suicide attempt. The study involved questioning 189 patients who attended North Shore Hospital's Emergency Room, during 5 months in 2003. Of the total number questioned, 70 agreed to participate in the study. Of that number, 70 people who had made a suicide attempt, ***17%*** *were found to be problem gamblers.*

Concurrent gambling and alcohol addictions radically increased the suicide risk, researcher Alison Penfold reported. "Gambling and alcohol problems together tended to dramatically increase a person's suicide risk," she reported. "Most of the problem gamblers primarily played poker machines," which is what most hot-line calls report as problematic. This study, although with a limited population, shows that gambling is another risk factor, another catalyst, toward efforts at self-harm or destruction. 59

Efforts in Canada to explore the percentage of gambling involvement in people who attempt or are successful in committing suicide have recently corroborated Penfold's research and have also demonstrated that gambling and suicide are much more intertwined than previously thought.

****

In Las Vegas, more than once a month, a visitor commits suicide, according to Clark County coroner records dating to 10/98. Atlantic City, N.J., has about a third as many as Las Vegas in a one year period. As Adam Goldman, of the Associated Press wrote on 2/9/04, "In the same six years, no one committed suicide at Disney World." 60 In 2001 Nevada ranked third behind New Mexico and Montana in suicide rate, according to the American Assoc. of Suicidology.

For many years it was number one. Sin City, "(Las) Vegas is a canvas for American neurosis," University of Nevada at Las Vegas, history professor, Hal Rothman said. "It's a place where we paint our hopes, dreams, fears and apprehensions...It's the city of excess. What could be more of an excess than killing yourself?"

More than 90 people, both tourists and locals, have committed suicide inside a casino or on hotel properties in Las Vegas since l998. *61 http://www.azcentral.com/news/articles/0209leavinglasvegas-ON.html*

From l991 to 2002, 4,994 people killed themselves in Nevada. Of those, about 11 % were from out of state. So locals, Nevada natives, are very vulnerable to the effects of compulsive gambling and show that in their suicide rate. Most suicides occur in Clark County, home to the city of Las Vegas, with its infamous Strip of decadence and debauchery. 62 AP 2/9/04, Adam Goldman

In Nova Scotia, statistics from the chief Medical examiner's office regarding suicides, have led the head of Nova Scotia's gaming corporation, the provincial government department in charge of gambling regulation, to adopt stricter new standards for VLTs and other gambling machines.

New provincial statistics show that 10 out the 159 suicides between January, 2001 and September, 2002, were linked to gambling addiction. In 2001, the chief medical examiner's office adopted new questions for relatives of suicide victims regarding whether gambling had played a role in the death. This is "devastating information," said Marie Mullally, head of Nova Scotia's gaming corporation to a legislature committee on May 12, 2004. ***"The VLT product, like any product, has the potential to be misused. The public has spoken about their concerns with problem gambling. We want to address that."*** *63*

In 2003, new gambling and suicide statistics collected by medical examiners in Nova Scotia and Alberta showed that suicides there were far more frequent than in Quebec, which was thought to have the highest suicide rate linked to gambling in Canada. Liberal finance critic, Diana Whalen, said that other jurisdictions have installed devices shutting down machines after a brief time of play, or only allow them to operate on weekends. These are beneficial ideas, she said, "That would make it more of a social or entertaining thing rather than something people are relying on all day, every day. That's where the addicts are."

The province of Quebec, has decided that small neighborhood bars will not be allowed to have VLTs in an effort to curb problem gambling. Loto-Quebec said that bars with VLTs will have to eliminate them by 32% over the next 3 years. 64

****

This is really a burgeoning **Public Health Crisis** *that's being ignored. Casinos say that they don't cause compulsive gambling. Instead they maintain that 'a certain small percentage of the population is predisposed to addiction'. But if the machines weren't there, people wouldn't be able to use them.*

My husband never sought to gamble until Atlantic City became so convenient and attractive. As the line from the movie, Field of Dreams, states, "If you build it, they will come." This can refer to both baseball and gambling. In the movie, the main character built a baseball field and the greats of baseball, long since dead, returned to play. Similarly, when we build casinos, people will also come to play. But gambling in Atlantic City isn't a fair game and only one side ever wins.

The high incidence of gambling problems in the population, whether 1 % or 20 % should be alarming to all Americans and especially to our **legislative leaders**. *This means that an epidemic, of at least, 5%, a generally agreed upon estimate, of Americans are addicted to gambling and the destructive effects that it incurs, a major Public Health Problem. As the psychiatrist, who testified in Great Britain's Parliament said, any health disorder, any illness, which was thought to affect so many people in the population would be considered a very serious public health issue. (Chapter 2)*

In life, if you build gigantic casinos, 'attractive nuisances', if you put in such 'addictive delivery systems' as VLTs and slot machines, they will come and they will become addicted. It's a sure bet, guaranteed. The Susan's, the Eric's and the Bob's, sons, mothers and fathers, previously law-abiding citizens, might well not have killed themselves if they had no accessibility to gambling.

How desperate does someone have to be to kill themselves? What do the survivors later feel when they know that their loved one killed themselves out of humiliation, hopelessness, and despair? The government licensed something that later killed them. Yes, I indict the governments and their depraved disregard for human life in making gambling available to the masses of citizens, on every street corner, so to speak.

This was my experience as spouse during the time that my husband was gambling. I never had any idea that his gambling was so out-of-control. I never had any inkling that he was spending such huge amounts of money. Alan later told me that he was careful to keep all knowledge from me. He said that he knew that if I knew what was happening, he knew that I would have stopped him from gambling. He didn't want to be stopped from his addiction. He wasn't ready to stop gambling. He added that he thought he could 'kick it' on his own, that he would sooner or later have 'the big win' that would let him pay the money back to me and to others he had 'borrowed' money from.

That statement in itself was not a rational one because he didn't play games that would have given him such a big win. He usually played craps and some slots. A big win wouldn't have given more than $50,000 at tops which wouldn't have paid all his debts back by any means. But in his unclear, addict's brain, all he was thinking about was being able to gamble more, to be able to indulge in his addiction and his fantasy even more. Subterfuge was just one more method of being able to continue gambling.

It's the same with alcohol or drugs. All the addict wants is his next fix. He doesn't really care how he manages it as long as he gets it. He's so enmeshed in his own denial, his own rationalization, his own fantasies, that he loses track of what reality really is.

Indeed we should raise questions about these euphemistically called, 'social costs' of gambling. When something can destroy an individual, his strength, fortitude, and adaptability, so much that he wants to end his own life, then what kind of monster is this that we've unleashed? This is the 'dark side of gambling,' 'the underbelly of the beast,' the side that no one talks about. It's not lit up with a million light bulbs, dazzling with neon signs. There are no limos or waiters in tuxes by the dozen serving shrimp and caviar. But it's there nevertheless.

We introduced the monster of legalized gambling and we continue to feed it with our governments never-ending, voracious need for more and more money, with the continual call to 'balance the budget,' never mind the incidental 'social costs...,' such as suicide.

Are we so morally bankrupt that we would accept money when there was even the hint of something corrupt, something life-threatening, someone who became so overwhelmed by the effects of gambling that they killed themselves? Or do we look the other way?

"We are not our brother's keeper," *said Maryland House Del. Terry Gilleland, on 3/30/04, a member of the Ways and Means Committee, State House, following testimony about the 'social costs' of gambling. Are our public officials now distancing themselves from responsibility for their constituency's problems? The Bible, source of both Jewish and Christian traditions, is clear about the fact that we are, indeed, our brother's keeper. Del. Gilleland seems to want to throw the whole Judeo-Christian tradition out the window and deny any responsibility or concern for 'our brother.' What kind of compassion for our fellow man is this public legislator modeling? What kind of values does he seem to hold?—Yes, Del Gilleland, we* ***are*** *our brother's (and sister's) keeper! Either we all swim together or we'll all sink alone.*

What a tragic, senseless end for people. What losses and wasted lives, what tragedies for their loved ones. What an indictment that speaks for itself on societies that license gambling in order to raise money. There must be something we can do to curb the excesses of this terrible addiction. My husband said he didn't commit suicide because he knew he was worth more to us, dollar for dollar, alive than dead. If he had committed suicide, I might have been tempted to do the same, a never-ending cycle of pain.

Gambling sets up a never-ending chain of misery and destructive actions. We need to put every limit we can think of to curb this tragic phenomenon. All the bans and the limits spoken about later in the chapters on Misrepresentation and Bans and Limitations, need to be carefully considered and implemented to save lives, to safeguard families. My heart grieves for these families and individuals whose lives were so cruelly torn apart by what their government licensed - gambling.

CHAPTER FIVE

GOVERNMENT & GAMBLING

*"It's a tax on ignorance...I don't like the idea of the government depending, for certain portions of its revenue, on **hoodwinking** citizens."*
Warren Buffett, Stockholders meeting, 5/2/04 1

I don't think we'll ever live to see anything more corrupting than gambling as far as governance is concerned."
Robert Coffin, lawyer, Native American Press/ Ojibwe News, 3/19/04 2

GOVERNMENT AND THE GENERAL WELFARE

*...**TO PROMOTE THE GENERAL WELFARE...***
(WE) DO ORDAIN AND ESTABLISH THIS CONSTITUTION FOR THE UNITED STATES OF AMERICA. 3
Constitution of the United States of America.

What is the role of the government in terms of gambling? Does the government have the right to legalize, to license, an activity acknowledged by many to be not in the best interests of a certain significant proportion of its citizens?

It's hard to believe that the government has the right to license an activity which is blatantly not in the common good, which will inevitably cause great harm either to some citizens or to the economic community of society, and which serves only to enrich the coffers of the already wealthy.

What does the term, 'the general welfare' mean? Does it mean the greatest good for the greatest number of people as John Locke, political philosopher, would say? If so, then what happens to the minority? If a law is good for a large percentage of the population, but bad for a small percentage of the population, are the rights of the minority abridged when the law is enacted. We know that in America the rights of minorities are watched over carefully by a variety of groups under our 'checks and balances' system of government. Whether the minority constitutes a small 5 % or a large 30 % of the population, is irrelevant to the exercise of their rights under law.

Gambling is not in the interest of the majority of individuals, except for the very few who get rich usually the owners or financiers, the Donald Trumps, or Steve Wynns. Gambling is against the law, except when the state licenses it, except when it serves the state's purpose to do so. That sounds to me like a contradiction in terms, or perhaps a specific exception made for someone's benefit. If it's illegal, i.e. not beneficial for people, then why wouldn't it be illegal at all times and in all places for everyone?

If it's illegal, presumably it was made illegal because it's not in the general interest of our citizens or of our country. Gambling is an activity which is illegal everywhere in the state, except for the narrow walls of a few casinos. Recently a judge in Wisconsin queried the district attorney as to whether the judge and/or the state of Wisconsin could get rid of gambling totally, because of the variety of ills that it brings to the community. The DA responded 'Maybe', since it would be an involved process to close down all the gambling in the state. Two months later, a Supreme Court judge there ruled the Governor-Indian tribal compacts null and void.

Can State legislatures or Governors license something normally illegal, and make it legal in certain places? Perhaps the State could make illicit drugs, child abuse, or even shooting senior citizens, legal if it was done in certain prescribed places? Does the special place make it acceptable? Sounds ridiculous, doesn't it? In the same way, if gambling is illegal in one place, then what makes a special place, a casino, okay to have gambling in?

In 1999, the National Gambling Impact Commission (NGIC), a Federal commission created to explore gambling's effect in America, found that there had been a huge increase in the numbers of people becoming compulsive gamblers in the prior 10 years. At that time, 5 years ago, the commission, after studying this issue of *gambling intensively for 2 years, suggested that states declare a **'moratorium on gambling expansion'** saying that the country needed time to assess the social impact of gambling. Yet states did not choose to abide by the Commission's recommendations and have been rushing to legalize this new activity, apparently seeing in it the answer to all their budget problems.*

A Harvard Medical School study, also found that compulsive gambling increased by 50 % from the mid-l980s to the mid-l990s. However, instead of a moratorium as suggested by the NGIC Federal Commission, the states have continued to legalize gambling at an alarming rate. The states have not looked at whether gambling is something beneficial or not for people, whether it's intrinsically good or bad. States, with tunnel-vision, appear to only see gambling in terms of the amount of revenue that it might bring in. Legislators and Governors only want to know 'how much money'. They look at it as a 'quick fix' to their economic problems. However this band-aid approach to the state's economic problems and to balancing the budget, is a short-sighted, 'lazy' way to solve the state's financial difficulties.

The NGIC found that 80 % of young people between the ages of 12 and 17 had gambled in the previous year. Now young people are not allowed in casinos but with the increased legitimacy that gambling has these days, gambling is more widespread than ever, and they find various ways to indulge, such as sports betting.

FOR THE GOOD OF ALL

I like to think that my government would generally go along with overarching moral law, with the Judeo-Christian tradition and the values espoused there, 'for the good of all'. I'd like to know how gambling can suddenly be turned into an acceptable activity after governments and religions throughout the ages have questioned and prohibited it. Perhaps it's felt that 21st century American Governors and legislators have some special insight into truth or a magic crystal ball where they can discern what is right and what is wrong. Or perhaps it's felt that what was wrong before can now be legislated to make it right, that the truth changes from time to time based on how legislatures in the United States vote?

Our elected officials have decided for themselves, that gambling is not only acceptable but even something to be encouraged, thus turning their backs on the wisdom of the ages and the insights of past scholars, academics, and theologians. In 1665, England passed a law against gambling, having experienced it for hundreds of years first. In 1698, they passed laws against all lotteries. Lord Beaconsfield in England in 1665 called gambling:

> ***a vast engine of national demoralization.***
>
> *Rex M. Rogers, "Seducing America: Is Gambling a Good Bet?"*

Quite a negative comment about something that Great Britain had experienced for so long already. What does history say about those who don't learn from it being destined to repeat it?

The people in our country have the right to recall their legislators and other elected officials including the Governor if they wish, if they feel that the legislators are not acting according to the will of the people. The people are the ones in the final analysis, who tell their legislators what they want them to do. It is assumed that legislators are acting in the best interests of all the people at all times, for the common good, for the good of the state. If this is true, then why and how has gambling proliferated so exponentially in the past 25 years without in many instances, citizens ever having voted for it? In many states, including both Connecticut and New York State, there have never been public referendums asking people if they want casino gambling in their state, much less in their neighborhoods.

State government's role is to watch out and to protect its' citizens, to help them make a better life for themselves and their families, to enable them to act "in the pursuit of life, liberty and the pursuit of happiness," to encourage them to achieve the highest they are capable of in all ways. However my husband ruined himself and his family financially while engaging in an activity not only condoned but encouraged by the state. If this activity was so dangerous, so potentially disruptive, then how could it have been legal? Why would it be permissible for any person over the age of 21 to indulge in? If my husband had taken drugs, he would not have hurt his family to the extent that he did. So why doesn't the government license drugs? Many experts feel that in the long run, drugs are less dangerous than gambling.

Gambling can destroy households exceedingly quickly. It can consume years and years of savings and investment in a short time. Money translates to a certain lifestyle and even survival in our society. If the money has been lost, a person's whole way of life will change. As the person's lifestyle changes, so do the lives of his family. As their lives change, family dynamics often change also. What was acceptable before, becomes unmanageable in the face of this new stress, gambling. Families break up easily. People break down quickly. A significant number of people affected by gambling losses commit suicide. The fall-out from gambling is documentable, incredibly pervasive and long-lasting.

By what authority can the Legislature pass laws not in the best interests of the people, of all the people? The government licenses cigarettes and alcohol, it makes money from their sales. Yet it's careful to provide certain stipulations, such as truth-in-advertising laws to regulate their sale and distribution.

In many areas of our society, government goes to considerable lengths to attempt to protect its citizenry. One such example is the widespread mandated licensing of professions. Such fields as real estate, accounting, medicine, teaching, social work, and many others have extensive training and education programs, all designed to protect the consumer, the public, from fraudulent and unscrupulous people or businesses that might take their money. Professions have extensive required licensing stipulations, educational credentialing and continuing education and staff development.

The state's authority to require licensure falls under its 'Police Powers', to protect the 'health, safety, welfare, and property' of its citizens. The purpose of licensing laws is to protect the public from dishonest dealings and from incompetency by representatives of professions. What about the misrepresentative advertising, the misguiding inducements, and overall misleading tactics of the gambling industry? In real estate, advertising has to follow certain, strict guidelines in order not to be considered misleading. In medicine, any activity or treatment where 5% of the patients had severe, traumatic reactions as inciting another illness, such as addiction, would certainly come under close scrutiny and regulation.

Casinos have government licenses, 'legal permission to operate', supposedly for the good and benefit of the community as well as their own self-interest. Licensees in the field of ***real estate****, Article 12-A of the Real Property Law of New York State, for example, are charged by the state as having a "****duty to the public to act with honesty and competency.****"* ***I****f found acting contrary to these expectations, a licensee is subject to having their license suspended or revoked and additionally fined, or even imprisoned for violations. The state scrutinizes and examines so closely behaviors and actions on the part of licensed professions yet gives the gambling industry practically carte blanche in much of their behavior and business practices.*

*The doctrine of '****parens patriae****' states that government has the right to litigate, and therefore protect citizens in the name of the public good. This is just one of many concepts that bear relevance to the true role and responsibility of government. Parens patriae is an old, and accepted concept in jurisprudence, our English common law tradition, that states that government has an obligation to exercise its powers for the common good, that this is the nature of government. Other concepts such as the government's fiduciary responsibility, legislation such as Fair Housing Codes, the exercise of police powers in health, education, and welfare, of the state, all call for the intervention of government in activities that uplift people and their overall standard of living.*

My husband wasn't cheated by any of the professions with whom he does business. But he was hoodwinked and completely taken advantage of, by another industry in our midst, the gambling entrepreneurs, the gambling shysters. Licensing professions is small change in terms of numbers of people and amount of dollars, and intensity of damage compared to the scope of activities that casinos are involved with. In the future, the gambling profession will be looked back as the real robber barons of the twentieth century.

Yet the problem is that State governments make money off of people gambling – 'mucho' money. *Gambling revenue is one of the 'sin' taxes, like the cigarette and alcohol tax. In the last 20 years, state governments have licensed casinos seemingly as fast as they could. The governors have been making compacts, contracts, with Indian tribes to allow gambling in many states. Many states have casinos with table games and thousands and thousands of slot machines - yet the people of the state have never been polled in public referendums as to their wishes in the issue of gambling. We'll see below how this could have occurred.*

Gambling is addictive. That's agreed upon and accepted. The gambling industry in their literature admits that 'a small percentage' of the population will become addicted. Then they go on to comment, judgmentally, that this small percentage is already a 'troubled group' with various other illnesses, that the individuals who become addicted to gambling are different from the mainstream, exceptions.

However this point of view, that gambling addiction only affects a select few who are already troubled in some way, understates the problem so greatly as to be on the very borderline of truth. This number of people that gambling affects in a very negative way number in the thousands and thousands and thousands!

In 1993, more than a ***100 Million people*** *gambled legally in the U.S. Of that number between 5 and 10 % were or became compulsive or pathological gamblers inflicting great damage on themselves or others. That's almost* ***10 Million people addicted*** *across the U.S. If this many people became addicted once gambling became available, then certainly gambling has messed up a lot of people's lives, people who were managing on a much higher basis than after gambling arrived.*

Whether it's 5 Million or 10 Million, the numbers are still incredible. Each of these individuals has felt incredible pain due to their addiction. They each would agree that gambling has led them down a path they would never have otherwise chosen. The emotional pain that each one of those 5 or 10 Million addicted people feels due to gambling is uniquely his own—yet it's also shared by his family and community. Its economic impact is felt by all of society.

Even one compulsive gambler who decides to take his life because of his losses, or one gambler who loses the family home to foreclosure because of his debts, or one compulsive gambler who embezzles from his employer, is one too many. People have, of course, engaged in self-destructive, fool-hardy acts from time immemorial. The difference here, however, is that the ***State*** *has made it possible for them to engage in such self-destructive behaviors by licensing, by allowing, by making legal, an activity which is known to be detrimental to a significant number of people. By legalizing gambling, the State has given people the means and the avenue to destruction.*

The State has voluntarily opened up the floodgates of hell, saying that this activity is acceptable and okay. It's given people a loaded gun and then said that target practice is 'entertainment'. If 100 people are given loaded guns, then probably only a small percentage of people will use it destructively. Perhaps 5 people will be stupid, use the gun in a misguided way, and end up inflicting great damage. But if the actions of those 5 people could have been prevented by the State not giving a hundred people a gun, then who is to blame for the damage they inflict? Would the State be morally liable for having sold guns for the purpose of making money?

We used to look down on 'gun-runners,' feeling that they were dealing in weapons of human destruction. So if the state is dealing in implements or means of human destruction or financial ruin, would we look down on the State also? Similarly, wouldn't the State be responsible for the vast numbers of Social Costs of suicides, or foreclosures, or divorces, for having licensed casinos for the purpose of making money? The fruit of the state licensing casinos is the revenue, the money, for them. This revenue is quite substantial, $400 Million annually in the case of Connecticut. With their money comes substantial financial ruin for their citizens. The state paved the way for the ruination of their citizens, making losers out of them...

Almost 100 million people participate in something that past societies outlawed, something that drains money out of the community, often out of the country, and something that leads to financial ruin and/or crime.

Now not everyone who becomes addicted, gambles away entire fortunes. Not everyone who becomes addicted, resorts to breaking the law to feed their habit. But people could be addicted and lose a lot of money, money needed to pay bills, to pay children's expenses, money to fulfill family responsibilities. Our state legislators have licensed an addictive activity, designed and carefully calculated to entrap citizens and incite them to spend their money in non-productive, frivolous, and reckless ways. This activity, gambling, is so tempting and so attractive that if someone succumbs to that temptation, it will put them at risk of losing all their money, their savings and doing great harm.

Is this what our government is supposed to be doing? To put a gigantic Temptation near people's homes and businesses? To balance budgets on the backs of its most vulnerable citizens? To provide the means and the avenues for people to do great harm and damage to themselves and others?

Legislators in the State of ***Georgia*** *in April, 2004, approved a House bill to make it even easier and more convenient for its residents to buy State Lottery tickets. Now people, both residents and out-of-state people, can buy tickets on-line, from their home or work computers. So if someone is working, decides to take a break, they can just stay at their computer and play the Lottery. Or people can decide to buy a few tickets a day without ever leaving their home. How Tempting! How convenient! How insidious! Georgia would be the first state with an Internet Lottery. It would be the first state to tempt its citizens to become losers without even leaving their homes. 6*

BALANCING STATE BUDGETS

I thought that government was about finding new and innovative programs for needy people to enhance their lives with, that government would seek to use the resources available to implement public works projects, such as low-cost housing, or the 'greening' of our cities through regeneration programs. Generally one hopes that government searches for new ways to meet the needs of its citizens. I never thought that government was in the business of providing the means for its citizens to indebt themselves, to become even needier than before.

If states need gambling revenue so desperately, perhaps they would like to do what legislators did 25 years ago, before casinos. Budgets got balanced then by either raising taxes or lowering the cost of running government, i.e. eliminate some programs. These are elementary concepts that every homeowner knows - you balance a budget by increasing income or decreasing outgo. The need for additional vast sums of money arise when one tries to increase outgo, i.e. increase programs, increase layers of bureaucracy, and decrease income, lowering taxes.

Legislators think they can increase programs and decrease taxes. The people want also to increase programs and decrease taxes. Yet economics, simple math, doesn't work like this. If you want to increase one, you must also increase the other. It's like a scale. It needs to balance. Since it doesn't balance now, it's felt that gambling revenue will allow it to balance.

So where can states look for additional revenue other than gambling? They can look at the ***creation of jobs****. In the short run, some revenue would have to be spent for the creation of jobs. Over the long haul, additional jobs would pay for themselves and then some.*

There are a wealth of ideas for the creation of new jobs in various alternative technology fields. These jobs would serve to generate additional revenue, i.e. create new money versus redistributed money as gambling does, for the state in terms of taxes and consumer spending. There are many projects in the fields of alternative energy, programs to decrease our dependence on traditional petrochemical sources, which further indebt our country to foreign gas and oil cartels. These innovative types of projects and ideas are going begging for people to explore.

Recent innovations in road building could be explored. Many of these programs and new ideas are not implemented for lack of interest in new products and a dearth of creative, can-do thinking. Alternative lifestyle and energy-conservation magazines, such as Mother Earth news, have a plethora of innovative ideas which could provide local jobs and even industry. But State government is almost reactionary in refusing to relinquish old ways of doing things, yet continuing to build expensive new layers of super-beaucracies and government regulation in order to raise revenue.

Another way of 'raising revenue' is by decreasing expenses. I would like to suggest that eliminating the annual rape of our landscape by State Highway Departments, the reconstructing and expansion of additional highways in our country, would save an avalanche of taxpayer monies. I constantly see highway crews demolishing roads and the sides of those roads in order to expand existing roads even further. I can only imagine wildly what the taxpayer expense for this Spring-Rite-of-Road-Construction costs the public. If you don't build or expand additional highways, people will make do with public transportation or perhaps not travel as far or as much. Less auto travel would help our overall pollution problem, as well as decrease American consumers dependence on foreign petroleum products, gasoline.

In addition to eliminating the needless road work, I might suggest that the exponential expansion of beaucracy be curtailed and eliminated. The government seeks to regulate citizens in everything from where they can put their garbage, to the color of their houses, to how many sheds they can put in their backyard, to how often they have to pay for additional license plates. Haven't regulations and the expense to the government of the additional staff needed to implement the countless restrictions in our society been overplayed today and taken to an absurd level. There are many ways to balance budgets other than gambling.

Many state programs that need revenue are undermined by the addiction of gambling. Such programs as welfare benefits, tax breaks for special groups such as seniors and lower income groups, government sponsored programs to help first-time home buyers, as well as other government-sponsored programs for the poor, are fighting the very thing that gambling incites, people's impulsive and poor use of their money.

As we noted, in 1999, the Federal National Gambling Impact Study Commission found in their research that the poor, the elderly and youth, are the segments of the population who are especially hard-hit by lotteries, who spend a disproportionate amount of their income and meager resources on lotteries as well as other forms of gambling. Lottery advertising encourages them to do so. State lottery advertising uses sophisticated marketing tools to get people to buy tickets. Ads are intentionally misleading and don't mention the incredibly small odds of winning. The government gives with one hand, in many programs for the poor, in fact, makes up much of its expenses in its budget with these types of programs, and with the other hand, it continues to license expanded gambling which will add more citizens to the ranks of the impoverished, necessitating the further expansion and expense of government programs.

As state agencies, lotteries are not subject to Federal 'truth-in-advertising' Standards! Amazing, isn't it! The State, itself, is not subject to its own truth-in-advertising laws! Lottery advertising promotes the **opposite** *values that the state government programs try to teach their clients. The Lottery rewards, or appears to reward, such profilgate values as 'luck' over hard work, instant gratification over consistent investment, and entertainment over savings. I thought the State was obligated to promote the public good, not to encourage false values and short-term strategies of making money that inevitably backfire in the long run.*

A typical scenario would include a state caseworker counseling poor families and welfare clients to conserve and to save their money for future goals, to forego immediate pleasure in favor of long-term savings, to put aside money for emergencies, all solid middle-class values. Meanwhile, the State Lottery Dept. spends big money on advertising to encourage them to blow their money on lottery tickets which they don't have a chance of winning!

When State Lottery Departments aggressively advertise their lotteries, it's tantamount to state governments themselves promoting gambling. States should be ethically opposed to being in the business of running lotteries, of promoting gambling. In 1997, state lottery departments advertising costs were about ***$400 Million,*** *about 1 % of total sales. (The amounts of money involved continue to be mind-boggling).*

In New York State, the infamous ad campaign, 'All you need is a dollar and a dream,' encouraged people to believe that lotteries provide an avenue for financial success, an investment in their future. How misleading, how false and phony is this. Yet the ad campaign was wildly successful—that is, successful in getting people to part with their money.

In New York State the possible recipient of 6 new VLT gambling sites would be the big Apple, New York City. The addition of a total of 8 new VLT betting halls is Governor Pataki's way of complying with the Court's demand to establish further school aid for New York City's embattled schools. But others in the state realize that providing gambling in such an accessible place as New York City would further impoverish thousands and thousands of poor people adding to existing Public Assistance rolls. State Senator Frank Padavan, a Queens Republican, has opposed gambling in the past and is continuing to fight against the expansion of gambling. He noted recently that:

> *A person can gamble any time, day or night, and not only is it perfectly legal, it's actually sponsored, supported and encouraged by the state. We're at saturation point now, but still some seek to increase access to gambling and to ruin more lives. 7*

Although legislative leaders have not embraced the Governor's endorsement of gambling as a source of revenue for New York State, they also are not discussing other ways of raising funds for the State general fund or for New York City schools. Pataki spokesman says that the Governor is hoping that Lottery expansion will create new jobs and revenue. Padavan responded that the ***"immoral expansion of state-sanctioned wagering will increase the social ills of compulsive gambling, such as personal bankruptcies, job losses and family turmoil."*** *8*

"This isn't economic development and it isn't an acceptable funding source for anything. What it is, is a life-shattering addiction for millions, and it's being fueled by a state that seems addicted to the promise of easy revenues." *9 Padavan*

The prevalence of people addicted to gambling in New York State *is already high. It's estimated that* ***750,000 New Yorkers*** *have experienced serious to severe gambling problems and that* ***250,000 people*** *currently are experiencing problems with issues as a result of gambling, according to the executive director of the New York Council on Problem Gambling, James Maney. 10 4/27/04, Joel Stashenko, AP*

In ***Maryland****, the lottery is the* ***3rd-largest source of state revenue****, right behind income and sales taxes. It's common knowledge that poor people spend more money on lottery tickets than affluent ones. Studies repeatedly show the high correlation between lottery ticket sales and poor neighborhoods. The biggest buyers of lottery tickets are minorities, elderly and working-class people. These are the lottery's constant buyers, the ones with no serious chance of winning, continuing to shell out their money over a lifetime. These are the ones who bought 'the ticket and the dream'. And they're also the ones who are often supported by government programs.*

Maryland Del. Luiz R.S. Simmons (D-Montgomery), said that: Over the last 30 years, the lottery has become a sharp instrument to harvest a horrible amount of money from our poorest and most vulnerable communities. 11

In an editorial, "Lure the Poor", 10/21/03, The Washington Post suggested that before welcoming thousands of slot machines, Maryland law-makers should examine the serious social aspects of gambling. Instead of debating where casinos would be located and the percentage to tax the casinos, legislators should first be asking the question, What does gambling do for the economy and for individual citizens. Debates and public testimony should be about the question of the true benefits of gambling, not the implementation of a gambling agenda as favored by some. www.washingtonpost.com/wp-dyn/articles/A56395-2003Oct20.html

*In **Maryland,** where Gov. Ehrlich Jr. is attempting to rally support for 8 'racinos', Republican U.S. Rep. Wayne Gilchrest, publicly stated his opposition to further gambling expansion in an editorial in the Baltimore Sun on 3/21/04. Rep. Gilchrest courageously crossed Republican Party lines to state his opposition to gambling expansion in Maryland and the reasons for his decision. He noted that*

> *Gambling should not be "a solution to our state's fiscal problems... (Gambling) is only short-term budgetary salvation. 12*

*Gilchrest asked about "setting priorities? about accountability? and about new ideas (to balance the budget)?" **He noted that gambling was illegal in the U.S. for almost 100 years and reminds us that "history tells us that there are no real economic benefits; our elected state officials should be aware of the fundamental economic principles governing gambling activities...Studies of that history conclude that gambling produces no product and no new wealth and thus makes no real contribution to economic development. It is inherently recessionary."***

Gilchrest even quotes noted economist, Paul Samuelson, Nobel Prize winner.

> *(Gambling) creates no output but does absorb time and resources. When pursued beyond the limits of recreation, where the main purpose, after all, is to kill time, gambling subtracts from the national income. Beyond the initial revenue boost from gambling, the social costs overwhelm that benefit. **Dr. Paul Samuelson,** Nobel Prize Economist. 13*

So various economists, Samuelson, Grinois, Garrett, all concur that gambling does not help areas or people economically. Samuelson added that one risk analysis *put the cost to taxpayers at "$3 for every $1 in new tax revenues." Gilchrest continues, stating that:*

> *the social costs are real, but their actual dollar amount will be hidden in the future budgets of state programs...*
>
> *Problem and pathological gambling affects not only the gambler and his family, but also society.*
>
> ***Economically for the state, this means added unemployment and welfare benefits, physical and mental health care, domestic violence costs and child abuse and neglect expenses.*** *14*

These are the very same reasons, all the studies cite, that experience has taught us is true. Representative Gilchrest knows from numerous, documented studies that bankruptcies increase radically, families are split up, people who are already precarious or marginal in our society whether because of already existing mental illness or for monetary reasons, cross the line, make poor and self-destructive life choices, and deteriorate further. Suicides increase, homelessness increases, and generally the quality of life degenerates for a significant number, for thousands and thousands and thousands, of the population. Whether we want to call this segment of the population 'vulnerable,' 'sick', 'weak' or whatever, gambling and its excesses take a very real toll in terms of money and basic human misery. This all translates to increased taxpayer dollars for social programs.

All of this, Gilchrest notes, is in addition to the "impact of increased bankruptcies and the extra money needed to respond to the crime that inevitably would follow." Gilchrest concludes that "the future of Maryland is in our hands."

> *We should not allow slots into our communities in order to permit governing to be easy and expedient just for the moment. Rather than surrendering the state's financial future to dubious revenue sources, we can meet the current fiscal challenge by using our initiative, ingenuity and intellect and work for a future that we won't come to regret. 14 http://www.baltimoresun.com/news/opinion/oped/bal-op.gilchrest21mar21,0,2025059.story?coll=bal-oped-headlines*

This is not only the future of Maryland, but the future of all states when it comes to the possible expansion of gambling. This research is true not only for one state but for all states, and in fact, all countries. South Australia recently has lowered the number of 'pokies' or slot machines as they are called there, by 20 % in January, 2004 as a result of the escalating social costs that they have seen that gambling incites.

****

So how did all this gambling-craziness begin? How did it happen that our society became so involved with gambling? The mixed messages by the State, the idea that gambling is bad but yet the State wants you to do it, that it wants your money - where and how did all these lotteries and subsequent casinos start?

I never voted for gambling in my state of New York. The New York State Constitution does not allow casinos. Citizens in the state of Connecticut voted for a lottery - but nothing more. So how did they wind up with 2 gigantic Indian casinos? What role did the State's legislators and Governors play in this incredible expansion of gambling in the past 25 years?

Before 1978, there was only one place to gamble in the United States - Las Vegas. Then In 1978, Atlantic City was licensed by the state of New Jersey in an effort to rehabilitate the ailing City and to bring economic development again to the boardwalk. No one expected it to take off as it did. When New Jersey voters approved casinos for the opening of Atlantic City, gambling interests told them there would be only table games, no slot machines. Now slot machines are the major source of income for casinos and table games have diminished. Atlantic City gambling has continued to expand since that time.

NATIVE AMERICAN PEOPLE AND CASINOS

The big impetus to provide gambling in an accessible and wide variety of places began in 1987, with the Federal Supreme Court decision, Cabazon Band of Mission Indians vs. California, 480 U.S. 202/1987. This ruling subsequently led to the extensive licensing of Indian tribal casinos and Congress's Federal Indian Gaming Regulatory Act, (I.G.R.A.) legislation implementing the decision in 1988. This is what opened Pandora's box. This ruling stated that states could not restrict traditional gaming on Indian reservations in states where there was 'already existing gambling.' Seeing the possibilities in this court ruling and in Congress' response, shrewd gambling industry entrepreneurs began to see the possibility of expanding gambling via this 'back-door' method.

Previous to this judicial decision, there was only Las Vegas and Atlantic City. Then came the Indian tribes and their expansion and proliferation across the states. States that allowed legalized games of chance, such as bingo or 'Las Vegas nites' with casino games, were then mandated to allow Indian tribes to also have gambling. Actually what the Court intended was probably not for Indians to open the largest casinos in the world, such as the 2 in Connecticut, but just to allow a little gambling. However, just as people are not a little pregnant, there is also not a little gambling. Bingo and Las Vegas nights, as we discussed, are completely different than casinos that operate constantly and whose only goal is to take your money for private gain.

Indian reservations have traditionally had 'limited' sovereign status and self-government privileges since they initially started negotiations with the Federal government. This has now come back to haunt us since it provides that Indian nations cannot be sued in civil court and are not subject to the laws of the land in which they live, the U.S. Something wrong with this picture?

Management companies and financiers, seeing this 'back-door approach' that Congress had legislated, then began to subsidize Indian tribes to organize themselves, and to start the process which would ultimately lead to gigantic casinos such as Foxwoods or the Mohegan Sun. They provided funding and expertise for various disparate factions to become recognized as the legitimate descendants of past tribes, by the Bureau of Indian Affairs (BIA), the Federal agency which licenses tribes and reservations.

These financial management companies are part of the reason why in February, 2004, Connecticut's congressional delegation asked the Federal Government Reform Committee for hearings on the influence of 'outside interests, especially wealthy gaming interests' on the tribal recognition process. These financially astute and well-endowed management companies have bankrolled and focused this entire process of Indian recognition into one whose ultimate goal is to build casinos to make money. This process is not about Indian rights, being recognized as tribal nations, or even about reparations for past injustices. It's about money. "Show me the money" could well be the mantra of the financing companies. It's their sole intention and goal. They're not about economic development, jobs or anything else - they're after the money!

In pursuing this costly and time-consuming process, these large and often multi-national gambling industry corporations such as Bally's Park Place, MGM Mirage, and foreign individuals and corporations first approach the tribes. They agree to finance the costs involved in the legal process of getting themselves identified as bona fide Indian tribes. The industry bankrolls the tribes in exchange for future involvement rights such as managing the future casino. The tribes are not opposed to being 'helped out' as the vast sums of money look very enticing and they have nothing to lose.

***The Federal Bureau of Indian Affairs in Washington** has established a recognition process and criteria for the tribes. This is a lengthy process but it's obviously paid off for many tribes. Many more tribes, in fact, are currently engaged* *in this process and about ready to be recognized shortly. Presently there are 291 tribal groups seeking federal recognition. Presumably all of these Indian tribes are ultimately seeking to open casinos, otherwise they wouldn't be so involved in obtaining Federal recognition. Many of these groups have signed contracts with investor groups, all seeking a share of the action, of the nation's $15 Billion dollar a year Indian gambling industry. There are about a dozen groups awaiting final determination from the BIA in the near future. Two-thirds of them have casino investors bankrolling them, reported the New York Times, on 3/29/04. The investment is huge but so is the possible payoff. After BIA recognition, they then make their claims on states for casinos, for a share of 'the pie'. Everyone is looking for a piece of 'the action'.*

In January, 2004, the **National Coalition Against Gambling Expansion (NCAGE)** *called for a national moratorium on gambling-driven tribal recognition and off-reservation casinos. NCAGE chairman, Guy Clark, charged that "The Bureau of Indian Affairs has transformed itself into a national facilitator for the uncontrolled and inexcusable proliferation of casino gambling." Clark added that "The last straw was the 'Christmas Eve Surprise' wherein the BIA granted land in trust to the Jena Band of Choctaw Indians for a casino in* **Louisiana** *without allowing hearings and procedures promised to Louisiana citizens." 15*

This is another instance of the proliferation of Indian tribal casinos without the consent of state citizens, without public referendums, or even legislative approval. This process of Federal recognition subverts the democratic process of citizen involvement and approval and allows Federal bureaucrats relative autonomy and tremendous influence in the lives of citizens in these communities.

This process of tribal recognition has been scrutinized lately as corruption appears to have made inroads into the BIA. We shouldn't be surprised that corruption has become part of the process. Wherever large amounts of money involved, people are going to become overzealous in promoting their own personal gain and aggrandizement.

Some investigations have raised questions about the authenticity of certain Indian tribes seeking federal recognition. The Hartford Courant, 1/5/04, wrote that some experts in this area question the authenticity of Indian bands in Connecticut. Recently it was alleged that corruption within the BIA had led to some tribes being recognized despite the lack of justification and documentation for them as a tribe.

Members of the California regional BIA office, had allegedly registered themselves as members of a California Indian tribe, the Ione band of Miwok Indians, in an attempt to add members to the tribe and, ultimately to enrich themselves. The then-acting regional director who approved this was added to the tribal roll along with 68 relatives including 2 other bureau staff members. Another bureau staff member also had himself and relatives added to the tribe. 16

The Pequots, owners of one of Connecticut's 2 big casinos, Foxwoods, "have little, if any, Pequot blood," Brett Fromson wrote in the Hartford Courant. "The typical tribal member is at most at most 1/64 Pequot and many are 1/128. Some may have no Indian blood at all." 16 So if they're only 1/64 Pequot Indian, then they're 63/64 not Pequot, not Indian.

*Connecticut Attorney General, Richard Blumenthal, said "**Money is driving the federal tribal recognition process.** These tribes have wealthy, powerful investors because the financial payback is potentially unending and immeasurable...We're talking about Billions (of dollars)." 17 Blumenthal added that many senior BIA officials have conflicts of interest because of past or future associations with casino developers. "The end result (of the tribal recognition process) could be that the resolution of tribal recognition cases will have less to do with the attributes and qualities of a group and more to do with the resources that petitioners and third parties (investors) can marshal to develop a successful political and legal strategy," said a General Accounting Office investigation in 2001.*

Most of the almost 300 groups seeking tribal recognition have presented themselves since Congress legalized Indian gambling. Private investors such as Las Vegas corporations or a South African corporation, have seen this an avenue to gambling in l988. Financiers have seen this as access to a gambling market that otherwise wouldn't be open to them. 18

In fact, the Rev. Sue Abrams, a Methodist minister and also of Indian descent herself, has commented that these newfound riches are not trickling down to the rank and file tribal members. They are not providing career opportunities for Indian people to establish a steady and honorable source of income. She also noted that the process of casino proliferation is making inroads into the destruction of what remains of Indian culture. She called for the repeal of the National Indian Gaming Act, IGRA, at the NCALG Baltimore conference in 9/03.

> *When Congress approved gaming for Indians across the country, it created a tool that destroys us. The Great White Father didn't do his job again. There is a better way of life. We need to teach our children there are values and morals and principles to live by, and that a quality of life is more important than making a buck off of a person who has an illness. Rev. Sue Abrams 19*

Thank-you, Rev. Abrams for saying it so well and for standing up for ethics and morality. When people do what they can to defraud and take advantage of other people, it's not beneficial for anyone. This is true regardless of anyone's color or ethnic origin. NCALG Bulletin, Vol 1, #5, 12/03. 20

It's ironic that ***American Indian tribes*** *have been in the forefront of this movement to expand gambling. In the past they were often thought of as a people with a spirituality that stressed being in tune and in harmony with Nature, the elements and with other people, that they believed in 'treading lightly' on Mother Earth. The impression was that they were not into materialism big-time but rather more into appreciating the fruits of today and living in accord with what is. Now in an effort to gain wealth and riches, they're in the forefront of this assault on the people of America encouraging them to gamble their savings and paycheck away in a false hope, a vain wish to make their lives easy by winning big money at a casino.*

We should remember that the Indian community is not a monolithic, homogeneous culture that agrees on all things but in fact, are often led by leaders not in sync with their people. The Rev. Abrams, doesn't believe gambling is good for American Indian communities. The move toward Indian casinos by sovereign Indian nations is "short-sighted" and tears "away at the fabric of our traditional values." 20 Rev. Abrams is concerned that Indian gambling has changed the values and priorities of American Indians. "When do we stop caring about the rest of the world and start caring only about ourselves? ***The traditional way is to care about the world and the Earth****," she said on 1/27/04 in a news article by Judith Davidoff. 21 http://www.madison.com/captimes/news/stories/66121.php.*

The Rev. Abrams is well aware of the need for economic development tools within Indian communities having grown up in poverty herself, but added, "When do we say enough is enough? Why is it that once you have a reservation casino, it's not enough?" It's not looking at what is best for the world of community. It's looking at how we can gain more financially." 22

Major financial moguls have spent millions of dollars backing Indian tribes and helping them get Federal recognition. They have done this for the purpose of contracting with them to open additional casinos when they otherwise wouldn't be allowed to do so. 'Back-door' financiers have bankrolled Indian tribes in the hopes of getting a share of the lucrative $15 Billion dollar Indian gambling industry. Four major financiers have supposedly spent almost $35 Million dollars in Connecticut alone, attempting to help tribes succeed in getting Federal tribal recognition.

Donald Trump has spent approximately $9.1 Million allegedly helping Connecticut's Eastern Pequots tribe seek tribal recognition. Tom Wilmot, a shopping mall developer, is a partner to the tune of at least $10 Million, of the Golden Hill Paugussett, an alleged tribe in Trumbull, Connecticut. Fred DeLuca, founder of Subway restaurant chain, invested about $10 Million in the Gold Hill Paugussett also. Lyle Berman's company spent almost $4 Million helping the Nipmuc Nation in Connecticut. "There's no question we make money," Berman said, "That's the American way." 23

Except the problem here is that Congress in 1988, didn't legislate IGRA for the purpose of helping wealthy investors seek additional places to make more money. This legislation was conceived to help destitute Indian tribes with a little gambling, not to open the way to force rural Connecticut or anywhere else to become the proving grounds for some of the world's largest casinos!

*Jeff Benedict, author of the book, Without Reservation: How a Controversial Indian Tribe Rose to Power and Built the World's Largest Casino, said in testimony on May 5, 2004, before the Government Reform Committee in Washington, D.C., that casino moguls and their lobbyists have exploited Indian tribes as well as the legislative tribal recognition process for financial gain. Benedict, director of the Connecticut Alliance against Casino Expansion, said that "**The Indian Gaming Act and tribal acknowledgment have become twin tools exploited by the casino industry to expand gambling throughout the country.**" "Donald Trump and other financiers...have invaded the acknowledgment process for personal enrichment."*

Benedict charged before the Government Reform Committee that the 1988 Congressional legislation has been misused by private individuals resulting in harm to the American public.

> *The Indian gambling law has the shameful distinction of being a boon to non-Indian millionaires and casino moguls that have exploited the law's loopholes to enrich themselves, often at the expense of needy Indian tribes. 34 www.connecticutalliance.org*

In testimony, Benedict noted that 2 influential Republican lobbyists, with ties to the Bush Administration White House, had been employed by the tribes to aid in the recognition process. The Eastern Pequots paid $645,000 to lobbyist Ronald Kaufman, brother-in-law to President Bush's chief of staff, Andrew Card and the Schaghticokes spent $500,000 on Republican insider Paul Manafort, as well as other lobbyists. 25

In 1988, when Congress legislated for Indian tribes, only 2 states had gambling, Nevada and New Jersey. Now over 300 casinos dot 31 states on the American landscape enriching the tribes and their financiers in outright, grab-the-money-and-go schemes. 26
NY Times, 5/6/04, Raymond Hernandez.

CONNECTICUT'S 2 TRIBAL INDIAN CASINOS

Indian tribes themselves have been subject to outside influences using them to become sources of gambling casinos. They have happily gone along with being used for the benefit of their finances. The Pequot Tribe of Connecticut, for example, was involved in a deal with the Malaysian billionaire, Lim Goth Tong, in 1991, to build Foxwoods Resort Casino. Lim's contract was confidential but recently some of the details were leaked.

The contract supposedly paid him 9.99 % of the casino's adjusted gross revenue for 25 years. 25 years was an unusually long period but it was one of the first contracts negotiated and there was some uncertainty as to how the casino would do. The Lim family reported lent the tribe $235 million to build the casino. They now receive interest on the loan plus almost 10 % of the casino's total profits. For 25 years, Lim will receive almost 10 % of the profits of this supposedly most profitable casino in the world! What is that about the rich getting richer and the poor getting...

A year later, the South African casino entrepreneur, Solomon Kerzner, negotiated an arrangement with Connecticut's Mohegan Tribe to build and operate the Mohegan Sun casino, as reported by Robert Little and Mike Adams, Baltimore Sun, 3/14/04. 27 The contract supposedly stipulated that Kerzner's group would receive 30 to 40 % of the net revenue for 7 years. Seven years is a more common contractual number than the Pequot's 25 year contract. Kerzner first began negotiations with the tribe when the tribe was not yet been recognized by the BIA. He spent 4 years helping the Mohegan tribe secure federal recognition, then he helped them negotiate a contract with the state of Connecticut, and finally he completed the deal by financing the last $50 million of construction costs.

*Kerzner's company, Trading Cove Associates, operated and managed the casino when it first opened in 10/96. The Mohegan Tribe bought out Kerzner's interest at the end of 1999 with another lucrative deal for him. The new deal gave him 5 % of the revenue for 15 years. This refinanced deal was estimated to be worth around $549.1 million at the time, Today it's projected to be near **$1 billion**!*

So in case Kerzner wasn't a billionaire before he became involved with the tribe, he certainly is today. The people of the state of Connecticut have enriched this South African individual handsomely to their own detriment. For such astronomical numbers and profits as are in the deal, for the Indian tribes to give this foreign investor almost a $1 Billion contract, what incredible amounts of money must be being generated at the casinos, what incredible amounts of money must first be lost by Connecticut's_citizens. http://www.baltimoresun.com/news/nationworld/balte, cordish14Mar14,0,3949703.story?coll=bal-nation world-headlines. 28

Remember, casinos neither create nor print money. There is no product that they produce. The money comes from their customers, the pockets of American citizens, the majority of whom live within 50 miles of the casino. Casinos are 'a black hole' for the communities with the money going down the hole, never to return.

Such deal-making between Indian tribes and private financiers is a common arrangement and, as we see, extremely lucrative for all involved. That is, lucrative for everyone but the American public. It's hardly lucrative for America's negative balance of trade, nor for the economy of the state of Connecticut with the casino profits leaving the state and the country. Both financiers for the two incredibly profitable Connecticut Indian casinos are out-of-country individuals and companies and have reaped incredible sums of money for their efforts.

The Eastern Pequots, a Connecticut tribe won federal recognition by the BIA in 2002. That decision is now being appealed by the state of Connecticut. They are backed financially by multimillionaire, William A. Koch. They also hired another influential Republican with White House ties, Ronald Kaufman, to try to get officials to support the tribe.

THE TRIBAL RECOGNITION PROCESS

*Indian tribal gambling has grown enormously since 1988 when Congress first enacted legislation to allow and regulate Indian casinos. Since that time, it has grown into a **$15 Billion dollar-a-year industry** with 330 sites in 29 states! There are fights across the states over tribal membership rights.*

***Foxwoods Casino**, it's estimated, has **revenue of $1.3 Billion dollars annually** and is acknowledged as the world's most profitable gambling casino.*

This movement of Indians and casinos began with a Supreme Court ruling saying that states could not restrict traditional gaming on reservations which were located in states that also had gaming. In other words, if the state had gaming, then the tribes could have it too. Tribes have limited sovereign status and self-government. Seeing this Supreme Court statement, the gambling industry started looking into funding Indian land-claim lawsuits. The overall strategy, in a simplified manner, has been that Indian tribes would sue states for historic land claims and treaties that were allegedly broken or disregarded long ago. Casino or other financier's money funds this costly and extensive land claim researching, the necessary BIA recognition process, and final lawsuit and subsequent state negotiations.

Tribes essentially sue states for broken treaties and illegal seizure of Indian lands often over a hundred years ago. When the state is unable to provide a defense or adequate documentation, the tribes are able to secure judgments in courts against the state. Once the tribes have a judgment against the state, they're able to go to the state and negotiate for a casino in payment of the judgment. A coalition of Apaches, and Cherokees recently sued the state of Colorado for **70 Million acres.** *Imagine the chaos this could create from people who have been living and paying taxes on this land. Then the tribes acknowledged they would settle their claim in return for the right to build a casino. Sounds like blackmail to me.*

Established gambling companies and even overseas investors provide the extensive money necessary to research the land claims, wait out and sponsor the BIA recognition process and negotiate the resulting court battles. This means of course, that when the time for profits comes, the investors also get a sizable share of the profits.

The casino companies are actually using the Indian tribes as a way to get a foothold into a state and to expand gambling operations. The financier, often casino companies such as Harrah's, together with the Indian tribes, split the subsequent and enormous profits resulting from these negotiations. Federal regulations state that the financing companies cannot take more than 30 % of the profits from the tribes. This is often not scrupulously observed and companies find various ways to subvert this arrangement. This is easy to do since the tribal-financier arrangements are not matters of public record and the figures of contractual deals are often kept silent, as are on-going annual profit and loss statements. Recently as the gross inequity of all this for many people has become more evident, people have started leaking financial figures to the newspapers.

In attempting to settle tribal lawsuits, States and governors often negotiate a percentage of the profits to go to states as revenue in exchange for the tribes having an 'exclusive' market share. In other words, the Indians pay the state a certain percentage as long as the state doesn't open its own casinos or allow other competition. This ***'monopoly'*** *then is highly lucrative for the tribes. Of course, these casinos, as all casinos, generate traffic, congestion, crime, and a multitude of other social costs.*

In fact, the **'social costs'** *are so exorbitant, that Connecticut at this point, is attempting to rid themselves of the 2 Indian casinos. As Jeff Benedict, president of The Connecticut Alliance Against Casino Expansion, said on 2/29/04, in an article in The Daily News,*

> *We are receiving 25% of the slot machine revenue, $400 Million a year, and we are a tiny state with 3 million people. Twelve other (Indian) groups are lined up, wanting to build more. But our Legislature, which gets all this money, said 'No Thanks.' 29*

Perhaps States that are rushing headlong to license more Indian casinos should pay attention to Connecticut's experience. In 2003, the Connecticut State Legislature became so alarmed by the threat of further casino expansion that it repealed its 'Las Vegas Nights' statute. Remember, Federal law only allows tribes to offer gambling where it's permitted under state law. As Benedict said:

Casino money costs us a lot more than it's worth.
When the Indian casino comes to town, nobody else does well. *29a*

As one local resident wrote in a Letter to the Editor of the Index-Tribune on 1/23/04, the casinos "were forced on us by a federal judge...The judge equated the once-a-year 'Las Vegas Nights' with full-scale round-the-clock casino gambling and said because we allowed charities the former, we couldn't deny 'tribes' the latter." 30

The letter writer wondered also about the ***authenticity of the tribes****. "No one believes the Mashantuckets are or were 'tribes' any more than the dozen other sudden 'tribes' that sprung up in the past decade. We all grew up with and went to school with these so-called 'tribal members' and they weren't a tribe in the 1950s and 1960s. No tribal (governmental) existence remained."*

There have been many ***local legal battles with the Pequot tribe*** *and local surrounding towns in the past 20 years over various issues such as land annexation within local towns, property taxes, land use regulations, and the extent of tribal sovereign immunity from lawsuits and police jurisdiction. Local people feel that the Pequots are encroaching into local community affairs and not being a good neighbor. As a sovereign nation, police cannot enter unless invited in. Indian casinos are also not subject to environmental regulations, property taxes or other state laws including smoking regulations.*

There are also the Social Costs, said Benedict. Who pays for the (increased bankruptcies, foreclosures, divorces, child abuse and crime)? The local and state governments." 31

The casinos have increased crime in the area towns. In fact, a town employee had to be fired in 12/03 after she admitted she embezzled almost $1 million dollars of the town of Stonington, Connecticut, funds over the past few years, gambling them away at the nearby Foxwoods Resort Casino.

> *Donna Allen was a staff accountant for Stonington's finance department located nearby the 2 Indian casinos. She'd worked for the town for 24 years and had had no prior criminal involvement up to this time. Another tragedy for an individual and her family, another significant loss for the taxpayers, more social costs incurred in her court case, possible imprisonment, etc. 32*

Gambling leads many down the slippery road of Temptation destroying incredible numbers of people, as we can see, both young and old alike.

Recently the BIA recognized the Schaghticoke Indians. They are claiming more than 2,000 acres in Kent, Connecticut, that they want to annex to their existing reservation. Wealthy investors, who hope to put casinos on the reservation, back this 273-member tribe. Towns in the area are not happy because they see themselves as losing more of their tax base to tribal land annexation as well as a host of other ills including traffic congestion, increased crime, etc. This is the fourth tribe to be recognized that lays claim to Connecticut's lands. People don't know where this is all going to end.

The Schaghticokes want to build a casino in Bridgeport, and are bankrolled by Subway Restaurants founder, Fred DeLuca. This site would be a short railroad ride from Manhattan and a half an hour from New Haven, Connecticut. They also hired Republican Party Washington insider, Paul J. Manafort, and spent more than ***$500,000*** *on lobbyists in recent years. If they can afford $500,000 now, imagine how much they anticipate future profits to be.*

Since the BIA have been recognizing Indian tribes, there has been much concern about whether the tribes really have the required Federal documentation to support their claims. Federal regulations state that tribes must have had 'political influence for 64 years in the 19th and 20th Centuries.' In the situation of a California tribe recently, an internal Bureau memo showed that agency staff knew the tribe lacked the required evidence. Knowing this, staff members in the BIA's Office of Federal Acknowledgment, provided the agency's director with direction on how to recognize the tribe anyway, even though it lacked 2 essential criteria.

The memo also showed that the Bureau had placed some of its own agency staff members on the list of tribal members! Attorney General Richard Blumenthal says that "This document says that the BIA was ready, willing and able to do virtually anything to recognize this tribe. The BIA staff in essence presented completely lawless and false options for the political leaders to pick." 33

If the Schaghticoke Tribal Nation spent more than $500,000 on lobbyists, and then in addition, the BIA acted in a seemingly haphazard and illegal manner, then the Tribe won recognition through political influence, not historical facts, according to Harford Courant writer, Rick Green, on 3/12/04. What incredible deal-making and manipulation seem to be the order of the day in Washington when such large amounts of money are involved. What happens to the little citizens of the towns involved? What happens to the individual gamblers involved? When these amounts of money and political influence are bandied about as if they were nothing, it's no surprise that our little gambler doesn't have a chance of winning, or just coming out even.

CALIFORNIA INDIAN TRIBES AND GAMBLING

In California, in 1998, Indian tribes that supported Proposition 5, a measure legalizing slot machines for tribes, and their adversaries, the Nevada gambling interests, spent a total of ***$92 Million dollars*** *getting this public referendum passed by the voters! This was a record amount of money on an initiative. This demonstrates the vast sums of money people are willing to spend to get 'a share of the action'. The state Supreme Court later overturned the measure so the tribes spent another $243 Million dollars in the year 2000 on Prop. 1A which ratified the casino compacts the tribes had agreed upon with the ex-Gov. Gray Davis. 34*

California Indian casinos *currently bring in approximately* ***$5 Billion a year.*** *Las Vegas' casinos only bring in slightly more at $7.7 Billion. This $5 Billion in revenue is an unstable and a morally questionable source of income. As Larry Berg, founding director of the Jesse Unruh Institute of Politics at the University Southern California, in an article in the Christian Science Monitor said on 2/9/04,* ***"It's a really sad state of affairs that a state of 36 million people with the fifth largest economy on earth is going to rely on gambling to help balance the budget."*** *35*

This statement reflects the incongruity and inappropriateness of a major world economy stooping so low as to rely on an historically known vice and a recognized addictive activity to balance their budget. Can't the world's richest nation do any better than this?

As California licenses more and more gambling venues, places for its citizens to lose their money, they are also finding that the sword of gambling cuts both ways. Citizens will not only lose their money, but they'll also lose the state's money. A story from the AP, 12/8/03, showed this to be true. An employee of the ***California State Employees Association*** *recently was discovered to have* ***embezzled almost $1 Million dollars*** *from the agency. The CSEA represents 140,000 California government employees.*

> *A 64 year old woman and bookkeeper, said she lost the money in California and Las Vegas casinos over a 5 year period. Gail Jones handled cash management and investments and wrote fraudulent checks to herself on CSEA accounts. As with many gamblers who embezzle, after she started embezzling, she said she continued gambling in an effort to try to win the money back to return it. Of course, she never made it back and it was never returned.*
>
> *She was sentenced to 30 months in a Federal prison. It's unusual for a 64 year old person to engage in criminal activities, especially one without prior criminal records. 36*

The addiction of gambling seems to bring out the worst in people. This person succumbed to the Temptation that the State licensed and provided, that the State made available. I would think that the state was culpable also. Chalk up another tragedy for gambling, another family destroyed by what the State licensed and allowed.

California Indians could eventually become the richest people on earth, according to Indian expert, Jan Golab, in an article 2/29/04 in The Daily News, Los Angeles. 37 Although Indian tribal casinos are called and treated as 'sovereign' nations, in fact, they depend on state, county and local governments for their basic needs such as power, water, fire and police protection. They need their 'host' country, to provide the currency and method of exchange, i.e. money. They send their children to public schools and they influence the political process in this country with large cash donations to public officials. So there's a wealth of detail to work through in deciding what exactly the term 'sovereign nation' really means.

Lobbying with huge cash subsidies has occurred in many states throughout the country. In California, the Morongo Bank of Indians has pledged $50 Million dollars to defeat one of the gambling initiatives there, should it be necessary. Nelson

Rose, California gambling expert, and a professor at Whittier Law School, said that this kind of money to be used for political purposes means tremendous power. Racing, which used to be among the leading campaign donors in California, has been dwarfed by the tribes' political influence, he said, in an article in the BloodHorse on 3/22/04. http://news.bloodhorse.com/viewstory.asp?id=21426. The compacts with Indian tribes have "created a gambling industry half the size of Las Vegas practically overnight." 37 ***Gambling wagering may reach $6 Billion dollars in 2004,*** *he said, noting California's* ***34 million residents****. 38*

Governor Arnold Schwarzenegger of California recently appointed a past police chief and law enforcement liaison to the office of director of the California Gambling Control Commission. Former police chief, Robert Shelton, said that the Commission actually has authority to ensure compliance with many of the Commission's requests that tribes haven't adhered to in the past. Shelton said he is beginning to 'convince' people (Indian tribes) to cooperate with the State. California has many different casino contracts with different tribes subject to different and competing interpretations.

Engaging a past police chief like Shelton is ushering in a new phase in the state-Indian casino relationship. Now tribes are now being pressured to pay higher percentages back to States as well as become 'a team player' with the State in terms of adhering to state regulations about various issues. Shelton, who has had experience with gambling for many years as a Police Chief, said he views gambling as a ***vice*** *to be controlled in all its legal and illegal variations.*

I don't gamble and I don't believe in gambling.
I wouldn't have any gambling whatsoever.

I don't believe in robbery and homicide and burglary either. Dir., Calif. Gambling Com. Robert Shelton 39

Shelton experienced gambling's impact as Police Chief of South Lake Tahoe Police Dept., another city where gambling has had free rein for many years.

In the State of ***Alabama****, the Poarch Bank of Creek Indians operate 4 video gambling halls. Under Federal law, the state of Alabama cannot tax this income. So the Indian tribes are getting very wealthy and the people in the community are getting very poor. Somehow America has to 'look at this picture and see what's wrong...'*

Not only is this ludicrous for Alabama's taxpayers, but it's terribly unfair to all struggling people who don't happen to be Indians and have not inherited a flourishing gold-mine in the form of gambling. It's also unfair to all of Alabama's citizens who would like to see the state's hard-won social programs go to help all the poor. It's unfair to see one group suddenly enriched by a quirk or a misinterpretation of a ruling. When the Supreme Court allowed amorphous Indian tribes, already wracked by chronic alcoholism and unemployment, to implement casinos and gambling, it started this monstrous industry throughout our states, now known as the Indian gambling and casino business.

When the Supreme Court said Indians could have traditional Gambling on their reservations, it had no idea of the ensuing proliferation of gambling. We called Indian nations 'sovereign' 100 years ago but today's tribes have largely assimilated and acculturated, and bear little resemblance to the Indians of a hundred years ago. The Court didn't envision that the gambling that they opened up would eviscerate existing government social programs and enrich a small group at the expense of the larger society.

Not all Indians are benefiting from gambling. Often tribal leaders don't share the largesse with all tribal members. Indian tribal members, so near to gambling casinos, gamble as do non-Indians. So when they gamble, they're hurt that much more. The tribal gambling programs are impoverishing, i.e. putting more citizens into poverty levels, than ever before. It's perhaps even more debilitating to their lifestyle.

Recently there have been news stories about the fact that the leaders of the Seneca Nation seem to be making vast sums of money, while rank-and-file people continue to live in poverty without access to many of the lucrative things associated with casinos. For example, although Indians were supposed to have gotten preferential hiring in the casinos, individual members of the Indian Nation haven't been able to get jobs or contracts there in the case of business firms there. Corruption grows everywhere, in our government as well as on Indian Nation land.

Government's job is to help all the citizens, the rich, the poor and the middle class. State government has an overview of all of society and is able to use this perspective to create and design new programs that will act as a catalyst to everyone's economic development and social consciousness, that will benefit the larger society.

Sometimes negotiations with Indian tribes become even more involved. In New York State, Park Place Entertainment Co., a casino company based in Atlantic City, negotiated with Indian tribes in the Monticello area. The agreement essentially enjoined the Indian tribes from actively pursuing this tribal recognition process in exchange for a huge payment every year. After the 5 year contractual arrangement expires, then the contract transforms itself into a deal for the management company,

Park Place casino, to 'help' the Indians manage and operate a new casino in the Monticello area. This gives some idea of the magnitude of the profits involved, that a gambling corporation can pay a tribe enormous profits just to wait and do nothing.

****

NEW YORK STATE—SENECA INDIAN CASINOS

In New York State, the Seneca Indians, along with its managing agent, the Seneca Gaming Corp., opened a casino 5 blocks away from Niagara Falls on 55 acres in the heart of the town of Niagara Falls. Financially, the casino has been extremely successful. The city of Niagara Falls gets $9.5 million dollars revenue annually and about 200 jobs have been spun off, according to a Niagara Falls Reporter article. Yet the city must cope with the extra police and many other services required for managing the constant influx of people that the casino generates. $38 million is paid to New York State annually under the terms of the casino compact, strictly from slot-machine profit.

All of the money spent on table games as well as sales of food, liquor, souvenirs, and everything else goes strictly to the Corporation and stays there. Figures released by the Niagara Falls Reporter show that the casino grossed hundreds of millions of dollars, the slots brought in almost 96 % of the casino's excess profits. Yet despite these astronomical figures, wages start at the minimum of $4.40/hour plus tips. Foods and beverage workers, slot attendants work at this below-minimum-plus tips level. Its estimated that half of the 'labor budget' goes to top casino executives.

The Seneca Gaming Corp. is not required by law to disclose any financial figures. The above figures were published by the Niagara Falls Reporter with information that their reporter uncovered. Even the members of the Seneca Nation, the tribal members involved, are not allowed access to financial data. According to Federal law, the management companies are not allowed to take any more than 30 % of the casino profits from the tribes. Yet if the financial data stays hidden from all except a few top executives, how will anyone be able to check on these percentages of profit and loss.

One thing is clear, top executives are doing well and low-paid labor in the casino is just that, low-paid labor. The casino also states that it's provided about 2000 jobs for Niagara Falls residents. They don't state 'full-time' jobs. By minimizing the number of full-time workers, the Seneca Gaming Corp. saves millions in health and other benefits they don't have to pay for and increases the number of jobs they're supposedly created. This gambit of creating part-time jobs also keeps people impoverished as it does not allow for any kind of a career ladder or long-term job expectations by employees.

The Rev. Sue Abrams, also a member of the Seneca tribal council, said that only about 75 tribal people are among the more than 2000 casino employees at the Niagara casino. Unemployment for the Seneca nation remains near 60 %. Some Seneca families still live without indoor plumbing and crammed into mobile homes. Within the tribe, the close proximity of gambling is already generating extraordinary addiction rates among tribal members, easily twice the rate of the great U.S. population.

Big money alledgely tampered with the rights of tribal members and manipulated tribal members into passing the election of whether the tribe should proceed into the gambling arena. Abrams said her group had defeated gambling in 2 earlier tribal elections. There is 'no money' coming down to the people, she told the NCL conference. No tribal member is allowed to see the books that show where the money goes and how it's distributed.

Estimates give the total number of jobs available to Niagara Falls residents as actually about 200 instead of 2000 as claimed by the management company. Interestingly, what has hurt these arrangements recently and made people so angry that they 'leak' financial figures, has been the attitude and actions of the managing companies. In the face of these enormous profits, one would hope that managing companies would strive to secure employee loyalty and contentment with well-paying salaries for everyone, a corporate 'everyone-shares-in-the-wealth-spirit'. So everyone could make money and feel they were doing well. However this has not been the case. Lower paid workers, waiters, cleaning people, even dealers, often receive minimum-wage salaries.

Knowing that casino executives are reeling in enormous sums, but that they are not being offered a share of the gigantic, 'windfall profits', employees understandably feel somewhat disgruntled and left out. As a result of this state of affairs, someone 'leaked' to a Buffalo newspaper confidential financial figures for the year 2003 for the Seneca Indian nation casino in Niagara Falls. These figures showed that while casino profits were higher than anticipated, and casino executives and management company administrators were well-paid, lower level casino workers were extremely poorly paid.

The Reporter article quotes a financial analyst who estimated that at least half of the labor budget went to casino executives. The analyst noted that "What's going to the actual workers, compared to total revenue, is pretty disgusting." Numbers can be twisted to serve anyone's point of view. But what cannot be twisted or subverted is the fact that this casino is making some people very wealthy, but it's certainly neither the rank-and-file tribal members nor the residents of Niagara Falls.

The state of New York has another Indian tribal casino, ***Turning Stone****, run by the Oneida Indian Nation, near the U.S. Canadian border. This casino is expanding and in Fall, 2004, the new expansion will nearly triple the square footage of the current resort, from about 500,000 to 1.3 Million square foot. This is 22 times larger than the original casino that opened in l993! The casino will be the tallest building between Syracuse and Albany. The expansion is costing $308 Million dollars. This represents money from customer losses, from Social Security checks of seniors, from life-time savings, from college tuition, from money earmarked for other purposes, more constructive pursuits. 40 The Post-Standard, 4/13/04, Glenn Coin, http://www.syracuse.com/news/poststandard/index.ssf?/base/news-5/108184680624853.xml*

The Seneca Indians are also seeking to open another casino in Buffalo, New York, about 100 miles from the Niagara Falls casino. How much money, we wonder, does the small tribe need to make? Or perhaps does it managing agent want to make? I never thought that big money and large bank accounts were one of the goals of Indian culture. Governor Pataki had negotiated a compact with the Seneca Nation in 2001 allowing them to establish up to 3 casinos in western New York State. ***Neither the State Legislature nor the voters ever approved the compact.***

When initially proposed, the Buffalo-Niagara Business Partnership had supported the Buffalo casino, feeling that it would generate economic development. However the compact only required the Seneca's to pay the state a percentage of profits as long as they had an exclusive franchise on those types of machines. If other locations open, then the Seneca's won't have to donate profits from slots to New York State. Presently the Buffalo-Niagara Partnership, having had experience with the Niagara Falls Seneca Casino, now a year old, doesn't want a casino.

The Business Partnership, noted that:

> *The Seneca casino could lead to disinvestment downtown. Most of a Buffalo casino's business would come from local people, not tourists. The Seneca casino, will not create a tourism destination, and will fail to bring 'out-of-town' dollars to Buffalo. 41*

So local business people recognize that local resorts, as opposed to destination resorts, take their profits from local citizens, essentially acting as 'black holes' in the local economy. They benefit no one but casino executives and shareholders. As Assembly member Sam Hoyt (D-Buffalo) said, ***"A casino would be bad for Buffalo's economy. A casino can actually result in a net loss of jobs for the region. Local***

residents will spend their money at the casino instead of on (sports) games, local restaurants, concerts, and clubs and other established businesses. Some will even gamble away money that they should be spending on food, clothing and housing." *42*

This is exactly what the big research studies state that we've quoted say. It's a welcome development that local leaders, such as Assemblyman Hoyt, are starting to understand the dynamics of gambling and the fact that gambling would bring more harm than good to their regions.

The ***state of Michigan has 20 casinos, 7 horse racing tracks, and a State Lottery****. Yet the state is not reaping the benefits even in terms of additional revenues from the casinos as much as they could. They're seeking to further expand gambling by allowing horse tracks to add slot machines and VLTs, and further to allow Internet and off-track wagering on races. The general opinion by State government there seems to be that since there's already betting, why not tax it more. This argument is fallible however since, as we've learned, the closer people are to gambling sites, the more often they'll go, and the more they'll bet. This 'enhanced' racetrack model is being opposed by the existing casinos as well as anti-gambling forces as additional competition.*

Only 3 tribes out of Michigan's 17 Indian-run casinos pay taxes to the state. These 3 pay only 8% as opposed to Connecticut's 2 tribal casinos which kick back 25% of their revenue to the state. This is because the state approved compacts with other tribes and with non-Indian casinos to open in Detroit in the late 1990s so the requirement that the casinos pay revenue to the state was null and void. State budget crises continue to make gambling expansion proposals very attractive to legislative leaders. 52

CASINOS WITHOUT VOTER APPROVAL

To satisfy judgments that Indian tribes are able to get against the States for alleged past treaty violations, many State Governors have entered into compacts or contracts with Indian tribes without constitutional or legislative approval. This is what happened in **New York** *where the State Constitution prohibits casinos. Yet the Governor entered into an agreement or compact with the tribes to open casinos without constitutional or legislative approval. This is why New York has casinos yet New York voters have never approved casino gambling.*

The same thing, Governors making compacts with Indian tribes without legislature or voter approval, has also occurred in other states. Connecticut voters never approved casinos in their state either but now have 2 giant ones.

***West Virginia** voters have also never been consulted on the issues of gambling yet they have casinos. In 1984 a public referendum approved only a simple paper-ticket lottery. So how could that have evolved into casinos? A lottery is very different than a casino. It's a relatively benign "game that doesn't rip apart families, sink citizens into bankruptcy, nor create and foster habitual, compulsive day and night gambling habits," according to an editorial entitled, Sodom and Gomorrah, in the Johnson County Sun newspaper, 2/26/04 by Steve Rose, Chairman. It's also, he added fairly low-profile as compared to the huge glitzy monuments surrounded with neon lights that are always open, called casinos. 43*

Since 1984 in West Virginia, the voters have never approved gambling, but "the legislature has expanded the definition of lottery ***six*** *different times without the approval of the voters. Today, the definition of lottery even includes slot machines," Stephen Reed, State Director for West Virginia Coalition Against Gambling Expansion (WV-CAGE) said on 2/13/04 in a press release. I also would like to know how a casino can be defined as a 'lottery' and how feeding table games and slot machines endless money can be re-interpreted as buying a ticket. Reed added that casinos are not what the West Virginia voters intended in 1984. Black jack, dice, and poker are certainly not lotteries. The addictive potential is very different with each and soars with the former. 44*

Reed stated that the gambling industry designs ways to deliberately make people psychologically addicted to gambling. The gambling industry spends millions of dollars every year to figure out how to get people addicted to gambling. 45

As we will see in the chapter discussing ways casinos misrepresent gambling to people, there are many ways and techniques that they utilize to do so. Casinos seek to hook people into gambling because that's their business. "If the gambling industry can prove there is no effort to create addictions then that helps their cause. They need to come clean on the addiction issue. Until they do that, we're looking at people who lost their life savings." This is a common occurrence. Consider how could casinos be built by people spending $50. or even $100. a night? 46

These are the millions and millions of addicted people who the gambling industry says are a 'small percentage' of the people who play. My husband and I lost life savings. So did many other gamblers who are now in GA and go faithfully every week to remain unaddicted. If gambling continues to expand, this number will be even further increased. Tomorrow it may be your husband, or your son, or your favorite 'Uncle Harry'. When it comes to addictions, no one is immune, no one is exempt. It's just a matter of time.

WV-CAGE director, Reed, also met with West Virginia's Attorney General, Darrell McGraw, on 2/26/04. McGraw announced in that meeting that his

Consumer Protection office had already started a file about West Virginia's gambling industry and that that office has been monitoring the state's gambling enterprises for a while. McGraw's Consumer Protection Division had recovered millions of dollars on the cigarette issue for West Virginians previously.

Even candidate for West Virginia Governor, Monty Warner, is also against gambling and sent out a public letter detailing his position. What Warner writes can well be applied to any State or municipality. The economics and addiction apply everywhere. On 2/13/04, he wrote that

> *West Virginia shouldn't grow dependent on a form of revenue that*
>
> *(1) encourages destructive behaviors amongst our citizenry,*
> *(2) is inherently unstable, and*
> *(3) undermines our economy.*
>
> *Dependence on gambling proceeds, makes the State complicit in the crime of looting our most vulnerable citizens. The State becomes an active agent in promoting behavior and attitudes that under-mine our greatest strengths and erodes our values.*
> *The expansion of legalized gambling destroys and undermines the best in us. It is shameful and disgusting. Legalized gambling becomes a vicious, insidious addictive drug; hastening the decline of honorable, respectable businesses and jobs. 47*

No one wants to see Appalachia or New York City, or Miami, Florida, become even more destitute and its citizens even poorer. No one wants to see what happened to Lesia Reed happen to other citizens of this state.

> *Lesia Reed's sister lived in West Virginia when slots were legalized a few years ago. Her sister's husband, Eugene Golden, was a compulsive gambler and lied to his wife for years to conceal his addiction. He tried to stop, Reed said, but then succumbed again when casinos moved nearby into his neighborhood. In towns in West Virginia, Keno and slots are easier to find than grocery stores or even doctors. Once to get money for his addiction, Golden even told his debtors he couldn't pay then because he was arranging for the funeral of his infant daughter, still very much alive.*
>
> *Then this compulsive gambler, who turned to crime by forging checks, robbed the town bank. He ended up in prison because of his gambling obsession.*
>
> *"My brother-in-law was a caring, loving father," Reed said. "He took his children to church, was never drunk, or violent and ever lifted a finger at my sister. But he had an addiction that was far more devastating." 47*

Another family ruined, children without a father, wife without a husband, all because of gambling. Does this man bear responsibly for his own action? Of course he does and he's suffering the consequences right now in prison. His family are also enduring the fruit of his actions, the cost of his addiction. Does the State have some culpability for putting an 'attractive nuisance' in this man's neighborhood? I would say 'yes.' The State legalized this activity, made it available, gave it its consent and its blessing.

What this family experienced, is the aftermath, the fruits of the State legalizing this activity of gambling. Addiction is what occurs, what happens to some people, when exposed to this activity. This is what state governments are rushing to legalize. This seems to be all we can think of, to solve our budget problems. Where are our resources, our creativity, our sense of can-do? If we decided to all work as a team, for a common goal, the upliftment of society, the betterment of all people, we would accomplish a great deal. If we all act alone, seeking our own material success, we may swim or perchance, we may sink, depending on the cards that night...

Whether it's a private casino, as in the Atlantic City casinos, or an Indian casino, which are proliferating without cease, casinos have the potential to hurt people in many ways. Gambling is an issue inadequately debated and questioned thus far and whose implications do not bode well for the American public.

For all of these reasons, namely Governors entering into tribal compacts without voter or legislative approval, as well as because gambling is so detrimental for both state economies and for individual citizens, and families, 2 Federal Congressmen courageously introduced a Federal bill in February, 2004, calling for a federal commission to study the economic and social impact of Indian gaming. They also asked the Government Reform Committee for hearings on the influence of 'outside interests, especially wealthy gaming interests' on the tribal recognition process.

Rep. Chris Shays, R-Conn. and co-sponsor, Rep. Frank Wolf, R-Va, said the bill would require state legislatures to approve Indian gaming compacts instead of governors. This legislation would also require communities and local areas to approve any new Indian casinos in their jurisdiction. According to this bill, local Communities that decided gambling was not something they wanted, would be able to prevent their incursion into their neighborhoods. Presently there is a process for appeal by local citizens and communities, but usually grass-roots movements gets started too late by too few and are unsuccessful against the enormous financially backed and superbly organized pro-gambling forces.

"Federal tribal recognition should not mean the end of local participation in decisions about casino expansion - especially because those decisions have enormous impacts on the communities in which casinos are built," Shays said. Wolf, a longtime critic of the gambling industry, added in a letter to his Congressional colleagues that, ***"Under current law, local communities often have little say about whether large gaming operations will open in their towns".*** *48*

"The bottom line is, citizens should have the final word on casino expansion in their communities." The Shays-Wolf bill would also establish an advisory committee to create minimum requirements for federal regulation of Indian gaming, he said on Friday, January 30, 2004. This legislation would enable communities to have jurisdiction over their own local affairs and not allow small tribes backed by large wealthy, foreign corporations to come and invade their areas without public consensus or approval.

Certainly the idea of local control over local affairs would seem to be an elementary one for communities in the United States. Local control is a provision of the terms of the U.S. Constitution and state's rights. Local citizens need to actively support such legislation by Shay and Wolf if they don't want to see electronic bingo and other types of gambling in their neighborhoods.

LOBBYISTS AND INFLUENCE- PEDDLING

Lobbyists are increasingly being turned to by the gambling industry in an effort to get their agendas, i.e. the expansion of gambling, passed by Legislatures. The gambling industry has plenty of cash flow, has connections with important legislators and influential lobbyists, and the knowledge of how to make the system work for them. Unfortunately when the system works for private interests whose agenda and goal is to make money, then it doesn't work so well for the average citizen.

In New York State in 2003, over $112 Million dollars was spent on lobbyists, according to the state Lobbying Commission. When the State Lobbying Commission was first formed in l978, total lobbyist spending was only $6 Million dollars for the year. Especially significant was the Seneca Nation of Indians which spent just under $2 Million dollars, as recorded in an article in the Buffalo Business Journal on 3/22/04. 49 http://buffalo.bizjournals.com/buffalo/stories/2004/03/ 22/daily14.html

The Seneca Indians hope to open a second casino in Cattaraugus County. This excessive cash flow is to influence the legislative process, to curry favor and gain access to state legislators in an effort to get favorable legislation and rulings for the Indian Nation. I wonder at the funds that the Indian Nation can make available to high-priced lobbyists, whether it's fair to others who don't have such cash reserves to allow the Indian Nation to throw their weight around with apparent impunity. I also wonder whether this kind of influence-peddling leads to the best, most thoughtful and carefully considered legislation with the good of all New York State citizens.

These incredible amounts of money are unlike anything else ever seen in America's political scene. What they will do to our government system of checks and balances is unclear. The fact is that they are doing all in their not inconsiderable power to affect the balance of power and to favor the interests of small groups over the majority of citizens. To have such money and hence power in the hands of small interests groups would seem to be precarious for American Democracy and to exert undue influence on the democratic process as we know it, and as it exists today.

- *Other states have even more casinos than Connecticut or New York. Illinois has **9** riverboat casinos with 4 casinos located in the populous but economically poor Chicago area. Guess who's funding the casino's profits there?*

- *There are currently 4 tribal casinos in **Kansas** and a state lottery. Governor Kathleen Sibelius is attempting to persuade the legislature to open 5 additional state-owned casinos to generate revenue for the state. An editorial against gambling's expansion noted that **"We have hit bottom and are now willing to sell our souls to make a buck."** 50*

Not everyone in Kansas is so enamored of casinos. Sen. Tim Huelskamp, R-Fowler, said that he was concerned about the social costs of increased problem gambling in the state.

***On the one hand, we're trying to see what we can do about skyrocketing Medicaid costs, and on the other hand, we're trying to see how many more families we can add to the welfare rolls.**" 51*

What a true expression of the tension and inconsistency in the role of the government in licensing gambling, as the addictive activity that it is, and yet trying to ensure that the state budget is balanced and that the costs of various public assistance programs for medical benefits to disabled citizens is constantly growing.

But to say that these two roles are polarities is to buy into the false values that gambling creates something, that gambling is not a parasite on the government's revenue. The State licenses gambling which serves to increase the money that government spends in various services, yet then gambling gives the state back a little money. Sounds like gambling buying its licenses from the State, which is what is exactly happening with some of the Midwest States especially. The states are considering charging Millions for a casino license which the gambling industry will pay in the relatively confident hope of future enormous profits.

Yet where do the vast sums of money come from that everyone is eagerly seeking? Out of whose pocket does this money come? The money comes from its citizens, the citizens of the State that licensed the gambling. The money goes to the casino owners, gambling industry operatives, and then they give a little back to the State. What a curious round-robin. What poor business this is for the government, not only poor morality. The State is creating an industry by their licensing. Then the industry, born an 'enfant terrible', turns and gives a little, perhaps 10 %, back to its creator. Pretty good deal for someone. Not the State, and not the individual. Harris News Service, 4/14/04, Gambling opponents warn of social costs, Chris Grenz.

*In Pennsylvania, Gov. Ed Rendell created in May, 2004, by executive order, the **Office for Financial Education.** Newspapers reported that the directors' office will have a salary of more than $90,000. Rep. Jerry Stern, 80th District, Pennsylvania House of Representatives, asked why the Governor thought it necessary to help Pennsylvania families manage their money, while simultaneously heading efforts to bring slot machines, known as being the most addictive form of gambling, veritable* *addictive delivery systems, to the State. Rep. Stern added that it was ironic that the governor, who is "pushing for expanded gambling, has just announced the creation of an office to help Pennsylvanians better balance their checkbooks and avoid the pitfalls that often lead to bankruptcy and foreclosures." 52 http://www.jerrystern.com*

In Pennsylvania, legislators have been inundated by gambling money with its poorly disguised efforts at influencing votes. Centaur, Inc., an Indiana gambling company has made political contributions of more than $200,750 since September, 2002. "Pennsylvania campaign finance sounds like that new HBO western show Deadwood, where there's no laws in the town and everybody's out for themselves," said James Browning, executive director of Common Cause, Maryland, a nonprofit government watchdog. 53

- *An Inquirer analysis of campaign finance records shows that gambling interests have contributed at least $5.8 Million into Pennsylvania's campaigns since 2000. "Centaur makes campaign contributions to support candidates whose policies are in line with the company," Centaur spokesman Rick Kelly said. In February, 2004, Centaur donated $42,500 to Democratic Rep. Michael Veon's campaign, Beaver County, where the company would like to build a racetrack. House Minority Leader William DeWeese (D-Greene), acknowledged that Pennsylvania needs to reform its campaign finance laws. Yet even he has gained money since 2000 from gambling interests.*

The result of this unquestioned political donation is that wealth gains access to influential people, to push their own agendas and ordinary citizens don't get their concerns addressed in as direct or supportive a manner. ***"Money has an undue influence on politics,"*** *said Sen. Allen G. Kukovitch (D-Westmoreland), who has backed campaign finance bills since 1977. "Especially in a state like Pennsylvania, where there are no limits.* ***It's a dagger in the heart of Democracy."*** *54*

- *Even Pennsylvania Gov. Ed Rendell himself, has benefited from gambling interests contribution to his campaigns, receiving about $1.7 Million since 2000. Rendell has been very enthusiastic in supporting the legalization of slots in Pennsylvania, according to the Philadelphia Inquirer, May 2, 2004.*

- *The infusion of gambling in Pennsylvania would only hurt the economy in the long run, according to experts in the field. It's estimated that if 15,000 slot machines were installed at the racetracks in Pennsylvania, problem gamblers would probably cost the state "more than $500 Million." University of Nevada gambling researcher, William*

> *Thompson, testified before the General assembly's finance committee in 2003 saying that "local areas will lose approximately $267 Million annually from their economies. The state economy will also lose $84 Million" as people spend money gambling rather than other purchases."*

These figures were estimated with 15,000 machines. Current proposals are seeking more than 30,000 machines so people in Pennsylvania can expect even further increases in problem gambling and money siphoned away from local and state economies. ***Legislators ought to take a look at the costs, not just the income of economic proposals,*** *noted an editorial in the Philadelphia Inquirer on April 28, 2004, by Robert Goodman, director of the U.S. Gambling Study at the University of Massachusetts. 55 http://www.philly.com/mid/inquirer/news/editorial/8535491.htm*

- ***Indiana has 10 riverboat casinos.*** *These generated $1.8 Billion in revenue during 2001. Annually there were almost 41 Million visits by people. We note 'visits' instead of people since people visit multiple times. In Illinois, the state is seeking to add 2 additional casinos in the Chicago area, to allow slot machines at horse-racing tracks and 15,200 more gambling positions at existing casinos. Currently there are 12,000 allowed.*

Low-income groups in the Chicago area will now have even more of an opportunity to support the state's budget in their own back-yard. Illinois Governor Rod Blagojevich had campaigned on a promise of no expanded gambling. However, with the state's budget worries, the revenue of $1 Billion Dollar in fees and hundreds of millions in new gambling tax revenues annually, look very attractive to all, as reported by Bob Tita in an article from the Crain's Chicago Business Newsroom on 3/29/04. Money is addictive, big money is very addictive.

Gambling revenue looks like 'easy money', a 'quick fix' for impoverished states dealing with bloated bureaucracies and overpaid politicians. Yet the 'chickens will come home to roost' and the Social Costs will show their ugly face in the not-too-distant future. Whose relatives and friends will become addicted and lose the family home to foreclosure, whose Uncle Fred or Aunt May is going to go there for a fun night out on the town and later end up spending their life savings in the casinos? Maybe the Governor's family?

- ***Missouri has 11 riverboat casinos*** *which opened in 1994. They generated $1.1 Billion revenue in 2001 with more than 51 Million visits by people annually. Gambling seems to be the way a lot of Americans are spending their leisure time and money. This dubiously-termed* *entertainment does nothing for people's minds and a negative something for their pocketbooks. Are Americans so wealthy these days that they can afford to throw money away without receiving some tangible value for it?*

- ***Mississippi has 29 casinos** that generate nearly $2.7 billion in annual revenue. If, as some studies indicate, casino gambling has a net social cost of $156. per person, then the states are paying for a lot of social costs, a lot more than the revenue they collect that looks so good. The social costs are more 'hidden', not as obvious, and not as amenable to being 'hyped' as the supposed revenue collected. 56*

***South Carolina** had video gambling but it was banned by the Courts in 2000. **"That industry sucked $3 to 4 Billion out of our people's pockets every year," said Rep. John Graham Altman, III, R-Charleston. "That was money that could have been spent in grocery stores, on wives and children.** We got out of that jungle once and we ain't going back." There have been efforts to revive gambling but so far have been beaten back. The Post And Courier, 12/23/04.*

South Carolina is another place, like Buffalo, New York, where local leaders, such as Assemblyman Hoyt, became well-aware of gambling's potentially disastrous impact on local businesses and people. As people become more aware and sophisticated in understanding what gambling really brings, they're realizing that gambling is not the panacea that its adherents claim. In fact, not only is it not a panacea but it becomes a voracious whirlpool sucking in money, energy, community resources and businesses, destroying all in its path.

We've heard all this before, again and again. It's not new. But it is hard for some people to believe. People who bother to examine the gaming industry's claims, realize that 'all that glitters is not gold' and that the only people a casino benefits, are its own executives and stockholders.

So the advent of tribal casino gambling has been destructive for communities in America, has led many people to ruin, and is certainly not a 'high point' in the history of Indian culture. Gambling and the large amounts of money that the casinos are bringing in, the money lost by naive citizens who actually think they can win, money that should have gone for other more constructive purposes, will wind up hurting the Indians more than they realize, will wind up "destroying a culture - the first people of this land," said Rev. Abrams.

Private corporate casinos, such as Harrah's or MGM Mirage, are different entities than Indian tribal casinos. Corporate casinos are private industries with their taxes regulated by the state. These types of casinos, although equally destructive of individual gamblers, generate more revenue for the State and hire more labor from the general labor market than Indian casinos do, noted Dr. Garrett, Federal Reserve Bank of St. Louis senior economist, in his thesis, "Casino Gambling in American and its Economic Impacts."

Corporate casinos, as opposed to Indian tribal casinos, are more amenable to state regulations and revenue. Indian casinos, being sovereign nations, don't usually return as much revenue back to the State. Indian nations, as part of their 'sovereign status' are similar to having a foreign nation, such as France or Spain, in our midst. They are immune from prosecution, and do not have to abide by U.S. laws and regulations such as smoking, child welfare legislation, sanitation, environmental, truth-in-advertising, etc.

Energy and time has been so consumed by debating the merits of more and more slot machine casinos, additional 'racinos', racing tracks with slots, that no one has ideas about other sources of income for the state or other constructive programs. There is not a lot of energy going into exploring different ways of finding more state revenue, other ways of cutting the excess pork-barrel in state budgets.

Not only has gambling usurped time and energy, it's consumed endless amounts of money that could have been spent more constructively, not only on the part of gamblers themselves, but on the part of states and politicians. As large amounts of money get bandied about, many people lose sight of the important things and start looking to see what they can get for themselves. The next step after gambling is Corruption which has reared its ugly head in quite a few places and threatens to become even more pronounced in the future.

Governors and some legislators get so enamored of gambling and it's possible revenue that they turn a deaf ear to everything else. They become sold on what gambling can do for the state and refuse to look at the overall picture, to explore other funding sources or various innovative programs to meet the needs of the state's citizens. Instead of examining the needs of the citizens, they examine the needs of the budget.

People are beginning to realize the negative effects of gambling all over. In ***Canada****, a group of downtown North Bay business owners has come together to oppose casino development. In a meeting on March, 2004, the business owners listened to retired pharmacist Bill Clark speak on gambling as an 'addictive process.' In Canada, the state itself owns and operates the casinos. Here in Ontario, Clark said referring to state casino ownership:*

The promoter is also the regulator. ***It's like having Dracula in charge of the blood bank****. A pathological gambler...will get up in the middle of the night to go and gamble.*
In a pharmacy, "If a drug exhibited side-effects that caused death, it would be pulled off the market in no time." 57

Clark added that the further a person is from a casino or slot machine, the better off they are, he added, commenting on the addictive nature of the activity. There were 4,000 suicides in Canada last year. "If gambling suicides were recorded, it would be one a day." Clark referred to Australia which has had casinos for 25 years. ***"Real estate went down a great deal because gambling addicts steal and don't make repairs to their houses,"*** *he noted in an article in the North Bay Nugget on 3/25/04. 58 www.nugget.ca.*

There are a great many ways in which a gambling addict brings down the community he lives in with his addiction. Gambling corrupts individuals, it corrupts state governments, and it even corrupts politicians in its endless drive for more and more money.

CORRUPTION AND POLITICIANS – SOFT MONEY, CAMPAIGN DONATIONS

The political impact of the tribes and of the gambling industry is significant and is an ominous sign for our democracy. Whether it's Indian tribes or private gaming management companies, they're starting to make startlingly big campaign contributions to politicians. The idea is that later they will receive favorable votes and other favors. This is Corruption - the buying of political influence with money.

- *Leaders of the Coushatta Indian Tribe of Louisiana have spent millions on lobbyists, and spent it without informing tribe members, according to news reports. "Chief Maynard Kahgegab of the Saginaw Chippewa Tribe and other tribe council members have spent more than $8 million in 2 years on lobbyists, according to tribal activists. Coushatta tribal Chairman Lovelin Poncho and council member William Worfel spent more than $18 million in one year on lobbyists. 59*

Two of the firms were Capitol Campaign Strategies and Greenberg Traurig. CCS is located in Washington and Greenberg Traurig has offices in more than 12 cities, including Washington DC. Fortune magazine once noted that Greenberg was one of the country's top lobbying firms, employing more than 385 lawyers. What do 385 lawyers do when they get together, what do they talk about? They talk about making money! http://www.thetowntalk.com/html/AE75ABA4-6A9D1-91BAAD31C3 B6.shtml

- *Common Cause, a politically active group campaigning for clean government, says that the gambling industry in California has spent $130 million in political campaigns, as reported by the NCALG Bulletin, in 12/03, Vol 1, No. 5, p. 3. 60*

- *In Colorado in 2003, Wembley PLC, a London based company, spent more than $8 million organizing and promoting an unsuccessful campaign to bring VLT terminals to racetracks there, as reported by John Accola, Rocky Mountain News, 2/26/04. Of the $8 million, $6 million dollars directly underwrote what appeared to be a local group called "Support Colorado's Economy and Environment." For Wembley PLC to surreptitiously support this grass-roots group is misleading. It led people to believe that this was an indigenous group with local people. The campaign was supposed to rally support for a ballot measure, Amendment 33, thus getting the people of Colorado to vote for gambling terminals, i.e. VLTs, at Colorado's 5 dog and horse tracks.*

This was incredibly self-serving in that Wembly USA, a subsidiary of Wembley PLC, operates 4 of the 5 horse-racing tracks in Colorado at which Wembly PLC wanted to put VLTs. Can we imagine the amount of money Wembly PLC would have made if its subsidiary both owned the racetracks and the VLTs there?

- *Corruption can occur very easily on a state legislature level. In April, 2004, checks totaling about $11,000 were sent to 8 GOP legislators in St. Paul, Minnesota. Most of the 8 legislators were members of a key committee overseeing gambling issues. Two of the checks were sent from Caesars Entertainment of Las Vegas, 3 were from a group connected with Caesar's in Indiana, 1 from a Washington, DC lobbyist, and 1 from a Minnesota lobbyist. 61*

*This is an on-going problem, the flashing and **donating of large sums of money by the gambling industry to legislators in order to receive favorable legislation**. State law clearly prescribes contribution to legislators, 'in session' especially from lobbyists or principals with matters pending before the Legislature and accompanying civil penalties. The checks were returned and no further action was taken.*

*"**Minnesota** has been relatively free of scandal and political graft. More casinos will deliver boatloads of cash into the political process to ensure that gambling only*

grows," said the executive director of the Joint Religious Legislative Coalition, Brian Ruschle, on April 28, 2004. Ruscle heads a coalition of religious and social justice groups which has joined with a conservative group, the Taxpayers League of Minnesota, to fight against expanding gambling in order to balance the budget. Plans are under consideration by House and Senate Republican leaders for gambling expansion to balance the State budget. Caesar's Entertainment is being considered for a proposal for a casino at the Mall of America. www.twincities.com/mid/twincities/news/8537563.htm, AP.

*In **Maryland**, where Gov. Robert L. Ehrlich Jr. is attempting to allow VLTs at 9 locations in an effort to get revenue for the state, there has been a great deal of money paid to lobbyists and PACs.*

- *During the 2003 legislative session, gambling interests paid $2.5 million to lobbyists. These lobbyists were paid to secure support for the agenda of gambling interests, as stated in an editorial in the Baltimore Sun, 2/5/04. (The pro-slots State Senate President, Thomas V. Mike Miller, is under FBI investigation after a national political action committee (PAC) that he heads, received $225,000 in donations from the gambling industry in 2002 and 2003. 62*

Even while the FBI investigation is occurring, that same PAC then took another $175,000 from the gambling industry in the last half of 2003. For the 6-month period ending 12/31/03, there was another $175,000 in gambling-related contributions to the Democratic Leadership Campaign Committee. This included $100,000 from Reno, Nevada-based International Game Technology (IGT), the world's largest manufacturer of slot machines, $50,000 from Las Vegas-based Harrah's Entertainment, and $25,000 from Trump Hotels Casino. 63

This is big money and big influence. It barely skirts the federal law against campaign contributions. This 'soft money' is supposedly allowed because it is said to be for 'party building' purposes, unrelated to influencing federal elections. This premise has been widely acknowledged as a 'legal fiction'. The Democratic and Republican parties accumulate such 'soft money' in an effort to fund election campaigns and to get politicians re-elected. After they're re-elected with the help of gambling money, who do we think they're going to be grateful to?

Del. Luiz R.S. Simmons, said the money given to the DLCC is further "evidence of a gambling juggernaut" that exerts too much influence on the political process. "It is in my mind a very perilous situation for states like Maryland that are going to be swamped by this kind of organized money," he said in an article in the Baltimore Sun, by Greg Garland and David Nitkin on 2/4/04. 64

Gambling interests have been criticized for some time for making large donations to influence political campaigns. This ***'soft money'*** *is not meant to be a part of the federal campaign finance system. Since 1974 it's been illegal for an individual to contribute more than $1000 to a federal candidate or more than $20,000 to a political party for the purpose of influencing a federal election. Soft money violates these rules. It's the corporate donations or even large donations by wealthy individuals. Soft money is given in such huge amounts that of course the donors expect to receive something in return for their money,* **Common Cause** *writes.*

- *Gambling interests have given more than $8.6 million in soft money donations to the Republican and Democratic parties since 1987 and almost $3.2 million in political action committee (PAC) contributions to House and Senate candidates. These contributions, to both parties, helped the gambling industry gain extraordinary direct access to the highest officials in our nation. Furthermore, these big-money contributions also helped persuade Congress to weaken the powers of a federal commission examining the impact of gambling on American society by appointing several commissioners representing pro-gambling interests. 65*
  http://www.commoncause.org/issue_agenda/familyvalues.htm

- *Common Cause reports that during the time period, 1995-2002, gambling interests gave total monies of $9,688,680 to the Democrats and $13,659,949. to the Republicans! 66*

I was surprised at the brazenness and the amount of the contributions. This is after tax dollars for the businesses and corporations. They're giving direct from their profits, so one could imagine that they expect a high rate of return on this money. Characteristically, the private businesses gave 30 % more to the Republicans than to the Democrats as business traditionally supports a more conservative viewpoint. As you can see, the gambling industry and associated Indian tribes gave to both political parties generously. The amounts are high starting with $1,208,086 given by MGM Mirage Inc. to the Democrats and $1,790,268. to the Republicans. 67
http://www.commoncause.org./laundromat/results.cfm

In ***Rhode Island****, there has been an interesting picture of financial influence, together with enormous multi-national corporations, with their 2 existing dog tracks. Several major corporations have had their eye on Rhode Island. It's seen as an opening into the lucrative Boston market, it has an existing foothold already, in the form of the dog tracks, and it's a possible back-door approach for companies which* *have few other opportunities to move into new territory. Dog tracks, incidentally, are really sleazy with frequent allegations of animal mistreatment.*

- *Harrah's Operating Co. is attempting to gain a foothold with the Narragansett Indians and has employed and is paying eight lobbyists whom it registered with the state. The price just for these 8 lobbyists? $381,000. per year, according to Scott Mayerowitz, the Journal State House Bureau. www.projo.com/news/content/projo 200400317 lobby17.17f892.html The Narragansett's are also spending $42,000/ year in lobbyists and have spent another $27,000 in expenses in their efforts to secure a West Warwick casino in Rhode Island. 68*

Top executives of Lincoln Park racetrack, and Wembley PLC were indicted last year on charges of bribery and conspiring to pay as much as $4.5 Million dollars to their Rhode Island attorney. The case was argued in Federal court on 3/25/04, with the Judge saying she will rule at a future date. The law partner of Wembley's attorney was the Speaker of the Rhode Island House of Representatives at the time. Prosecutors said that Wembley tried to deprive the public of fair and honest government services, that devising a scheme to defraud the public is in itself sufficient to bring charges whether the deal was finally actualized or not.

MGM owns a dozen casinos in the U.S. and Australia. In 2003 New York racing officials selected the company to operate 4,500 slot machines at ***New York's Aqueduct racetrack in Queens****, one of the 5 boroughs of New York City. This new facility hasn't opened yet but when it does, who do we really think are going to betting at these slot machines? The size and scope of this industry is beyond our limited comprehension and certainly beyond the awareness of the American public.*

However, the citizens of Rhode Island have become somewhat savvy and have responded to the threat of possible casinos by MGM and other groups. Opposition has started to build in Newport County and specifically in Middletown. The Town Council of Middletown passed a resolution on 4/7/04 opposing the expansion of casino gambling in Rhode Island and also opposing efforts to have a public referendum in November, 2004. This resolution states that it represents both state residents and their municipal representatives in their 'unalterable opposition" to the expansion of any kind of gambling in the state.

The resolution says that Legislation has been introduced in the Rhode Island General Assembly which is contrary to the expressed statements of the citizens and councils of Middletown. 69

Council member Charles J. Vaillancourt said that "In reality, ***you do see the poor get much, much poorer," when a casino comes to town.*** *70*

Tourism officials throughout the state have also expressed concern that a large gambling facility could harm the state's tourism industry. Also in support, against gambling is the Newport County Chamber of Commerce and the Preservation Society of Newport County. This amount of organized support contrary to the expansion of gambling is somewhat unusual and says to me that the honeymoon is over with gambling, that people are becoming wise to what gambling is all about, and are ready to stand up for what is right and for what is best for all.

So we see that although citizens and town Chamber of Commerce's are beginning to understand how gambling really works, the incredible amounts of money thus far have served to influence a lot of people favorably. Gambling has expanded exponentially in the last 7 years because people had idealized fantasies about the money it could bring in and also because gambling paid money for the right to approach high elected officials in this country. These donations are influencing our democratic political process in a big way! When industries give these amounts of money, they're going to want something substantial in return. Remember - there's no such thing as a free lunch, especially with these corporations who are not in business for 'Entertainment.' They're 'not playing with us.'

The executives in these management corporations, past gambling directors, money financiers and management companies, are perhaps not the 'choirboys' that they present themselves as to the American public. This industry has historically been associated with money and with criminal elements in our society. It has ties with Hollywood, Frank Sinatra's Rat Pack often performed in Las Vegas, with the Mob, they often used to visit Las Vegas, and generally with prostitution and sleaze. So why would people take their word for anything now?

Given the actual documentable history of this industry in Court case after Court case, one would wonder at why we accept anything that the industry's says at face value. Anyone would be unwise and ill-informed to accept anything that was said without 100 % documentation.

In fact, the gambling industry has been prone to exaggerate, to wheel-and-deal, to manipulate. With their Intention and Goal clearly stated to be the acquiring of money by gambling, then could we be surprised if they turn, twist, bend, and even break, the truth in their comments? Actually is this so contrary to human nature, anyway? Human nature is to want what you want, when you want, our first primitive desire, the force behind materialism. You want what you want and you think it can make you happy. The gambling industry has as its roots, the desire for money and power. They're interchangeable, each leads to the other. So why would we believe anything this industry said.

This pattern of large donations to Political Action Committees is full of Money and Corruption. *It's a subversion and undue influence on our political process,* *bribery of individual legislators and governors, and finally, dishonesty and fraud of the high ideals and goals that this country was founded on.*

Corruption, graft, and fraud. What fruit of gambling, what further evidence do we need to know that this is not something that is going to take anyone higher, is not going to contribute anything worthwhile to the American people or to our society.

Other people call this corruption also. Dr. James Dobson, a former federal gambling commissioner on the National Gambling Impact Study Commission (NGISC), also commented about the corruption inherent in this whole process and in the industry. Dobson said that because of their unlimited financial resources:

> ***...gambling representatives can influence elections dramatically and entice political leaders to do their bidding...***
>
> ***The gambling lobby is the most powerful force in government today, and its master is not reluctant to use it."*** *71*
> *http://www.hotel-online.com/News/PressReleases l999_1stJan99_Dobson.html Hotel Online Special Report, Federal Gambling Commissioner Speaks on State of Gambling in the U.S.*

Dr. Dobson noted that leaders of both major political parties have accepted many campaign contributions.

- *Steve Wynn, sent his private jet to Washington DC to bring politicians to lucrative fund-raisers. His guests have included Bill Clinton and Bob Dole in l996 who each received checks for* ***$500,000****. Ultimately they received more than a million dollars in 'soft money" said Brett Pulley, in an article in the New York Times, 3/4/98, "Casinos Increase Their Contributions to U.S. Campaigns." New York Times, 3/34/98, "Vegas Bob: Nevada Gambling Interests and Bob Dole," The Nation, 2/12/96. 72*

- *Others who have benefited include Newt Gingrich, Jon Ralston, "Terms of Surrender," Casino Journal, 6/96. Trent Lott, Richard S. Durham, "Guess Who's Raking it in From Gambling," Business Week, 10j/12/98, Al Gore, "Gore, Gephardt Head to Vegas," The Hotline, 3/10/98, Thomas Daschle," The Casino-Campaign Connection," The Hartford Courant, 7/7/97, p. lA8, Richard Gephardt, Robert L. Koenig, "Trips*

Gephardt Takes Frequent Flights in Corporate Jets," St. Louis Post - Dispatch, 6/26/91, p. 1A, Tom Delay, German, op.cit., 73

- *Other political leaders have also been treated to this or other similar 'courtesies'. Other legislators have had large amounts of money given to them, including Sen. Harry Reid, (D-Nev) $348,459, Rep. John Ensign, R-Nev, $214,686, Rep. Frank LoBiondo, R-NJ, $77,150, Rep. James Givens, R-Nev, $75,100, Sen. Robert Torricelli, D-NJ, $70,600, Sen. Frank Lautenberg, D-NJ, $36,250, Rep. Richard Gephardt, D-Mo, $24,000, and others." Top 1996 Donors by Industry," Center for Responsive Politics. 74*

- *We shouldn't be surprised that Congress has rarely opposed the gambling industry and their multitude of requests. Washingtonian magazine said, "Lott has cozied up to Steve Wynn, who not only has provided Lott with use of his private jet but also has given him thousands in campaign contribution in 1997-88." 75 Kim Eisler, "Local Lawyers and Lobbyists Have Big Stakes in Gambling," Washingtonian Magazine, 11/98.*

- *Dr. Dobson adds that Bill Clinton first favored granting subpoena power for the NGISC. Then he changed his mind shortly after flying off to Vegas for a golf junket with Steve Wynn. Martin Koughan, "Easy Money, Mother Jones, July/August, 1997, p. 37. 76 Consequently the NGISC was not allowed to require testimony from key witnesses, as Federal commissions usually are.*

Dr. Dobson adds that ***no special interest group should have such power over the electoral and legislative process.*** *But money seems to set the agenda, and gambling continues to grow and shape the fabric of American culture in a negative way. Gambling is also shaping the fabric of the millions of American families who have been hurt by the excesses of gambling, who have had to file for bankruptcy, or whose families were ripped apart by divorce and separation due to gambling problems by a spouse. Dr. Dobson, President of Focus on the Family, said that* ***'gambling fever' has engulfed the nation. "It now threatens the work ethic and the very foundation of the family."***

What a powerful foe to influence the American scene. We don't even see most of its machinations and don't even hear its voices yet it affects us in countless unseen ways. What is our little gambler, faced with just wanting to have a fun night out, to do in the face of all this powerful and undue influence. There's no way to come out even in the fight against such strong influences and such enormous money.

This is truly big corporations gone amuck. As former deputy attorney general of Nevada, Chuck Gardner said,

> *I don't know if there has ever been a situation with* ***so much power concentrated in one industry ...government gone berserk***
>
> *Boomtown's Big Land grab: Las Vegas, Nevada," George, March, 1998. 77*

George magazine named Las Vegas as "One of the 10 Most Corrupt Cities in American." The Yellow Pages in Las Vegas list 136 pages of advertisements for prostitution by various names. Barry M. Horstman, "New Vegas: Original Sin City Tries Family Values," Cincinnati Post, 9/16/97.

For a while Las Vegas tried to appeal to families. Hotels such as Circus Circus and MGM opened amusement theme parks with rides inside the hotel. Other casinos such as The Mirage built outdoor shows such as a Pirate ship that sinks in front of the hotel and had Siegfried & Roy do 'family' shows with endangered white tigers before Roy got injured.

The development and the expansion of the gambling industry in the U.S. in the past 25 years is without precedent. We've seen from state to state, the activities of the Federal government, its BIA Dept., past Supreme Court rulings, the involvement of Indian tribes, that all have been involved in gambling's establishment and expansion. The active involvement of our State Governors, and Legislators has spurred the rapid establishment of this new industry into an accepted heavy-hitting player in the American business landscape.

States and legislators think that they are obtaining low-cost revenue that will enrich their states and allow their constituents to think that they 'brought home the bacon'. Unfortunately what has really happened is that they have unleashed the hounds of hell. The lack of proposed economic development will bring their economies even lower than before.

This is what West Virginia CAGE, Communities Against Gambling Expansion, and director, Steven Reed, are seeking to bring public awareness to. This is what Rev. Sue Abrams, what Assemblyman Hoyt, what Rev. Tom Grey, what Dr. James Dobson, what Assemblywoman Peoples, what Former Police Chief, Robert Shelton, what economists Earl Grinois, Paul Samuelson, and countless others are all seeking to bring to public awareness.

Addictions threaten some of the basic tenets of our government noted Taylor Branch in an article in the Baltimore Sun on 3/28/04. Any addiction is a potential threat to good government since an addict, by definition, is not self-governing. Every addict succumbs to a cheap high that progressively saps his and others strength.

> *"**Addiction is the mother of corruption in people and government alike.** Self-government requires us all to look beyond the moment and safeguard the integrity of clear choice." 78*

Our political discourse values hard work, opportunity, investment, sacrifice, cooperation and fair play. Would State advertising in the case of Lottery advertisements, for example, get the citizens the truth about slots odds and the real possibility of winning. Or do we think that we don't deceive and exploit citizens with advertisements for the Lottery. Branch noted that "Slots proposals fail all 3 enduring lessons of our democratic experiment. If we exercise self-government, public trust and accountability, we will reject a bad gamble that also threatens our political health. 79 http://www.baltimoresun.com/news/opinion/bal-op.slots28mar 28,0,884284.storoy?coll=bal-pe-opinion

Gambling is not beneficial for the gambler, for the State, for the economy, for businesses, or for anyone except for gambling's owners and operators. Even for them, who are certainly getting very wealthy, I would doubt that it's worth the sale of their souls to do so. We've unleashed a new addictive activity and we will suffer for it until we put it back in its cage and bolt and lock the door. Gambling is bad for everyone except for the 'House.' Gambling is no one's friend.

****

CHAPTER SIX

CHURCHES & TEMPLES RELIGION & GAMBLING

"The Devil invented gambling," St. Augustine 1

ORGANIZED RELIGION AND POPULAR VALUES

***

Gambling is a menace to society, deadly to the best interests of moral, social, economic and spiritual life and destructive of good government.
As an act of faith and concern, Christians should abstain from gambling and should strive to minister to those victimized by the practice. 2

United Methodist Bishop,
Michael J. Coyner, 3/14/04

***

Churches, synagogues, and temples in our society are traditionally one of the main avenues for the dissemination of values in our society and in most communities. In the early days of America, the churches were the only vehicle for the propagation of faith, for spreading ideas about man, his space and place in the world, and his actions. People were church members and that was the extent of their activities. They listened to their pastor or priest give weekly sermons, and they attended Sunday school. Church was where they and their parents received their moral education. Scriptural injunctions about what to do and what not to do, constituted people's guidance about how to handle their lives.

These days it's a little different with many kinds of faiths and ethnic and cultural groups all competing for peoples' participation. These varied groups espouse and promulgate values of one kind or another, many with moral overtones and implications. Environmental, Women's, Gay Rights and Meditation societies, all have messages to bring to people about quasi-moral issues. These groups instead of churches, have become ways people identify themselves in the world and in fact, direct or influence their 'stance' toward the world.

Such groups, while excellent resources of enrichment in the world, sometimes offer less of a 'world-view' and overall moral perspective than traditional organized religion. These groups would agree, admitting freely that they are not meant to be 'religions,' or to guide people's behavior in the world. They focus on their own particular segment or world perspective. Overall they don't provide clear values and insight into what is morally right and wrong.

As people participate less in organized religion, they are subject to less directive, commandment-type injunctions about what activities to indulge in. Some activities, such as gambling, are one of those issues that languish in the realm of uncertainty. We've found ways to rationalize many behaviors that the commandments would not always be favorable toward.

Additionally, fewer people are associated with churches these days. Often Protestant churches are more than half empty. With churches half full and pastors seeking to increase attendance, perhaps they won't preach sermons that might alienate people if they're too hard-hitting.

So the question remains, where are people getting their values and moral orientation from? Since churches are unclear about moral imperatives, people are also vague in their feeling about morality, or dharma, about what is the right course of action, the right thing to do for the benefit of all. I've gone to church for many years yet I've never heard a minister say one word about gambling. Ministers and priests are hard-pressed to be emphatic about the negative things about gambling, when government and the gambling industry have extensive advertising campaigns extolling its virtues, stating that it's all just 'entertainment'.

These kinds of 'rationalizations', can be seen frequently in our world with its laissez-faire codes of conduct and relaxed personal self-discipline. Sometimes people refer to gambling as a 'victimless' crime, alluding to the fact that although it's illegal outside of certain venues, it doesn't appear to hurt anybody nor does it appear to involve violence. However, our casual standards and 'feel-good' mentality leave a lot to be desired in terms of justice for all.

Gambling erodes family values, personal integrity and community spirit. Note the innumerable tragedies and personal horror stories that come out of gambling as detailed in this book alone. A relaxed orientation toward values, a lack of clarity and integrity doesn't help anybody negotiate the intricate web of life with its myriad ethical questions.

State governments also give unclear and misleading ideas about gambling. They advertise their lotteries as being so wholesome, for the good of all, that it seems practically a civic duty to buy tickets. After all it's for 'Education', who could argue with that? This whitewash, or sanitizing, of gambling in the past 30 years has radically changed Americans' view of it and contributed to the overall feeling that it's okay when used with restraint.

At this point, almost ***60 % of Americans*** *say that there's nothing wrong with gambling done in moderation. The 21st century phenomenon of taking a relaxed view toward many social issues has been a new and novel way of looking at things. The current laissez-faire viewpoint of 'it's-okay-as-long-as-you-don't-hurt-anyone', has not been the long-standing traditional stance. The stance of organized religion on this issue has historically been very different. Previously, church authorities were very free and quick to tell people exactly how to live their lives.*

Organized religion has traditionally had definite, clearly defined views of right and wrong. In the current wave toward letting people make their own decisions, being more casual and relaxed about what previously was called 'sinful' behavior, we've forgotten about the fact that some things are clearly harmful for people. Religion's traditional directives and rules were in the service of people's present and future well being. They really were for the good of people.

Today, the lure of 'easy money' has infiltrated both people and groups. When budgets are difficult to balance, and salaries continue to rise, many groups, including organized religion, feel a lot of financial pressure. It's felt that a little 'Bingo' or 'Las Vegas nites' might be a way out. When religious groups have Las Vegas nights and State governments have Mega Lotteries, it's hard to see how gambling could be a 'sin' and destructive of people's lives. Yet that happens to be the truth.

Religious doctrine evolved over thousands of years as a means of helping people see what was right and beneficial in the long run. Rules for behavior weren't made to constrict people and impede their freedom, but in fact to allow them to thrive, to prosper, and thus to have the freedom of choice that sufficient finances and a clear conscience brings. It's hard for priests and pastors to get up and ban gambling when churches are sponsoring it!

As Protestant ministers are quick to point out, Christianity's scriptural source, the Bible, notes in several places that there are a few acceptable ways for people to gain money, i.e. by inheritance, by planning, by accumulation - but never by gambling. The Protestant view of wealth has been that money and everything all belong to God first and that it's all His in the long run. The Catholic Church, long more monolithic in its approach to various social questions, has been somewhat more vague in its precise proscription of gambling.

From a theoretical point of view, there's little difference between organized religion pursuing Las Vegas nites, and individuals going to Atlantic City casinos. If gambling is okay for local churches, then why isn't it okay for individuals? Both are gambling. Yet both are different entities. The ***Intention*** *is different with both. With churches, the intention is to have fun, bring people together, and do some fund-raising. It's done for a limited time period, by a small-scale group, with everyone knowing each other.*

With Atlantic City, the intention and the goals are different. The intention is to ***make money****, a self-serving activity. It's billed as a recreational activity, entertainment, and the possibility of getting rich, is heralded loudly. Atlantic City is run by large-scale private industry whose intention very definitely is to divest people of all their money. It's a different ballgame.*

Church bingo *doesn't bankrupt people nor does it lead to crime and prostitution. It doesn't lead to people being obsessed with gambling and how they can get money to do it. Bingo doesn't lead to the excesses so destructive of people and families. Although a game of 'chance', bingo does not involve drinking, it doesn't have repeated games within seconds of each other, and it doesn't encourage people to go to the nearby ATM machine to get out more cash. It's a different scenario than a Billion-dollar casino.*

This criterion that people apply to gambling, ***moderation****, allows people to feel that gambling is an acceptable activity. This makes a lot of sense. The problem here is that, by definition, gambling is 'progressive'. In order to get the same thrill, or high, that you did the first time, it's necessary, at least for some people, to bet more and more money. The thrill is not in betting nickels after the first time. Part of the thrill comes from the 'risk' involved. Risk translates to something that can make an impact one way or another, create a major change, thereby justifying the risk. Either it will help a lot or hurt a lot. Without the risk, the thrill is minimized.*

Moderation is a difficult road to travel when it comes to gambling. Church bingo, while perhaps not the most ideal form of fund-raising and not the most productive of activities, is not the demon in disguise that casino gambling or horse-racing can be. Church bingo doesn't lead to individual addiction and it doesn't sow the seeds of destruction. I don't have a problem with bingo, Las Vegas nights, although it could be said that this kind of thinking, that moderation makes gambling okay, is what led to our situation.

Some things just cannot be done in moderation. You're either pregnant or you're not. In moderation, gambling can be seen as entertainment. The problem is, with any activity that has the potential to be addictive, it's progressive, difficult to be done in moderation over the long haul. It inevitably leads to betting more and more. That's its nature. That's what gives it, its 'kick' or its 'high'. The risk is the adrenaline rush, the 'risk' or the 'chance', of hitting it BIG, the possibility, of making a lot more.

With us, Alan went to Atlantic City on a regular basis, once a week. That was his 'night out'. But gradually, incrementally but steadily, the gambling 'progressed' to the point where it was out of control. It wasn't something that allowed itself to be done 'in moderation'. Alan never really increased the frequency of his trips. What he did increase over time, ***was the size of his bets. He 'fed' his addiction by increasing one of the two variables in the equation****. He couldn't increase the frequency because of his home situation, so he increased the other variable, bet size. This gave him his 'hit'. The end result was that great damage was done, even though it began innocuously enough and continued in moderation for a long time.*

Gambling is seen to be innocuous because, after all, so the thinking goes, even local churches and state governments allow and encourage it. The problem comes after people partake of this seemingly innocuous activity, Bingo, Las Vegas nites in churches and then progress to large-scale casinos with all the slot machines, the VLTs, the lights, music and the friendly 'reps'. This is where the casinos do their dance, where they begin to addict you. Everything there is calculated to addict. Then the activity that was innocent enough to begin with, playing 'just for fun', and perhaps even beneficial when done with neighborhood churches, becomes addictive for the individual.

What becomes addictive for the individual, leads to his self-destruction and financial demise. What started out as an innocent pastime, then leads the person to become exclusively focused on this activity as a way of life. The activity leads the person to change his ideas and thoughts about how one handles money, leads him to forget that he must work to support and provide for his family, and instead incites him to fantasize and behave recklessly, dreaming of winning imaginary riches, allowing his ego, his little me, full rein to get in trouble.

No more does he have a philosophy that accepts a Higher Power as the source of all good things. Rather than trusting that all will be provided, with the appropriate amount of involvement and effort on his part, the individual changes toward a philosophy that says, he's going to win it himself, if he just plays 'hard and smart' enough.

For these reasons, organized religion has been less than forthcoming in providing a clear statement about whether people should indulge in gambling. They've not done so for reasons of not wanting to alienate people, not wanting to drive people away with gloom-and-doom scenarios, and finally because they themselves have become addicted to the extra revenue from gambling. They've become addicted, just like our governments have become addicted, to the money that can be made from gambling. This all leaves people unclear about whether gambling is a 'moral' activity, whether one that a Supreme Deity would smile on.

Recently though, as increasing numbers of people are sharing their stories of hardship, bankruptcy, financial and familial ruin with their pastors, churches are becoming more aware of gambling as being very harmful to people. Finally some of our church leaders are beginning to sit up and take notice. It's unfortunate that church leaders weren't sensitive to this trend of increasing Social Costs previously but seeing things differently often requires being hit over the head. Catholic Church leaders were beleaguered on other fronts, and Protestant leaders are always seeking to counteract empty pews. Besides, in this day of multi-challenges, few people are interested in taking on another fight, acknowledging yet another difficult situation that needs attention.

POTESTANT CHURCHES

***Protestant Baptist churches** are beginning to take a strong, more public stance against the excesses of gambling. On 10/28/03, the Orangeburg-Calhoun Baptist Association, comprising 42 Southern Baptist congregations, publicly said that*

> We have always opposed gambling of any form and we continue with our consistency in that position. *Gambling promises you something for nothing as opposed to the ethic that you work hard and earn your living. Gambling's 'big promise—and lie'—is that you're going to win back your money. But this doesn't happen, gamblers "just dig (themselves) a hole".*
>
> ***God calls us to work diligently, to be frugal and invest wisely rather than depend on luck. Gambling today is not simply harmless family entertainment.*** *resolutions committee chairman, Rev. Quinn Hooks 3*

This is a hard-hitting, no-holds barred resolution and states the Baptists' point of view well. It would probably encompass the positions of many churches. People don't realize the depth of damage to both individuals and communities that is inflicted by problem gambling in our country. I would even suggest that run-of-the-mill gambling, gambling within the individuals control and justified by their budget, is even harmful as it siphons off resources from the community and puts them into an activity which has no product and does nothing for anyone. So both regular and problematic gambling are activities intrinsically harmful to all. If more of our society were aware of the scope and extent of the harm inflicted, many people would take notice and conclude, as the resolution states, gambling is not just 'harmless entertainment'. Yet gambling has gained a 'social acceptability' as a result of the state's involvement and the gambling industry's constant advertising blitz 'whitewashing' and legitimizing it.'

The Baptist position is further enumerated:

> *Gambling can encourage the sins of greed and covetousness and can lead us to misuse stewardship over our time, talents and resources... Jesus calls his followers to make wise investment of their talents, time and money. Gambling is predicated on a very different philosophy of getting something important for nothing...The emphasis on* ***chance*** *can be an occasion for despair and distrust in God's promises.*

Gambling can place vulnerable members of our communities at risk of great harm. *Lee Hendren, 4 http://www.thetandd.com/articles/2003/10/28/news/news1.txt*

The Baptist Press in a column on 2/1/04, added that gambling is:

> ***often connected with other vices**, such as prostitution and drugs, is always associated with get-rich-quick motives, discourages work, and manifests a **heart of greed and love of money** which ...is the root of all evil. Gambling is preying on the weakness of others, contrary to the instructions of Scripture.*
> *The Baptists recognize 'the wages of sin' to result in family breakdown, individual crises, and community chaos. 5*

In a column on 1/21/04, Howard Dayton, CEO of Crown Financial Ministries in a column from the Baptist Press noted that:

> ***At least a quarter or maybe more of all family disruptions, neglected or abused children, divorces, impoverishment, mental breakdowns and suicides can be traced back to the negative effects of gambling.***
>
> *An Employee Assistance Program report, from the University of Texas at Austin, indicated that approximately $14 billion dollars per year worth of productivity is lost by business and industry through absenteeism, wasted time, poor work performance, loss of income, criminal acts such as theft, accident, rehabilitation and recovery and medical treatment due to gambling and gambling-related problems. 6*

The Georgia Baptist Convention's office of ethics and public affairs, Dr. J. Emmett Henderson, was also quoted in the column. He noted that lotteries are not without harm either even though the amounts spent are much less.

> *For the poor, the **lottery** is not harmless entertainment. It is a desperate but vain attempt to survive. The odds of winning are so cruel—roughly 13 million to one is typical for state lotteries throughout America—that lottery turns out of be theft by consent. Almost all players lose money. 7*
> *http://www.sbcbaptistpress.org/bpcolumn.asp?ID=1270*

This is similar to what Assemblywomen Peoples said in Chapter 2, that for the state to encourage poor people to buy lottery tickets, can be another way of throwing away the little money they have. ***The state is essentially suggesting that poor people make poor and ill-informed choices with their money.*** *Often there is heavy state promotion of the lottery, or the 'Lootery', as it's been called. Dr. Robert Goodman as quoted in a Christian Science Monitor article by Jane Lampman on 2/18/04 recalled that government can suffer from the same addictions as individuals. "We talk about people becoming addicted to gambling, but essentially governments have become addicted to these revenues. Even increasing the revenue annually will never be enough" because, as we've learned, it's 'progressive'. 9*

> *The Illinois lottery had billboards in poor black neighborhoods saying,* ***'This is your ticket out.' 8***

In an admirable let's-put-our-money-where-our-mouth-is move, the Baptist General Convention of Oklahoma in May, 2003, called on its 700,000 Southern Baptists and 'all people of faith', to sign a petition referendum bringing SB 553, a legislative law passed by the State Assembly to a popular vote. SB 553 passed the Legislature during the 2003-4 session, and was signed by Gov. Brad Henry in February, 2004. It sought to expand gambling at Oklahoma's horse racing tracks and Indian tribal casinos.

The Baptist General Convention of Oklahoma is one of the groups in the Oklahomans for Good Government coalition, founded by Rep. Forrest A. Claunch (R-Midwest City, Oklahoma). Claunch led successful anti-gambling campaigns in 1994 and 1998. The petition drive required SB 553 to be voted on by Oklahoma's citizens. Claunch said that gambling is never good public policy,

> *"Inherent in its very nature is that those conducting the gambling and supplying the means to gamble win, while everyone else loses." 10*
> *The group had 90 days to collect 51,781 signatures to force a statewide vote of the issues.*

Other churches are also concerned about the spread of gambling and the impact it is having on people of lower income. The Rev. Janet Jacobs noted that the ***United Methodist Church's official position*** *is that people should not gamble. She added that* ***"People with chronic gambling addictions are part of a group with the highest suicide rate." "Participation in religious activities and religious attitudes are protective factors against gambling addiction in the senior population"*** *11.*

The Rev. Jacobs, director of Gambling Recovery Ministries, South Indiana Conference, United Methodist Church quoted) a 1998 survey by Louisiana State University that said that 5.3 % of Indiana adults are problem gamblers, and...almost 1 % are pathological gamblers. 12

An article in the Roanoke Times by Tim Thornton noted that pastors of ***9 churches*** *there had signed an* ***anti-betting statement*** *on 10/22/03. The statement declared that:*

> ***It is our belief that gambling is a menace to society, deadly to the best interests of moral, social, economic and spiritual life.***
> ***(Gambling) is morally wrong because it preys on the poor and fosters the belief that people can get something for nothing. 13***

As a member of that group, United Pentecostal minister, Gerald Adams, said what many of us believe, that:

> ***We need to make a stand and say we don't want this for the next generation, for the children coming up."*** *14*

What parent would want to know that their child is going to a casino and gambling? As a parent myself, I'm sure I speak for most parents when I say that I want to know that my children are saving their hard-earned money or spending it on needed, long-range items, not blowing it on gambling in the name of entertainment. I don't worry that my, now grown, children don't get enough 'entertainment'. I do worry that they're not going to be able to afford houses, that their families will be broken up by divorce or that their children will not get all the attention and love that they need.

*So we see that churches are speaking out much more so these days as they're witnessing the social costs in parishes. In Maryland, where Governor Ehrlich has been seeking to expand gambling and bring slot machines into the state, an article by Robert Redding Jr. in the Washington Times, 2/17/04, News World Communications, Inc., showed that church ministers there had some cogent comments about the governor's idea. "****I have been working to try to stamp out this immorality (gambling****), said* ***Pastor Kennedy,*** *Walker Mill Baptist Church in Capitol Heights. "And instead of helping, the* ***legislature is trying to increase it****." 15*

Yes, the legislature is trying to increase gambling in a big way despite the fact that legislators have access to these same studies also. In 2004, gambling opponents defeated an attempt to expand gambling in Maryland but gambling forces are already gearing up for 2005. Gambling seems like a quick-fix for the budget, it's touted as what everyone wants. And legislators are getting plenty of encouragement from gambling interests in the form of campaign donations, special invitations, and overall attention.

Governor Ehrlich thought that he could persuade the African-American caucus to vote for casinos if they were offered ownership of one of the casinos. Sounds like a bribe to me. In discussing the issue of whether gambling would be acceptable if some of the casinos were owned by Black Americans, Rev. Gregory Perkins, pastor of St. Paul Community Baptist Church took a strong position saying that race is not an issue.

> *The fact is, we don't need gambling in our community, regardless of who the owner may be.*
> ***A predator is a predator is a predator. 16***

Rev. Perkins added that the introduction of slots will mean more personal bankruptcies, crime, prostitution, and other problems - regardless of the owner's race or nationality.

The Rev. Kevin McGhee, president of the Laurel Clergy Association, an alliance of 20 churches, also agreed with his colleague condemning the activity of gambling. He said:

> *We are not willing to lose* ***even one family*** *to this addiction, and especially to have the state bring it to us. 17*

Many of the ministers involved in the alliance are bringing their message to their congregations seeking to have people show elected officials that they don't want more gambling. It's hoped that if legislators feel they will be hurt in elections by their support for gambling, then they will reconsider their views.

Such strong, forthright, clear, compassionate thinking on the part of these church pastors helps people know and act upon what's good for them and what's not. These pastors are concerned about the needs of the whole community, their mandate is for the long-range good of all. They know about the weaknesses of people, about how Temptation can play its part only too willingly. They're not so concerned about 'entertainment', as about food and shelter, not so involved in having a good time, as about caring for children and the homeless.

The ***Bishop of the United Methodist Church in the Minnesota*** *area wrote a public letter to the Governor and Legislators of the State on 2/23/04. In his letter the Bishop, the spiritual leader of 90,000 United Methodists in Minnesota, urged the Legislature to "avoid the tempting option of expanding legalized gambling in Minnesota." He stated it is "both a simplistic and deceptive alternative." He writes,*

> *Gambling victimizes people. It can quickly become addictive, leading individuals to risk their families' livelihood, for the highly unlikely chance at easy money. 18*

Here Bishop John L. Hopkins is taking a hard-hitting stance at gambling and its negative repercussions. And isn't this all true? As we've now seen, it certainly is a menace to society. Now that we know what gambling and addiction can do, we can certainly see it lead individuals to risk families money and hence survival. He adds that ***"The majority of gambling revenue is linked to pathological and problem gambling."*** *He quotes a study by Grinols and Omorov, Univ. of Illinois Dept of Economics that states that:*

52 % of casino revenues come from about 4 % of the population, the pathological and problem gamblers. 19

Bishop Hopkins is well aware that the majority of casino income is from a minority of players, and is concluding that these are ***the addicts*** *who pump up casino revenues. The addicts are the ones who've given all their money to the casinos. The addicts are the 'victims' and the vulnerable ones. He notes that the state "victimizes vulnerable people to boost the state budget." He includes the social costs on the rest of society and quotes a study that found that each problem gambler imposed a cost of at least $13,200 annually on government and private businesses for various costs. Finally he also wonders whether "governments themselves become addicted to gambling." He urges the state legislature:*

to seek revenue sources that strengthen
rather than tear away our social fabric. 20

The United Methodist Church, Minnesota Area, 122 W. Franklin Ave., Suite 200, Minneapolis, Mn. 554004-2472

Other Protestant ministers feel similarly and are beginning to advocate against this new addictive activity. The Protestant position generally is that 'everything belongs to God.' In an article by Jane Lampman in the Christian Science Monitor, Dr. Tony Campolo, head of the Evangelical Association for the Promotion of Education, noted that when you gamble, "you're not using what God has placed in your hands in a responsible way." Dr. Campolo and more than 150 other religious leaders sent an open letter to the U.S. Congress in 2002 urging that it begin to address "the ***pain and devastation****" that gambling has wrought on society. 22*

In the state of North Dakota, Methodist Bishop, Michael J. Coyner, wrote an editorial in The Forum, regarding gambling and the proposed state lottery that will open soon there. In an announcement on 3/14/04, the Bishop noted that he wanted to warn the residents of North Dakota that –

"The lottery is coming! The lottery is coming!" 23

The Bishop noted that he shared the news as a warning similar to the bad news warning first shouted by patriot Paul Revere in 1776, saying that the first 230 outlets would be selling lottery tickets soon. He added that now the state of North Dakota:

> *is joining hands with the gambling industry and will pour thousands and thousands of dollars into* ***advertising*** *to entice the citizens of North Dakota to spend their money...Rather than the state of North Dakota promoting the health and welfare of its own citizens, the state will be working hard to get its citizens to* ***waste their money*** *on other* ***false hopes*** *of 'getting rich quick.' How sad...When our own state government tells us that lottery tickets are a good thing, who can resist that allure?"*

The Bishop added that United Methodists are clear that just because the lottery is legal, that doesn't make it right. He quoted the *Methodist Social Principles* *saying that*

> ***Gambling is a menace to society, deadly to the best interest of moral, social, economic and spiritual life and destructive of good government.***
>
> ***As an act of faith and concern, Christians should abstain from gambling and should strive to minister to those victimized by the practice.*** *24*

The Bishop called upon all United Methodist pastors in North Dakota to remind congregations not to participate and to warn people not to be caught in the allure of state-sponsored gambling, not to waste their hard-earned money on this 'nonsense'. The Forum, 3/14/04, Editorial by Michael J. Coyner. 25

The Bishop's address leaves no lack of clarity in anyone's mind what he thinks of gambling and what he expects Methodists to do in this regard. It's a clear statement of the church's position on it. The church's position has been hammered out by church leaders over time, people who had nothing to do but sit and contemplate what was best for people, and try to translate theological principles into best practices on a daily basis for the common man.

It's helpful for organized religion to take clear perspectives on a certain issue and then to make that position known to parishioners and even the larger community. In this fast-paced world, it's hard for every 'average Joe' to contemplate and make ethical judgments about everything that crosses his path. We all don't always have the time to 'reinvent the wheel', in terms of ethics and morality, about every life decision. I never heard any ministers taking any positions about gambling or treating it as an offshoot of one of the 7 deadly sins. I would certainly have begun to contemplate gambling from this different light had I ever been challenged to think about it. We did discuss the gambling and I was opposed to it from various points of view but to equate his winning with others losses, to believe that it victimized people, I never considered.

My husband never thought about the moral implications of gambling or whether his actions meant anything in the larger scheme of Heaven and Earth. He just didn't think...The whole scene was just so much fun and so appealing, lights, actions, like an adult play-ground or amusement park, that he didn't stop to contemplate the implications of his actions, whether or not the activity was dharmic, right action and thinking, or not. This seems to be the approach of many in our society. If others are doing it and it generally looks okay or fun, they're not going to give the issue a lot of serious consideration.

*One of the **central religious arguments against gambling by religions is that it puts something else, gambling, as higher, more important than God.** Theorists postulate that it breeds 'idolatry' in that a compulsive gambler will see gambling and not God, as the most important thing in his life, as his priority and his passion. Gambling turns our attention to things of this world, to ephemeral, transitory things, that only satisfy sense cravings, that don't stay with us, are not enriching, cannot be taken to the next world, and that don't appear to be particularly soul-enhancing, or awareness-nurturing. This is so true, that if we're concentrating on winning, we're not thinking about God, we're not 'constantly in prayer,' we're not involved in good works of charity or love for others.*

*Another prime issue about gambling for many religions is that **gambling preys on the weak and poor. These are the very people that scripture and other sacred writings repeatedly tell us are the very people identified as 'the apple of God's eye',** not the rich or powerful who already have trouble getting into heaven, according to scripture. Gambling entices someone to **gain money at the expense of another,** thus violating just about every principle taught by Christ or any great being whose message is about Compassion and Love for one's fellow human beings. Rather gambling encourages thinking and obsessing about money for the individual, promoting one's own selfishness, greed and covetousness.*

The Rev. Tom Grey, head of the National Coalition Against Legalized Gambling, and a Methodist minister, states that gambling is contrary to 'social morality.' His argument makes sense both morally and economically. He said recently about gambling:

> *It's not good economics, it's not good public policy, and it's not good for the quality of life.*
>
> ***Any society that preys on the pathology of some people to support education or another cause, that's not just.** 26*

Pastors and priests are becoming more outspoken about gambling after years of deafening silence. They have first-hand experience with it. The Rev. Bill White, pastor Bethel Lutheran Church, Wisconsin, said that all 9 pastors on his staff are opposed to gambling because of the social costs. "We've all counseled families where there has been a member who has jumped into the gambling pool. ***We've seen the damage,*** *" as reported in an article by Judith Davidoffon1/27/04. 27*

Traditional organizations like the ***Salvation Army,*** *who have a strong faith foundation and clear service philosophy have always been opposed to gambling. In an interesting change of pace, the Salvation Army* ***rejected a $5 Million dollar donation from gambling industry giant, Tattersall's*** *in Australia. Salvation Army spokesman, John Dalziel, said Tattersall's Casino approached the Salvation Army with the offer a while back. In an article by Nick Papps, 10/16/03, Dalziel said Tattersall's was 'very angry' with the rejection. The Salvation Army felt however, that they couldn't accept the money because they would have been seen "to be in partnership with a group that causes so much misery. How would we be able to face the people that we were seeking to help that were victims of Tatts?" The Salvation Army is careful not to 'sleep with the enemy' nor to rationalize that the end justifies the means. 28*

Dalziel said that ***40,000*** *people come to the Salvation Army in Australia every year with gambling-related problems.* news.com.au *Thank goodness that the Salvation Army, at least, has integrity and the courage of their convictions, principles that can neither be bought nor swayed by money. Perhaps some of their staff would like to become state legislators.*

Christian theologians have had their own views on gambling which were not fraught with laissez-faire twentieth century thinking. ***Martin Luther****, the Protestant reformer said, "****Money won by gambling is not...without sin.****" 29 Traditional Christianity, being aware of these statements, would not have endorsed gambling as 'entertainment' or as anything else. Rex M. Rogers, "seducing America: Is Gambling a Good Bet?" Baker Books, PO Box 6287, Grand Rapids, MI 49516, p. 55.*

In ***Minnesota,*** *a similar drive occurred when it appeared that gambling expansion efforts might be successful. The Taxpayers League of Minnesota, joined with the Joint Religious Legislative Coalition, to urge people to oppose expanded gambling. Coalition leaders said they escalated their efforts as it appeared that gambling expansion might pass in the Legislative session. Leaders added that a recent University of Illinois study showed* ***$34 dollars in benefits from gambling, yet $190 dollars in social expenses from additional crimes and their many attendant costs*** *to net jobs lost, despite casino promises of the creation of additional employment. 30*

When different groups in our society join together for a common goal, they can defeat the mammoth appearing forces of big business and government which seem bent on expanding gambling even in the face of public acknowledgment of social costs.

CATHOLICISM

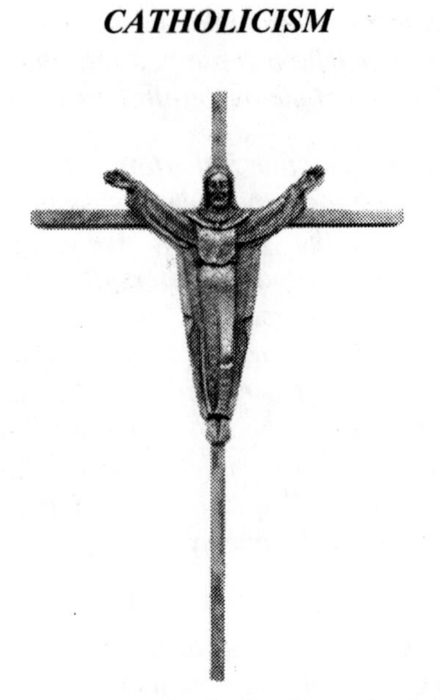

In terms of Catholicism, the **New Catholic Encyclopedia** *notes that "***A person is entitled to dispose of his own property as he will…so long as in doing so he does not render himself incapable of fulfilling duties incumbent upon him by reason of justice or charity. Gambling…is not sinful except when the indulgence in it is inconsistent with duty."** *31*

If Gambling is an addiction similar to drug addiction, I wonder if the authors of the Encyclopedia would say that 'Drug addiction is not sinful except when the indulgence in it is inconsistent...' No, I don't think so. What the New Catholic Encyclopedia perhaps overlooked in their definition is that the indulgence in gambling ***inevitably*** *leads to 'dereliction of duty'.* ***Gambling addiction*** *is a by-product of gambling and for a significant number of people, is something that creeps up and then takes over before a person even realizes that they're in its clutches.*

This definition seems to be on shaky ethical ground. It seems to say that people can gamble, as long as they spend their own money and fulfill their duties. The end, the person's functioning and fulfillment of duties, are more important than the means, what happens in the interim, as long as the job gets done.

Yet the job won't get done, and we know that both drugs and gambling can lead to increased crime. After the gambler or the druggie has lost all his money, the addict steals to support his habit, and many gamblers embezzle to support their addiction. Both are similar. Gambling addiction is a progressive illness and as such "the indulgence in it" inevitably leads to rendering the person "incapable of fulfilling (his) duties." Both drugs and gambling lead to people being unable to fulfill their roles and duties, whether as parents supporting children, as spouses, paying for household bills, or fulfilling other obligations. The addiction of gambling incapacitates people from being available for the performance of their jobs as productive members of their community. In most Catholic parishes, opposition to gambling is substantial but not universal.

At Gesu Church in Milwaukee County, Wisconsin, they're well aware that gambling leads to crime and embezzlement. An article in the Journal Sentinel, 10/17/03, by Tom Held, noted that at Gesu church, a bookkeeper in the parish office stole more than ***$500,000 to feed her gambling habit.***

> *The bookkeeper gambled the money away at the Potawatomi Bingo Casino, a local Indian gambling casino. The embezzlement first began in 2001 and continued for 2 years when the bookkeeper, Rebecca Piekarski, was given check writing responsibility.*
>
> *Thereafter she wrote 154 checks to herself totaling $201,549. She also kept about $317,000 from parish collections. So in 2 years, she stole over $500,000. dollars from the church, probably destroyed any attempt at balancing the church's budget, ruined her life and her family's, and enriched the coffers of the local Indian tribes immeasurably.*
> *These tribes could be accused of trafficking in stolen goods, the embezzled money, except for the difficulty tracing it. 32*

This is a tragedy not only for the parishioners of Gesu Church, who lost $500,000. dollars of their hard-earned and donated money, but also for Rebecca, this poor soul herself, who now has had her life and her family's life ruined. She must live with the knowledge of what she's done for the rest of her life. It's a tragedy that should have been avoided by our government not always seeking to leap through hoops to license and further expand something that's been illegal throughout most of recorded history. theld@journalsentinel.com

Churches and businesses who've had employees embezzle from them, or businesses that don't get paid for services because people have filed for bankruptcy, cannot afford these kind of losses. Many businesses operate on a slim profit margin. If a few major accounts become uncollectible, what's going to happen to that business? Gambling hurts everyone, not only those who gamble. Everyone becomes a victim, not only the perpetrator. The winners, industry owners, casino entrepreneurs, get richer, at everyone's expense, at the cost of people's personal ruin and overall social decline.

In February, 2004, the ***New York State Catholic Conference*** *took a first step toward the state's chronic efforts to expand gambling. They began a campaign saying that the state can't afford the many social costs of widespread gambling. The conference, representing* ***Catholic bishops, urged New York State legislators and Governor Pataki, not to expand gambling*** *from its current already widespread venues in New York. Pataki wanted a constitutional amendment repealing the New York State's constitutional ban against gambling and expanding VLT casinos.*

Spokesman for the conference, Dennis Proust, said that more casinos lead to more compulsive gamblers who may well turn to crime or other things to support their habit:

The state should not be in the position of promoting addictive behavior. *33*

Conference Executive Director, Richard E. Barnes, also noted that the social ills that come with increased gambling are not in the state's moral or economic interests. Although Catholic churches make extensive use of 'Bingo Nites', Proust added, and I agree, that bingo doesn't have the addictive potential or the inherent destructiveness of casinos. "It doesn't have social drinking and bright lights. It has a set time and then it ends. Bingo players are exercising charitable giving. They just have fun doing it." 34

> *There was one Catholic parish that managed to survive and even prosper without Bingo. In May, 1963, Father William J. Witt, arrived as pastor for the parish of Our Lady of the Holy Rosary in Lowellville, Ohio. A small Bingo game had been going on for years before he arrived.*
>
> *One night Father Witt announced that bingo would be discontinued. He said hearing people's complaints about the small jackpots made him feel that the church was contributing to people's greed for money. He explained that, in fact Bingo worked "against the teachings of Jesus in that it was encouraging greed or lust for money."*
>
> *He asked the parishioners to tithe, to give 10% of their salary to the church, "to return 10% from the 100% He (God) has given you." The collection progressively increased until it went up to 500% of what it had been.*
>
> *The church was able to build an education center soon and a new church in 4 years. Many churches feel they can't manage without Bingo but in fact, everything is possible when looked at from the right perspective. 35*
> *2000 NCALG/NCAGE Conference, Sioux Fall, SD*

Other groups associated with the Catholic Church have also begun to take action against the destructive aspects of gambling. In Alberta, Canada, the ***Knights of Columbus,*** *a Catholic fraternal organization, recently declared in* ***April, 2004****, that they would* ***stop raising money through charity casinos.*** *Alberta's Catholic bishops have been opposed to gambling for the past 6 years because of the social costs.*

The Knights of Columbus acknowledged that it was a difficult decision as gambling money was lucrative and paid for large ticket items such as a $70,000 roof. "It's big money and quick money," Knights official Michael Casavant said. Charity casinos generate about a Million dollars annually for the Knights in Alberta alone. But the social costs weighed on the mind of the Knights. As Knight Raymond Cyre said, without casinos, "it won't be as large amount of money as was raised before, but everybody will be able to sleep better at night." 35

Six years ago, the ***Alberta bishops wrote that "anything that contributes significantly to addictive forms of gambling…should be banned or substantially altered in order to diminish the addictive power."*** *Father John Gallagher, president, Newman Theological College in Edmonton, added that casino gambling and lotteries had "reached a stage in which a lot of people are spending a lot of money...some of them...****money that they can't afford****." 36 Perhaps an understatement, 'money they can't afford,' not 'some of them', but many or all of them.*

Perhaps the Canadian government where these Knights are located, which is also addicted to gambling, will take its cues from this example, and seek to turn away from gambling revenues and toward other, morally palatable source of revenue. But as the columnist, Glen Argan, for Mustard Seed, *Canada's largest religious weekly, questioned,* ***if the bishops said this 6 years ago, why has it taken so long for the Knights to act on it?***

The answer, of course, is that their reluctance was fueled by the ease of fundraising where casinos are involved and the large amounts of money involved. This wasn't easy to turn away from. Other non-profit groups, the columnist hopes, will follow suit, and also turn to raising funds in other ways. This kind of moral outrage, clear thinking, and decisive action is what is needed for people to see that gambling is more than just 'a little Entertainment', and potentially very harmful to millions. 37

JUDAISM

"HEAR, O ISRAEL, THE LORD OUR GOD, THE LORD IS ONE."
OLD TESTAMENT

With a statement like the above, as one of the primary tenets of faith, it's not hard to understand that Judaism would not be in favor of gambling. As with the Christian ethic that one should be 'constantly in prayer,' and always thinking of God and serving one's fellow man, in its theoretical principles, Judaism is concerned about man's relationship to his God, not how much money he has.

Although Judaism doesn't have scriptures specifically opposing gambling, most rabbis are not advocates of gambling and generally look down upon it. However, as we know, many temples have high-stakes bingo and Las Vegas nights. Different branches of Judaism, just as in Christianity, have different proscriptions about behavior, with more orthodox branches being more adamant against gambling.

*Judaism does have some interesting takes on gambling showing it to be wrong by virtue of the fact that gambling is intrinsically **unfair.** It notes that for one person to win, means that others must lose. Since religions are about the best and the highest for everyone, gambling, creating losers, would be incompatible with their views.*

> *A story from the Chafetz Chaim shows this position. Someone once asked the Chafetz Chaim, a revered rabbi, to bless him so he would win the lottery. The rabbi refused saying that he would bless stock investments because if the stock goes up, no one loses money. But the rabbi wouldn't bless a lottery ticket because it would amount to a 'curse' upon the other lottery tickets. 38*

This, eminently fair and just position, reflects the heart of the true religious leader who cares for the good of all, and wouldn't want to bless one individual at the expense of others, who wouldn't want to help one, if it meant hurting others in the process

Similarly in the Talmud, it's stated that ***gamblers are not to be relied on as witnesses*** *in trials. Rabbi Bar Hamma suggests that for gamblers to take winnings, is a kind of* ***'theft'*** *from others. For one to win, others have to lose, so it's really an activity incompatible with the good of all, certainly not conducive for the welfare of the whole community. So Orthodox Jews would be very much against gambling. When we were in the Atlantic City casinos, it was very unusual to see men wearing yarmulkes.*

The Talmud, one of Judaism's scriptural texts, further says that the gambler is a person who 'cannot give testimony in a rabbinic court'. This indicates that that person is seen as unreliable, untrustworthy, as having allegiance to something other than the whole truth. Rabbi Daniel Horwitz, president of the Rabbinical Association of great Kansas City, says Judaism doesn't object to such things as raffles, however historically those who gambled for a living were regarded as inherently untrustworthy and their testimony not accepted in religious courts. He added that Judaism would condemn gambling that became a habit, since it would take time away from studying Torah and living by its commandments, the rabbi noted in an article by Bill Tammeus in an article in the Kansas City Star on 3/27/04. 39

In fact, that's the basis for the Biblical injunction that man cannot serve 2 masters, God and mammon (money). As the Bible says, you serve the one, and spurn the other. If we're on this earth to study Torah, to love and serve God, then anything that distracts us from our basic goal is essentially not beneficial. This is similar to the Christian value that one should be in constant prayer, focused on God, certainly not on gambling and the fruits of this world.

As the rabbi said, business transactions rest on the principle of fair exchange, value for value. Money changes hands with an exchange of material goods or services. Business produces value for both buyer and seller - everyone benefits. Gambling however, has no product, the gambler loses, and the community must absorb the social costs. The only winner is the casino owner, the gambling industry. So true business and gambling are very different entities. Business is a player in the overall picture of trade, giving and getting. Gambling is a parasite, only taking, giving no product, giving nothing back. Again, ancient wisdom that we disregard at our own peril.

Islam, on the contrary, makes clear and definitive statements against gambling. In fact, Islam is so clear against gambling that its people are not allowed to invest in the stock market, likening it to gambling. In Islam, Allah or God, is all-important and supposed to guide all of people's actions and even thoughts. Pious Muslims wouldn't dream of gambling.

> *O ye who believe!...* ***Gambling (is) an abomination*** *of Satan's handwork; Eschew such, that ye may prosper. Satan's plan is to excite enmity and hatred between you, with intoxicants and gambling...will ye not then abstain?*
> *Qur'an, Al-Ma'idah, Surah 5:90-1.*

It's interesting that in the Qur'an, one of Islam's major scriptural texts, written 1200 years ago, gambling is coupled with intoxicants, alcohol or drugs, other addictions. Islam outlaws these addictions as a scourge against people, as something that will bring them to ruin. The Qur'an exhorts its people to 'eschew', or stay away from gambling, in order that they may do well, that they may prosper. So people 1200 years ago, without the benefit of sophisticated economic studies or computer analyses, knew that if you wanted to 'prosper', i.e. do well economically, then you shouldn't gamble, that gambling was not the way to good fortune and wealth, that it was a poor economic choice for all. Sound familiar?

Raeed Tayeh, public affairs director of the Muslim American Society's Freedom Foundation described Muslim opposition to gambling saying that:

> ***"As people of faith, we deal with the aftermath of gambling: the destruction of families, their impoverishment."***
> *Tammeus, Kansas City Star Article, 3/27/04. 39*

****

The wise people of old knew that gambling did not bring riches but only self-destruction. Intoxicants - alcohol, drugs, and gambling, named the 'devil's handwork', did not bring joy but only sorrow. They didn't need to go to college to understand how gambling affected society.

Note that St. Augustine, "The devil invented Gambling", said the same thing 500 years later in western Europe. People knew this truth a long time ago and we're just rediscovering it again. Yet people among us would dress up Satan in fancy clothing and call him Entertainment. They would disguise his face and call him 'Family Fun'. And in that guise of Entertainment and Fun, the demon of gambling has raised national bankruptcy levels to twice what they've been in 20 years, and laid the seeds of destruction in many homes and families.

So, as we see, the feeling among communities of faith is that gambling is a social evil and should not be indulged in. If this is so, then why do most states allow and even promote gambling? Do church members refrain from making their opinions known at election time? Or do they feel that the revenue outweighs the social harm? Or have church leaders kept their opinions to themselves about this vice?

It's heartening that now church leaders are finally taking a look at what gambling is doing to members of their congregations. They're realizing that a little gambling can undo a lot of efforts to save individuals. Although religion has not been perfect in our society, at least it's been a leading force in seeking truth and encouraging people to do good acts and help each other.

As the promulgator of values for the common good in our society, we would do well to listen and hear what the leaders of religion say about such important issues in our lives as gambling. We can judge gambling by its fruits, by whether it leads to better ways of doing things, to improved lives, to a higher perspective of seeing what's right, to individual happiness and peace of mind. Or does gambling lead to ruin and pain? Simply put, does gambling help people or not? I think the answer is clear.

The statements throughout this chapter, by an aggregate of religious leaders and scriptural sources, seem to cut through a lot of the fluff, the carefully worded, politically correct statements of politicians and political leaders. The above statements have been thought through, often prayed over, and certainly come from the heart of religious leaders who only want the highest and the best for all people. They have no hidden agendas, no self-interest here, they're going to make their salaries regardless of what they say or do not say.

But they have seen, from a broad perspective, what gambling has done to many individuals and their families. They want to eliminate this harm from also occurring to others. They seek the members of their congregations to live upright and righteous lives dedicated to God and their fellow man. These truly are the statements of wise counsel, from people who are our best 'well-wishers.' We would be prudent to heed their advice, to truly not allow ourselves to be involved in endless scenarios about money. We need to turn away from gambling's single-minded obsession with the riches of this world, at whatever cost.

****

CHAPTER SEVEN

SLOT MACHINES

and Other Examples of

CASINO MISREPRESENTATION

'...Gaming machines are relentless. Just keep feeding and they will continue to swallow. Only rarely do they spew up more than you have sunk in their multi-coloured maws' 1

(Forell, 1997).

Casinos "want people to get addicted, they want them to lose every last drop of money they have." Rev. John Eades. 2

SLOTS...AND PROFIT!

When we speak of addiction, when we're inquiring as to how someone becomes addicted, the discussion inevitably turns to electronic machines, slots and VLT's, video lottery terminals. Slots and VLT's are video machines that people drop their money into hoping to win 'big,' 'to hit a jackpot', to make a life-changing bet.

These are the devices that spawn addiction, that turn loving husbands into crazed machine junkies only thinking about their habit, that turn Mothers into neglectful Moms, leaving babies in cars. These machines have been found to addict people much more rapidly than any other method of gambling. They're the 'crack cocaine' of gambling.

***In 2003, state and local governments gained about $6 Billion in revenue from casino gambling,** according to a USA Today, 7/26/04 article. 3 Slot machines accounted for about two-thirds of that revenue. Only 15 states have no legal machines. The goal of casinos **is "to hook people on gambling** because that's where they make most of their money," according to the National Coalition Against Legalized Gambling, vice chair, Dianne Berlin.3 www.sbcbaptistpress.org/bp news.asp?ID=18800, 8/3/04*

- *Nearly 40 Million Americans played slots in 2003, according to a Harrah's Entertainment survey noted in the New York Times Magazine, 5/9/04 article.*
- *Slots take in an average of more than $1 Billion dollars a day in wagers.*

Slots gross more annually than McDonald's, Wendy's, Burger King and Starbucks combined.

Casinos "want people to get addicted, they want them to lose very last drop of money they have," Rev. John Eades, a United Methodist pastor and addiction counselor in Murfreesboro, Tennessee, said recently on 10/11/03. He recalled one 70 year old man whose habit cost him everything. "He started gambling when he was 68 years old, and he lost his home, his retirement and he was left with whatever his Social Security would bring in," Eades said. Casino getaways for seniors, with bus rides and free meals, can quickly become a costly mistake.

This is the 'product' that casinos offer, the bitter end result. This is their goal, their intention, and usually what happens even to good people...even to normal and sane people. This ties into Dekker's hypothesis, that anyone, given the addictive qualities and ambiance of the whole casino-gambling set-up, can become hooked. 5

The free-wheeling atmosphere that casinos set up, the slot machines as addictive delivery systems, the total ambiance, all contribute to the speed with which people become addicted. The external stimuli of lights, noise, actions, the free drinks, free giveaways, the 'on vacation' scenario, the structuring of slot machines their intermittent reinforcements, speed of play, all contribute to the gambler acting in non-discerning, foolish, self-destructive and thoughtless ways.

> *"The* ***social, environmental, and stimulus features*** *of mechanized gambling...affect* ***the speed with which people develop Pathological Gambling,"*** *Breen and Zimmerman, Brown University School of Medicine 6*

It's the total atmosphere of the casino scene with its glitziness, it's hype, the total package the casino throws in your face, the selling, including the reinforcement features of the machines that are the prime determinants of addiction according to these two Brown University Medical School psychiatrists.

In other words, the created, fantasy world of casinos, the illusionary facade that's produced and ambitiously marketed, the glamour and the opulence, are all the ***social*** *features of casinos. The hype, the lights, the noise, the action, the convenience, the appeal to sense pleasures, the accessibility, and the stimulus features of the machines themselves, all these are the addictive elements, and are to blame for people becoming pathologically addicted. The world created by the architects of gambling, the designers of this new plastic charade called Entertainment is the culprit in people becoming hooked. This is exactly what the British psychiatrists said, what the Sandra Dekker thesis noted, and what our common sense would tell us.*

This artificial world of gambling has sprung up, in the last 25 years and is based on the greed of state governments, gambling financiers, and even the 'regular Joe' who thinks he can become a millionaire. Now the goddess of gambling, powerful and willful that she is, exercises more influence and more of a pull, than the traditional gods of home and hearth. Just as the moth is attracted to the fire, so people are attracted to this goddess of Gambling. She's seems more powerful than any gods before her and capable of unleashing the blessings of wealth or the fire of economic destruction at her command. Yet she's a mirage just as her power is. We must take back our power and realize that the future is governed by ourselves alone, that her blessings can neither give life nor can her ire bring death. It's all in ourselves.

If someone bets on the lottery or even goes to Atlantic City and concentrates on table games such as baccarat or blackjack, they take much longer to become 'hooked' than the infamous slots. My husband played table games for many years appropriately using gambling as entertainment. Once he started slots, it was the beginning of addiction 'big-time'.

Then he started acting crazy, throwing thousands and thousands of dollars at a machine in hopes of the big win. Of course, it never came. When someone is 'hooked', addicted, they start doing reckless things with their money, like throwing it away, like flushing it down the toilet, or like feeding it to slot machines.

Different forms of gambling vary widely in their intensity and in their ability to addict people. Someone playing slot machines plays in a different way than bingo or card games. The machines are hypnotic and people who play them fall into a 'semi-trance', standing there for many hours totally fixated on the action of the machine. These machines have lights, visual stimuli, sounds, and music, all contributing to the total mesmerization and entrancement of the game.

These all act as strong reinforcers. ***Reinforcers****, as noted, are what make you continue doing whatever you are doing. The machines pay off sometimes and other times not. They pay off in different amounts depending on what symbols appear on the reels. This 'intermittent reinforcement' is the strongest kind of conditioning. In other words, if you want a habit to develop, you reinforce it selectively, not always - but often. Then the person gets 'hooked' on the reinforcer thinking that maybe, this time, it's going to be a winner.*

These reinforcers are what keep people coming back. Each time the person wins, they are reinforced. The lights, sound, the whole picture goes off. We like to hear the lights, we know that we've won, that we are going to get paid, we're going to get 'fed'. Bets are made in rapid succession, within seconds of each other. This reward, or motivational item, then becomes what the person is looking for. Lights, sound, bells all presage winning—maybe a jackpot. So he's getting stroked, rewarded, in some way, for his efforts. So we see how the patterns of the gambler's mind is being shaped to conform to follow in the addictive patterns set up by the casino.

*The machines also have a '**high event frequency**', that is you can bet many times a minute. This internalizes the bond of the reinforcement inside you. Just as a dog salivates when he knows he's about to get fed, a gambler's adrenaline flows when he thinks there's a chance that he's going to win. He becomes **very** focused, playing in a very concentrated way.*

*The speed of play, perhaps as little as 3 seconds, the illusion that winning is a possibility, the lights and noise, all add up to an ability to addict almost instantly. "**This intermittent reinforcement policy...works really well,"** said University of Alberta professor Garry Smith, a gambling research specialist. "It (playing the machine) gets ingrained in people. **You don't know when you're going to win...so you keep playing until you win**." 8 In the long run, said Smith, **it's virtually impossible to win on the slots.***

*In **Canada**, one person is very vocal about his VLT addiction. Donald Swinimer claims that he's been addicted to VLTs since he first dropped a coin in the machine. "I've been losing since I first dropped a loonie into a machine."*

*"It became an addiction that has cost me many thousands of dollars and in the end I'm the big loser. The **machines are everywhere and people are losing their homes and families on a regular basis"** Swinimer, 34 years old, has a wife and 2 children, and has been gambling for the past 13 years. He first began gambling on the VLTs when he was 21 years old and the machines were in a corner store near his home in Nova Scotia.*

"In the past 10 years, a large subculture of people have developed with many on government assistance, all who do nothing but place money on VLTs," he added. Swinimer mentioned the names of 5 nearby establishments that have VLTs in his neighborhood saying that they all attract many gambling addicts who spend their own money, the government's money and everything they can get their hands on. Recently Swinimer spent his entire $825 income tax refund on a VLT. The same thing happened last year with an even larger refund check. Swinimer said he doesn't drink but that in the past few years, he's lied, stolen, and become estranged from his parents as the addiction increased.

*"**I'm not a bad person**," he said. "**I want to be a good parent**...but **I just cannot stay away** from the machines. this is **a sickness...an addiction.** This is **not who I am**. **I am a better person than this, but I need help**." 9*

Chalk up yet another tragedy for gambling, another family where everything was spent on gambling, food budget, rent, savings, everything for gambling. I wonder what children think about a father who spends money on gambling rather than on his children. I can only guess what children think about a government that places an adult's right to choose where he spends his money as more important than insuring that children have what they need.

This is addiction in its raw, uncut version. Not the cleaned up version the casinos would have you believe, that gambling addiction affects only a 'small' percentage of its people and people gamble what they can afford. Hungry children, parents committing suicide, mothers without sons. This is what gambling addiction does.

Any gambler will readily testify that when you're at the machines, it looks like others are winning. People see the multitudes and the hordes of players feeding their machines as fast as they can. They appear to be winning because the lights and noises continue to sound. The clink of the sound of the coins dropping into the metal basins seems constant. Yet overall these people are losing. They are 'throwing good money after bad' in the vain hope that they'll be that one big winner. They stay there for hours and hours. When they go to the bathroom, they put things on their machine to let everyone know that this machine is theirs and not to touch it. They talk to the machine and try to influence it by whatever means they know. However, the random number generator is the only thing any machine ever 'knows'. And that random number generator is totally beyond player control in any way.

Gambling is not a game of ***skill****, as you're led to believe. It's a game of* ***chance****, and your 'chances' of winning big are about* ***1 in 8 Million****. Do you really want to play with those odds?*

The frenzy and the intense feelings that the player brings to his addiction are partly a result of the tactics and gambits used by the machines. When we play a machine, we're sowing the seeds of our addiction. We're opening ourselves up to the demons of addiction, inviting them to find a place to enter and find a home in us, in our souls. The means of addicting someone is inherent in the activity itself. The ability to bet so intensely on the slot machines and so rapidly is a critical factor in drastically shortening the amount of time it takes people to become problem gamblers.

*These machines do their job, of addicting the player, efficiently and fast. They are economical to run and maintain, requiring no constant staff attendance. "****The average slot machines pays for itself in the first 100 days.*** *For the rest of its useful life, it's all gravy." Quite a nice return on money, don't you think? I can't think of* *any other investment where the returns are so high and so quick! And the investment is a sure money-maker. As David Davila points out from an article in Gaming Today,*

> *The longer you sit in front of one, the more you lose. Next to prostitution, it's the world's business. In no other business do people budget money to lose (just) to you. What would make people 'budget money' 'just to lose?' 10*

It hardly makes sense for people to budget their money to lose when it seems we all work so hard for our money. But this is the final circle of the argument. They budget money to lose in their hopes of winning. They hope to ultimately hit the jackpot, to change their lives from the reality of their present one to a Madison Avenue illusion filled with materialistic dreams and grandiose schemes.

If the slots have done their job according to casinos, then they have addicted plenty of people. In a speech regarding the impact of gambling and slots at the 9/28/2002 NCALG/NCAAHE Conference in Texas, Maura Casey noted that

> *Slots increased addiction incredibly.*
> *Slots are an incredible combination of computer*
> *technology, psychology, video games and*
> *Madison avenue marketing.*
> *The human race has gambled for thousands of years,*
> *but these machines are entirely new.*
> *They have no resemblance whatsoever to the slow,*
> *mechanical, one-armed bandit of 20 years ago. 11*

Other reasons why slots are so popular include the fact that machines are non-threatening to the gambler. It's just the person and the machine. At table games, people are often intimidated by the dealers or others watching. With machines, people withdraw into their own worlds and stay there for hours with no one bothering them. Machines are 'user-friendly' to the uninitiated. Betting with these machines can be rapid, continuous, and repetitive. They give partial reinforcement in the form of small wins and near misses, but almost never do people 'hit the jackpot'. Playing these kinds of machines enable a person to have a 'solitary', experience, i.e. the social chatter, interaction, and banter of some of the other games doesn't occur here. Even if they hit the jackpot, they don't stop playing.

SLOTS—AND PROFIT

Earl L. Grinols, economics professor at the University of Illinois at Urbana-Champaign agrees that slots are the "most addictive and most problematic form of gambling, far more so than the lottery or horse racing. ***"You can't easily lose $30,000 on the lottery in a night, but you can on a slot machine."*** *12. Dr. Grinols sees machines in terms of creating a multitude of social ills that often get ignored. Speaking before the Maryland House Ways and Means Committee, offering his expert testimony recently, he said that although additional slots would generate millions of dollars for the state, they would also entail heavy* ***social costs that outweigh any potential benefits.***

Dr. Grinols added that the state can expect ***$3 in costs for each $1 in benefits.*** *The costs of social problems far outweigh the benefits, "It's not even a close call," he said. The problems he listed include an increase in crime, including robbery, embezzlement, fraud and other as well as violent crimes, lost productivity in the workplace, bankruptcy filings, and gambling-related suicides. 12*

At that same hearing before the ***Maryland*** *House Ways and Means Committee,* ***Attorney General*** *J. Joseph Curran Jr. also spoke to give his views about the impact of legalizing slots. He added that legislators can't look at slot revenue without also considering the social costs. Additionally he warned that legalizing slots inevitably leads to their proliferation, just as the lottery grew from a single weekly drawing to one with many drawings daily and even 'instant' tickets. 13*

In ***Maryland,*** *Gov. Robert Ehrlich, Jr.'s., latest proposal involves expanding the number of slot machines at a series of slot emporiums at 2 non-racetrack venues along side I-95. The Gov. proposed 11,500 slot machines last year at 4 racetracks year estimated to generate 1.6 billion for the state in revenue. This year, 2004, he added an additional 4,000 machines to his proposal. This would increase revenue to about 1.3 billion dollars according to industry analysts. Four states in the U.S. have casinos with annual revenues to the states that exceeded $2 billion in 2002: Nevada, Mississippi, Louisiana, and New Jersey.*

*As we've seen, in the past 20 years, casinos themselves have shifted the use of these '****addictive delivery machines****', as Rev. Tom Gray called them. Casinos now rely heavy on slot machine winnings for most of their profits. In the past, table games were the primary profit making means for the casinos, especially table games, such as blackjack, baccarat, and craps which used to produce 60%, of the casino's revenues. Now slots produce the majority of revenues. Slots are especially profitable for casinos when the reduced number of staff required to run them are* *factored in. Christiansen Capital Advisors, 2000, noted that of the 2 Connecticut Indian casinos, 73% of their revenue comes from machines.*

This form of gambling, machines, whether slots or VLT's, are the most profitable for their owners. They amass more money than table games, sports betting or lotteries. The casinos just have to get us addicted, and then they can rake in the profits. Whatever is most addictive, is what is being implemented. It's our own addiction that brings us down. Our own addiction makes us lose our values, our judgment, our sense of discernment. Whatever will make the casinos the most money is what they'll use. ***It's all about Addiction. It's all about Money.***

There are currently more than ***750,000 slot machines in the U.S****. The slot machine mania has progressed from simple one-armed bandits in the early days of gambling in the late seventies, to video lottery terminals, to electronic bingo devices. As the fast-paced machines proliferate, there are many issue which need to be discussed regarding* ***casino responsibility, manufacturer's product liability, and governmental regulation.***

> *"The machine is telling us we can win*
> *and we are going to win big soon.*
> *That is the crux of the fraud.*
> *The players are being* ***deceived****.*
> *It is deceptive entertainment." 14*
>
> *Roger Horbay, Canadian researcher*

A 1984 U.S. Patent Office document for modern computerized slot machines notes that encouraging gamblers to play by convincing them they have a legitimate shot at winning is part of the plan. The documents noted,

> ***"It*** *is important to make a machine that is* ***perceived to present greater chances of payoff than it actually has.***
>
> ***U.S. Patent Office*** *15*

So machines deal in perception – not reality. These machines have, as we've seen, an incredible addictive potential to hook-in players and to keep them at the machines. "With a possible bet every 3 seconds on these machines, it's over-stimulating," said Robert Breen, clinical psychologist and director of the Rhode Island Gambling Treatment Program. "In terms of whether your mind can handle that, it's overwhelming." 16

Breen adds that video slots are "the ***most virulent strain of gambling in the history of man."*** *Have we heard this before from other researchers? Breen is co-*

author of 2 studies that found that the machines create problem gamblers 4 times faster than any other form of gambling. "We measured the period of time between regular gambling and pathological gambling," Breen said. "The machines addict people much quicker, about ***13 months*** *in between the time when they started gambling regularly and when they developed a pathological gambling disorder." Actually it's surprising that its that long.*

People can enjoy different form of gambling as part of their routine, leisure activities for many years. But when exposed to video slots, the problems progress very rapidly. "People transitioned from being non-problem gamblers to losing lots of money, having bad relationships, losing their jobs, their freedom and their good mental health." 17

Slot outcomes are predetermined*, i.e. the moment the spin button is pressed, the result is determined, not when the video reel slows to a stop. Computer-driven slots arrived in the 1980s in the U.S. and handed manufacturers the chance to create a totally controlled environment, with the outcomes determined by whatever the manufacturer decides. "The reels displayed don't represent what the odds of winning actually are," said Horbay.* ***Slot machine design "encourages a false impression of one's chance of winning."*** *18*

Connecticut's director of problem gambling services for the Dept. of Mental Health and Addiction Services, Chris Armentero, said the ***new fast-paced machines are 'absolutely' producing more pathological gamblers, the same way a high-nicotine cigarette hooks a smoker.*** *19 Sound familiar, this is becoming a refrain. http://www.ctnow.com/news/local/hc-slotmachine.art may09,1,5044301.story?coll= hcbig-headlines-breaking, Rick Green, Hartford Courant*

Slot machines have payouts dictated by a ***computerized random number generator****. This means that every combination of possible reel outcomes has certain numbers associated with it. Higher payouts have fewer possible combinations. When the reels land on a certain symbol, it's because those symbols have been* ***pre-assigned*** *to that combination of random numbers. The machine symbols on each reel are irrelevant. The outcome is determined at the time each bet is made, not when the reels stop spinning.*

Machines have no memory – each spin is completely independent of past outcomes. So the odds of hitting a jackpot are the same each play regardless of whether the machine has just hit or not. To think that you've been playing the machine for 6 hours straight and 'it's got to pay off soon,' is erroneous. The machine may pay off at any time or it may not pay off for 2 more years of constant play.

The probability or possibility of winning the larger jackpots is very slight. In 1997, a researcher showed that to obtain 5 Black Rhinos, the top jackpot, the probability of winning is ***1 in over 8 million****. If one plays 9 instead of 5 lines, the probability decreases to about* ***1 in 1.2 million****. Of course that's additional money bet too. Slots are wholly based on chance. There is* ***nothing*** *the player can do to increase his odds of winning. The r-n-g (random number generator) is all the machines knows. But – and this is the thing – the casino tries everything in its power to persuade you that you do have the power to influence a win, a win of BIG money.*

CASINOS & TV

Casinos like slot machines and the addiction they bring. They like them so much that in November, 2003, Tropicana Casino and Resort in Atlantic City made playing slot machines even more attractive and opulent than ever before. In an unprecedented step toward meeting ***all*** *of a person's sense pleasures, they attached* ***TV monitors*** *to each of the 94* ***slot machines*** *in their newly refurbished Crystal Room slot parlor. Patrons of this exclusive area, high-rollers, can now sit down in a fully adjustable seat, raise their feet onto a footrest, grab a remote control, don complimentary earphones, and enjoy TV, while they drink free drinks and eat the casino's free food. So they eat, drink, gamble and watch TV while they throw away their money! What decadent opulence. The free food, incidentally, isn't hamburgers and hot-dogs either, it's trays of shrimp and other delicacies. Some sybaritic pleasure palace! Even the Roman emperors didn't have it so good!*

Of course the casinos are 'betting' that people will be so busy imbibing their drinks, watching their favorite programs, and feeding their faces, that they won't notice how much money they're losing. The casino spent $3 Million dollars just outfitting this room. We can bet that if the casino spent that much money outfitting this room, they anticipate making a whole lot more money in profits. After all, said casino representative Dennis Gomes, this new room is foremost a vehicle for Tropicana to 'make money'. 20 Remember the casino's primary directive - to make money!

21 http://www.trumptaj.com/default.asp

MISREPRESENTATION

> *(Gambling) is* ***licensed banditry*** *in the guise of entertainment, given the imprimatur of legitimacy because the victims are presumed to be willing and able (to pay) and because the community shares in the profits through taxation. 22*

The above logo, in dark, sultry red and black colors, is on the front of Taj Mahal's web site. It gives some feeling as to what gambling is about, implied promises, dark connotations, suggestive implications, with nuances of amorality and sexuality. This is not what America is about to me and to billions of other hard-working citizens. I don't think such advertisements should be public on the Internet nor a part of casino advertising at all. But this is what casinos are about. To make money in any way they can. If it means selling sexuality and darkness, that's fine with them. Whatever it takes, would be their mantra.

23

Implicit in this book is the understanding and assumption that the gambling industry and especially casinos, have overstepped their bounds, that they have breached the boundaries of truth and honesty. Casinos and the gambling industry have gone overboard in seeking to make exorbitant profits. The average person is no match for the research, the smarts, and the money the casinos throw at the gambler in order to get him to stay and continue to pump his money into the machines.

24

No one argues with an industry trying to make a dollar. In terms of casinos, however, there's no such thing as an 'honest dollar.' It seems that they're out to make profits, regardless of how they do it, and regardless of who gets hurt in the process. But while casinos try their utmost to give the impression of being upfront, above-board and open, the fact is that their methods are based in subterfuge and duplicity, manipulation and pretension.

25

Let's look at exactly how the casinos do this. We're all intelligent people, not accustomed to being played for fools. If we say we're going to a casino, surely we know that there's **risk** *there. So how do they get us to part with our money so quickly and so constantly? What are the tricks of the trade that induce us to throw away our money, to give it away to casinos. And if we give it to casinos, we're not offering it to our families or loved ones? How do casinos get to be more important than our families?*

26

Gambling is not a homogeneous activity. Pari-mutual betting at dog and race tracks is different than casinos which are again different than sports betting. Even within casinos, some forms of gambling, slot machines and VLTs, as we know, are very different, more addictive and dangerous than other forms, such as poker, table games or keno. In this chapter, we're focusing on casinos and some of the strategies and machinations used to entrap the player and his money.

The difference between table games at a casino and the slot machine is what contributes most to addiction, to people getting 'caught up in the moment' and letting go of their customary controls and self-discipline. This critical difference is the amount of ***time between the bet and the outcome, between the risk-taking-behavior and the reinforcement****. This* ***time-lag*** *between the act of wagering, placing the bet, and the outcome, losing, determines how reinforced the activity is. In Lotto, one might not find out for a week if they were a 'big' winner. With BlackJack, the whole table and dealer has to receive cards so the time-lag is at least a few minutes.* ***In slot machines, the time-lag is negligible, the time interval between starting the game, pushing the button, and the reels stopping, can be as little as 3 seconds, almost instantaneous!***

With slot machines, after you put your coins in, or even quicker, after you pushed the credit button which works on money stored inside the machine, if you blink slowly, the reels have stopped turning already. The machine's action is incredibly quick. Many slot machines these days are capable of new games with a 6 second interval, the industry standard. Machines are capable of a 3 second interval, but it's felt that's too fast for people to play. Then people lose their money too fast and it becomes obvious it's not a game but a massacre.

With machines, you win 'a little' money,' thus teasing and tempting the gambler to play even more. This 'little' money is negligible. Often the machine tries to excite you by returning 2 coins. However since you just put in 3 coins, it's still an overall loss – but manipulated to look like a win. The machine gave you money, didn't it? You got 2 coins back and another chance at the Big Jackpot.

Players continue to put money in a machine because they're seeking the Big Jackpot. Anything that lets them keep playing, keeps them in the golden-opportunity-aura, let's them stay 'in-the-game'. People know they can't win unless they're playing. So they keep playing because then they at least have a ***chance*** *at the top prize. This is more of the rational-thinking-that-seems-logical-but-really-isn't scenario.*

The player rationalizes that he's staying in the action. Compared to the top Jackpot, the money that he's gambling is small potatoes. He thinks he's being 'smart' by gambling the maximum bet, that way he can get the maximum jackpot. But this is another example of unclear thinking. The odds of him hitting the top prize are so slight as to not be realistic. So he's throwing his money away if he's there for the Big Win. If the gambler has set a limit, let's say $50. dollars for the evening, and just wants to be there for the exciting atmosphere, the lights, and the fun night out, then that's a different story.

The problem here is twofold. First, $50. can be lost in 10 minutes if you happen to have a bad night. Or it can last for 2 hours. So you don't know if your pre-set money limit will actually last the evening and fill your time. If it doesn't, the temptation to add more money to play more is very strong. Once you've added more money to a pre-set limit, self-discipline and control have just been co-opted. So right away, you may spend more than you meant to.

Secondly, the excitement of gambling doesn't seem to stay, for many people, by taking the same amount of money each time and playing until it's gone. In order for the excitement to continue, for the 'hit' to come, the player needs to bet a little more than he knows he should. Here's the risk, the excitement, the kick. The need here is for ever expanding quantities of the stimulator, the addictive substance. This what makes for ***addiction****. Remember, it's progressive. It needs to* ***increase in intensity in order for the hit to stay the same****. It's like the blob in the old sci-fi movies. To maintain itself, it needs to grow in size and intensity.*

The machines operate so fast, and with such reinforcement on each play, i.e. lights, sound, the total picture, as discussed, that the possibility of losing money and becoming addicted, escalates rapidly. The play on machines is 'continuous' and as such, incite 'persistent' play. The machines are played fast, people get hooked quickly, and players lose a lot.

The combination of the uncertainty and excitement of the unknown combination of these variables seems to serve to focus the individual's mind completely on the machine and on what's going to happen on the next spin. And the next spin, and the next spin, until oblivion. The player himself is now in the twilight zone, mindlessly throwing his money into the machine, forgetting his limits, his responsibilities, other people in his life.

This continuous action puts people's minds into the 'zone,' into a zombie-like-state of intense concentration on the machine, to the exclusion of everything else, to the detriment of other pressing responsibilities. We've just turned the corner into a problem gambler. As we continue on this machine, we're rapidly approaching becoming a pathological gambler.

This strategy, of machines paying small amounts at varying times, is the ***intermittent reinforcement*** *that makes for addiction. The player never knows when he's going to 'hit'. It appears to him like* ***he's always about to hit****. He often almost gets it, 2 reels out of 3, near misses. So combining the rapidity of the payout interval, event frequency, and the variable ratio schedule, it's no surprise that a high rate of responses occur, namely that he keeps playing, and consequently, gambling excessively.*

Near misses utilize a psychology of their own related to operant conditioning. Near misses occur when a machine lines up 2 winning symbols but not the third and final, crucial one. The near miss acts as an 'intermediate' reinforcer because the player is led to believe that he 'almost made it.' In fact, for a few moments, when the player is seeing the first two symbols coming up the same, he begins feeling the hope and subsequent elation of the win. Poker machines are designed to ensure a 'higher than chance frequency' of near misses. These encourage future play because the gambler feels he was 'almost there'. He was almost at the place where he'd been trying so hard and for so long to get to, the jackpot.

Yet it's not true that he almost won. A near miss is as far off as 3 completely unrelated symbols. It just appears that way. The psychology is that the ***player is not always losing but constantly almost winning.*** *The feeling of almost getting it, the regret, the frustration which the player feels at not winning, is mitigated and eliminated by playing again, which is another chance at winning, at staying in the* *game. It's also another chance at losing, though. Just because it looks close, it's really not. Remember that the random number generator which decides what symbols will come up is the only thing that matters. Nothing else!*

The ***multiplier potential*** *is another* ***structural characteristic*** *that allows the players to bet or wager different amounts. A player can bet a quarter on a machine and become eligible to win a certain amount of money. If he bets 3 quarters, though, he becomes eligible to win more than 3 times as much as his quarter bet. He learns that 'smart money' bets the 3 quarters. The player becomes highly motivated to bet the maximum amount in order to win the maximum amount. If a player bets a quarter and wins, it's felt that he's been ill-advised, because by betting the max, he could have won more than triple the win. Gambling 'wisdom' always says to bet the max amount on the machine. Of course this is another way that the gambler and his money are soon parted. Changing the amount of the bet gives another 'illusion of control'. The gambler feels that it's his '****skill*** *and smart judgment' that allows him to affect the gambling outcome, to win BIG! The propaganda has done its bit. Yet remember, skill is not a factor.*

Casinos know that the more the person is ***involved*** *and* ***engaged*** *in what he's doing, the more tied into the whole process he's going to be. Personal participation in the game, bettor involvement in terms of making decisions about how much to bet and when, and the exercise of 'perceived' skill, all contribute to our gambler thinking that he is actively involved in making money. When players believe that their actions affect the outcomes, they're hooked. Then they feel they can make winning possible for themselves. If it's their skill involved in winning, they think they think they can make a difference in winning and that it's something that's doable. 27.*

This aspect of believing that it's his skill that's affecting the outcomes is ***the 'illusion of control.'*** *The illusion is achieved by allowing the player to decide the amount of his bet, and how many lines to play. The gambler's '****expectancy of success****' is inappropriately higher than the objective probability would warrant. This is what casinos are striving to create, the illusion on your part that you're going to win the jackpot, the life-changing win. As we've seen, the odds of winning are so infinitesimally small that it's not a realistic probability for one to strive after.* ***This illusion of control and expectancy of success are at the heart of the unrealistic thinking that casinos imbue players with****. Casino advertising says that you can win a jackpot, anyone can. You know you're a relatively skillful person in certain areas. If others can do it – and you've seen them do it—then there's no reason why you can't do it also, win a jackpot. Sounds logical and realistic. So let's forget the real odds of winning, the reality of the situation. This is the beginning of 'Denial'.*

Some machines even have 'nudge', 'hold' and 'gamble' buttons which enable a player to improve their scores. These, 'specialist play features', take longer to learn how to play and so induce longer, more losing play. They also give the illusion of more control over the outcome. In fact we know that the outcomes of machines are based wholly on chance.

Most players believe their activity to be skillful and their actions to affect the outcome of the machines. They believe that it's a matter of trying hard enough and playing smart enough to win. But this isn't accurate. Machines are based on **chance** *alone. But it's a chance carefully manipulated and controlled* ***by the casino****. Nothing the player can do, whether touching the button in a certain way, whether praying at the moment of inserting the coins, whether clutching his stomach muscles or not breathing, (a common phenomenon), nothing can make a difference in winning. Only the random number generator can do it. And it only does it when it wants to.*

Misleading advertising is not the only instiller of misleading thoughts in the individual. The whole ambiance, of light, sound, and noise effects is contributory towards increasing gambling play. But even if he wins, it's not enough to pay off past loses. So it's really not a win. Companies like International Gaming Technology spend millions of dollars making sure that you feel good about playing. They spend months deciding what tunes to put in machines and after what plays to do so.

All of this commotion inhibits our player's customary good judgment. It induces him to play for longer times and for larger amounts since he's being so strongly reinforced by all these varied stimuli. It also induces others to play more to emulate his (apparent) success. Often when someone wins, i.e. when lights and sounds go off, other players or casino staff will congratulate the winner. As if it had anything to do with him as a person, either his skill or smarts or anything of that nature. Human nature being what it is, people glow in this attention. It serves the purpose of having them gamble even more.

Light and color variables affect behavior in a variety of ways with players often not really aware of how they're being influenced. Red is known to stimulate behavior and to provoke excitement. Many studies have found color variation to affect human physiological reactions such as blood pressure and breathing rate. Red appears to be associated with increased frequency and intensity of responding as compared with blue or green. In gambling arcades of 'fruit machines', the English term, the color of the arcades' interiors were often red with dim lighting. The machines were a series of flashing red lights. The effect was to increase gambling and to create a feeling of being in a cocoon, 'away from it all', totally spaced out, certainly oblivious to your own concerns. The dim lighting served to decrease social and verbal interaction which would inhibit concentration on gambling.

This kind of total ambiance could certainly get someone to dissociate and to let go of their normal conservative judgment. Flashing lights, especially red, have been found to affect people who are pre-disposed to seizures. Seizures, neurological lapses within the brain occur because of neuron mis-firings. The total effect of all of these sense stimuli could well influence sensitive brain cells in many different ways.

Another psychological strategy that casinos use as a subtle inducement to gambling, includes the gambit of 'Naming machines'. This makes them more familiar to people, and allows the player to choose a machine that is supposedly in sync with their own tendencies. Players feel they have a tie with their machine and more readily engage with it. They remember the machine and look for it when they visit in the future. The first machine was called, ***'The Liberty Bell',*** *a symbol of American Independence. Many machines refer to money such as 'Piggy Bank' or 'Cash pot' implying that the machine is holding money just waiting for the player to tap it. Other machines have been called things like 'Fortune Trail', and 'Silver Chance' implying that the odds of winning are favorable. It's one more thing to get the player and the machine into a perceived relationship. Alan often had a 'favorite machine', one where he thought the odds were especially favorable.*

So a player is nonverbally encouraged to 'individualize' and 'personalize' his machine. He identifies with it and becomes further enmeshed in his unclear thinking. He forms a relationship, an affective bond, with the machine. So you see players talking to machines sometimes, certainly not allowing others to play them when they go to the bathroom. Often players tie up 2 machines simultaneously feeding both at the same time. This personalization of a machine, something we don't normally do, contributes to the whole unreality of the situation, the TV-Hollywood-Las Vegas mentality. Suspension of judgment, the disruption of a gambler's value system, all these stimulate irresponsible gambling and the further loss of money.

Everything is not as it seems in casinos. This is true with the ***'buy-in'*** *for machines also. Machines tout themselves as just being a quarter or fifty cents to play, implying that it's just a 'little' money. However that fifty cents needs to be tripled in order to hit the maximum jackpot in case one wins. Then each 'spin' of the reels costs $1.50. Because the machines are programmed to play so rapidly, one can play 5 to 10 times in a minute. That brings it up to $15.00 a minute. Then if a player stays a few hours, that ends up being in the hundreds and thousands of dollars. All from what was first touted as a quarter or fifty cent bet! So you have to account for the* ***Total Bet****, not your initial buy-in.*

***Machine speed** is also designed to hinder and halt thought processes. It's hard to be exactly rational with lights, bells and music playing loudly in response to the slightest win. It's like trying to be coherent and rational when you've had a drink and whistles and bells are gone off in your ear and people are yelling. Sensory overload. Why do we like to watch movie thrillers, scary movies. It's the hit, the adrenaline rush.*

*These **structural characteristics** of slot machines are designed to elicit certain similar responses in people. These phenomena are calculated to engage and addict people. Just as BF Skinner's rats were always hitting a lever to get a reward, addicts feed machines to get their reward. **Anyone who chooses to play, to gamble, will experience similar responses to these phenomena."** 23 These are natural, scientific deliberately incited phenomenon. The problem is that these 'natural responses' are then called **addiction.** The gambling industry then calls the addicted players, deviant or compulsive, when in fact they have just had a **natural reaction** to a series of carefully calculated phenomenon built into machines.*

*Machines in general are programmed for players to lose. Slots generally are configured that they return 85 to 92 cents out of every dollar. So to start with they return 92% of your money. Then they return 92% of your 92 cents and so on until you get nothing back. **Continuous and persistent play guarantees economic loss.** This is what the machine is programmed to do. Yet casinos advertise jackpots as frequent events guaranteed to happen to everyone.*

*So **economic loss** is programmed into the machines, with the probability of jackpots rare but presented as frequent, with the machines presented as profitable to the player but really not. This range of operating techniques and psycho-structural characteristics, such as naming machines, increased event probability, and strategies for persistent and continuous play are typical of slot machines. In the past 10 years, the machines have been exceedingly fine-tuned with state-of-the-art graphics and psychedelic effects guaranteed to addict everyone. The casinos have been given a license to exploit, justified by the basic capitalist profit maximization principle. 24 No wonder that slot machines are making millions for their owners and conversely, increasing numbers of people are filing for bankruptcy.*

With all of these incentives to gamble, as well as the pre-education that casinos indoctrinate people with, gambling seems quite a rational activity. In fact, we know that it's really an irrational activity. The gambler himself feels that he is acting within reason, that his actions are rational. If one would believe all the advertising, or even half of the advertising, then gambling would appear to be a rational activity. One believes that one might well make money if skillful and smart enough.

The gambling industry presents this economically irrational activity as an economically productive one. Overt appeals are made in the form of advertising to economic motives, i.e. that the gambler has a good chance of winning, to recreational motives, 'it's just a night out,' 'aren't we allowed to have some fun', etc., and prestige motives, people are catered to, and treated deferentially as if they were royalty or Hollywood stars.

***Marketing strategies** create the impression that gambling results in financial gain. Casinos announce by loudspeaker, big Keno and slot-machine 'jackpot' winners—overt evidence that others are winning. If they are winning, then so the assumption goes, then you too can win. Casino advertisements cite that they have the 'most generous slots', i.e. advertising that they minimize the house's percentage.*

Other inducements, proffered eagerly by casinos, include cheap meals, 49 cent breakfasts, inexpensive buffets, complimentary meals and drinks, free 'stakes' for gambling, a few dollars worth of change for the machines, free junkets for selected players, including free accommodations, meals and transportation, free baby-sitting, free souvenirs, provision of free financial services, lending facilities, personal check cashing, and the provision of entertainment at bargain rates in lounges or shows.

Sometimes casinos distribute vouchers for free lunch or dinner, 2 hours before dinner is available. Then you feel you have to stay there otherwise you're throwing away a free meal. In those 2 hours, you could conceivably throw away the value of 20 free meals.

Inside casinos, traffic patterns wind their way through gambling areas, to the dining areas, and then back through the gambling areas. Often the lines for top entertainment Shows or other big ticket events wait beside the machines. While people wait, they feed the machines. As people stand in line to get in the show, they're in a jovial mood, feeling expansive, dressed up, about to see big-name entertainment, so they indulge in a little play. Then what happens is that in addition to the price of the show ticket, you might lose another 30 or 50 or a hundred dollars while waiting to get in. We might feel that this is penny-ante to the casinos. But as we see, nothing escapes their gaze, nothing is too big or too small for them to focus on as a means to get your money.

*Staff walk around offering **free alcoholic drinks.** Free drinks impair your concentration and makes you think, 'Hey, I'm on vacation, let me have a little fun.' Not a good idea to follow such impulses when it comes to your hard-earned cash. Free credits on machines are another common form of prizes. These, in turn incite more persistent and continuous play. Various incentives and promotions are advertised and people have to be there to win. Casinos have their own private* *'clubs' which offer free sumptuous buffets, drinks, and often wide screen TVs with sports events.*

One gains access to these private clubs, a very valued benefit, by having played there in the past. The advantage to the casinos of these 'clubs' is that being buffets, players get in and out fast, thus returning to the tables sooner. Plastic player cards which allow one access to clubs, earn 'comps' when inserted in machines or given to the pit boss in table games. The Taj Mahal Casino, one of Donald Trump's own, has ***3*** *separate private player clubs, the Bengal Club, the Maharajah club, and the President's Select club, all with large-screen TV's, opulent buffets, and hosts to answer your every whim. The Casinos design these clubs as additional 'freebies' that they can comp players with and seem to be giving them select, VIP treatment.*

The other side of the coin, however, is that they also allow the casinos to monitor the players, their gambling habits, their preferences in play, the amount of money spent, the player's patterns of behavior. They accumulate data about you which they later use in various ways, including figuring out the most effective way to market to you.

Other strategies the casinos use include, ***free Turkeys*** *at Thanksgiving, and small and large gifts at various other times. Every year the casinos would give us a free turkey at Thanksgiving. Each year we would seriously consider making a special trip down to Atlantic City from Long Island, just for the free Turkey. Realizing that the turkey's value was about $12, we saw that we'd be spending more to get down there, even if we subsequently didn't play, than the turkey itself. But each year we considered it. The casinos don't stay in business by 'giving it away'.*

So food, gambling and drinking are now established. The cashiers where one cashes out, exchanges one's chips for money, often have long lines and require a wait. While you're standing in line waiting, you're watching the other machines continuously (apparently) hit for other players and second-guessing yourself as to whether you cashed out at the right time.

ATM and other credit machines *are plentiful in casinos. Regulations to remove ATMs from casino floors and put far away would be helpful. Then it wouldn't be so easy to give in to the impulse to withdraw additional cash. One Western Canadian province did take machines out of casinos to inhibit some of the excesses of addiction. This is an important part of limiting people's free rein to act impulsively spending more than they should.*

The practice of playing with ***'chips'*** *rather than real money makes people think they're not losing as much. Alan and I always had a running commentary on the* *definition of the money that one wins. When you win, and you're ahead that night, is it your money or the casinos money that you have. Some people think that when they're winning, since it wasn't their money to begin with, they can afford to be freer and less cautious with it, to take more chances. On the other hand, once it's in your hand, it's yours and if you choose not to play wisely with it, then that's your problem.*

Also, the advertising of casinos includes many appeals to the ***recreational value*** *of gambling. The assumption is that leisure and recreation are highly valued and a necessity. People often rationalize that they want 'to have a little fun', or 'we're entitled to take a vacation.' Other slogans such as 'Take time out of fun,' or 'Go where the action is' are common. However the truth is that we're not here for 'fun' and no one gets anywhere by gambling.*

Gambling is promoted within the same context as sporting activities, for example, various kinds of sporting events, golf, or boxing. Thus the legitimacy and sportsmanship of the sporting activities seem to be extended to gambling. The casinos themselves are noisy, bustling environments with important looking people, hustling around. Top entertainment from small musical groups to Broadway shows is hyped. These were often 'comped', for us, giving the gambler the impression of being 'important'. My children and their friends saw the world-famous magician, David Copperfield, many times, with complimentary drinks as well.

The elaborate architecture, decorating and landscaping of many casinos reminds you you're in fantasyland, not Mayberry U.S.A. anymore. You're treated as a VIP in a castle. The Taj Mahal in Atlantic City with the plushest carpeting and the largest chandeliers is giving a clear message, an appeal to prestige and to wealth. People usually don't see such opulent surroundings.

The rooms all give the impression of heightened activity, fun, glamour, opulence and excitement. Overall, it's an extremely alluring environment with the overt promise of wealth. Often one hears and feels the heavy beat from a nearby lounge area with a group or singer performing. These places are open 24/7/365, i.e. all the time. You can walk down to the casino at 5 am and there are people, bleary eyed, nursing a drink, looking like hell, and still popping their money into a machine. Holidays are no problem for the casinos. You can walk into a casino on Christmas Eve or Easter morning and there are people there losing their money. The casinos are happy to accommodate you any time day or night.

The overall impression is of sociability and fun. Before I became aware of the destructiveness of gambling, I used to think that gambling was good for some people, seniors, for example. I thought, well, it gets them out of the house, gives them something to do, and be around other people. Yet this isn't really true. When we scratch the surface, we see individuals standing alone at machines for long hours, not really talking to anyone except perhaps perfunctory comments. You can't have any intelligent or meaningful conversation around a blackjack table, and certainly not around a craps table. In Baccarat, the silence is deafening with everyone intensely focused on the next card to come up. Gambling is about money. It's not about being social, fulfilling your role in society, being a good parent, being constructive, helpful, or anything else. It's all about money.

Despite being billed as promoting sociability, gambling is a solitary activity between you and the machine, or you and the dealer. If one could have a relationship with a machine in the realm of sociability, then it would be sociable. But alas, machines don't respond no matter how much one talks, bribes, prays, exhorts, or begs. It's really something you do by yourself, with your own money as your prime consideration and your own drama as your hit.

The gambling industry presents gambling as a ***rational*** *economic and leisure activity. They make sure that every player is attended to, feels welcome, and important. Their aggressive advertising strategies project every one as winners, implying that gambling is prosperous for all. In their advertising, the industry has 'glamorized, normalized, and sanitized' what used to be regarded as sinful or as morally wrong. Advertising promotes the idea that this is an easy, quick opportunity to 'get rich'. This advertising, this inciting of desire, is the* ***'marketing of dreams'*** *demonstrating the goal of great wealth for the common man. This provides a powerful motivation for all to play. In fact, people think that if they don't play, they missing an opportunity to accumulate wealth.*

Glossy pictures portray all players as 'happy winners.' There are no pictures of the losers who really constitute almost everyone who plays. Advertising shows sophisticated men and women interacting socially in exciting, glamorous surroundings. Casino advertisements invite people to 'Come and join the party'. The reality is that you're going to go in and you're going to lose your money. Casinos are presented as an 'entertainment center for all the family,' with childcare included. Gambling has been made socially acceptable and respectable for men and women as well. Why not women, we would say, their money is as green as anyone else's.

The illusion created is that all your needs will be met, financial, social, recreational, and emotional. This has a powerful lure for people who might be socially isolated or lonely, needy, bored with their lives, hard-up for money, or uncertain what to do or where to go. Gambling is shown to fulfill all your needs 'on a silver platter'. Remember, if it's too good to be true, it probably is.

Overall, given the appeals to both social and economic needs used to encourage people to play, that the machines are psycho-structurally designed to incite 'continuous' play, that they are programmed for all to lose, in fact, guarantee financial ruin upon persistent play, there is no way for people to win. Perhaps the gambling industry has abused the knowledge of human sciences? Players are powerfully manipulated into continuous play guaranteeing financial ruin. In view of the incredible ***profits*** *generated from people psychologically manipulated into losing their money, who are then scape-goated as deviant and morally weak, the situation is exploitative and abusive for the gambler.*

To think that we invited and continue to invite these very powerful and destructive forces to enter our states, in the guise of balancing the budget, is to wonder whether we've lost all common sense and good judgment—in the name of filthy lucre. Are we acting for the good and the general welfare of all or for the economic enrichment of a few? Is this where our advanced knowledge of psychology and human sciences has led us - to be able to manipulate the masses into throwing away their money in the name of having 'a good time'?

When do we start to look out for the welfare of all, to seek the upliftment and the enlightenment of all people, to insure that everyone in our society and in our world, has a good life, sufficient food, clothes, a shelter, and freedom from want? I would like to see communities come together to build for everyone, to engage in constructive projects for the good of all.

This is all about ***Misrepresentation****. It's about making something, gambling, seem like something it's not, an activity that will bring you money and feed your social and recreational needs. It's a tainted product. It's deliberately pretending one thing and then delivering another, playing with perception, playing with your 'head'...It's appealing to people's emotional needs, for money, for attention, for prestige, sense pleasures, sucking people into the game-plan, and then taking advantage of them. It's setting up one scenario, that a person will be a winner, and ending with another, making the person not only a loser but an addict. So then the casinos have a consistent loser. A chronic gambler is a constant money-maker for casinos. He's their bread-and-butter. They're not about to let him get away.*

****

CHAPTER EIGHT

BANS & LIMITATIONS

ON GAMBLING

So what can we do about this modern-day addictive, many-headed Medusa, this Trojan Horse of gambling that only serves to bring people down? What can we do to ameliorate its excesses, protect our citizens, safeguard our children from it's evils?

Gambling and the extent to which it's become so available is a real problem both for people in the U.S. and around the world. Based on an incalculable amount of research done in the lat 20 years, I would suggest a ban on gambling totally. Illicit drugs like heroin, and cocaine are prohibited because of their destructive impact. There's no difference with gambling. We don't need any additional social costs or any negative addictive avenues for people to travel down in our society. Life in our fast-paced society is already replete with plenty of attractive nuisances that get people into trouble, already sufficient temptations without adding more.

Gambling takes energy away from people seeking more constructive solutions to society's problems of housing, food and education. Legislators argue endlessly about what kinds of gambling to allow, where to put it, and what kind of compacts and conditions for Indian tribal vs. non-Indian casinos. While they debate incessantly, while they 'fiddle, Rome is burning', our society is skewering itself on the stake of money, profit, and luxuries. We need legislators to stay up nights planning new social programs to help the poor, to rehabilitate the prisoner, to ameliorate addictions, not to debate endlessly on what additional gambling to allow, what percentages to give Indian tribes, or where to put casinos.

If we decide not to do the right thing and totally ban gambling, then we at least have to implement some appropriate and rational regulations and guidelines for companies to abide by, if we're to keep the monster of profits at bay. There are many small regulations and other measures that can be implemented to help people stop and pause, to think and wonder, about whether they've gone far enough in their gambling for the night, for the year, or for their life. Australia has already begun to grapple with the gambling problem and to begin to implement guidelines that might inhibit the worst elements of addiction. ***Truth-in-advertising laws, self-exclusion bans*** *which don't allow a gambler to enter gambling areas,* ***loss limits****, are all part of the package that we have to start to implement if we're not to allow this colossus to continue its relentless march toward addiction.*

If we're going to let the wolf prowl loose in the barnyard, if we're going to make gambling so available, so accessible, then we've got to protect the chickens and the sheep. We're got to call a wolf a predator and not a chicken. We must let people know they're playing with fire when they gamble, that they're playing with their lives, their homes, their reputations, their marriages, the lives of their children. We've got to fight fire – addiction, with something equally powerful, and not call a fire, a light sprinkling of needed rain – such as Entertainment.

The idea of giving Indian tribes 'reparations' in the form of gambling licenses was short-sighted when it was first suggested and its equally out-of-place today. The harm that was done to Indian Nations can never be undone, just as the pain of countless injustices in the world can never be rectified. We can never make the past up to the Indian Nations. But reparations is not what gambling is all about. It's about Money, the dollar.

Americans have better things to do than to build marble and glass edifices, i.e. casinos, for people to throw away their money in, gigantic caverns as odes to people's inability to manage their money and stay away from temptation. We need to find entertainment in hundreds of different, more upright, honest ways than the act of gambling. As we know, when one wins, others must lose. By definition we're creating losers and we'll have to live with the fall-out that will inevitably occur. Is this what we dream of for our children? Are our highest visions centered around winning and losing money? Are we on this earth to amass more money at the expense of our fellow man?

As gambling proliferates, the market-savvy "Family Entertainment Centers", which include places for adults to gamble while children engage in other entertainment, continues to proliferate. This is another poorly disguised way to create the next generation of gamblers from the children who watch their parents get carried away by gambling's hype. Is our society teaching and modeling good parenting skills when we make gambling a legitimate and accessible activity? People get excited by the prospect of winning money but do they get equally thrilled when they lose? We ***know*** *that they will* ***probably*** *lose their money in the short run and* ***definitely*** *in the long run.*

The gambling industry is dismayed by all this bad press and every once in a while try to show that they're 'really good guys at heart'. On ***12/12/03,*** *Park Place Entertainment, which operates 29 casinos across the country, including giants such as Bally's, Caesar's, and the Flamingo, advertised that in a move toward* ***'Responsible Gaming'****, it would compile a list of problem gamblers who would theoretically be banned for life from its casinos. This, their "Responsible Gaming Program," would create a computerized, lifetime list of people that casinos will stop marketing to. The terms of the program indicate that people excluded might have to forfeit future winnings should they sneak into casinos and play. This is one of the few alternative remedies that the casinos have come up with to try to inhibit the compulsive gambler. Yet it's a program that hasn't been implemented in most places and doesn't work where it has been operational.*

Rev. Tom Grey, National Coalition Against Legalized Gambling*, called the move* ***'a ploy'*** *to help mitigate and deflect lawsuits. Chad Hills, gambling policy analyst at Focus on the Family, said the term 'responsible gaming' is an oxymoron, a contradiction in terms, a paradox. Rather we should call it 'responsible suicide', or 'responsible bankruptcy', or 'responsible domestic violence,' Hills said. "****Responsible irresponsibility doesn't exist****." http://www.family.org/forum/fnif/news/a0029378.cfm*

In fact, although this program was announced in 12/03, even now, 1/2005, more than a year later, the casinos haven't yet made up any such national list. With the casinos sophisticated computers, and their highly trained computer technicians, they could create a list in 24 hours if they really wanted. The casino's gigantic computers themselves could be enlisted to let casinos know when people are betting in a way as to be dangerous to themselves just as bartenders know when someone is imbibing too much and don't continue serving drinks to already drunk patrons.

Yet they haven't made up such a list as my husband and I can well attest to. Despite 3 casinos having sued him for unpaid markers and loans, and despite our filing for bankruptcy, we still frequently get promotional mailings from the casinos, and calls and mailings from various casino reps.

Through their sophisticated computers, the casinos chart meticulously how much people spend and lose while they're gambling. They have a good idea of individual's net worth. So for them to continue to target my husband sending him promotions and having reps call, tells me that they're constantly seeking additional profits, no matter where they come from. They don't care what damage gambling has inflicted on a person or on a family, they're just concerned about their bottom line, their profits, their money.

In ***England****, there is growing sentiment on the part of legislators there to modernize antiquated gambling laws and for the government to reap additional revenue as a result. As in the U.S., there is growing opposition to this idea. Research by The Henley Centre, a strategic marketing consultancy, estimated that the number of compulsive gamblers could double to* ***750,000 people*** *if liberalizations were implemented.*

*As Public Health Association chairman, Geoff Rayner said, "****There are major poverty problems because if you are putting a proportion of your very meager income into gambling, you are not actually providing other things like fresh fruit and vegetables to your children."*** *What a telling comment, that money spent gambling does not go towards providing the highest and best, or even what's necessary, for children.*

Rayner has proposed ***limiting casino size****, clearer and more explicit* ***health messages*** *about gambling's potential risks,* ***additional funding*** *for gamblers who get in trouble, and Government* ***goals of reducing the numbers of problem gamblers. The liberalization of gambling laws, the public health chairman added, "flies in the face of the other anti-poverty, pro-public health policies of this government."***

*English Culture Secretary, Tessa Jowell, who is leading the shake-up for modernization of the gambling laws in England, insisted that the plan be done in a 'socially responsible manner', with a "****very clear obligation on all gambling businesses to act in a socially responsible way."*** *Here, in the U.S., we don't have government representatives stating emphatically that gambling businesses will act in a socially responsible way. Rather it's more of a barroom-anything-goes-mentality, caveat emptor, let-the-buyer (the gambler) beware mentality. http://news.bbc.co.uk/1/hi/uk politics/3641207.stm*

In Australia, pokies (Australian term for slots) player and addict, John Clements, knows well that ***Bans do not work****. He has banned himself from every gaming room in Australia but yet he continues to be able to walk in unchallenged. On 10/20/03, he* *was accompanied by a staff member of The Advertiser, a South Australian newspaper, to 5 gaming sites. Each time he walked in unchallenged and was able to stay and play. "The policy does not work," he said.*

The Australian Hotels Association admitted bans were difficult to enforce. Australian Hotels Association President, John Lewis, said gambling sites could face fines of up to $35,000 for failing to evict barred gamblers. But he also added that "It's unreasonable to expect an employee to recognize someone from tens of thousands of people who frequent their hotel," he said. John Clements' wife, Vicky, however, said she put her faith in the program and was crushed that it had failed her husband. She said that in the past when her husband was asked to leave, he went home, rather than move on to another venue indicating that the program did work, that the moment of time to think that the program installed, had the desired effect of inhibiting the compulsive gambler.

It's that brief window of opportunity to make
the gambler think, 'what am I doing?' she said.

Two former gamblers in Detroit, Michigan casinos also know about self-exclusion programs, voluntarily bans and the fact that they don't work. Virginia Ormanian and Norma Astourian both signed up for the voluntary bans. Yet the gambling companies didn't enforce the rules of the self-ban list. Both of these players continued to gamble and ended up losing fortunes including retirement and life savings playing slot machines.

I was counting on the casinos to honor their contract,
I had to get my life back together, said Ormanian.

Now both addicts are suing the casinos for breach of contract saying that the gambling companies didn't enforce the rules of the list on which they placed themselves, as noted in an article, February 26, 2004, by Adam Goldman, Associated Press, on 2/26/04.

*Six states, **Missouri, Louisiana, Indiana, Illinois, Michigan, and New Jersey** have self-exclusion lists with more than 8,600 names. **Nevada**, the nation's largest gambling state, has no self-exclusion list*

Harm minimization, or harm reduction,** is the new term to describe strategies or efforts to help moderate the deleterious health, social and economic consequences of gambling for the compulsive gambler. Australians have looked at this issue for a while and have seen clearly some of the depths of destructiveness of the so-called social costs. The director of the Sydney University Gambling Research Unit, Michael Walker, said on 11/29/03, that many of the measures suggested to reduce harm from gambling would not deter serious players. He added that 80% of clients* *who came to the Sydney University gambling treatment centre had substantial debts, ranging from a few thousand to over $200,000, he said. "If you could stop that* ***debt *from occurring, you can stop (the problems) dead in their tracks." Of course, if there's no debt, there's no problem, as we can well understand. Yet the nature of the beast is that the addiction leads to debt, which leads to bankruptcy, which all leads to an on-going string of social problems. www.smh.com.au/articles/2003/11/28/1069825992480.html*

So the question is ***how to stop the debt from occurring****. If the maximum poker machine bet was decreased from $10 to 10 cents, that would eliminate the problem, Dr. Walker told the National Association of Gambling Studies conference. But this would also deter recreational gamblers and hurt the industry as well as government revenues. A* ***smart card****, with bank-approved monthly gambling limits would be effective as it wouldn't affect those who gamble within their means, he added. However, if the government and the industry "are serious about harm minimisation, they have to accept that there are serious impacts on revenue." So we see readily that this is a complicated issue full of implications for all parties involved.*

In ***South Australia****, there is a new gambling code of practice aimed at reducing the risk of problem gambling. This new code began in March, 2004. Serving* ***alcohol*** *to gamblers while at machines is banned, along with warning stickers on hotel ATMs. Staff will be trained to report neglected children, among other measures. Australia also will reduce the number of slot machines and/or VLTs by about 20%. Sites will be required to prevent intoxicated people from gambling and there will be* ***substantial restrictions on advertising*** *by the gambling industry.*

Independent Gambling Authority chairman, Stephen Howells, is confident the measures will work. But 'No Pokies MP Nick Xenophon, isn't convinced. "I'll start being happy about gambling codes when the gambling industry starts squealing like stuck pigs," he said. "The fact that they're comfortable with these codes makes me very uncomfortable." abc.net.au.news.australia/sa/metsa-8dec2003-5.

A study in Canada*, "VLT Gambling in Alberta: A Preliminary Analysis," noted several harm reduction features and proposals including:*

1. ***Restrictions*** *on age, alcohol consumption, hours of operation, bet size, advertising, number of gambling location in a jurisdiction, and number of opportunities in a gambling venue.*
2. ***Education*** *in the form of* ***warnings*** *on machines and problem gambling modules in school curricula,*

3. ***Interventions*** *targeting high-risk groups such as self-exclusion programs, problem gambling awareness program for gambling industry employees, and ministering to problem gamblers in gambling venues,*
4. ***Alteration of the structural design*** *of electronic gambling machines, especially their addictive potential, possible* ***machine modifications****, to structure in certain controls such as warnings regarding amount of money gambled, size of bet, and time spent without a break at the machine. 1*

All strategies designed to give the message of ***Moderation****. These efforts are designed to reduce excessive gambling by helping gamblers exert control over themselves and the gambling situation, by calling their attention to the need for awareness of these factors and for the establishment of inner discernment and judgment on the gambler's part.*

Canada, *has also had some serious considerations of gambling's negative effects and how to stem its destructiveness. In Manitoba, a western province, a proposal to install ATMs in Winnipeg casinos was rejected due to concerns from the province's addictions foundation, a Globe and Mail Update article reported. According to a study published by Statistics Canada in December, 2003, Manitoba has a high concentration of problem gamblers. The study reported that almost 1 in 10 Manitoba gamblers have some type of addiction to games of chance. That's* ***10 %*** *of the population! Another University of Manitoba study suggested that problem gamblers cost the government about $56,000 each in such expenses as lost wages and health care. ATMs are still available for gamblers using VLTs in Manitoba hotels and bars, just not casinos. http://www.globeandmail.com/servlet/story/RTGAM.20040121.wlott)121/BNStory/National/.*

All of these harm reduction features would involve significant changes both for gamblers, for the gambling industry, and even for the governments in terms of revenue and would not be implemented easily. Yet the Social Costs, the bankruptcies, the divorces, the suicides, the increase crime and embezzlement, have not been easy for all involved either.

In ***Missouri****, the State Senate held hearings in February, 2004, to decide whether to remove the state's* ***$500 per-session loss limit.*** *Removing the limits would increase the state's revenue by at least* ***$45 Million dollars*** *as reported in a St. Louis Post-Dispatch editorial 2/19/04. Missouri gambling interests state their loss limit makes it harder for them to compete with casinos in adjoining states with no limits. (Remember the states 'arms race of gambling'?) They also stated that the limits are expensive to enforce and aren't effective with serious gamblers easily finding various ways to skirt the limits. The editorial suggested that the Legislature should* ***leave the***

loss limits intact, "if only to prove the state hasn't completely sold its soul to the gambling industry."

The editorial further added that these limits are almost the last vestige of the restrictions placed on casino gambling when it was first introduced in Missouri in 1992. At that point, the state wanted to ensure that people did not get hurt too badly on the, as envisioned, little-riverboat-gambling-cruises.

> *"Instead we got giant boats-in-moats. Compulsive gamblers found a way to get in trouble, either by reboarding or by returning to the boats night after night.* ***This is an industry flush with cash, an industry that…adds only to social ills,…an industry that has fleeced Missourians for a dozen years****. A better idea is to keep the limits where they are and find another way to pay for the state's needs," the newspapers editors courageously added.*
> *http://www.stltoday.com/stltoday/news/stories.nsf/News/ Editorial*

Other measures *discussed, include large* ***signs in casinos, employee training, credit restrictions*** *and* ***loss limits****.* ***Self-exclusion program, helplines, and treatment programs*** *are after-the-fact measures which strive to pick up the pieces but not to ameliorate damage before it occurs. Gambling addiction is a "****Public Health problem*** *that must be examined thoroughly and without prejudice," said Dennis Eckart, National Center for Responsible Gaming Chairman, and a six-term former congressman from Ohio, in an article in the Las Vegas Sun on 12/9/03. http://www.lasvegassun.com/sunbin/stories/gambing/2003/dec/09/515992268.html. The National Center for Responsible Gaming, of which Eckart is chairman, is viewed with some caution by most people as it was formed and is supported by profits from casino companies.*

Various possibilities are currently being discussed in many countries around the world regarding how to effectively minimize the damage from this very destructive activity. There are measures that attempt to ensure that when someone sits down at a machine, that he gambles in moderation and with his own customary judgment. Other measures try to limit access to sources such as ATMs where a gambler can get impulsive additional supplies of money. Treatment programs seek to offer alternative life-styles to the compulsive gambler showing him that life without gambling can be more enticing and productive than he thinks.

Having lived through this very destructive phenomenon and felt more pain than I ever thought existed, I would seek to reverse the hands of Time and go back to a society with only 2 destination spots in the country for people to gamble, Las Vegas and Atlantic City. Even this would be destructive enough for people to get themselves in trouble but it wouldn't be casinos and lotteries on every corner, so to speak. Then in those 2 major destination resorts, there would be additional limitations, as discussed above, such as self-exclusion lists, external warnings on machines in the form of signs as well as internal structures within machines that would post notices to gamblers alerting them as to how long they had gambled, annual mailed statements of loss.

I would like to see a ***mandatory percentage of casino profits*** *such as 40 % dedicated to treatment programs and to various other supports for problem gamblers including loans against home foreclosures and bankruptcies. Casino employees could be trained in spotting the self-destructive gambler. Dealers and pit bosses knew my husband well. If the casino kept such close tabs on people, they must have known that he was gambling way over his head.*

Perhaps casinos could mail ***annual or monthly notices*** *to gamblers alerting them as to how much money they had lost that year, similar to organizations that mail forms to people notifying them of money donated. Then gamblers' spouses or children could simply demand to see the forms to know how money had been spent. This would also reinforce for gamblers themselves the amount of money lost, bringing it to their awareness and interrupting their cycle of denial. Also important would be to limit gambling companies from making large contributions to political action committees, PACs, to law-makers, and to employing lobbyists. This is a crucial part of the democratic process which is getting stomped upon by gambling corporations and which needs to be rectified.*

Another idea I like is Great Britain's idea of ***'regeneration' benefits*** *in their plans, in return for gaming licenses. Casinos would be responsible for consulting with regional planning bodies over what substantial benefits were needed for the area as a result of the initiation of gambling and the resultant physical changes that would occur. For example, improved transportation services, restoration of historic buildings, reclaiming derelict land, and the provision of new jobs, could all be looked at intensively as a way of ameliorating a casino's impact.*

Some of the hotels in Atlantic City that the casinos took over, such as Bally's Park Place, for instance, were historic hotels with elaborate detailing as old marble stairways and sundecks for enjoying the ocean. While Bally's reclaimed the building, it did nothing to preserve the historic character of the site.

Other limitations on gambling corporations would include leveling the playing field with anti-gambling groups. Our society could refuse to allow corporate gambling giants to use their money to bully-influence various segments of society whether by bribery or attention or the many other ways that casinos manage to get what they want. ***Equal time*** *could be given to both gambling and anti-gambling groups in terms of newspaper and TV advertising.* ***Truth-in-advertising laws*** *could apply both to casinos and to state Lotteries with the odds of winning posted conspicuously, just as cigarette packs have conspicuous warning signs. Sites would be required to have* ***clocks*** *on walls and prevent patrons from playing more than one machine at a time.* ***No ATMs*** *would be allowed in casinos or limitations on the amount of money that can be withdrawn on them.*

Other suggestions about limiting the amount of destruction that gambling brings include having players get cards which act as ***licenses*** *permitting them to gamble. These licenses then could be scanned by computers to insure that people already in financial difficulty according to credit reports, or late with child support payments, or the recipient of government programs, such as Welfare, not be allowed to squander money, theirs or that of others, in gambling. I like this idea because it reserves the right to restrict gamblers from people already receiving credit from government sources. What a foolish idea to allow people on welfare or other public programs to gamble.*

Another idea advocated by Bill Kearney, author of the book, Comped, suggests that there be ***no credit*** *allowed by casinos. He notes that no other industry gives out loans and doesn't charge interest. He questions "Is it because the profit margin is so great or...because they're really giving casino* ***chips, along with a very slim chance of winning****." Casinos don't mind giving credit because they well know that the probability is that* ***people are going to turn around and give it right back*** *to them. And then they'll still have to pay off their credit, their 'markers', as the industry calls it. So in fact, the casino make out like a bandit when it gives loans on the spot. They have nothing to lose. Kearney also espouses dispensing with casino chips and coin-less slot machines thus forcing people to use* ***actual money****. This will be a very real reminder that the money you lose is not 'funny money' but real.*

He further advocates ***no free alcohol*** *where gambling is allowed. He says "Imagine how many lawsuits (would occur)...if financial transactions, at your bank, insurance company, mortgage or stocks, happened while you were being served free liquor while doing business?" "How many DUIs have occurred from a night out at the casinos?" Looked at from this perspective, the idea of drinking alcohol while gambling with your hard-earned money is ridiculous. Who among us would transact business while downing a couple of Scotches. Yet we think nothing of it while in a casino. A fool and his money are soon...*

This book is primarily about the economics of gambling and the psychology of addiction. Both are areas in which the truth or the reality of what occurs in gambling venues has yet to come out, has yet to be confronted in an open spirit of public inquiry and debate. When the facts about what is occurring become known, then the hundreds and hundreds of thousands of people who have become addicted and lost substantially will know that it wasn't only their own particular moral weakness, it wasn't only their own unique impulsiveness that got them into trouble. There were other potent and powerful forces impacting upon them in seen and unseen ways that were responsible for bringing them to their knees.

Gambling addiction is a burgeoning ***Public Health problem*** *that needs to be addressed on many levels, state and federal government, churches and temples, and individual and family groups. With* ***5 or even 10 Million people*** *suffering from various forms of gambling addiction in the U.S. alone, the addict is not alone. And if 5 Million people could have gone so far wrong, so far astray as to lose great sums of money, to squander life savings, to cause houses to be foreclosed upon and marriages to wind up in divorce, to commit substantial crimes of embezzlement, theft, and even murder, then we have to wonder if gambling addiction is really something we want in the U.S.*

Why would we license something that we know in advance, is going to addict ***at least 5 %*** *of the population that engages in it. Five percent is an extremely high number when the numbers are tallied up. Even that number of 5% is not a top limit. It may well increase to 10 % given additional time and availability just as it has done with alcohol. Already some segments of the population have gambling addiction rates of 10 %, such as youth and senior citizens. At this point, we know that that 5 % will inevitably commit crimes, will hurt themselves and others significantly, and generally commit grievous acts upon their fellow citizens whether they happen to also be gamblers or not. Can't we find other forms of amusement, of entertainment, that are not so destructive.*

We don't allow suicide to be legalized and neither should we allow people to gamble away inheritances, life savings, retirement accounts. Engaging in this type of behavior, similar to the one-thing-leads-to-another scenario, will also then prompt people to do other foolish things. If we don't allow suicide, we shouldn't allow the path to it to be open and welcoming, adorned with flowers and champagne, and with casino reps whispering to 'just come on down, and have a good time.' We don't license Russian roulette, and we don't license illicit drugs. Gambling is another destructive phenomenon that tries to paint itself in rainbow hues, 'to paint the pig', but in fact is just as black as any other addiction.

We've opened Pandora's box and invited in all of the dark forces of the night. Gambling needs to be recognized for what it is—a highly risky and reckless way to try to have fun, one that will inevitably get you in trouble. It's the theft of other people's money cleverly disguised under the rubric of 'fun and games'. If we continue to get in bed with this industry, we will only give birth to chaos, corruption and destruction. People who know this to be an immoral, ungodly activity must speak up, let others know the nature of the beast, and let legislators know that gambling is not what America is about.

America has been a haven for oppressed people across the world, a hero for multitudes of tyrannized and burdened individuals and families. We don't have the time or the energy to allow the forces of evil to take us over, to invite in the chaos of greed and corruption, to let the splintering effects of divorce and neglect consume us. Americans have stood for the highest, for Democracy, Truth and Justice, for individual freedom, we've sought the best in mankind. Let's not turn our back on our principles in the name of money.

****

SUMMARY

WHAT CAN WE LEARN?

We have now learned what a terrible thing gambling can be. To recall and focus on the most cogent data from increasing numbers of groups, approximately 3-5% of people who start gambling will become pathologically addicted in some form or fashion. That addiction will take the form of everything from gambling one's own money, earmarked for other purposes, to embezzling, stealing, neglecting one's family, other responsibilities, and generally causing a high amount of crime, human misery, and personal ill fortune.

We know that the more ***accessible*** *gambling is, the more likely people are to become addicts. An addict causes great destructiveness to himself and to at least 4, and possibly 12 other people in various ways. So why have we licensed something that will cause great misfortune to at least 5%, if not more, of the general population? Whatever happened to us being 'our brother's keeper?'*

Is the revenue that the state gets from gambling 'worth' the destroyed lives, the financial misfortunes, the crimes against other citizens who didn't even gamble? Is that revenue 'worth it?' Is the government bound to protect all its citizens or just the smart 95% that have the brains to stay away from an institutionalized and legal bona fide addictive activity?

As people have said, it's not about our moral choice to gamble. ***It's about casino's moral and democratic rights, in our 'democracy', to create harm,*** *i.e. to yell 'fire' in a crowded theater, to advertise, 'A jackpot won every 10 minutes!' What jackpot, the one dollar jackpot, after you put 6 quarters in?*

If casinos create addiction, if they deal in stolen goods, if their product is 'tainted', do they have the right to continue to sell their products*? Can government, duty-bound to legislate for the 'general welfare', continue to allow casinos, the harbingers of harm and destruction? Casinos deal in stolen goods, they're 'accessories after the fact' in so many crimes, and are implements for the destruction of so many lives? Can legislatures, now knowing all this from reputable studies, continue to allow the expansion of casinos and other types of gambling? Legislatures do this without even having polled the people in public referendums as to their desires?*

The other addictive activities or substances in our society, alcohol, smoking, and illegal drugs, have all wrecked and destroyed many people's lives. Our government spends great amounts of money in the Dept. of Health, Education and Welfare, HEW as well as other government agencies, on some aspect of handling the problems these substances create, or in educating citizens against these demons.

Government is duty bound, has a responsibility to act in the interests of all its citizens. Judging by the huge amounts of money that it spends every year associated with other addictions, such as drugs, cigarettes, and alcohol, it seems to feel its responsibility keenly in these areas. This money, by the way, is taxpayer's money, my taxes, your taxes, your money and my money.

When the government initially started the licensing process, of Las Vegas in 1931 and Atlantic City in 1979, little was understood of the impact of gambling would have on our lives and in our society. Little was known of the terrible and significant blow to many people's lives that gambling would show itself to be. But now we know.

Many of us have learned the hard way, have experienced the excesses that gambling addiction brings. It hasn't been a kind teacher or a gentle lesson but it has been an emphatic education. Professor of Economics at the University of Nevada, William Thompson, said 7/19/04 on Washingtonpost.com that:
*"**gambling addiction** is considered the **strongest addiction** affecting our society. The **forces of the addiction dwarf people hooked on alcohol, drugs and tobacco**. It is disturbing that governments...fail to recognize the addictive qualities of gambling."*
1 http://www.washingtonpost.com/wp-dyn/articles/A55 444-2004Jul16.html

SUMMARY

Now that we most certainly know, we have to implement what we've learned, we must do something about it. We have to do the right thing. Government must protect its citizens through legislation "promoting the general welfare", protecting their environment, quality, highway safety, licensing, building codes, school standards, and other areas deemed to be in the public interest.

Now our government in the form of its legislators must realize that gambling is a dangerous and a damaging area for a significant portion of the population. We would hope that the government would be eager to pick up the ball and enact legislation at least curbing some of the harmful impact of this modern menace, if not shutting it down entirely. Although gambling has existed for thousands of years, that is not to say that governments have profited from it for that long.

The fact is that governments in the past usually either ignored it, or tried to stamp it out. Yet our country, as it's been said, is run for money and by money. There are powerful interests behind gambling and its expansion throughout society. These interests want their lucrative and prodigious profits to continue, if not increase. Look at how much money gambling has given to these influential policy-makers, i.e. our Federal elected representatives, in the form of Senators and Congressmen.

In the 2003 campaign to allow casinos in Maine, gambling interests contributed $300,000 to each campaign. 2 So if one side didn't win, the other would and thus be indebted for quite a substantial amount of money. That's certainly 'hedging your bet' if there ever was one.

Yes, gambling interests have shown that they want certain things and are not shy about 'paying' for them, at whatever price is necessary. If political influence is what is needed, they're not reluctant to buy that too. But is money really so important that we should we allow some people to profit outrageously, 'windfall profits', at the expense of other people's weaknesses?

The stories in this book and their frequency are saddening, and genuine human tragedies. These stories have shown how gambling was the catalyst responsible for ruining many people's lives.

These are not the only stories. See the Appendix for a list of many more. These stories are 'a dime a dozen.' People's lives are 'a dime a dozen,' according to the casinos. Each of these stories is one crime statistic, or more. Each story is one person's life, one mother's child, one child's parent. Gambling is creating an incredible amount of personal tragedy in many people's lives.

But surely, you say, not every gambler is going out and shooting his wife? Or, had it not been for gambling, might it have been something else? Crime statistics are instructive in this regard. Before and after crime statistics show us whether gambling motivates new and additional crime, or whether there is any change in crime statistics at all. In fact, **there is a conclusive and significant upward rise in crime every year in areas close to gambling sites***.*

In our own case, gambling was certainly the catalyst leading to crime that otherwise would never have occurred. My husband never committed crimes of any kind before he started gambling nor after he stopped. Yet during the time he was gambling, he stole from family and business clients alike.

How has this affected my life and my family, my daughter, my son, our adopted child? It's made our lives a living hell. At a time when we were anticipating relaxing, we had to seek part-time jobs in addition to our full-time jobs, undergo bankruptcy, almost lose our house, lose one side of our family. It's also given us less time available to make a more positive and constructive impact on society.

It's also almost killed my husband in the form of a heart attack a year after this all surfaced. Our life was so difficult during that time, with him suffering guilt and depression, myself also having my own issues, that I think our very cells recoiled from the constant and never-ending pain. He had a major heart attack almost a year after the gambling truth came out. I feel his very sensitive and eager-to-please nature found it difficult to live with how he had hurt his family and his heart 'broke' with the overwhelming pain. Our bodies and our minds are so tied in together that for his thoughts to be always in turmoil, always in pain translated naturally to his heart being in physical pain also.

It's personally hurt us both internally and externally. It has hurt others financially whom we would have come into contact with. For example, the way we spend our money and how much we spend, affects many others in a ripple, or 'multiplier' effect. So we spent $5000 for a lawyer to protect us - instead of spending 1 million on building a new house. ***$5,000 vs. $1,000,000****. Quite a difference in the amount and direction that this money would have taken. Quite a difference to ourselves and to society as a whole.*

We like to think that we all contribute in our own small way towards the most humane, loving, uplifting society dedicated to all citizens in economic, social and mental ways at all times. This search for the highest, in whatever area, should be the foremost duty of our elected officials. After that, within the broad framework of government, and overall guidelines of society's needs, then their duties would include enacting laws providing for the greatest good for the greatest number, that is, the general welfare and well-being of all. After this is insured, then our legislators can direct their attention to the nitty-gritty of implementation including balancing the budget.

If 5% of the population are disabled in one way or another, whether with health or physical challenges, alcoholic, mental illness, drug addiction, alcohol or gambling, then that 5% will 'pull down' the other 95%. This minority of addicted people will exercise an influence far beyond their numbers.

We have created, in the last 25 years, a new Sodom and Gomorrah, ancient biblical twin cities of sin, a new addiction and we will 'reap the whirlwind,' experience the consequences of this act. Five percent of people now are addicted. How about the people who are gambling now but not yet addicted yet, i.e. part of the 95 %? What is going to happen to them in the next 25 years?

Theory tells us that it's a question of ***Accessibility****. We continue to make it more accessible to even greater numbers of people. Accessibility means* ***Frequency****. Frequency of visit translates to more* ***Time*** *involved. Time is money, as we well know. Increased visits lead to increased addictive tendencies and increased numbers of people succumbing to its powerful pull. This figure, 5%, will increase in the future, if it hasn't already. In 25 years, the number of people gambling will not stay constant but rather expand, the percentage of people involved in gambling at a detrimental level will increase. So instead of, for example, 5% of 200,000 gamblers, or* ***10,000*** *people, there will be 10% of 500,000, or* ***50,000 people.***

The last major blight upon our society in the recent past was, and still is, AIDS. This modern 'plague' has killed more people than the sum total of all the plagues in history. We still haven't been able to contain it, yet it's been around for 20 years. Where will it go in the next 20 years? And where will gambling go and the harm it causes - all in the name of lower taxes.

Gambling is an institutionalized way of robbing from Peter to pay Paul, a 'redistribution' of money *as the economists suggest. We license groups (large corporations) to offer this activity which we know will cause a certain percentage of people to have serious personal issues. All of this happens in order that the first group of people, the escalating gambling industry, will make a lot of money and the government will make a little revenue.*

So ***government must take responsibility*** *for educating people about this new activity, which it has allowed, and to begin to 'pick up the pieces', in terms of the overall 'social costs.' We remember that various studies have shown that the social costs range from $1.00 per person to $10.00 / gambler per member of society.*

William Thompson notes that his studies have shown "that typically a compulsive gambler imposes costs of ***$10K (10 thousands) a year*** *through theft, bad debts, missed work, public welfare, criminal justice costs."3*

Thompson notes that should gambling be allowed in ***Washington D.C****., there will probably be an extra* ***5,000*** *compulsive gamblers generated. These gamblers will then "impose costs of* ***$50 Million dollars*** *through theft, bad debts, missed work and other social maladies on their fellow citizens every year. This is in addition to the negative economic flows from slots." 4*

The whole society foots the bill for the weaknesses (gambling addiction) of a small group of people and the greed (revenue seeking governments and profit making large corporations) of two other groups of people. The whole society, in the form of the taxpayers, foot the bill, the taxes necessary to pay for the social costs to society of that small group of addicts, whether 5 % or more.

As ***Donald Trump*** *said in an interview with CBC Venture in 1993:*

> *"Gaming doesn't come cheap and I have to agree with a lot of the critics on that. It brings* ***crime****. It brings* ***prostitution****...There's a* ***big cost to pay****. Most jurisdictions have considered gaming and most...have rejected it. The ones that have accepted it, many of them, if you gave them their choice again, they would have turned it down." 5*

What a shame that this intelligent and erudite person couldn't have chosen something more positive to do rather than to increase and expand gambling sites throughout this country.

Society pays for allowing the other groups, businesses, and state and local governments, to make money. The first group, the addicts, lose money while the second group makes money. Yet the first group, addicted gamblers, must then be subsidized by the larger societal group while the second group, financiers, become very wealthy and walk away with their extra money. It's the institutionalized implementation of the concept, the rich getting richer and the poor getting...

Yet I don't believe that there are evil people and weak people. This is all a matter of ***AWARENESS****. Before our legislators can know how they ought to legislate, they must become aware of all sides of an issue, of all the possible implications and ramifications of legislation. This is the first 30 years of this path of legalizing gambling. We're beginning to learn that it's a path with plenty of pitfalls, quicksand, and very little firm ground to get a footing. The path looked great at the beginning, spacious, amply endowed with food and drink for all. Yet as we walked,* *we saw the path was no more permanent than the sands of the Atlantic Ocean, no more stable than the tides of the sea, shifting, swirling, endlessly undercutting the beaches, and the people walking there.*

Incidentally, that 'weak' person who succumbs to the glitter, the lights, the action, the hype about 'Entertainment', that person may not be you, but it may be your child, or your Uncle Harry who just blew his life savings, or that nice little senior citizen who lives across the street, or that first grader's father you see at the bus stop. We all have an Uncle Harry. Or maybe we'll become Uncle Harry ourselves when we get older.

When we're not sure what to do and we're a little bored or lonely, the lights of Atlantic City can look pretty bright, enticingly beckoning. It's easy to rationalize, 'what's the harm of just one bet, what's the damage would there be of taking just one drink, or just one hit of crack?'

To demonstrate what a worldwide Public Health issue problem gambling has become, we see increasing numbers of conferences and symposiums on this burgeoning problem. In Auckland, New Zealand, May 11-12, 2004, 50 of the world's leading gambling authorities met to discuss such questions as "At what point does gambling become problem gambling? How is problem gambling defined and measured? To what degree should the gaming industry encourage responsible gambling and minimize potential harm?" At this first International Think Tank, scientists, researchers, policy makers, and regulators, service providers and gambling industry members met to discuss a range of globally significant issues.

The meeting was hosted by the Auckland University of Technology's Gambling Research Centre. Chief Executive of Gambling Problem Helpline, Gary Clifford said he hopes that participants would form an international network to advance the understanding of gambling as a ***Public Health and social and economic development issue.***

Such leading experts attended the Think Tank as Adrian Scarfe, clinical practice manager, GamCare, UK, Dr. Jeff Derevensky, McGill University, editor of the Journal of Gambling Studies and co-director of the International Centre for Youth Gambling Problems. Montreal, Canada, and Dr. Jim Westphal, University of California, San Francisco General Hospital, Director of the Division of Substance Abuse and Addiction Medicine. These are all people who have an interest in the betterment of society, in the upliftment of people's lives.

This is what we should be about - combating the evils of society, seeking the upliftment of lives. As society has evolved, we've gradually enacted more laws seeking to assure quality-of-life-issues for citizens. We have laws seeking to minimize pollution, increasing the protection of children from abuse, striving to raise the standards of society in regards to bringing up children and protecting animals. We even have laws protecting people from the detrimental effects of other's smoking. Now we must make laws protecting our citizenry, ourselves, from the rapacious grasp of profit seeking large corporations bent on separating people from their own very needed and necessary money and income.

This is the next higher stage of evolution for our society, to strive to support and take care of those who need taking care of, in whatever way it is. The numbers of homeless tell us clearly that some people cannot manage for themselves, have difficulty functioning in our fast-paced, challenging society. We don't want to have to provide the fish, the food, for them forever, but we do need 'to teach them how to fish.' We need to throw them a line to fish, not a rope to hang themselves.

As we grow wiser as a society, we need to learn to protect our weak, our mentally and physically challenged, our aged, our children, our alcoholics, and our gamblers, from themselves and from large business and other groups in our society whose single-minded intent is to ensure that people lose their money. This is what our legislators need to do, to create and implement programs helping people learn to be useful, productive citizens, how to provide a helping hand, not to debate endlessly, where to allow casinos and how many slot machines to permit.

We've allowed the wolf to come into the flock, provided that he only consumes a few - 5%. Are we deliberately sacrificing the few for the entertainment of the many? But we had better beware, because the wolf has a never-ending appetite, the fire is not content to stay at the perimeter, but consumes everything in its path. The demons do not rest at half a pie, they'll continue until they've consumed the whole pie, the whole person, all the money, and the whole society.

Then we'll go down in history along with the fall of Rome, from the invading forces. Only this time, we unlocked the door and invited the barbarian forces in. Sodom and Gomorrah were small potentates compared to Las Vegas, the 'city of sin', where they take pride in the fact that 'what goes on here, stays here,' The forces of darkness, always with us, were unleashed and allowed to consume the society that fell into the mistaken thought that 'something could be had for nothing', and gambling was just a little 'fun'.

What would help? It's going to be hard to get it back in the box now that the lid has been opened. What would help would be to abolish this new blight upon society. What would help would be to give a resounding, 'No' to the forces of darkness and the greed that surround us. What would help would be truth-in-advertising laws, and equal advertising time for gambling's opponents.

*We need opportunity for gambling's opponents to raise our awareness and educate us, after gambling interests have sold us their bill of goods. Signs on machines – **"Warning: this machine may increase the likelihood of bankruptcy, divorce, suicide, and the overall neglect of personal responsibilities..."***

*We need signs prominently displayed in casinos, machines that give **'time-outs'** to players losing large amounts of money, **loss limits** / day and per week at casinos, **full disclosure laws** for casinos, laws detailing where large amounts of money come from, to avoid money laundering operations, limitations upon number of machines, sites, and venues. We need acknowledgement of gambling as the tremendous bane upon society that it is, just as smoking has been acknowledged as a killer. We need increased monies from casinos to fund and staff, mental health and counseling facilities on casino floors. My vote, and the consensus of all truly compassionate, concerned citizens should be simple, to **shut down** something that hurts so many in so many different ways.*

*To shut down gambling, to 'Prohibit' it, would be the best thing for our nation in so many ways. As Dianne Berlin, vice chair of the **National Coalition Against Legalized Gambling**, said,*

> ***"When 'Prohibition' is mentioned, it's slammed as a 'disaster'. This was really not the case. All the negatives associated with alcohol use took a nosedive. The more sober people in the nation experienced more savings, more young people staying in school, fewer divorces, etc.***

*Our nation's two largest killer drugs are 'legal' tobacco and alcohol. **Prohibition** is in place for many actions such as murder, use of LSD, heroin, etc. Laws will probably always be broken but a civilized society needs law and order to prevent chaos." 5 E-mail from Dianne Berlin, 8/4/04. We need to be not afraid to stand up and say, 'Yes, something is wrong, it hurts people and we won't allow it.'*

*We need a change of the 'wild-west-anything-goes-mentality, to the casinos taking a **responsible corporate outlook,** a beneficent overview of their patrons to **truly insure** that people 'gamble with their heads,' and 'not above it', as casinos say they advocate. The casinos are able to calculate, often to the penny, the amount of money won or lost by an individual in a certain night. So they can easily extrapolate this to amounts won and lost over time, and ascertain easily, whether people probably had the amount of money they wagered or whether they obtained it from various other illegal sources, as so many people have.*

The casinos are ***complicit*** *in accepting money, funds, that often have been* ***'taken'*** *from unsuspecting family,* ***'embezzled'*** *from unaware businesses, illegally obtained in one way or another. They really should have judicial action against them for being accessories after the fact. They're* ***enablers****, facilitating the process of people addicting themselves.*

Yet they represent themselves as 'all-American', cordial, friendly, and just in the business of giving you a good time, gourmet food, fancy restaurants, top-name-Entertainment, shows, and 'a little gaming,' if you choose. But it's not like this, all the focus, the concentration, is on getting people in the casino and gambling. Everything else is an afterthought. And it's almost impossible to get people to partake of one and not the other. This is exactly what casinos strive for.

They provide child care for parents to 'abandon' their children in, while they throw away their precious resources and scarce money. The casinos provide easy access and enticing places for us to spend our hard-earned salaries. The shift is to gamble any extra income rather than putting it to more constructive use, such as investing in one's community, or further education, in family, house, or personal self-edification or fulfillment. They make it really easy to destroy yourself; they've paved the walkway down the road to ruin. And many skip merrily down the path to the detriment of themselves, loved ones and communities.

****

Footnotes

INTRODUCTION

1. Rex Rogers, "Seducing America: Is Gambling a Good Bet?" Baker Books, PO Box 6287, Grand Rapids, MI 49516, p. 30.
2. Sen. Frank Padavan, R-Queens, New York.
3. Star Telegram, 10/22/03.
4. Toronto, Canada, CNEWS, 4/30/04.
5. Judge Bucki, www.buffalonews.com/editorial/20040106/1023803.asp
6. *(American Gaming Assoc. www.americangaming.org*
7. Dr. Joel S. Rose, Speech, 11/21/02., CACGEC website.
8. Thomas A. Garrett, Casino Gambling in America, p. 6.
9. Lesieur, www.gamblingprolem.org/kidsgamblin.htm Christiansen, op. cit. p. 3.
10. Gambling Causes Economic Decline, CACGEC website, p. 1.
11. US Census Bureau, Stat. Abstract of the US; 1997, 117th ed., Wash., DC p. 769.
12. Rogers, p. 30.
13. Alcamo, p. 56.

CHAPTER 1 – 'OUR STORY'

1. Charles Munger, vice chairman, Berkshire Hathaway, shareholders meeting, 5/1/04.
2. State Rep. Matt Baker, Pa. The Herald Standard, April 29, 2004 htt;://www.phillly.com/mid/inquirer/news/local/states/pennsylvania/cities_neighborhoods/philadelphia/8544562.htm
3. Maura J. Casey, Buffalo News, 11/19/03
4. Newsday, 2/12/04. Dealer Rapes Granddaughter.

CHAPTER 2 - ADDICTION

1. Warren Buffett, chairman, *CEO*, Berkshire Hathaway *Inc. 1*
2. Diagnostic and Statistical Manual of Mental Disorders, fourth Edition. 1994 American Psychiatric Association).
3. Bob Arndorfer, NYT Regional Newspapers, http://www.herldtribune.com/apps/pbcs.dll/articlle?AID=/20040111/NEWS/401110685/1060
4. www.suntimes.com/output/health/cst-nws-gamb01.html
5. Dr. Suck Won Kim, Univ. Minnesota
6. Ibid.
7. Marc Potenza, Yale Univ.www.boston.com/news/globe/health_science/articles/22003/10/28/pills_to_treat_gambling_ills/
8. Robert B. Breen and Mark Zimmerman, Brown Univ. School of Medicine, p. 1.
9. National Gambling Impact Study Commission (NGISC, 1999. Federal Government.
10. Pat Fowler, Florida Council on Compulsive Gambling, says: www.palmbeachpost.com/news/content/auto/epaper/editions/today/nbews 04a751069040608a007e.html
11. Ibid.

11A. Hartford Courant, 8/10/04

12. Custer, Robert, When Luck Runs Out, Harry Milt, p. 102.
13. Ferguson, Laurie, Green Bay, Wisconsin,12/23/03
14. Custer, p.90.
15. Jacobs, 1986, p. 15.
16. times.hankooki.com/lpage/culture/200402/kt200-4021219363911700.htm Putting Gambling Addiction Into Perspective, by Lisa Hanson.
17. Ibid.
18. Sandra Dekker, Commercial Gaming The Unfair Deal, Graduate thesis, 9/97, The Univ. of So. Australia,

22. "SeattlePost-Intelligence, SamSkolnik,2/24/04, seattlepi.nw source.com/local/161827_gambling24.html
23. Dickerson, M.G. (1984). *Compulsive Gamblers.* Longman: London and New York.
24. (Lesieur, H., & Custer, R. (1984). 'Pathological gambling: Roots, phases, and treatment. Annals of the American Academy of Political and Social Science, *474.* Pgs. 146-156.
25. Dickerson.
26. Dekker, Sandra, Chapter 1, p…3,
27. Ibid.
28. Maura Casey said to the NCAL on 9/28/02,(28)
29. Glenn R. Pascall, Puget Sound Business Journal, 6/9/03
30. Assemblywoman Peoples, 1/26/04, Buffalo News, Vanessa Thomas,
31. Foreel, C.1997, The Gambling Fix in The Sunday Age, 3/9/97, p. 8.
32. Tim Sullivan, columnist noted. 70 eco
33. Assemblywoman Peoples, 1/26/04, NY Times,.
34. Senior Fellow Charles E. Greenawait, of the Susquehanna Valley Center for Public Policy, 10/20/02
35. 12/31/03, www.rcpsych.ac.uk/college/parliament/responses/subgamb2003.htm.
36. Transcript of oral evidence, House of Commons, 139 iii1/8/04.
37. Ibid,
38. Joel Rose, Speech.
39. www.thoroughbredtimes.com/todaysnews/newsview.asp?recno=41054&subsec=1
40. www.nctimes.com/articles/2003/09/29/news/top_stories/0_28_0322_21_53.txt, 9/28/03
41. Ibid.
42. Milwaukee Journal Sentinel, 10/18/03.
43. Ibid.
44. The Wall Street Journal, Christina Binkley, 2/24/04.
45. Assoc. Press, 11/19/03, Compulsive Gambling on the rise in La.
46. Ibid.
47. Boston Globe, 10/28/03. Pills to Treat Gambling Ills. 15, Potenza, Yale
48. Wash. State Gambling Commission.
49. Ibid.

50. Pat Fowler, Florida Council on Compulsive Gambling, says: www.palmbeachpost.com/news/content/auto/epaper/editions/today/nbews 04a751069040608a007e.html
51. Ibid.
52. http://seven.com.au/todaytonight/story/pokiefight
53. www.springharbor.org/press_detail.php?pressrelease_id=40
54. www.healthunit.org/adults/php_gambling.htm
55. times.hankooki.com/lpage/culture/200402/kt200-4021219363911700.htm Putting Gambling Addiction Into Perspective, by Lisa Hanson.
56. www.signonsandiego.com/sports/sullivan/20040126-9999_ 1s26sullivan.html
57. Wyoming__House Speaker, Pro Tem Rodney Anderson, R-Pine Bluffs, said recently on 2/27/04,
58. "http://www.projo.com/opinion/columnists/content/projo 200040127-clacho.19ca07.html
59. *www.projo.com/ap/ne/1084380348.htm, Associated Press, Michael Mello*
60. NCAG Website
61. Breeen & Zimmerman, Brown Univ. School of Medicine, p. 1.
62. Press Release from the Office of Congressman Mike Rogers, 12/11/03
63. Ibid.
64. AP, Don Thompson, 1/26/04, http://www.signonsandiego.com/news/state/20040126-1657 -ca-indiangambling.html
65. www.theunionleader.com/articles_showa.html?article=31992
66. Fla. Sheriffs Assoc., 3/04.

CHAPTER 3 - ECONOMICS

1. William Thompson, professor, public administration, Univ. of Nev.
2. John Kindt, Univ. of Illinois, Ibid., p. 52
3. Christiansen Capital Advisors NY Times, 1/18/04, George Vecsey.
4. Harrah's survey.
5. Joel S. Rose, in a speech on 11/21/03 to the League of Woman Voters of Buffalo, NEWSDAY, 2/5/04, P.
6. Sacramento Bee, Sheldon Carpenter, source, Christiansen Capital Advisers. http://www.wtol.com/Global/storoy.asp? S=1471285,
7. recent newspaper bus advertisement for the Indian casino in Connecticut, Mohegan Sun, Newday newspaper.
8. www.ncalg.org. www.Casinowatch.org
9. St. Louis Post-Dispatch, "1 in 5 of Homeless in Survey Blame Gambling, by Tim Poor, 3/15/98, p. A9.
10. Fox News, 8/3/04, "Sin City Has Become Homeless City http://www.montanaforum.com/rednews/2003/05/13/build/gambling/atlantic-city.php?nnn=6,10/14/03, AP

10a. www.iht.com/articles/530255.htm

11. Joel Rose speech, p. 2.
12. Tim Poor, "1 in 5 of Homeless in Survey Blame Gambling" St. Louis Post-Dispatch, 3/15/98, p. A9
13. Joel Rose, p. 2.
14. Maura J. Casey, Buffalo News, 10/19/03. Special art. On Gambling.
15. CACGEC WEBSITE, http://nocasinoerie.org/jobques.htm
16. http://ncalg.org/library/l995-factsheet.htm. Dr. James C. Dobson, 1/99, htt;://www.hotel-online.com/News/Press Releasesl999_1st/Jan99_Dobson.html, Hotel Online,
17. Dr. Robert Goodman, "Legalized gambling as a Strategy for Economic Development." Christiansen Capital Advisers, LLC; U.S. Department of Commerce; Fortune magazine; Variety magazine; Recording Industry Association of America; Association of American Publishers http://www.buffalonews.com/editorial/2004016/1023893.asp, Buffalo News, Focus
18. Christiansen Capital Advisers.
19. www.kycage.org/Crime.html
20. Ibid.
21. Ibid.
22. www.thestar.com/NASApp/cs/ContentServer?pagename=thestar/Layout/Article_Type!&call, 4/20/04
23. as quoted in www.hotel-online.com/News/PressReleases1999_1st/Jan99_Dobson.html
24. Ibid.
25. Dark Side of Gambling, WorldNow, WIVB.
26. Dr. Jeffrey Marotta, Ph.D. presented to the Lane County Commissioners 8/12/03
27. Dekker, p. 4.
28. Star Telegram, 10/22/03, www.dfw.com/mid/dfw/7077825. htm, Jay Root
29. Ibid.
30. Tom Grey, Executive Director of the National Coalition Against Legalized Gambling, NCALG,
31. Star-Telegram, 10/22/03, Jay Root.
32. Ibid.
33. CACGEC Website, http://nocasinoerie.org/jobques.htm
34. Ibid.
35. Ibid.
36. Ibid.
37. "
38. Erie Times-News, 11/18/03, Michael Geer.
39. http://www.smartmoney.com/consumer/index.cfm?story=gaming, Ten Things the Gaming Industry Won't Tell You, Brian O'Keefe, 7/17/00
40. Ibid.
41. Garrett, p. 8-10.
42. Ibid.
43. PACT.
44. Dobson, p. 2.
45. "
46. Greg Garland, Baltimore Sun, 2/16/04.
47. Ibid.
48. "
49. "
50. "
51. "
52. Garrett, p. 11.
53. Larry Harless, The Hill Report, l995.
54. PACT, Florence, Oregon, 2/12/04 – e-newsletter
55. Spring/2003 Stanford Journal of Law, Business and Finance, Vol. 8p. 185, John W. Kindt, Prof. Univ. of Illinois.
56. Ibid.
57. Ibid.
58. Rose, p. 29.
59. Charles Greenawait, Senior Fellow at the Susquehanna Valley Center for Public Policy,

FOOTNOTES

60. The Hill Report, Christian Science Monitor, 11/6/03.
61. 30
62. Joel Rose.
63. "
64. quoted from the National Opinion Research Center, Univ. of Chicago, 1997, p. 6.
65. www.kycage.org/Crime.html
66. Ibid.
67. "
68. Optimal Solutions, CAGE. www.kycage.org/Crime.html
69. Iowa Seminar on gambling, Clay County, 11/26/03 KICD News.
70. Ibid.
71. www.kycage.org/Crime.html
72. Ibid.
73. Les Bernal, NCALG website.
74. Ibid.
75. Newsday, 2/15/04.
76. Christian Science Monitor, 11/5/03
77. The Times Record, 10/28/03, High Stakes for Maine, Leslie Talmadge.
78. www.timesrecord.com/website/main.nsf/ news.nsf/oD85E58BooBB5256DCDOO5A9487? *Opendocument.*
79. Ibid.
80. Judge Bucki, www.buffalonews.com/editorial/ 20040106/ 1023803.asp
81. "The Impact of Casino Gambling on Personal Bankruptcy Filing Rates, Barron, Staten, Wilshusen, 8/2000, p.6.
82. Baltimore Sun, 2/8/04, Bill Atkinson, Rising Debt draws millions to refuge of bankruptcy.
83. Barron, Staten, Wilshusen,
84. "
85. Morse & Goss, A County Level Analysis, Creighton Univ.
86. Baltimore Sun, 2/8/04, Bill Atkinson, Rising Debt draws millions to refuge of bankruptcy.
87. Australian accountant,
88. Administrative Office of the U.S. Courts, *chart in Barron, Staten, and Wilshusen.*
89. Ibid.
90. Ibid.
91. Ibid.
92. TheBaltimore Sun,12/28/03, Michael Dresser. http://sunspot. net/news/local/bal-te.md.embezzle28dec28.0.3286170.story? coll=bal-local-headlines.
93. Ibid.
94. "
95. Milwaukee Journal Sentinel, 2/8/04
96. Ibid.
97. Baltimore Sun, 2/8/04
98. Ibid.
99. Baltimore Sun, 12/28/03.
100. Baltimore Sun, Michael Dresser, 12/28/03
101. Ibid.
102. "
103. "
104. "
105. "
106. "
107. Maura Casey, 10/19/03, Buffalo News.
108. Mary Ellen Godin, Record-Journal, 4/17/04, Workplace Gambling can lead to Problems.
109. *www.shawanoleader.com/articles/2003/12/29/news/n ews2.txt, Tim Ryan.*
110. Ibid.
111. Press Conf., Madison, Milwaukee, 2/10/04, DA Blanchard.
112. *http://www.badgerherald.com/vnews/ display.vART/2004/ 02/10/402864e5ccb99*
113. Baltimore Sun, 12/28/03, Michael Dresser.
114. Sen. Padavan, R-Queen, NY
115. Assemblyman Ssteven Sanders, Manhattan-NY
115A. Newsday, 8/10/04.
116. William Duncombe, Syracuse Univ. study on NYS state education financing, 2003
117. Buffalo News, Women's risky gamble, editorial, 4/26/04
118. Ibid.
119. Delaware Health and Social Service Substance Abuse and Mental Health Division, study, 2002 re: costs of gambling.
120. 11/04/03 for the Times-News, Delegate DeRoy Myers
121. Ibid.
122. Letter to the Editor, Jefferson County Journal, Jefferson, Missouri, 10/11/03. Ben Bradshaw, Imperial.

CHAPTER 4

1. McGill University's International Centre for Youth Gambling, Dr. Jeff Deverensky
2. *Ottawa Citizen 10/14/03 by Sarah Schmidt*
3. Ibid.
4. www.abc.net.au/news/newsitems/s1070325.htm
5. editorial, Sunday, Maine Today newspaper on 11/2/2003. Blethen Maine Newspapers Inc. http://news.mainetoday.com/ indepth.casinos/031102casino.shtml
6. 2/22/03 in the Daily News by Heidi Evans
7. Ibid.
8. Ibid.
9. "
10. *Buffalo News article, 7/02*
11. Ibid.
12. http://pokermag.com/managearticle.asp?C=150&A=6 400.
13. Rev. Tom Grey, spokesman for the National Coalition Against Legalized Gambling,
14. the University of Chicago Divinity School. sightings-admin@listhost.uchicago.edu.14
15. "College Campuses Rife with Gambling. Http://www.family. org/cforum/fosi/abioethics/faqs/a0027734.cfm
16. *Adelaide University psychologist, Dr. Paul Delfabbro, Sunday Mail, 3/21/04, So. Australia.*
17. *Ibid.*
18. *Cynthia Abrams, pastor, Dir. Drugs and Other Addictions Program, United Methodist Church.*
19. *Director Pat Fowler, in an article in the Sun-Sentinel by Diane C. Lade, on 3/20/04. 20*
20. *Ibid.*
21. *www.tcpalm.com/tcp/palm_beach/news/ar ticle/0,1651m TCO_1020_2745470,00.html.*
22. *Michael Pollock, publisher, Gaming Industry Observer, newsletter.*
23. *www.abc.net.au/news/newsitems/s1070325.htm*
24. *Ibid.*

25. *The Bristol Press, 4/26/04, Adam Wittenberg, The Herald Press*
26. *http://www.detnews.com/2003/business/ 0310/15/b01-298338.htm*
27. Valerie C. Lorenz, Compulsive Gambling Center, Inc., Maryland.
28. Earl L. Grinols, Gambling in America: Costs and Benefits, Cambridge University Press, 2003
29. www.gazettetimes.com/articles/2004/03/ 27/news/the_ west/satwst04.txt
30. Grinois
31. Ibid.
32. Sightings, 12/18/03, Marty Center at the University Of Chic. Divinity School
33. http://www.wvgazette.com/section/News/ Today/2003100617
34. www.gazettetimes.com/articles/2004/03/ 27/news/the_ west/satwst04.txt
35. Ibid.
36. www.detnews.com/2004/metro/0405/02/b01-139561.htm
37. Ibid.
38. http://www.thestar.com/NASApp/cs/Cont entServer? pagename=thestar/Layout/Article Type1&call pageid= 971358637177&c=Article &cid=1082412612698 Apr.20,2004.
39. www.belfasttelegraph.co.uk/news/story.js p?story=517113
40. Ibid.
41. Custer, p. 49
42. David Phillips, study, 12/03, Suicide and Life-threatening Behavior," the American Assoc. of Suicidology Journal.
43. Robert Hunter as quoted in Study Links Gambling, Suicide, 12/17/97, Shaun McKinnon, Review-Journal,
44. http://www.capitalonline.com/cgi-bin/read/2004/03 30-42/Gov
45. Dark Side of Gambling, 2/5/042004 WorldNow and WIVB
46. ibid
47. "
48. The Guardian, 1/2/04, Manchester, England
49. Rev. Tom Grey, feeding frenzy
50. http://news.statesmanjournal.com/article. cfm?i=77307, 3/19/04
51. *Jaszczynski, A. & Farrell, E. study of suicides, Journal of Gambling Studies, 1998,14(2), 93-*
52. *Ibid.*
53. The National Post, 2/20/04, by Tom Blackwell.
54. Canadian Press, Bailey and Elliott, 2/23/03
55. The Gazette, 12/31/03,, Aaron Derfel
56. Dominique Bourget, Quebec, University of Ottawa. December, 2003, bulletin of the Canadian Psychiatric Association
57. Ibid.
58. National Post, Tom Blackwell, 2/20/04
59. The **New Zealand** Herald reported on May 12, 2004
60. Alison Penfold, 5/12/04, The New Zealand Herald.
61. David Phillips, study,12/03, Suicide and Life-threatening Behavior," the American Assoc. of Suicidology Journal.
62. http://www.azcentral.com/news/articles/ 0209leavinglasvegas-ON.html
63. *AP 2/9/04, Adam Goldman*
64. www.canada.com/health/story.html?id=5 5B14A7A-9B8A-4414-BBE7-410877D3896BC, Murray Brewster, Canadian Press.
65. *Ibid.*

CHAPTER 5

1. Warren Buffet, Stockholders Meeting, 5/2/04
2. Robert Coffin, lawyer, Native American Press/Ojibwe News, 3/19/04
3. Constitution of the United States of America.
4. Rex M. Rogers, "Seducing America: Is Gambling a Good Bet?" Baker Books, PO Box 6287, Grand Rapids, MI 49516, p. 30.
5. Barron, Staten, and Wilshusen
6. http://www.latimes.com/news/nationworld /nation/la-na-lotto5mar05,1,7049552.story, 3/5/04.
7. Padavan
8. Ibid
9. "
10. htt;://cbsnewyork.com/nynews/NY—GamblingGlut-on/resources news html, 4/27/04, Joel Stashenko, AP
11. "Lure the Poor", 10/21/03, The Washington Post. *www.washingtonpost.com/wp-dyn/ articles/A56395-2003 Oct20.html*
12. U.S. Rep. Wayne Gilchrest, *editorial in Baltimore Sun on 3/21/04.*
13. Economist, Paul Samuelson, as quoted by U.S. Rep. Wayne Gilchrest, in an editorial, Baltimore Sun, 3/12/04.
14. http://www.baltimoresun.com/news/opinion/ oped/bal-`op.gilchrest21mar21,0,2025059. story?coll=bal- oped-headlines
15. *The New York Times 3/29/04.*
16. *1/5/04,* Hartford Courant, http://www.ctnow.com/news/ opinion/op_ed/ hc-fromsonoped0105.artjan05,1,1507600.story
17. Ibid.
18. *Ibid.*
19. *NCALG Bulletin, Vol 1, #5, 12/03. Rev. Sue Abrams.*
20. *4 wealthy financiers*
21. *Jeff Benedict, in testimony, May 5, 2004, before the Government Reform Committee, Washington, D.C*
22. *www.connecticutalliance.org*
23. *Jeff Benedict, president of The Connecticut Alliance Against Casino Expansion, 2/29/04, The Daily News.*
24. *Ibid.*
25. *letter to the editor of the Index-Tribune on 1/23//04*
26. *Benedict, The Connecticut Alliance, www.connecticut alliance.org*
27. *Harford Courant writer, Rick Green, on 3/12/04.*
28. *www.csmonitor.com/2004/0209/p02s02-usec.html*
29. *CSEA embezzler*
30. *Nelson Rose, www.csmonitor.com/2004/0209/ p02s02-usec. html*
31. *Shelton, Ca., Police Chief*
32. *1/27/04 in a news article by Judith Davidoff. http://www.madison.com/captimes/news/stories/66121 .php*
   www.connecticutalliance.org *an editorial, Sodom and Gomorrah, Johnson County*
33. *Ibid., Sun newspaper, 2/26/04 by Steve Rose, Chairman.*
34. *Ibid., news-register.net/news/story/022882 02004_new02.asp, 2/28/04, Tom Diana*
35. Ibid. *NY Times, 5/6/04, Raymond Hernandez,*
36. *http://www.baltimoresun.com/news/nation world/balte, cordish14Mar14,0,3949703.story? coll=bal-nationworld-headlines.*

FOOTNOTES

37. *Jeff Benedict, president, The Connecticut Alliance Against Casino Expansion, 2/29/04, The Daily News.*
38. *Ibid.*
39. *letter to the editor, the Index-Tribune, 1/23//04,*
40. *Jeff Benedict, president, The Connecticut Alliance Against Casino Expansion, 2/29/04, The Daily News.*
41. http://www.mlive.com/newsflash/michigan/index.ssf?/base/news-14/1082292241257990. xml, Tim Martin, AP, 4/18/04
42. *http://www.sacbee.com/content/politics/ca/story/8930743p-9857072c.html, Sacramento Bee, Steve Wiegand, 4/17/04*
43. *www.csmonitor.com/2004/0209/p02s02-usec.html*
44. *CSEA embezz.*
45. *Jan Golab, in an article 2/29/04 in The Daily News, Los Angeles.*
46. Nelson Rose, www.csmonitor.com/2004/0209/p02s02-usec. html
47. Shelton, Ca., Police Chief
48. *The Post-Standard, 4/13/04, Glenn Coin. http://www.syracuse.com/news/poststandard/index.ssf?/base/ news-5/108184680624853.xml*
49. *htt://maggiore.homestead.com/JBM.html*
50. *Ibid.*
51. *http://www.mlive.com/newsflash/michigan/index.ssf?/base/ news-14/1082292241257990. xml, Tim Martin, AP, 4/18/04*
52. editorial, Sodom and Gomorrah, Johnson County Sun newspaper, 2/26/04, Steve Rose, Chairman
53. *news-register.net/news/story/02288202004_new02.asp, 2/28/04, Tom Diana*
54. *Ibid.*
55. *Ibid.*
56. *Monty Warner, 2/13/04, Candidate for Governor, W. Virginia.*
57. *Lescia Reed, W. Virginia,*
58. *Congressman Frank Wolf, R-Va., 1/30/04 http://www.reviewjournal.com/lvrj_home/2004/Jan-30-Fri-2004/business/23110342.html, Friday, Jan. 30,2004.*
59. *http://buffalo.bizjournals.com/buffalo/stories/2004/03/22/ daily14.html*
60. *Harris News Service, 4/14/04, Gambling opponents warn of social costs, Chris Grenz.*
61. *http://www.jerrystern.com www.jerrystern.com*
62. *James Browning, executive director of Common Cause, Maryland.*
63. *Centaur spokesman Rick Kelly*
64. *Sen. Allen G. Kukovitch (D-Westmoreland), Pennsylvania.*
65. *the Philadelphia Inquirer, May 2, 2004.*
66. *http://www.philly.com/mid/inquirer/news/ editorial/8535491.htm*
67. *The Post And Courier, 12/23/04, htt;//www.heraldtribune.com/apps/pbcs.dll/article?AID=/20031223/APN/312230754*
68. *North Bay Nugget on 3/25/04. 55 www.nugget.ca.*
69. http://www.thetowntalk.com/html/AE75 ABA4-6A9D1-91BAAD31C3B6.shtml
70. *NCALG Bulletin, in 12/03, Vol 1, No. 5, p. 3.*
71. *John Accola, Rocky Mountain News, 2/26/04.*
72. *www.rockymountainnews.com/drmn/business/article/0,1299, Drmn_4_2683659,00.html*
73. executive director of the Joint Religious Legislative Coalition, Brian Ruschle, on April 28, 2004.
74. *editorial in the Baltimore Sun, 2/5/04.*
75. *Baltimore Sun, by Greg Garland and David Nitkin on 2/4/04.*
76. *Ibid.*
77. *http://www.commoncause.org/issue_agenda/familyvalues.htm*
78. *Ibid.*
79. *http://www.commoncause.org./laundromat/results.cfm*
80. Scott Mayerowitz, the Journal State House Bureau. www.projo.com/news/content/projo 200400317 lobby17. 17f892.html
81. *The Town Council of Middletown passed a resolution on 4/7/04*
82. *Council member, Charles J. Vaillancourt, Rhode Island.*
83. *http://www.hotel-online.com/News/PressReleases1999_1stJan99_Dobson.html Hotel Online Special Report, Federal Gambling Commissioner Speaks on State of Gambling in the U.S.*
84. *Brett Pulley, in an article in the New York Times, 3/4/98, "Casinos Increase Their Contributions to U.S. Campaigns." New York Times, 3/34/98, "Vegas Bob: Nevada Gambling Interests and Bob Dole," The Nation, 2/12/96.*
85. *"Terms of Surrender," Casino Journal, 6/96. Trent Lott, Richard S. Durham, "Guess Who's Raking it in From Gambling," Business Week, 10j/12/98, Al Gore, "Gore, Gephardt Head to Vegas," The Hotline, 3/10/98, Thomas Daschle," The Casino-Campaign Connection," The Hartford Courant, 7/7/97, p. lA8, Richard Gephardt, Robert L. Koenig, "Trips Gephardt Takes Frequent Flights in Corporate Jets," St. Louis Post -Dispatch, 6/26/91, p. 1A, Tom Delay, German, op.cit., 86*
86. *"Top 1996 Donors by Industry," Center for Responsive Politics. 87*
87. *Kim Eisler, "Local Lawyers and Lobbyists Have Big Stakes in Gambling," Washingtonian Magazine, 11/98.*
88. *Martin Koughan, "Easy Money, Mother Jones, July/August, 1997, p. 37.*
89. *Boomtown's Big Land grab: Las Vegas, Nevada," George, March, 1998.*
90. *Taylor Branch in an article in the Baltimore Sun on 3/28/04.*

CHAPTER 6

1. Rex M. Rogers, "Seducing America: Is Gambling a Good Bet?" BakerBooks, PO Box 6287, Grand Rapids, MI 49516, p. 30.
2. *United Methodist Bishop, Michael J. Coyner, 3/14/04.*
3. *resolutions committee chairman, Rev. Quinn Hooks,10/28/03, the Orangeburg-Calhoun Baptist Association*
4. *http://www.thetandd.com/articles/2003/10/28/news/news1.txt*
5. *Baptist Press, 2/1/04,*
6. *1/21/04, Howard Dayton, CEO of Crown Financial Ministries, Baptist Press.*
7. *http://www.sbcbaptistpress.org/bpcolumn.asp?ID=1270*
8. *Dr. Robert Goodman as quoted in a Christian Science Monitor article, Jane Lampman on 2/18/04.*
9. *Ibid.*

10. *Baptist General Convention, Oklahoma, May, 2003, Petition referendum.*
11. *http://www.zwire.com/site/news.cfm?new sid=10573728&BRD=2075&PAG=461& dept_id=386538&rfi=6*
12. *Ibid.*
13. *Roanoke Times, Tim Thornton,10/22/03.*
14. *Ibid.*
15. *The Washington Times, 2/17/04, Pastor Kennedy, Walker Mill Baptist Church in Capitol Heights, Maryland.*
16. *Ibid...*
17. "
18. *Bishop of the United Methodist Church, Minnesota, public letter, to* **the** *State, 2/23/04.*
19. *Ibid.*
20. *The United Methodist Church, Minnesota Area, 122 W. Franklin Ave., Suite 200, Minneapolis, Mn. 554004-2472*
21. *Jane Lampman, Christian Science Monitor, Dr. Tony Campolo, head of the Evangelical Association.*
22. *Ibid.*
23. North Dakota, Methodist Bishop, Michael J. Coyner, editorial, The Forum, regarding gambling 3/14/04.
24. Methodist Social Principles, Methodist Bishop Michael J. Coyner.
25. *The Forum, 3/14/04, Editorial by Michael J. Coyner.*
26. *NCALG.*
27. *http://www.madison.com/captimes/news/ stories/66121.php*
28. *news.com.au, Nick Papps, 10/16/03,*
29. Rex M. Rogers, "seducing America: Is Gambling a Good Bet?" Baker Books, PO Box 6287, Grand Rapids, MI 49516, p. 55.
30. www.in-forum.com/articles/index.cfm? id=56749§ion= News
31. New Catholic Encyclopedia, Journal Sentinel, 10/17/03, by Tom Held, Milwaukee County, Wisconsin. theld@journalsentinel.com
32. February, 2004, New York State Catholic Conference, Dennis Proust, Spokesman. http://timesunion.com/AspStories/story.asp?storoyID =222792&category=STATE&newsdate=2/26/2004
37. *http://www.wcr.ab.ca/columns/glenargan/ 2004/glenargan 042604.shtml*
38. *beliefnet.com*
39. *Bill Tammeus, Kansas City Star, 3/27/04. Ibid.*

CHAPTER 7

1. *Forell, 1997* Forrell, C. (1997). 'The gambling fix' in *The Sunday Age, 9th March, 1997.* P.8.
2. Rev. John Eades, 10/11/03www.news-star.com/stories/101103/rel_9.shtml
3. USA Today, 7/26/04
4. *Dianne Berlin, NCALG www.sbcbaptistpress.org/bpnews.asp?ID=18800, 8/3/04*
5. Eades, John.
   34. Breen and Zimmerman.
   35. University of Alberta professor Garry Smith, 12/8/03Vancouver, Canada, William Boei
   36. The Halifax Herald Limited, 5/5/04, Bill Power, VLT's Ruined his Life.
10. *David Davila, Gaming Today,*
11. *9/28/2002 NCALG/NCAAHE Conference in Texas, Maura Casey noted that*
12. *Dr. Earl L. Gambling in America: Costs and Benefits, ", Cambridge Univ. Press, 2004.*
13. *Ibid.*
14. *Roger Horbay, Canadian researcher*
15. U.S. Patent Office
16. *Breen and Zimmerman*
17. *Ibid.*
18. *Horbay.*
19. *http://www.ctnow.com/news/local/hc-slotmachine.artmay09,1, 5044301.story?coll=hcbig-headlines-breaking, Rick Green Hartford Courant*
20. *Ibid.*
21. http://www.trumptaj.com/default.asp
22. Sandra Dekker., ch. 2, p. 1.
23. http://www.trumptaj.com/default.asp
24. Ibid.
25. "
26. "
27. Sandra Dekker. Ch. 4, p. 3.

CHAPTER 8

1. http://www.washingtonpost.com/wp-dyn/articles/A55444-2004Jul16.html
2. Ibid.
3. "
4. Ibid.
5. Donald Trump, quoted from the minutes of the Toronto Police Services Board, 4/19/01.
6. Dianne Berlin, 8/4/04, e-mail, NCALG.

References

BOOKS

Robert B. Breen and Mark Zimmerman, The Rapid Onset of Pathological Gambling in Machine Gamblers, Brown Univ. School of Medicine.

Custer, Robert, When Luck Runs Out, Harry Milt,

Sandra Dekker, Commercial Gaming The Unfair Deal, Graduate thesis, 9/97, The Univ. of So. Australia,

Earl L. Grinols, Gambling in America: Costs and Benefits, Cambridge University Press, 2003

Rex M. Rogers, "Seducing America: Is Gambling a Good Bet?" BakerBooks, PO Box 6287, Grand Rapids, MI 49516

SOURCES

Constitution of the United States of America.

Garrett, Casino Gambling in American and its Economic Impacts, Sr. Economist, Fed. Reserve Bank of St. Louis
Diagnostic and Statistical Manual of Mental Disorders, fourth Edition. 1994 American Psychiatric Association).
Tom Grey, Executive Director of the National Coalition Against Legalized Gambling, NCALG,
William Duncombe, Syracuse Univ. study on NYS state education financing, 2003
Delaware Health and Social Service Substance Abuse & Mental Health Division, study, 2002 re: costs of gambling.
McGill University's International Centre for Youth Gambling, Dr. Jeff Deverensky
Barron, Staten, Wilshusen, The Impact of Casino gAmbling on Personal Bankruptcy Filing Rates, 8/2000.
www.belfasttelegraph.co.uk/news/story.jsp?story=517113
David Phillips, study,12/03, Suicide and Life-threatening Behavior," the American Assoc. of Suicidology Journal.
Robert Hunter as quoted in Study Links Gambling, Suicide, 12/17/97, Shaun McKinnon, Review-Journal, http://www.capitalonline.com/cgi-bin/read/2004/03 30-42/Gov
Dark Side of Gambling, 2/5/042004 WorldNow and WIVB
National Gambling Impact Study Commission (NGISC, 1999. Federal Government.
Joel S. Rose, in a speech on 11/21/03 to the League of Woman Voters of Buffalo, NEWSDAY, 2/5/04
William Thompson, professor, public administration, *Univ. of Nev* ...Dr. Robert Goodman, "Legalized gambling as a Strategy for Economic Development."
Wyoming House Speaker, Pro Tem Rodney Anderson, R-Pine Bluffs, said recently on 2/27/04, Spring/2003 Stanford Journal of Law, Business and Finance, Vol. 8p. 185, John W. Kindt, Prof. Univ. of Illinois. Dark Side of Gambling, WorldNow, WIVB. PACT, Florence, Oregon, 2/12/04 – e-newsletter NCALG Website *The Impact of Casino Gambling on Personal Bankruptcy Filing Rates, Barron, Staten, Wilshusen, 8/2000, Charles Greenawait, Senior Fellow at the Susquehanna Valley Center for Public Policy,* The Hill Report, Christian Science Monitor, 11/6/03. Administrative Office of the U.S. Courts, Press Conf., Madison, Milwaukee, 2/10/04, DA Blanchard. Sen. Padavan, R-Queen, NY Assemblyman Ssteven Sanders, Manhattan-NY William Duncombe, Syracuse Univ. study on NYS state education financing, 2003 Delaware Health and Social Service Substance Abuse and Mental Health Division, study, 2002 re: costs of gambling. McGill University's International Centre for Youth Gambling, Dr. Jeff Deverensky Charles Munger, vice chairman, Berkshire Hathaway, shareholders meeting, 5/1/04.

ARTICLES

www.boston.com/news/globe/health_science/articles/22003/10/28/pills_to_treat_gambling_ills/
http://www.herldtribune,com/apps/pbcs.dll/articlle?AID=/20040111/NEWS/401110685/1060
www.suntimes.com/output/health/cst-nws-gamb01.html
www.palmbeachpost.com/news/content/auto/epaper/editions/today/nbews
Hartford Courant, 8/10/04
Newday,. 8/10/04
times.hankooki.com/lpage/culture/200402/kt200-4021219363911700.htm Putting Gambling Addiction Into Perspective
SeattlePost-Intelligence, SamSkolnik,2/24/04, seattlepi.nwsource. com/local/161827_gambling24.html
Milwaukee Journal Sentinel, 10/18/03.
The Wall Street Journal, Christina Binkley, 2/24/04.
Assoc. Press, 11/19/03, Compulsive Gambling on the rise in La.
Boston Globe, 10/28/03. Pills to Treat Gambling Ills.
seven.com.au/todaytonight/story/pokiefight
www.springharbor.org/press_detail.php?pressrelease_id=40
www.healthunit.org/adults/php_gambling.htm
www.signonsandiego.com/sports/sullivan/20040126-9999_1s26sullivan.html
http://www.wtol.com/Global/storoy.asp?S=1471285,
www.projo.com/opinion/columnists/content/projo200040127-clacho.19ca07.html
www.projo.com/ap/ne/1084380348.htm, Associated Press, Michael Mello
Dr. James C.Dobson,1/99, htt;://www.hotel-online.com/News/PressReleasesl999_1st/Jan99_Dobson.html, Hotel Online,
www.theunionleader.com/articles_showa.html?article=31992
Christiansen Capital Advisors NY Times, 1/18/04, George Vecsey
www.Casinowatch.org
St. Louis Post-Dispatch, "1 in 5 of Homeless in Survey Blame Gambling, by Tim Poor, 3/15/98, p. A9.
Fox News, 8/3/04, "Sin City Has Become Homeless City
Maura J. Casey, Buffalo News, 10/19/03. Special art. On Gambling.
CACGEC.
www.kycage.org/Crime.html.
www.thestar.com/NASApp/cs/ContentServer?pagename=thestar/Layout/Article_Type!&call, 4/20/04

www.hotel-online.com/News/PressReleases1999_1st/Jan99_Dobson.html
Star Telegram, 10/22/03, www.dfw.com/mid/dfw/7077825.htm, Jay Root
CACGEC Website, http://nocasinoerie.org/jobques.htm
http://www.smartmoney.com/consumer/index.cfm?story=gaming, Ten Things the Gaming Industry Won't Tell You, Brian O'Keefe, 7/17/00
Greg Garland, Baltimore Sun, 2/16/04.
Erie Times-News, 11/18/03, Michael Geer
Baltimore Sun, 2/8/04
Les Bernal, NCALG website. Optimal Solutions, CAGE. www.kycage.org/Crime.html
Baltimore Sun, 2/8/04, Bill Atkinson, Rising Debt draws millions to refuge of bankruptcy.
Buffalo News, Women's risky gamble, editorial, 4/26/04
Newsday, 2/15/04.
Christian Science Monitor, 11/5/03
The Times Record, 10/28/03, High Stakes for Maine, Leslie Talmadge.
www.timesrecord.com/website/main.nsf/news.nsf/oD85E58BooBB5256DCDOO5A9487*?Opendocument*
www.buffalonews.com/editorial/20040106/1023803.asp
Baltimore Sun, 2/8/04, Bill Atkinson, Rising Debt draws millions to refuge of bankruptcy.
TheBaltimore Sun,12/28/03, Michael Dresser. http://sunspot.net/news/local/bal-te.md.embezzle28dec28.0.3286170.story?coll=bal-local-headlines.
www.shawanoleader.com/articles/2003/12/29/news/news2.txt, Tim Ryan.
http://www.badgerherald.com/vnews/display.vART/2004/02/10/402864e5ccb99
www.abc.net.au/news/newsitems/s1070325.htm
editorial, Sunday, Maine Today newspaper on 11/2/2003. Blethen Maine Newspapers Inc.
http://news.mainetoday.com/indepth.casinos/031102casino.shtml
2/22/03 in the Daily News by Heidi Evans
The Bristol Press, 4/26/04, Adam Wittenberg, The Herald Press
http://www.detnews.com/2003/business/0310/15/b01-298338.htm
Valerie C. Lorenz, Compulsive Gambling Center, Inc., Maryland.
Ottawa Citizen 10/14/03 by Sarah Schmidt
http://pokermag.com/managearticle.asp?C=150&A=6400.
the University of Chicago Divinity School. sightings-admin@listhost.uchicago.edu.14
"College Campuses Rife with Gambling. Http://www.family.org/ cforum/fosi/abioethics/faqs/a0027734.cfm
Adelaide University psychologist, Dr. Paul Delfabbro, Sunday Mail, 3/21/04, So. Australia.
Adelaide University psychologist, Dr. Paul Delfabbro, Sunday Mail, 3/21/04, So. Australia.
Cynthia Abrams, pastor, Dir. Drugs and Other Addictions Program, United Methodist Church
www.gazettetimes.com/articles/2004/03/27/news/the_west/satwst04.txt
Sightings, 12/18/03, Marty Center at the University Of Chic. Divinity School
32. Ibid.
33.www.gazettetimes.com/articles/2004/03/27/news/the_west/satwst04.txt
34. Ibid.

Letters to the Editor,
Jefferson County Journal, Jefferson, Missouri, 10/11/03. Ben Bradshaw, Imperial letter to the editor of the Index-Tribune on 1/23//04

William Duncombe, Syracuse Univ. study on NYS state education financing, 2003
Delaware Health and Social Service Substance Abuse and Mental Health Division, study, 2002 re: costs of gambling.
McGill University's International Centre for Youth Gambling, Dr. Jeff Deverensky
www.belfasttelegraph.co.uk/news/story.jsp?story=517113
David Phillips, study,12/03, Suicide and Life-threatening Behavior," the American Assoc. of Suicidology Journal.
Robert Hunter as quoted in Study Links Gambling, Suicide, 12/17/97, Shaun McKinnon, Review-Journal,
http://www.capitalonline.com/cgi-bin/read/2004/03 30-42/Gov
Dark Side of Gambling, 2/5/042004 WorldNow and WIVB
The Guardian, 1/2/04, Manchester, England
http://news.statesmanjournal.com/article.cfm?i=77307, 3/19/04
Jaszczynski, A. & Farrell, E. study of suicides, Journal of Gambling Studies, l998,14(2), 93-
The National Post, 2/20/04, by Tom Blackwell.
Canadian Press, Bailey and Elliott, 2/23/03
The Gazette, 12/31/03, Aaron Derfel
Dominique Bourget, Quebec, University of Ottawa. December, 2003, bulletin of the Canadian Psychiatric Association
The **New Zealand** Herald, May 12, 2004, Alison Penfold.
61. http://www.azcentral.com/news/articles/0209leavinglasvegas-ON. html
AP 2/9/04, Adam Goldman
www.canada.com/health/story.html?id=55B14A7A-9B8A-4414-BBE7-410877D3896BC, Murray Brewster, Canadian Press
Robert Coffin, lawyer, Native American Press/Ojibwe News, 3/19/04 http://www.latimes.com/news/nation world/nation/la-na-lotto5mar05,1,7049552.story,
3/5/04.htt;://cbsnewyork.com/nynews/NY—Gambling Glut-on/ resources news html, 4/27/04, Joel Stashenko, AP
"Lure the Poor", 10/21/03, The Washington Post.
www.washingtonpost.com/wp-dyn/articles/A56395-2003Oct20.html
U.S. Rep. Wayne Gilchrest, *editorial in Baltimore Sun on 3/21/04.*
Economist, Paul Samuelson, as quoted by U.S. Rep. Wayne Gilchrest, in an editorial,
Baltimore Sun, 3/12/04.
http://www.baltimoresun.com/news/opinion/oped/bal-`op.gilchrest 21mar21,0,2025059.story?coll=bal- oped-headlines
The New York Times 3/29/04.
1/5/04, Hartford Courant, http://www.ctnow.com/news/opinion/ op_ed/hc-fromsonoped0105.artjan05,1, 1507600.story
NCALG Bulletin, Vol 1, #5, 12/03. Rev. Sue Abrams.
Jeff Benedict, in testimony, May 5, 2004, before the Government Reform Committee, Washington, D.C
www.connecticutalliance.org
Jeff Benedict, president of The Connecticut Alliance Against Casino Expansion, 2/29/04, The Daily News.
www.connecticutalliance.org
Harford Courant writer, Rick Green, on 3/12/04.
www.csmonitor.com/2004/0209/p02s02-usec.html

REFERENCES

Nelson Rose, www.csmonitor.com/2004/0209/p02s02-usec.html
1/27/04, news article by Judith Davidoff.
http://www.madison.com/captimes/news/stories/66121.php
www.connecticutalliance.org *an editorial, Sodom and Gomorrah, Johnson County Sun newspaper, 2/26/04 by Steve Rose, Chairman.*
news-register.net/news/story/02288202004_new02.asp, 2/28/04, Tom Diana
NY Times, 5/6/04, Raymond Hernandez,
http://www.baltimoresun.com/news/nationworld/balte, cordish14Mar14,0,3949703.story?coll=bal-nationworld-headlines.
http://www.mlive.com/newsflash/michigan/index.ssf?/base/news-14/1082292241257990.xml, Tim Martin, AP,
http://www.sacbee.com/content/politics/ca/story/8930743p-9857072c.html, Sacramento Bee, Steve Wiegand,
www.csmonitor.com/2004/0209/p02s02-usec.html
Jan Golab, in an article 2/29/04 in The Daily News, Los Angeles.
The Post-Standard, 4/13/04, Glenn Coin.
http://www.syracuse.com/news/poststandard/index.ssf?/base/news-5/108184680624853.xml
htt://maggiore.homestead.com/JBM.html
52.*http://www.mlive.com/newsflash/michigan/index.ssf?/base/news-14/1082292241257990.xml, Tim Martin, AP, 4/18/04*
editorial, Sodom and Gomorrah, Johnson County Sun newspaper, 2/26/04, Steve Rose, Chairman
news-register.net/news/story/02288202004_new02.asp, 2/28/04, Tom Diana
Monty Warner, 2/13/04, Candidate for Governor, W. Virginia.
http://www.reviewjournal.com/lvrj_home/2004/Jan-30-Fri-2004/business/23110342.html, Friday, Jan. 30, 2004.
http://buffalo.bizjournals.com/buffalo/stories/2004/03/22/daily14.html
Harris News Service, 4/14/04, Gambling opponents warn of social costs, Chris Grenz.
http://www.jerrystern.com www.jerrystern.com
James Browning, executive director of Common Cause, Maryland.
the Philadelphia Inquirer, May 2, 2004.
http://www.philly.com/mid/inquirer/news/editorial/8535491.htm
The Post And Courier, 12/23/04,
htt;//www.heraldtribune.com/apps/pbcs.dll/article?AID=/20031223/APN/312230754
North Bay Nugget on 3/25/04. 55 www.nugget.ca.
http://www.thetowntalk.com/html/AE75ABA4-6A9D1-91BAAD31C3B6.shtml
NCALG Bulletin, in 12/03, Vol 1, No. 5, p. 3.
John Accola, Rocky Mountain News, 2/26/04.
www.rockymountainnews.com/drmn/business/article/0,1299,Drmn_4_2683659,00.html
executive director of the Joint Religious Legislative Coalition, Brian Ruschle, on April 28, 2004.
editorial in the Baltimore Sun, 2/5/04.
Baltimore Sun, by Greg Garland and David Nitkin on 2/4/04.
http://www.commoncause.org/issue_agenda/familyvalues.htm
http://www.commoncause.org./laundromat/results.cfm
Scott Mayerowitz, the Journal State House Bureau. www.projo.com/news/content/projo 200400317 lobby 17.17f892. html
The Town Council of Middletown passed a resolution on 4/7/04
Council member, Charles J. Vaillancourt, Rhode Island.
http://www.hotel-online.com/News/PressReleases 1999_1stJan99_Dobson.html Hotel Online Special Report, Federal
Gambling Commissioner Speaks on State of Gambling in the U.S.
Brett Pulley, in an article in the New York Times, 3/4/98, "Casinos Increase Their Contributions to U.S. Campaigns." New York Times, 3/34/98, "Vegas Bob: Nevada Gambling Interests and Bob Dole," The Nation, 2/12/96.
Terms of Surrender," Casino Journal, 6/96. Trent Lott, Richard S. Durham, "Guess Who's Raking it in From Gambling," Business Week, 10j/12/98, Al Gore, "Gore, Gephardt Head to Vegas," The Hotline, 3/10/98, Thomas Daschle," The Casino-Campaign Connection," The Hartford Courant, 7/7/97, p. lA8, Richard Gephardt, Robert L. Koenig, "Trips Gephardt Takes Frequent Flights in Corporate Jets," St. Louis Post -Dispatch, 6/26/91, p. 1A, Tom Delay, German, op.cit., 86
"Top 1996 Donors by Industry," Center for Responsive Politics. 87
Kim Eisler, "Local Lawyers and Lobbyists Have Big Stakes in Gambling," Washingtonian Magazine, 11/98.
Martin Koughan, "Easy Money, Mother Jones, July/August, 1997, p. 37.
Boomtown's Big Land grab: Las Vegas, Nevada," George, March, 1998.
Taylor Branch in an article in the Baltimore Sun on 3/28/04.
United Methodist Bishop, Michael J. Coyner, 3/14/04

resolutions committee chairman, Rev. Quinn Hooks,10/28/03, the Orangeburg-Calhoun Baptist Association
http://www.thetandd.com/articles/2003/10/28/news/news1.txt
Baptist Press, 2/1/04,
1/21/04, Howard Dayton, CEO of Crown Financial Ministries, Baptist Press.
http://www.sbcbaptistpress.org/bpcolumn.asp?ID=1270
Dr. Robert Goodman as quoted in a Christian Science Monitor article, Jane Lampman on 2/18/04.
Baptist General Convention, Oklahoma, May, 2003, Petition referendum.
http://www.zwire.com/site/news.cfm?newsid=10573728&BRD=2075&PAG=461&dept_id=386538&rfi=6
Roanoke Times, Tim Thornton,10/22/03.
The Washington Times, 2/17/04, Pastor Kennedy, Walker Mill Baptist Church in Capitol Heights, Maryland.
Bishop of the United Methodist Church, Minnesota, public letter, to **the** *State, 2/23/04.*
United Methodist Church, Minnesota Area, 122 W. Franklin Ave., Suite 200, Minneapolis, Mn. 554004-2472
Jane Lampman, Christian Science Monitor, Dr. Tony Campolo, head of the Evangelical Association.
North Dakota, Methodist Bishop, Michael J. Coyner, editorial, The Forum, regarding gambling 3/14/04.
Methodist Social Principles, Methodist Bishop Michael J. Coyner.
The Forum, 3/14/04, Editorial by Michael J. Coyner.
http://www.madison.com/captimes/news/stories/66121.php
news.com.au, Nick Papps, 10/16/03,
www.in-forum.com/articles/index.cfm?id=56749§ion=News
The New Catholic Encyclopedia, Journal Sentinel, 10/17/03, by Tom Held, Milwaukee County, Wisconsin.
theld@journalsentinel.com

February, 2004, New York State Catholic Conference, Dennis Proust, Spokesman.
http://timesunion.com/AspStories/story.asp?storoyID=2227 92&category=STATE&newsdate=2/26/2004
http://www.wcr.ab.ca/columns/glenargan/2004/glenargan04 2604.shtml
beliefnet.com
Bill Tammeus, Kansas City Star, 3/27/04.
Forell, 1997 Forrell, C. (1997). 'The gambling fix' in The Sunday Age, 9th March, 1997. P.8.
Rev. John Eades, 10/11/03www.news-star.com/stories/101103/ rel_9.shtml
SA Today, 7/26/04
www.sbcbaptistpress.org/bpnews.asp?ID=18800, 8/3/04
University of Alberta professor Garry Smith, 12/8/03 Vancouver, Canada, William Boei
The Halifax Herald Limited, 5/5/04, Bill Power, VLT's Ruined his Life.
David Davila, Gaming Today,
9/28/2002 NCALG/NCAAHE Conference in Texas, Maura Casey noted that
http://www.ctnow.com/news/local/hc-slotmachine.artmay09,1, 5044301.story?coll=hcbig-headlines-breaking,
http://www.trumptaj.com/default.asp
http://www.washingtonpost.com/wp-dyn/articles/A55444-2004Jul 16.html
Donald Trump, quoted in an extract from the minutes of the Toronto Police Services Board, 4/19/01.
Dianne Berlin, 8/4/04, e-mail, NCALG.
Star Telegram, 10/22/03.
Toronto, Canada, CNEWS, 4/30/04.
American Gaming Assoc.www.americangaming.org
Dr. Joel S. Rose, Speech, 11/21/02., CACGEC website.
Thomas A. Garrett, Casino Gambling in America.
Lesieur, www.gamblingprolem.org/kidsgamblin.htm
Christiansen, op. cit. p. 3.
Gambling Causes Economic Decline, CACGEC website, p. 1.
US Census Bureau, Stat. Abstract of the US; 1997, 117th ed., Wash., DC p. 769.
Charles Munger, vice chairman, Berkshire Hathaway, shareholders meeting, 5/1/04.
State Rep. Matt Baker, Pa. The Herald Standard, April 29, 2004
htt::/www.phillly.com/mid/inquirer/news/local/states/ pennsylvania/cities_neighborhoods/philadelphia/8544562.ht m
Maura J. Casey, Buffalo News, 11/19/03
Newsday, 2/12/04. Dealer Rapes Granddaughter.

****

Appendix

1. Gamblers Anonymous offers the following questions to anyone who may have a gambling problem. These questions are provided to help the individual decide if he or she is a compulsive gambler and wants to stop gambling. TWENTY QUESTIONS

1. Did you ever lose time from work or school due to gambling?
2. Has gambling ever made your home life unhappy?
3. Did gambling affect your reputation?
4. Have you ever felt remorse after gambling?
5. Did you ever gamble to get money with which to pay debts or otherwise solve financial difficulties?
6. Did gambling cause a decrease in your ambition or efficiency?
7. After losing did you feel you must return as soon as possible and win back your losses?
8. After a win did you have a strong urge to return and win more?
9. Did you often gamble until your last dollar was gone?
10. Did you ever borrow to finance your gambling?
11. Have you ever sold anything to finance gambling?
12. Were you reluctant to use "gambling money" for normal expenditures?
13. Did gambling make you careless of the welfare of yourself or your family?
14. Did you ever gamble longer than you had planned?
15. Have you ever gambled to escape worry or trouble?
16. Have you ever committed, or considered committing, an illegal act to finance gambling?
17. Did gambling cause you to have difficulty in sleeping?
18. Do arguments, disappointments or frustrations create within you an urge to gamble?
19. Did you ever have an urge to celebrate any good fortune by a few hours of gambling?
20. Have you ever considered self destruction or suicide as a result of your gambling?

Most compulsive gamblers answer yes to at least 7 of these questions. Reprinted with the kind permission of Gamblers Anonymous. E-mail isomain@gamblersanonymous.org.

2. ***Would Jesus have played the lottery???...****An interesting perspective that both Christians and non-Christians could find meaningful. As you read, include the name of your own figure of divinity to feel the truth and reality of the article. Write Pastor, at the bottom, with comments.*

In recent years lotteries have gained acceptance and popularity in many states. State governments promote them as "fun" and "entertaining," urging people to play. Some states designate lottery generated revenue to fund specific purposes such as education. State officials tout the benefits of these revenues. Slick ad campaigns encourage citizens to 'risk a little in hope of winning a lot'.

There were no state-run lotteries in Jesus' day, but there was gambling. The gospels do not directly say whether Jesus gambled for money, but they do say... ***what Jesus taught about God, people and money.***

- *that you cannot love God and money at the same time.*

"No one can serve two masters;... You cannot serve God and wealth." (Matt. 6:24) Is it possible to play the lottery and not hope to win money? Isn't the dream of winning a large amount of money the major appeal of the lottery? Could the desire to win money lead a believer away from trusting and serving God?

- *That you should love your neighbor as yourself. (Mark 12:31)*

Where does the prize money come from when someone wins the lottery? Doesn't one win at the expense of others who lose? Does playing the lottery measure up to the golden rule: "Do to others as you would have them do to you?" (Luke 6:31)

- *That our possessions are gifts from God, we are stewards of sacred trusts.*

(Luke 12:15) Jesus encouraged his followers to be generous and to give gratefully. (Luke 6:38) What sort of attitude toward money and possessions does the lottery foster? Does it encourage faithful stewardship and trust in God or does it foster greed, desire for more, needless and heedless spending?

- *Jesus had a special concern for the poor.*

He told the impoverished that they were not forgotten by God, but were blessed and loved by God. (Luke 6:20) He did not abuse the poor nor prey upon their weaknesses or desperation. To whom do lotteries appeal the most: the well-to-do or the down-and-out? A recent poll revealed that the poor in America spend twice as much on lotteries than any other income group. (Gallup Poll, Dec.11-14, 2003) Lotteries appeal most to those who can least afford to risk their money.

Jesus healed those who were afflicted and rescued those enslaved to outside forces. (Mark 5:1-20) Sadly, for some people gambling becomes a snare and causes self-destructive, compulsive and addictive behavior. Problem gambling negatively impacts not only individuals, but spouses, families, businesses, and communities. Studies have shown that young people are especially vulnerable to gambling addictions. Gambling problems can lead to higher rates of suicide, divorce, bankruptcy, and crime. Isn't prevention the best cure? Does buying a lottery ticket give unspoken approval of gambling? Might you lead others into temptation if you do? So would Jesus have bought a lottery ticket? Should you? You decide.

If gambling is causing problems in your life, marriage, family or job, or someone you know has a problem with gambling and you would like to get help: In ND, 211 or 1-800-472-2911. In SD, 1-888-781-HELP or 1-800-522-4700

For more Biblical perspectives on gambling's morality, see "The Lottery: A Good Bet or Bad Bet for North Carolina" by John Fonville of Truth Talk Live. http://www.830wtru.com/gambling.html. For an overview in brief, "Gambling: The Odds Are Against You, http://www.family.org/pastor/resources/sos/a000 6404.html, e-mail: mttoepke@bektel.com

© 2004 Pastor Marty Toepke-Floyd. Permission to reproduce and distribute this article for free is granted without charge as long as this disclaimer is included.

Stop** Gambling's expansion in the U.S., call the **National Coalition Against Legalized Gambling (NCALG)**, 1-800-664-2680, **www.ncalg.org.** Also excellent, **www.Casinowatch.org

3. ***This is a terrific Letter to the Editor (LTE) by someone with long experience in this field.***

***Sir:** In response to the letter 'Where **does the Bible prohibit gambling**?' published Wednesday, July 28/04. Before real discussion begins on gambling, one has to get behind the glitz and false hope pushed by the gambling promoters. **Gambling** is **NOT entertainment**, as touted by the pushers. It is a **predatory activity**. When one gambles, he or she wants to take what belongs to others without earning it or it being given freely as a gift would be. Under any other circumstances, that is robbery or theft.*

In fact, gambling has been called theft by consent or robbery with permission. The 10 Commandments address both coveting and stealing. Gambling undermines, and even destroys, the work ethic. Labour is advocated in the Bible. Ordinary activities all have an element of risk-taking in them... even crossing the street does. This is very different from gambling.

Gambling's negatives include addiction, bankruptcies, crime, corruption, divorce, violence, child abuse, homelessness, etc. Gambling recycles wealth, usually from many losers to the pockets of the gambling kingpins. It does not create new wealth.

The recent legalization of gambling has desensitized people to its harmful effects and the reasons it was an illegal activity in most countries. Wise people learn from the mistakes of others. There are many people and countries which have made the mistake of embracing gambling to their detriment. The Bible advocates wisdom whether Jewish or Christian, that's not bad advice for any person or government. **DIANNE M. BERLIN, DMBerlin@aol.com, Penryn, PA, USA**

Dianne sends out newspaper articles from around the U.S. and the world daily about gambling in her **FREE e-mail service.** To sign-up for this incredibly valuable service, mail a request to her e-mail above.

4 *How does **Gambling Addiction Feel?** Why would anyone allow themselves to continue? Read this and see. Winning this one - Winfield woman overcoming her gambling addiction. Cassie Means. <cassie@dailymail.com> Daily Mail staff, 7/23/2004.*

***What began as a childhood game of poker** ultimately led Winfield's Kim Murphy into a life-consuming spiral of thrilling wins and agonizing losses. Murphy, now 44, took her first shot at lady luck when she was only 13. Although her hobby began as playing cards, it resulted in feeding $300 a day into video lottery machines. As a truck driver, Murphy said she became enthralled with the slot machines of Las Vegas and Reno. After returning to the Mountain State, she found similar slots within driving distance. Pouring money into machines at Tri-State Greyhound Park in Nitro then became another full-time job.*

*"**For four years, I went every day and spent an average of $300 a day,**" she said. "I would beg, borrow, steal and con to get gambling money." Murphy said the thrill of gambling is inexplicable. Something comes over you," she said. "You are hypnotized by the machine." Although Murphy occasionally won small sums of money, she always left the track a loser. "Every dime I won, I put it right back into the machine," she said. "I never walked away a winner. "Murphy said the monetary toll of gambling pales in comparison to the emotional effects. "I didn't just lose dollars," she said. "I lost myself and that's hard to find again "I didn't want people to know how stupid I was," she said...*

*During secret road trips, Murphy's life began to crumble. Her **gambling binges had caused her to lose her apartment, furniture and even her dog, Captain.** The problem gambler then hit "rock bottom." To boost her* *floundering emotions, Murphy said she visited a track to spend away her sorrows. Although Murphy won $300 that night, she still wanted to drive her car in front of a tractor-trailer. "I had been a truck driver and I knew what would happen," she said. "I thought there was no other way out." Rather than committing suicide, Murphy called a help line she found listed in a track pamphlet. Unlike the current line that exists in West Virginia, the hotline Murphy contacted was for general emotional assistance. "All they told me was to go back to the track," she said.*

Luckily, Murphy failed to follow their advice. Instead, a friend took her to a hospital... where she was admitted for depression. After being released from the hospital, Murphy joined Gamblers Anonymous. Although Murphy has stumbled occasionally, she has not gambled for 18 months. Her last gambling spree was Dec. 12, 2001. During the two-day binge, Murphy dropped $3,000 worth of change into video lottery machines... Murphy takes precautions to prevent future setbacks. When she gets the urge to gamble, Murphy contacts friends or travels away from gaming facilities.,,, "We just offer peer-to-peer support. She stays three or four days or however long it takes to get over the hump," Roberts said. To keep away from slot machines, Murphy was advised to find another thrilling pastime. "I took up bungee jumping, but you can't go bungee jumping every day," she said. Murphy then purchased a four-wheeler in hopes of finding outdoor recreation thrills. "Rainy Saturdays were always my bad days, though," she said. "No one wants to ride a four-wheeler on a rainy Saturday."

Murphy was careful not to swap her gambling addiction for another harmful dependency. "I didn't want to turn to the bottle or to drugs," she said. "But I finally did find a replacement. My replacement now is talking about my problem." Since then, Murphy has not been ashamed to share her story. Murphy is also attempting to form a council on problem gambling that would represent the Lottery Commission, addicted gamblers and gaming facilities. Murphy said the council would create preventative education, educate about treatment centers and establish safe houses.

Despite the agony Murphy has faced, she still feels very fortunate. "I could be living in a mansion on the hill right now, but I live in a house in the valley," she said. "But I didn't gamble today, and I didn't gamble yesterday. That's enough to make me happy." Writer Cassie Means can be reached at 348-4850. © Copyright 2003 Charleston Daily Mail

4. *Look at the incredibly long list of Indian tribal casinos throughout the U.S. You can find the list online in the* ***NCALG Document Library.*** ***www.ncalg.org*** *This doesn't include Las Vegas, Atlantic City or non-Indian privately owned casinos. This is truly, 'a casino on every block'. Accessibility + Convenience = Frequency = Addiction. Indian Gambling Magazine, 2003 Indian Gaming Facilities, by State.*

5. *Read these stories and weep for the blindness and self-destructiveness of so many poor souls, 'suffering humanity', sold gambling's delusionary promises, misguided people motivated by money and casino hype. It could be any of us. These stories are neither unusual nor infrequent. Thousands and thousands more stories just as horrendous are happening every day.*

Gambling Addiction Suicides

Michigan - A small-business owner, had just returned from a trip to the Las Vegas Strip's MGM Grand Tuesday when he allegedly killed his pregnant wife and three children (under 7 years old) before turning the gun on himself. In his Mich., home, police found a suicide note blaming gambling addiction - and $225,000 in shredded casino markers. His business was $500,000 in debt because he withdrew the money to cover his gambling. Las Vegas Sun, 11/22/00, Las Vegas Review-Journal, 11/23/00.

Atlantic City - An 11-year-old Herndon girl died yesterday after initially surviving the slayings of her mother and brother and the suicide of her father, who authorities now say defrauded area banks of nearly $2 million and had $10 million in gambling and other debts. Washington Post 8/6/98

LA - On Thursday, another fight about gambling steeled Jueliene Butler's determination to leave her husband, as her children raced down the street on their bicycles. Two shots resounded through the neighborhood ending Rodney and Juelience Butler's stormy 26-year marriage in a murder-suicide heard by their 13-year-old daughter. Times Pica 5/8/98

IL - Each turned on the ignition of their Olds Regency after stretching a vacuum hose from the exhaust pipe into the car's interior, climbing in and rolling up the windows. Carol, 63, was the obsessive gambler. Disabled and saddled with the monstrous debt she had created, Skip, 69 had wanted to join her. Undone by a ravenous habit that cost them $200,000, a house, a nest egg and two lives, it was Carol who left a terse hint of the forest of guilt and fear that had grown around them. Bexson and Carol Warriner chose suicide as a last exit from gambling habits. LA Times, 6/22/97

ATLANTIC CITY—An unidentified man hanged himself under the Boardwalk on Thursday, the third suicide outside a casino in the last three months, police said. The Associated Press 6/9/00

ATLANTIC CITY—A 50-year-old Ventnor man apparently committed suicide Tuesday afternoon by jumping off the parking garage of a casino, police said. LAS VEGAS SUN 4/5/00

ATLANTIC CITY, N.J. (AP)—A German tourist jumped to his death off a 10-story casino parking garage Wednesday in the third such suicide in eight days. The Associated Press 8/25/99

Atlantic City - Ex-casino worker leaps to death from roof of Trump Marina. He is the fifth person to jump from a casino here and die since August 1999. South Jersey Publishing CO 5/27/00

Atlantic City - A bloodied body was found at the entrance to the Sands Casino Hotel parking garage just before 8 a.m. Investigators believe he fell two stories to his death but don't know much more than that. So Jersey Publishing 7/30/00

Atlantic City - The 36-year-old Florida man leaped seven stories to his death Tuesday after losing between $50,000 and $87,000 at Trump Plaza. South Jersey Publishing Co. 8/19/99

CT - He had gambled over the past few months beginning on a Las Vegas trip this summer. Police believe he was driving home from Foxwoods Resort Casino when, in desperation, he killed himself by hanging. The Day Publishing 9/9/00

A Long Island teen who had a "death wish" because of a $6,000 World Series gambling debt used a $1.75 toy gun to force cops to shoot and kill him, police said yesterday. New York Post 11/16/97

Detroit - A gambler losing big dollars in the high-roller area of the Motor City Casino in Detroit pulled out a gun Wednesday, shot himself in the head and died, police said. He was playing double hands at $500 per hand, and lost $10,000 that night. Detroit Free Press 1/27/00

BILOXI, Miss.—Police are trying to determine what caused a gambler down on his luck to shoot three people before killing himself at a busy Gulf Coast casino. A P, 1/15/01

Miss - In May 1996, Bay St. Louis, Miss., resident James Shamburger, a casino regular, hanged himself with a dog leash.

IL - No one knows why Howard Russell took his life, but authorities found he had taken more than $13,000 in advances on his credit cards during an eight-hour gambling spree on the riverboat. Sun Times 7/28/97

IL - Since casinos opened in Joliet five years ago, Will County Coroner Patrick O'Neil said he has handled three suicides involving people who had racked up debts on the riverboats. But there are others, he said, such as the Kankakee couple who killed themselves outside O'Neil's jurisdiction. Sun Times 7/28/97

IL - 27-year-old Larry ruined his career, maxed out his credit cards and finally killed himself after gambling away his girlfriend's rent money. TODAY 8/13/01

IL - Gambler, Robert Jewell, threatened to shoot in casino, then returned home and shot himself. LA Times 6/22/97

IL - Kate, 40, gambling addict, mother of 2, committed suicide, shot in the head. St. Louis Post-Dispatch 2/22/95.

TAMPA—The night Hillsborough State Attorney Harry walked into a darkened field carrying his gun, he already was mired deep in gambling debt and facing an investigation. He committed suicide. St. Petersburg Times, 11/28/00

AZ - Harrah's Indian gambling director committed suicide over a jackpot dispute. The A P, 1/21/98

LA - After a night of drinking at a Kenner casino Saturday night, a Ponchatoula man, 21, apparently shot himself to death in his car outside the gambling boat, police said. Times Picayune 11/8/99

MO - Mother commits suicide after secret, failed trips to Casino St. Charles, St. Louis Post-Dispatch 3/3/96

Las Vegas - Pierce was the second prominent actor to take his life in a little more than a year. In 3/99, David Strickland hanged himself, the Oasis Motel, 1731 Las Vegas Blvd... Strickland, TV series "Suddenly Susan." L. V. Rev-Jour. 7/12/00

LAS VEGAS (AP) - A 24-year-old Utah man scaled two security barriers and jumped to his death from the observation deck of the 1,149-foot Stratosphere Tower hotel-casino, police said. Las Vegas Sun 1/6/00

LAS VEGAS (AP)—The bullets fired by the family man and Alabama Power employee struck three people he'd apparently never met inside the 23-story hotel and casino, and sparked a panic that didn't end until a dozen other people were injured in the melee. McConnell then shot himself in the head. A casino employee said he had been in the casino before and was upset after losing at the slots. Alabama Live 1/15/01

Las Vegas - They have bank statements showing that Batdorf drained his $17,000 Florida bank account in 11 days. Between August and September he made $600 daily ATM withdrawals as often as three times a day and maxed out his credit cards that put him $72,000 in debt. A pawn shop ticket with his name and thumbprint on it prove he hocked the last of his things, among them the ceramic W.C. Fields and Marx Brothers figurines his mom gave him for Christmas. All activity stopped on his credit cards and bank statements a little over two months later in Las Vegas—the same time a man's body matching his description surfaced in the desert, dead of a gunshot wound in the head. Las Vegas SUN 10/31/98

CA - A compulsive gambler shot and killed himself in San Diego. It was at least the second such suicide in that city within the past few months, yet these events are rarely reported and when they are, the connection with gambling is often overlooked. The Los Angeles Times 6/30/97

Iowa - a 19-year-old, Jason Berg, killed himself 6/94, despairing over gambling habit. Los Angeles Times 6/22/97

A Long Island teen who had a "death wish" because of a $6,000 World Series gambling debt used a $1.75 toy gun to force cops to shoot and kill him, police said yesterday. New York Post 11/16/98

Pergament, depressed over $6,000 in gambling debts, got himself shot Friday night by threatening officers with what turned out to be a toy gun, police said. They call it "suicide by cop"—and say they've seen it before. The A P, 11/17/97

My father, a successful lawyer in Los Angeles, was also a compulsive gambler, and he killed himself in 1976, shortly after one of his many trips to Las Vegas. WARD M. WINTON St. Paul, Dec. 16, 1997

SALEM, Ore. - A Eugene woman blamed her brother's suicide on the state lottery's video poker network. She filed a lawsuit to constitutionally invalidate the lottery. The Register-Guard 7/25/01

RI - Hours after Police Chief Thomas Moffatt was found dead Nov. 20, apparently a suicide, in the basement of the police station, four city officials were told of reports that the chief had been borrowing money from subordinates to pay gambling debts. The Providence Journal 11/30/98

Miss. - After two losing days at the Tunica gambling tables, Ronnie Austin told his wife he was ready to leave. By the time she caught up to him in the Horseshoe Casino parking garage, the Cordova resident was dead from a 9 mm gunshot wound to the chest, an apparent suicide captured on security camera videotape. The Commercial Appeal 3/17/98

Las Vegas - Tillander became immersed in a gambling habit. While no one knows the extent of Tillander's debts, his inability to stop gambling left him unwilling to go on. "His finances were getting out of control," Flatt says. "Gambling is a tough addiction because when you confront someone about it, there is usually very little evidence." authorities found Tillander's body in his apartment. He had crafted the cyanide gas concoction, stuck his head in a pup tent and inhaled the deadly fumes. Las Vegas Review-Journal 11/16/98

CT - A bank employee and father with a gambling habit, in desperation, killed himself by hanging after leaving the casino. The Day Publishing Online 9/9/00

CT - The body of 28-year-old John Diakos was found in a casino parking lot after he committed suicide by ingesting a mixture of drugs and cutting his arms. The Day Publishing Online 9/9/00

CT - 38-year-old woman of Stamford drowned herself by wading into the Thames River after losing hundreds of dollars gambling and maxing outr credit cards at the casino. The Day Publishing Online 9/9/00 http://www.casinowatch.org/, NCALG Document Library

6. Gambling is incredibly tempting for seniors, yet so potentially lethal and exploitative. www.dunnconnect.com/articles/2004/07/26/ourtime/time02.txt 7/26/04, Neighbor Link.

Seniors may deal with loneliness by gambling.

Loneliness and the Elderly - Most people are aware of the physical losses that accompany old age, but many don't realize that older adults also can experience a loss of communication that is just as debilitating as any physical ailment. The ability to communicate is not enough. People also need opportunities to communicate and partners who are actively engaged in the conversation. These conditions become increasingly difficult to find. Individuals who feel cut off from normal society experience loneliness and depression. Lack of social contact and sensory stimulus can cause some older individuals to become paranoid, hostile, even delusional—the very same symptoms used to identify senile dementia.

Sources: News release from The University of Arkansas "Loneliness and the Older Adult"

Ministry of Citizenship, Ontario

For most seniors heading over to the slot machines at the casino, gambling is an entertaining excursion. But for an estimated 5-20% percent, it's an addiction that could cost them their life savings. It is an addiction that is on the rise. American studies asking the elderly why they gamble have confirmed that the opportunity to socialize makes gambling attractive. The most common response is that "it's a change to feel alive again, deal with loneliness and loss, and it brings back the days when they were younger." Casinos provide seniors with a rare opportunity to socialize and, particularly in the U.S., older individuals are courted by the industry.

Casinos offer to bus them, give them a discount on their meals, and make them feel important. Some casinos even offer the person a roll of quarters to get them started.

Sad scenario - Sitting in her own urine, the elderly woman continued to play the game. Observers concluded she had some sort of bladder disorder, but the real problem was actually staring the woman in the face: the slot machine. Her gambling, addiction had reached the point where she ignored everything—even her own bodily functions—so she could keep playing.

Seniors with gambling problems are known to stop taking medications, steal money, gamble with credit card money, gamble with money earmarked for utility bills, or even skip meals. When seniors rely too heavily on gambling for entertainment, it can lead to addiction. Growing numbers of older Americans find themselves grappling with problems arising from gambling.

Case in point - A 78-year-old woman had maxed out her credit cards—something like $40,000. As a result she had to file bankruptcy. The real tragedy is that people like her can't recoup these large sums of money. Seniors are reluctant to seek help for a gambling problem. They need encouragement to recognize addiction problems and to act help. If you have questions or know someone who could benefit from talking with someone about gambling, please contact The Dunn County Department of Human Services at 232-1116. Submitted by the Neighbor Link in conjunction with the Menomonie Community Health Foundation.

7. Gambling as Public Health problem is shown by this article, see the widespread tragedies accountable to people's addiction.

Money a factor in suicides, Thursday 3 July 2003, 10:30 AM Money troubles are second to relationship woes as the main reasons for attempted suicides in Australia, a suicide researcher said.

An ongoing World Health Organisation (WHO) study, which has so far included data on 15,000 Australians, shows financial pressures as a new factor in suicidal behaviour, Australian Institute for Suicidal Research and Prevention (AISRP) director Diego De Leo said. De Leo said while relationship pressures and breakups were still the most common cause of suicide attempts, ***financial troubles*** *were second on the list. "People frequently mismanage their finances. We need to pay much more attention educating people to deal with finances," De Leo told ABC Radio.*

"(Gambling) *ranks very high as the second most important factor for determining a suicidal crisis, which also has something to do, not as much with depression, but much more with shame and with aspects of stigma that can be attached to, for example, bankruptcy or serious difficulties, endangering other people in your family. "This, at least with this evidence, is quite a new factor." Prof De Leo said most research into suicide was conducted overseas and a national strategy was needed for Australia, incorporating local information. Australian Bureau of Statistics data shows about 2,400 Australians die as a result of suicide each year, the AISRP said on its website. The number of people who attempt suicide could be 10 times greater than that figure. Suicide is now the leading cause of death among young people under the age of 30, with men four times more likely to commit suicide than women.*

The AISRP, based at Griffith University in Queensland, conducts and promotes research for the prevention of suicidal behaviours in Australia. ©2003 AAP This story can be found at:
www.theage.com.au/articles/2003/07/03/1057179068971.html

8. *Another article about what gambling does. Opposition to Indian Gaming Grows, 88 Keith Peters, Washington, D.C., correspondent, SUMMARY: Some in Congress are questioning the wisdom that casinos are a boon for tribes.*

A new bill in Congress would make it more difficult for states to receive a portion of the profits from Indian casinos—but debate on the measure has led some to question the advisability of tribal gaming. Congressional proponents of the Indian Gaming Regulatory Act, sponsored by Sen. Ben Nighthorse Campbell, R-Colo., say it will put more money in the hands of Native American tribes. Others say any possible good done by the bill is more than outweighed by the harm brought by the gambling proliferation on Indian reservations. Sen.Brownback, R-Kan., is one lawmaker who thinks it's time to aggressively review the gambling statutes. "I've seen in my own state where, outside of the state, tribes have come in to purchase land to establish casinos—they say, on Indian ground, but...just for the purposes of expanding gaming."

Chad Hills, a social issues analyst at Focus on the Family, said the research on gambling is clear – and should be taken into account. "Gambling comes with costs," he said. "There's increased crime, there's increased bankruptcy, increased child neglect, there are requirements for more roads, traffic control, more police—all these things need to be taken into account." Hills called for ***a moratorium*** *on Indian gaming expansion, saying it is counterproductive for both Native Americans and the nation. "Now, Indian gambling is spreading across our country like wildfire, with little accountability."*

FOR MORE INFORMATION: "You Bet Your Life: The Dangerous Repercussions of America's Gambling Addiction". http://www.family.org/resources/itempg. cfm?itemid=453&refcd=CE04DCZL&tvar=no

9. *http://www.casinowatch.org/addiction/angie_&__ stevens_story.html Log onto this* ***website*** *for an* ***incredible story*** *about a young lawyer and his family's struggle with his gambling addiction. Their story, similar to ours, gives the true flavor and insidiousness of a gambling addiction and its destructive impact on all.*

10. Another great Letter to the Editor, **Numbers show lottery a loser, The Forum** - 07/24/2004

If a **scam** that cost North Dakotans over $5 million in about four and a half months were uncovered, and if that scam were reported to the Attorney General, you could count on headlines, an investigation, and action of some sort. The scam exists, but nothing will be done because it is **the lotteries** introduced this year that are **responsible.**

As of July 14 of this year, North Dakota's lottery sales totaled $6,597,173 and winners recovered $1,471,410. That is a direct loss of $5,125,763 from the pockets of North Dakotans.

In a state that is low wage, with a large percentage of families with two or more jobs just to meet living expenses, that is annually at or near the bottom for teacher salaries, that has a frighteningly high number of children and families lacking health insurance, and that has to resort to raiding state trust funds to balance the budget, promoting a scam like the lottery shows complete disregard for fiscal or social logic.

If nothing changes, **North Dakotans will lose about $1.4 million a month** and recover about $300,000 a month, for a net loss of about $1.1 million a month or about $9.1 million this year.

The state will get part of the take, about $3.3 million if the lottery office's estimates are correct. The ticket retailers will get about $580,000, leaving about $2,9320,000 (per BB correct number should be $2,932,000) for expenses. The rest goes out of North Dakota. And it will get worse as more games are added.

As the state's newest industry, the lottery can't be considered an investment by or for the citizens of North Dakota. There is virtually nothing to show for the investment. No products, no productivity increases, nothing but a gambling high for those who participate – a small portion of whom beat the odds and win, and an absurdly small share for the state treasury.

But the people wanted it, and the proponents claimed that there was no harm because it was a tax on the willing. The real problem is that not just the willing players lose money. The unwilling also lose, just not directly since the loss must be made up in ways that cost all North Dakotans.

Bruce Brooks, Minot, N.D.

11. Another telling **Letter to the Editor**. Times Picayune, Sunday, July 25, 2004, Re: the article, "State rakes in $600 million as gambling revenue rises," Money, July 21.

A mother writes:

Hip, hip, hooray for Harrah's. I wish I could consider this something to be proud of. How true it is that the **love of money is the root of all evil!**

Evil is exactly what gambling has meant to my family and me. Those numbers may represent grand accomplishment to the state, but for the millions of people who, like myself, are suffering due to a loved one's addiction to gambling, there is nothing to celebrate.

What exactly does it cost to gamble? A quarter? A dollar? Several thousand dollars? What exactly are we bringing to the table? I am not a gambler, but I will tell you **what it has cost me: two cars, a house, a 20-year marriage and enough tears from my three kids to fill a swimming pool in every casino in this state.**

Sure, money matters, but **people count, too**. The next time a gambler tries to figure out when to hold 'em and when to fold 'em, keep me in mind. All I have left to hold are my broken-hearted children. And to fold? The Times-Picayune article about the wonderful financial returns on gambling. Hip, hip, hooray.

Nina Mondy Jones, New Orleans

12. **Gambling in PA** - Letter To the Editor, by **PA**. **State Representative Clymer** www.zwire.com/sitenews.cfm?newsid=12463608&BRD=2311&PAG=461&dept_id=482260&rfi=6 7/24/2004,

"**We the People**" begins the words of our Constitution, reflecting a government "...of the people, by the people and for the people." With Gov. Ed Rendell signing the slots bill into law, **Pennsylvania is changing from a people's government to one dictated by the rich, the powerful and the politically connected.**

"Life, Liberty and the Pursuit of Happiness" are special freedoms to be protected by government for the enrichment of its citizens. And yet, the social havoc created by 61,000 addictive slot machines (with more to follow) will literally deny to thousands of our fellow citizens the opportunity to fulfill these constitutional opportunities.

A dark shadow of doubt and suspicion is cast over Harrisburg with the enactment of this bill. Gov. Rendell, in signing into law this gambling legislation, will sadly but surely destroy the American dream for many.

But there is more. The legislators who voted for the gambling bill allowed themselves to invest up to one percent in each of the 14 gambling venues. Surely, a conflict of interest, changing the meaning of government from the "common good" to "our legislators' common good." Let the feeding frenzy begin. The public should be outraged.

The seven-member Pennsylvania Gaming Control Board has been given enormous power. Without the usual Senate confirmation, this board can usurp local authority by approving the locations of the two remaining casino licenses. The board has the power to subpoena, write its own regulations and finance new indebtedness, without legislative oversight.

In addition, a huge financial windfall is provided with the 14 racino and casino licenses. Each license is worth between $300 million and $550 million. A $50 million fee is required. Do the math. **Greed and the politically connected win again. The $2 billion windfall coming from licensing should be in the state treasury rather than in the pockets of these powerful special interest groups**.

Property tax reform? Possibly in 2006, and for many, don't expect more than a 10 percent reduction. Indeed Gov. Rendell has kept his promise to give us a new Pennsylvania. We are now being labeled "Nevada East." With inadequate law enforcement, we can expect prostitution, illegal drugs and all manner of crime. Oh, yes! These gambling places will provide "wonderful" job opportunities for our college ad university graduates!

Whether a person is pro or con on the gambling issue, this bill deserves only one place of habitation—the garbage can. If you agree, contact Gov. Rendell and tell him 61,000 slot machines and the one percent investment by legislators is wrong for Pennsylvania. We are still in the fight.

Paul I. Clymer, PA House of Representatives, 145th Legislative District, ©*The News Item 2004*

13. CACGEC Website, http://nocasinoerie.org/jobques. htm
http://www.smartmoney.com/consumer/index.cfm?story=gaming, Ten Things the Gaming Industry Won't Tell You, Brian O'Keefe, 7/17/00. A terrific article. E.K.

****

***Elisa Korsi**, her maiden name, is the wife of a 'big' ex-gambler on Long Island. She is also a psychiatric social worker and a licensed real estate salesperson. She works for the New York City schools as a social worker-therapist with a private practice in psychotherapy on Long Island.*

She has been married for 32 years and has 3 children.

Comments and inquiries are very welcome. She thanks the kind reader for their patient attention and hopes that the book has raised some level of awareness. You may get in touch with her by e-mail at LisaKorsi@aol.com.

****